Sociocultural Theory and the Teaching of
Second Languages

Studies in Applied Linguistics

Series Editors: Srikant Sarangi, Cardiff University, and Christopher N Candlin, Macquarie University

This new series publishes books that are innovative applications of language and communication research; it is a companion series to the recently launched *Journal of Applied Linguistics*.

Advisory Board:
Charles Goodwin (University of California, Los Angeles)
Jim Martin (University of Sydney)
Kari Sajavaara (University of Jyväaskyläa)
Gabriele Kasper (University of Hawai'i)
Mary McGroarty (Northern Arizona University)
Ron Scollon (Georgetown University)
Gunther Kress (Institute of Education, London)
Merrill Swain (OISE, University of Toronto)

Published in the series:
Language, Identity and Study Abroad
Sociocultural Perspectives
Jane Jackson

Please note that Kari Sajavaara is deceased.

Sociocultural Theory and the Teaching of Second Languages

Edited by
James P. Lantolf and Matthew E. Poehner

LONDON   OAKVILLE

Published by
Equinox Publishing Ltd
UK: Unit 6, The Village
101 Amies Street
London SW11 2JW
USA: DBBC,
28 Main Street,
Oakville, CT 06779

www.equinoxpub.com

First published 2008

© James P. Lantolf, Matthew E. Poehner and contributors 2008

British Library Cataloguing-in-Publication Data

A catalogue record for this book is available from the British Library.

ISBN-13   978 1 84553 249 9   (hardback)
           978 1 84553 250 5   (paperback)

Library of Congress Cataloging-in-Publication Data

Sociocultural theory and the teaching of second languages / edited by James P. Lantolf and Matthew E. Poehner.
    p. cm. — (Studies in applied linguistics)
  Includes bibliographical references and index.
    ISBN 978-1-84553-249-9 (hb) — ISBN 978-1-84553-250-5 (pb) 1. Language and languages—Study and teaching. 2. Second language acquisition. I. Lantolf, James P. II. Poehner, Matthew E.
    P51.S545 2008
    418'.0071—dc22
                        2007037249

Typeset by S.J.I. Services, New Delhi
Printed and bound in Great Britain by Lightning Source UK Ltd, Milton Keynes, and Lightning Source Inc., LaVergne, TN

Contents

Part I: Mediation and the Zone of Proximal Development

Contributors

Co-editors

James P. Lantolf
Department of Applied Linguistics
305 Sparks Building
The Pennsylvania State University
University Park, PA 16802
jpl7@psu.edu

Matthew E. Poehner
Department of Curriculum and Instruction
Chambers Building
The Pennsylvania State University
University Park, PA 16802
mep158@psu.edu

Contributors

Rumia Ableeva
Department of French and Francophone Studies
Burrowes Building
The Pennsylvania State University
University Park, PA 16802
rxa180@psu.edu

Ruth Ban
Barry University
Miami Shores, FL
and Universidad Autonoma de Aguascalientes
Aguascalientes, AGS, Mexico
rban@mail.barry.edu

Tony Erben
Department of Education
University of Tampa
401 W. Kennedy Blvd.
Tampa, FL, 33606
terben@ut.edu

Marilia M. Ferreira
Department of Modern Languages
FFLCH-University of São Paulo
Av. Prof. Luciaon Gualberto
403 São Paulo, SP 05508-900
mmferreira@usp.br

Paula Golombek
Program in Linguistics
4131 Turlington Hall
University of Florida
Gainesville, FL 32611
pgolombek@ufl.edu

Howard Grabois
Department of Foreign Languages and Literatures
East Carolina University
Greenville, NC 27858-4353
hgrabois@gmail.com

John R. Haught
Department of English
Wright State University
Dayton, OH 45435
john.haught@wright.edu

Ibtissem Knouzi
Modern Languages Center
Ontario Institute for Studies in Education
University of Toronto
252 Bloor Street West
Toronto, ON M5S 1V6
Canada
iknouzi@oise.utoronto.ca

Sharon Lapkin
Modern Languages Center
Ontario Institute for Studies in Education
University of Toronto
252 Bloor Street West
Toronto ON M5S 1V6
Canada
slapkin@oise.utoronto.ca

Sally Sieloff Magnan
Department of French and Italian
University of Wisconsin, Madison
Madison, WI 53706
ssmagnan@wisc.edu

Holbrook Mahn
212 Hokona Hall
College of Education
University of New Mexico
Albuquerque, NM 87131
hmahn@unm.edu

Steve McCafferty
Department of Curriculum and Instruction
University of Nevada, Las Vegas
Las Vegas, NV 69154
mccaffes@unlv.nevada.edu

Eduardo Negueruela
Department of Foreign Languages and Literatures
University of Miami
Coral Gables, FL 33124-2074
eneguereula@miami.edu

Jonathon Reinhardt
Assistant Professor
Department of English
University of Arizona
P.O. Box 210067
Tucson, Arizona 85721
jonreinhardt@yahoo.com

Maria Serrano-Lopez
Edgaging: Empowering Education
1400 Jackson St
Hollywood , Florida
mserranolopez@gmail.com

Robert Summers
University at Albany
HU 238
1400 Washington Avenue
Albany, NY 12222
rsummers@albany.edu

Merrill Swain
Modern Languages Centre
Ontario institute for Studies in Education
252 Bloor Street West
Toronto ON M5S1V6
mswain@oise.utoronto.ca

Steven L. Thorne
Department of Applied Linguistics
305 Sparks Building
The Pennsylvania State University
University Park, PA 16802
sthorne@psu.edu

Leo van Lier
Graduate School of Language and Educational Linguistics
Monterey Institute for International Studies
Monterey, CA 93940
lvanlier@miis.edu

List of Figures

List of Tables

Introduction

James P. Lantolf and Matthew E. Poehner

Introduction

In concluding her very interesting and insightful chapter comparing Vygotsky to the American social psychologist, George Herbert Mead, Edwards' (2007: 98) asks the following question: 'Why is it taking so long for Vygotsky's pedagogical influence to be felt in the West?' Although in the present volume we are not directly concerned with the answer to Edward's important question,[1] we do nevertheless see signs that Vygotsky's theory is having an increased influence in Western education. For example the work of Hedegaard (1990, 1999) and her colleagues (Hedegaard, Chaiklin and Pedraza 2001) is certainly attracting the attention of educators in Denmark and other European countries. In the UK the work of Mercer (1995, 2000) and Daniels (1993, 2001) has surely had some impact on British education. In North America, the Fifth Dimension literacy project spearheaded by Michael Cole (see Cole 1996 for a discussion of the project) as well as the efforts of Moll and his colleagues in working with 'funds of knowledge' in multilingual communities in the US Southwest has certainly borne some fruit (Moll and González 2005). Finally, the recently edited volume by Kozulin, Ageyev, Miller and Gindis (2003) reports on numerous Vygotskian inspired pedagogical studies carried out in a variety of different sites around the world.

Despite its growing influence, Vygotskian-based pedagogy is a long way from becoming part of the mainstream of educational practice in the Western world. It remains to be seen if it will continue to expand or will remain more or less on the fringes of the educational establishment. As van Lier (2004) has somewhat cynically speculated, certain pedagogies such as those associated with Mead, Dewey, Montessori and Vygotsky may be destined to remain on the margins precisely because their effectiveness promises to disturb the status quo. Be that as it may, an aspect of the Vygotkian educational enterprise that should not be overlooked is the fact that it is has focused almost exclusively on children and adolescents. To our knowledge, with the notable exception of the work that has been and is continuing to be carried out in second and foreign language instruction, it has virtually ignored adult educational settings. In our view this is unfortunate. It most likely has its origins in the assumption that because Vygotsky's own empirical work often involved children, his developmental theory is, or should be, restricted to the childhood and adolescent years of life. Clearly, Vygotsky did not intend the theory to be limited to only the early years of life; otherwise, he would not have sent Luria (1976) to Uzbekistan to test the principles of the theory among the adult population of this region of the former Soviet Union. In addition, Luria's (1973) work with adults suffering from various forms of brain injury was also firmly grounded in Vygotsky's theory of mental functioning.

It must be kept in mind that there is an important distinction between Vygotsky's theoretical writings and his research agenda, which focused almost entirely on children (normal as well as handicapped) developing the capacity to mediate their thinking through the appropriation of cultural tools, including, of course, language (see Davydov and Radzikhovskii 1985). Much of Vygotsky's own research was no doubt motivated by the very real problems he faced as a psychologist and educator confronting the dramatic social upheaval in Russia following the 1917 Revolution, which resulted in a large and diverse population of children who needed to be brought into a formal system of education (see Gindis 2003). Moreover, Vygotsky's primary goal was to explain human consciousness rather than child development per se. As he discusses in Vygotsky (1978), in order to research consciousness, it had to be studied while it was in the process of formation and not once it had attained its adult form. Vygotsky (1978) referred to the research methodology he designed to investigate and assess the statements of his theory of mind as 'the genetic method' or at times as 'genetic-experimental' research, where the goal is to explain thinking by tracing its development over time.

With the above in mind, the current volume is intended as a contribution to both the L2 pedagogical literature and to the general sociocultural literature. The 13 chapters contained in the volume deal with the extension of principles of SCT to the adult foreign/second language instructional setting. The majority of the chapters report on classroom-based studies where the theoretical principles were implemented in extensive, often semester-long, courses of instruction in English, French, or Spanish in North America. In particular, these chapters focus either on the zone of proximal development and its derivative notion of *dynamic assessment* or concept-based instruction. Two chapters, however, are concerned with expansion of FL pedagogy beyond the boundaries of the classroom setting and represent a sociocultural challenge to more traditional approaches to Communicative Language Teaching. Another chapter examines the implementation of SCT principles in an ESL teacher education program. We will have more specific descriptions of the chapters contained in the volume later in the introduction. First, however, a brief overview of Vygotsky's theory will be presented with particular reference to those principles that are most relevant for formal educational settings. It is well beyond the scope of this introduction to consider all of the nuances of the theory. The interested reader should consult any of a number of comprehensive discussions of sociocultural theory that have been published in recent years, including Cole (1996), van der Veer and Valsiner (1991), Ratner (2006), Langford (2005), and Lantolf and Thorne (2006), among others.

The dialectics of mind

To appreciate the theoretical claims of sociocultural theory and in particular the positions it argues for with regard to education in general and language pedagogy in particular, it is important to understand that unlike other psychological theories, it is grounded in a dialectic rather than a dualistic approach to the relationship between humans and the world. The problem confronting philosophy and eventually psychology was how to explain how humans were able to know the world, comprised of physical substance, given that the mind, apparently, was a representational spiritual entity. In short, as Valsiner and van der Veer (2000) explain, psychology adopted either of two solutions to the mind-body problem, both of which are ultimately reductive in nature. One position, which Valsiner and van der Veer describe as 'upward' reductionism, assumes that all human mental processes are derived from the environment and are therefore in some way or other physical in nature. These authors term the other position 'downward' reductionism (ibid.) as it posits that all mental functions are innately specified in human genes.[2]

The dialectic orientation to the problem starts from the assumption that there is no mind-body dualism in the first place. The Dutch philosopher, Baruch Spinoza, whose writings had a strong influence on Vygotsky's thinking, rejected the dualism and proposed instead that mind and body are not two different and contrary objects, but 'one single object, which is the thinking body of living, real man [*sic*]' (Ilyenkov 1977: 31). This single object can be observed and studied from two different perspectives (body or mind) but this does not mean that the reality of human beings consists of 'two Cartesian halves – thought lacking a body and a body lacking thought' (ibid.). Thinking is not a reality that exists independently of the physical body, but is instead a mode of existence of the body itself. Just as the mode of action of the legs is walking, the mode of action of the human body is thinking (Ilyenkov 1977: 35).

Vygotsky, following this line of reasoning, proposed that human consciousness was the result of neither upward nor downward reduction but emerged from the organic (i.e., dialectic) unity of our biologically endowed brains and our culturally created symbolic artifacts and activities. Humans develop the capacity to use cultural means to gain intentional control over their brain rather than being controlled by this biological organ. Thus, for instance, instead of remembering only what the world presents to us as direct stimuli, we can remember voluntarily by creating what Vygotsky (1987) called 'auxiliary stimuli' of a physical (e.g., tying a string around our finger) or of a symbolic (e.g., telling ourselves linguistically in oral or written form) nature.

Marxian dialectics pervades Vygotsky's thinking about the nature of human consciousness and its development. We want to stress, however, that dialectics is not a set of procedures to be followed in order to attain a particular result. It is rather a 'general conception of the sort of intelligible structure the world has to offer and a program for the sort of theoretical structure which would capture it' (Bakhurst 1991: 138). Dialectics 'attempts to grasp things in their interrelationships and in the totality to which they belong, in the process of change, of being born and of dying, in their conflicts and contradictions' (Acton 1978: 392). As such it eschews the 'the role of comparison in thinking' (Davydov 1984: 24) that has characterized Western psychology in general and SLA research in particular. For example, instead of trying to determine which member of the following pairs – input/output, implicit/explicit knowledge, learning/acquisition – is more relevant for SLA, a dialectic orientation asks the interesting question: What would SLA be like if each pair of the dichotomy were in fact part of a unified process?

Dialectic thinking begins from the perspective of the unity of seemingly contradictory processes or entities and attempts not to disentangle that unity into what appears to be its component parts but to understand how the unity itself functions to achieve a particular end or goal.

Indeed to render the unity asunder is to destroy the very object of study one is attempting to understand in the first place. To be sure, one may undertake to focus attention on the components that form the unity but this must always take place within the scope of the totality that one is trying to explain. For example, to attempt to explain the physical process of magnetism by focusing on either positive or negative electrical charges independently from magnetism itself (i.e., the unity of positive and negative electrical charges) makes no sense. Magnetism depends crucially on the attraction and repulsion of positive and negative electrical charges. One of Vygotsky's favorite examples that illustrates the importance of dialectic unity relates to the capacity of water to extinguish fire. To explain this capacity it does no good to solely and independently study the elements, hydrogen and oxygen, that comprise water, since the former burns and the latter promotes combustion. The appropriate way to approach the problem, according to Vygotsky, is with the unity formed by hydrogen and oxygen in mind. At the heart of this unity is difference whereby each component possesses properties that the other does not and it is this difference that binds the components together. The same dialectic principle, 'unity in difference,' that explains magnetism and water's capacity to extinguish fire, is at the core of human society: 'two absolutely equal individuals, each of which has the very same set of knowledge, habits and inclinations, would be absolutely uninteresting to one another and the one would not need the other. They would simply bore each other to death' (Ilyenkov 1977: 350).

One of the foundational unities of dialectic logic is formed by 'the abstract' or theoretical domain and 'the concrete' or empirical realm. Indeed, this unity is often discussed in terms of the principle of 'ascent from the abstract to the concrete' (Bakhurst 2007: 70). This principle plays a central role in Vygotsky's theory, particularly with regard to the relationship he posits between everyday and scientific concepts (Vygotsky 1987). Everyday, or what Vygotsky often refers to as 'spontaneous', concepts are formed on the basis of concrete experience and are based largely on generalizations from superficial features of entities. For example, children often classify whales as fish on the observation that they appear to have fins and live in the ocean. Scientific concepts, on the other hand, are based on systematic observation of entities often at levels that are deeper than their superficial characteristics. The scientific concept 'whale' does not depend on surface features open to common sense observation but is instead based on a set of criteria established by biological theory, which encompasses not only its behavior of suckling its young, but also includes its genetic composition. These concepts generally bring into relief aspects of the world that are frequently hidden from, or distorted by, the gaze of everyday experience. Thus, while our commonsense observations tell us that the sun moves in the sky (and indeed in many languages this is captured through such terms as 'sunrise' and 'sunset'), scientific observations reveal something quite different about planetary motion. As Bakhurst (2007: 70) points out, 'because such scientific concepts are verbally articulated, theoretically embedded and tightly related to many other concepts, they seem abstract, general and remote from concrete experience.' However, understanding of scientific concepts 'properly integrated into a system of knowledge' (ibid.), 'actually facilitates the understanding of objects in their particularity' (ibid.). Indeed, as will be discussed in several chapters, Vygotsky understood this to be the principle task of formal education. Consequently, abstraction, in the form of scientific concepts,[3] 'allows us to ascend to a detailed understanding of the concrete and particular' (ibid.).

The unity formed by concrete experience of the world and scientific experience of the same world is essential for full development of human consciousness. Without concrete experience, as Vygotsky (1987) forcefully argued, we are left with a purely verbal and contemplative view of the world, which fails to provide full understanding. On the other hand, concrete experience alone, restricts our understanding to specific contextualized ways of knowing and prevents us from systematically generalizing across contexts. From the perspective of the dialectic unity formed by everyday and scientific experience, a concrete object is not an isolated thing, but is instead a 'unity of singular, particular and general characteristics, as a unity of manifold aspects, features and relations, etc., as a system' (Lompscher 1984: 294). Likewise, theoretical thinking does not disregard the empirical or concrete level. It is on this level that theoretical thinking looks to 'test, to enrich and to develop knowledge about substance and regularities' because such knowledge does not simply appear 'out of the blue,' but rather it has a history 'realized in the activity of which the concept is part' (Lompscher 1984: 334).

Vygotsky's dialectic understanding of human consciousness and mental development is at work in all of the chapters comprising the present volume. In some cases, as for instance the chapters by Negueruela and Ferreira and Lantolf, it is more clearly visible than it is in others. Nevertheless, the fundamental principle that the human mind is a dialectic unity of biological and cultural processes underlies thinking of all of the contributors to the volume. In the following section we will briefly discuss the concept of mediation, which Vygotsky proposed to account for the dialectic unity of biology and culture that gives rise to human consciousness.

Mediation

The concept of mediation has been widely discussed in the general SCT literature (see Wertsch 1985; van der Veer and Valsiner 1991; Cole 1996) as well as in SCT L2 research (see Lantolf 2000; Lantolf and Appel 1994; Lantolf and Thorne 2006). As Wertsch (2007: 178) notes, for Vygotsky, 'a hallmark of human consciousness is that it is associated with the use of tools, especially 'psychological tools' or 'signs.'' This means that our contact with the social and physical world is not direct but is indirect or 'mediated' by signs. Cultural tools, which have both a social and psychological function, are appropriated 'by acting upon and with them … in the course of actively reconstructing their meaning and function' and this is possible 'only through interaction with other people who already have the knowledge of a given cultural tool' (Stetsenko and Arievitch 2002: 87).

Sign-based mediation does not merely result in 'quantitative improvements in terms of speed or efficiency,' it gives rise to 'a qualitative transformation' in the thinking process (Wertsch 2007: 17). As Vygotsky put it: 'by being included in the process of behavior, the psychological tool alters the entire flow and structure of mental functions' (Vygotsky 1981: 137). Such tools, or cultural artifacts, are 'embodiments of certain ways of acting in human communities' which means that 'they represent the functions and meanings of things as discovered in cultural practices'; in other words 'they are 'objects-that-can-be-used-for-certain-purposes' in human societies' (Stetsenko and Arievitch 2002: 87). If the goal of psychological research is to understand human mental functioning, we must therefore understand how humans appropriate and deploy signs to organize and control their own and others' social as well as mental activity.

Two perspectives on mediation

Wertsch (2007) suggests that Vygotsky incorporates two different perspectives on mediation (implicit and explicit) in his writings. Implicit mediation, given this label because it is relatively transparent, 'less easily taken as objects of conscious reflection or manipulation' and generally not 'artificially and intentionally introduced into ongoing action' (Wertsch 2007: 180), is based on what Clark (1998) calls the 'supracommunicative' view of language, which contrasts with the traditional communicative perspective whereby speaking and thinking are two completely autonomous processes and speaking functions only to express and communicate thought. The supracommunicative position and the one argued for so forcefully by Vygotsky in chapter 7 of *Thinking and Speech* (Vygotsky 1987), maintains that speech, while not identical with thinking, is implicated in the thought process. In other words, thinking and speaking form a dialectical unity in which they butt up against each other in a 'developmental struggle' at the microgenetic level (Wertsch 2007: 183). In this struggle, thinking, according to Vygotsky, is synthetic and unpartitioned (Vygotsky 1987: 251), while speech is discrete and analytic and consequently partitions thought as thought comes into contact with speech, first at the level of inner speech and even more so at the level of social speech.

Vygotsky characterizes the struggle as between the psychological and the grammatical structure of communication whereby the psychological structure attempts to maintain the synthetic and unpartitioned quality of thinking while the grammatical structure partitions thought as the individual undertakes to express the thought, either privately or socially (see Vocate 1994). Not only is thinking partitioned into discrete units as it is communicated, the units themselves (i.e., words) are the site of conflict between the generalized, abstract and more or less, stable meanings sanctioned by the 'semiotic community' to which the individual belongs and the 'unique, spatiotemporally located intention of the individual' (Wertsch 2007: 185), who often reshapes these meanings to fit the local concrete circumstances. Vygotsky explicitly captures the distinction between a word's meaning and its sense as follows:

> In contrast, meaning is a comparatively fixed and stable point, one that remains constant with all the changes of the word's sense that are associated with its use in various contexts. Change in the word's sense is a basic factor in the semantic analysis of speech. The actual meaning of the word is inconstant. In one operation, the word emerges with one meaning in another, another is acquired ... Isolated in the lexicon, the word has only one meaning. However, this meaning is nothing more than a potential that can only be realized in living speech and in living speech meaning is only a cornerstone in the edifice of sense. ... The word absorbs

> intellectual and affective content from the entire context in which it is intertwined. It begins to mean both more and less than it does when we view it in isolation. It means more because the scope of its meaning is expanded; it acquires several zones that supplement this new content. It means less because the abstract meaning of the word is restricted and narrowed to what the word designates in this single context. ... The word is an inexhaustible source of new problems. Its sense is never complete. Ultimately, the sense of a word depends on one's understanding of the world as a whole and on the internal structure of personality. (Vygotsky 1987: 276)

As is clear from the preceding quote, the relationship between word and thought is indeed dynamic and unstable. This instability operates in two dimensions. One is very much shaped by the speaker's concrete, goal-directed communicative intentions and the other is influenced by the fact that the meaning itself develops as the individual engages in different culturally organized activities. For instance, in early childhood the word 'rose' may be generalized to mean what in adult speech is imparted by the word 'flower.' As the child's communicative experiences expand, the meaning of 'rose' is increasingly specified to reference a specific type of flower. This shift, of course, which takes place more or less subconsciously, is accompanied by a shift in thinking about a particular category of plant. However, a more explicit and perhaps more profound, meaning development occurs as a consequence of formal education – the leading activity in industrialized societies from age 6 or 7 to early adult life. This leads us to consideration of explicit mediation.

Explicit mediation

Explicit mediation, according to Wertsch (2007: 180), is explicit because it is intentionally and obviously introduced into the course of an activity either by the individual or by someone else (e.g., a teacher). Explicit mediation is a topic of intense research interest both in cultural psychology and in cognitive anthropology, where focus is expanded beyond autonomous individuals functioning alone in a laboratory setting to individuals functioning in real world activities with other individuals and with culturally created tools (e.g., paper and pencil, abacus, computer, charts, diagrams, instrumentation, etc.) (see Tobach, Falmagne, Parlee, Martin and Kapelman 1997; Salomon 1993).

One of SCT's classic and often-cited studies on explicit mediation is the Forbidden Colors Task (Leont'ev 1994), where a group of children of different ages were asked to respond to a series of questions posed by a researcher and in so doing they were forbidden to use specific color terms (e.g., yellow, green, blue, red). To help the children remember which colors were forbidden, they were given colored cards that matched the forbidden words.[1] The youngest group of participants, ages 5 to 6 were unable to use the cards to assist them and in fact, as Leont'ev reports, the cards made the task more confusing for this group. On the other hand, older children, ages 8 to 13, were able to use the cards to mediate their performance (i.e., avoid saying the forbidden terms). These children glanced at the cards before responding to the questions and were thus able to successfully avoid the forbidden colors. Adults who took part in the study did not need to use the external stimuli as they were able to rely on their intentional memory (i.e., inner speech) to tell themselves which color terms were forbidden.

Although the forbidden colors task may appear to be an artificial and perhaps extraordinary situation when compared to normal everyday activity, for Vygotsky and Leont'ev it demonstrated in an overt way how our ability to use auxiliary means to mediate thinking develops over time and eventually becomes interiorized as we become adults. The point is that even implicit mediation, which relies heavily on linguistic signs, is assumed to develop in a similar way. Luria (1982) documented the development of our capacity to use speech to mediate our mental and even physical behavior. Luria showed, for instance, that very early in ontogenesis speech, including the speech produced by others and directed at young children has no effect on controlling their activity. Over time, however, speech merely by virtue of its presence and regardless of its semantic content, begins to impact on child behavior. In one study, for instance, Luria showed that when directed to press a button when a green light flashed and to stop pressing when a red light flashed, young children had a difficult time inhibiting their pressing behavior even when the light flashed red. Even when the researcher reminded them with the utterance 'stop pressing' when the red light appeared, the children continued to press and in some cases the utterance resulted in intensified pressing behavior. Eventually, the children's behavior responded to the semantic content of the researcher's utterances, but at this point, they were unable to use their own speech to mediate their own activity. At a later age, however, their pressing behavior was indeed responsive to their own utterances and, as expected, at pre-teen and teen years, children no longer need to verbalize the self-instructions to control their pressing behavior, an indication that the locus of control had been interiorized.

As revealing as Luria's and Leont'ev's research is, there is another aspect of explicit mediation that is more relevant for the present volume. This has to do with the quality of the semantic content of mediation for organizing and controlling behavior. Early in life, when speech first begins to make its influence felt on the thinking process, its content is generally unnoticed in the sense that we appropriate meanings from our semiotic surroundings while we are at the same time participating in the everyday activities of our sociocultural community. As we mentioned earlier, this is part and parcel of implicit mediation. However, when children enter school and begin to participate in formally organized educational activity, they are exposed to what for Vygotsky is a very special type of explicit mediation – scientific concepts. We discuss these in the next subsection.

Mediation through scientific concepts

In addition to the implicit-explicit distinction noted by Wertsch (2007), Karpov and Haywood (1998) argue that Vygotsky distinguished meta-cognitive from cognitive mediation. The former deals with the process through which humans control their thinking through the use of signs, whether implicit or explicit. This is nicely characterized by Vocate (1994) as the conversation between 'I' and 'Me' that comprises inner and private speech. The latter has to do with the domain specific quality of the semantic content of self-directed speech (Karpov and Haywood 1998: 29). It is here that the difference between everyday and scientific concepts becomes salient.

Everyday concepts, as we've already mentioned, are formed during concrete practical experience largely on the basis of 'an immediate observable property of an object' (Kozulin 1995: 123). They are empirically based and require lengthy periods of practical experience to develop. Scientific concepts, on the other hand 'represent the generalizations of the experience of humankind that is fixed in science, understood in the broadest sense of the term to include both natural and social science as well as the humanities' (Karpov 2003: 66). These concepts arise as a consequence of *theoretical learning*, which is 'aimed at selecting the essential characteristics of objects or events of a certain class and presenting these characteristics in the form of symbolic and graphic models' (Karpov 2003: 71). The developmental value of scientific concepts is that because of their abstract and generalized nature, they liberate us from the constraints of context specific everyday experiences and allow us to function appropriately in any concrete circumstance in which the concept may be relevant.

The activity, par excellence, where scientific concepts develop is properly organized formal education. Mastery of scientific concepts, which takes place through explicit and systematic instruction, leads to a deeper understanding of and control over, the object of study. However, as Vygotsky (1987) cautioned, mastery of such concepts entails much more than merely memorizing verbal definitions of the concept, which as Vygotsky (1987) warns, gives rise to verbalism, or the inability to connect the concept to specific concrete practical activity. Education, then, is the systematically organized experience of ascending from the abstract to the concrete.

Stetsenko and Arievitch (2002: 91) offer an excellent example which illustrates the difference between traditional empirically based education and education based on scientific concepts. In traditional instruction numbers are presented as discrete objects that stand for other concrete objects, such as one apple and two oranges, but the 'logic and function of the concept of number – that is, how and why numbers have evolved in human practices – are not revealed' resulting in the confusion of 'mathematical numbers with discrete objects' (ibid.). Systematically organized theoretical instruction, on the other hand, first presents numbers as 'specific sociocultural practices' that emerged from the need to measure quantities in normal everyday human activity, such as the amount of merchandise to be sold in stores, the weight of a bag of beans, or the size of a space needed to accommodate a piece of furniture, etc. From this need, students are instructed how to select and use appropriate measurements (e.g., cups or liters for volume of water, rules in inches or centimeters to measure length, etc.) 'as an analytical tool with which to derive fundamental concepts in elementary mathematics' (ibid.). Next the number of cups of water that fill one container can be compared to the number needed to fill a different container by converting these into a more easily countable set of artifacts, such as plastic chips. This conversion of volume into a material quantifiable representational form makes it easy for students to understand 'how the properties of objects can be transformed into quantities as a result of measurement' (Stetsenko and Arievitch 2002: 92). In this way additional concepts such as 'more,' 'less,' 'equal to,' 'larger,' 'smaller' 'become operationally clear' to the students (ibid.).

As we have said scientific concepts are not restricted to those domains traditionally grouped under the heading 'science,' but includes all areas of the world, physical and human, that have been investigated in a systematic and principled way and that have resulted in generally accepted belief about how the relevant segment of the world functions. Several chapters in the present volume deal with instruction in linguistic concepts: Negueruela considers mood in Spanish; Lapkin, Swain and Knouzi deal with passive voice passive in French; Serrano-Lopez and Poehner focus on locative prepositions in Spanish; Thorne, Reinhardt and Golombek address the pragmatics of hedging in English; Ferreira and Lantolf look at the concept of genre as it informs writing in English.

We want to stress two points as a way of concluding the discussion for the time being. Concept-based instruction is guided by the concept that is the object of learning in its full form. The concept should not be simplified as a rule of thumb – a common pedagogical practice precipitated by the belief that beginning level students are unable to cope with complex grammatical or pragmatic notions. Compromising the integrity of the concept, as Negueruela and Lantolf (2006) argue, ultimately compromises the quality of learning. The second point is, as Vygotsky certainly would argue, memorization of the definition of the concept is insufficient knowledge to promote language development. Full mastery of a concept progresses through a series of concrete activities that results in its internalization. These activities normally include verbalization of the concept to oneself and to others and materialization of the concept in a form that can be used by students to guide their understanding and performance. For adult learners this most often consists of a two dimensional diagram or model, as illustrated in the chapters by Negueruela, Lapkin *et al.*, Ferreira and Lantolf and Thorne, *et al.*; however, it may also be represented as a 3-D model, as shown in the chapter by Serrano-Lopez and Poehner. Finally, the concept must be connected to specific communicative (spoken and/or written) activity in order to be fully proceduralized.

Vygotsky argued that mediation, especially as it was organized in formal education, was optimally carried out in what he called the 'Zone of Proximal Development.' Although the ZPD has been widely discussed and explored in the psychological, general education and L2 literature, we believe it is still useful to present a brief overview of the concept in the introductory chapter for those not familiar with the ZPD, given that it forms the organizing notion of several of the chapters.

The Zone of Proximal Development

As Poehner points out in his chapter, although the ZPD has achieved great popularity in the research literature, there continue to be multiple and sometimes conflicting interpretations of this concept. Chaiklin (2003: 43) for example observes that Vygotsky himself did not write a great deal about the ZPD and in fact, as he notes, the concept only appears for the first time in Vygotsky's writings a year before his death and then he only refers to it in eight different places in the totality of his remaining work. To avoid misusing the concept, Chaiklin advocates a close interpretation of Vygotsky's ideas, suggesting that the ZPD be restricted to discussions of age periods in child development and that alternative terminology be employed to describe other forms of learning and development (Chaiklin 2003: 48–50). This line of thinking leads Negueruela, in his chapter, to an intriguing theoretical distinction between a zone of *proximal* development and a zone of *potential* development, with the latter concept underscoring the non-linear and indeed revolutionary, nature of development that is the goal of Vygotskian pedagogy.

While we share Chaiklin's concern about the overuse and misuse of the term ZPD, in our view, one may be consistent with Vygotsky's understanding of the concept while applying it to areas of cognitive development not specifically addressed in Vygotsky's own empirical research. As we argued at the outset of this chapter, Vygotsky's theoretical contributions, including the concepts of human cognition he proposed to understand, are relevant to all aspects of mental development, not only early childhood.

The enduring appeal of the ZPD may be attributed to its simplicity, on the one hand and explanatory power on the other. In keeping with his dialectic view of consciousness, Vygotsky formulated the ZPD as a way of capturing the dynamic interactions humans have with their environment and how this brings about development. As previously mentioned, Vygotsky understood development as a process of transforming physical and symbolic tools into psychological tools with the result that we gain intentional control over our cognitive functioning and consequently our relation to others and to the world (see Kozulin 1998, 2003). Vygotsky (1978) argued that because human consciousness arises as a consequence of culturally organized interaction with others and with symbolic artifacts it means that human mental abilities emerge twice – first on the intermental plane of social interaction and then on the intramental plane.

The ZPD arose in Vygotsky's clinical work with so-called normal and special needs children as he realized that observation of individuals' independent performance does not adequately reflect the full range of their abilities. His insight that intermental functioning precedes intramental functioning led him to critique conventional approaches to assessment on the grounds that requiring individuals to perform without dialogic interaction with a mediator limits the scope of the assessment to only those functions that have already fully developed and ignores functions that are still in the process of forming (Vygotsky 1998). He charged that 'to establish child development by the level reached on the present day means to refrain from understanding child development' (Vygotsky 1933: 119, cited in van der Veer and Valsiner 1991: 329). Vygotsky argued that abilities that are ripening can only be revealed by exploring individuals' responsiveness to various forms of mediating support. He thus advocated a double method of evaluation that includes both independent performance to reveal an individual's *zone of actual development* and performance in cooperation with a mediator to uncover the ZPD.

Importantly, through this approach Vygotsky discovered that solo performance varied independently from cooperative performance. In one of his favorite examples, Vygotsky (1956) describes two children whose independent problem-solving abilities are quite similar but who, with support from a mediator, attain different levels of performance. Vygotsky concludes:

> From the point of view of their independent activity they are equivalent, but from the point of view of their immediate potential development they are sharply different. That which the child turns out to be able to do with the help of an adult points us toward the zone of the child's proximal development. This means that with the help of this method, we can take stock not only of today's completed process of development, not only the cycles that are already concluded and done, not only the processes of maturation that are completed; we can also take stock of processes that are now in the state of coming into being, that are only ripening, or only developing. (Vygotsky 1956: 447–448, cited in Wertsch 1985: 68)

Vygotsky's first reported application of this double method of assessment was as an alternative to IQ testing, in which case he found that the 'size' of an individual's ZPD (i.e., how responsive they were when offered mediation, including hints, prompts and leading questions) was a better predictor of academic performance than IQ (see van der Veer and Valsiner 1991: 336–341).

Dynamic assessment

The fields of psychological and educational measurement were first introduced to ZPD-based assessment years after Vygotsky's death when his illustrious colleague, Alexander Luria (1961), reported the success of this approach with learning disabled children. According to Luria, traditional assessments failed to differentiate between various groups of learners, offering only documentation of their poor performance. By co-constructing a ZPD with the learners, it was possible to uncover the source of their difficulties and to tailor an appropriate remediation program. This work has given rise to a number of assessment approaches that have come to be known as Dynamic Assessment (DA). Over the last 40 years, DA has been actively pursued by researchers around the world and applied with various populations, including children with special needs, gifted learners, patients suffering from Alzheimer's Disease and other forms of dementia, penitentiary inmates, immigrants and language learners (Tzuriel 2001; Haywood and Lidz 2007). Although important differences exist among DA approaches, they share a commitment to uncovering abilities that typically remain hidden during assessment by requiring the assessor to abandon his/her traditional role as a dispassionate observer in favor of collaborating with learners to actively intervene in development (Feuerstein, Rand and Rynders 1988). That is, cooperation between mediators and learners not only reveals potential future abilities but also helps learners develop those abilities. As Vygotsky (1986: 189) explains, mediation, or teaching, should target the range of what learners are not yet able to do independently but can do in cooperation because it is here that tomorrow's development lies. Thus, DA is an assessment to the extent that it enables learners to display their abilities but it does so through teaching interaction that is attuned to learners' ever-changing (i.e., dynamic) level of development (see Poehner 2008, for extensive discussion of this issue).

In the present volume, three chapters (Ableeva; Erben, Ban and Summers; Poehner) each bring DA into the domain of L2 teaching, learning and assessment. Ableeva and Poehner both emphasize mediator-learner interactions in the L2 classroom while Erben *et al.* reorganize assessment practices according to DA principles on a college-wide scale. In all three cases, the authors maintain a clear focus on DA as a development-oriented unification of assessment and teaching.

Finally, it is worth noting that teaching and assessment in formal schooling was not the only context in which Vygotsky discussed the ZPD. To be sure, Vygotsky understood schooling to be a specially engineered, artificial environment for promoting development by helping learners bring together their everyday understandings of the world with abstract theoretical knowledge, as previously explained. However, Vygotsky (1987) also viewed play as a leading activity in early childhood development. As children engage in play that involves taking on adult roles (parent, teacher, soldier, doctor, etc.) they are performing through imagination what they are not yet able to do in reality and it is through this form of play that they come to appropriate more adult-like ways of being. Thus, play emphasizes the transformative potential of creativity in the ZPD, a feature of Vygotsky's work that is often overlooked in ZPD research, but that is taken up in interesting ways in the present volume in the chapters by Mahn and Haught and McCafferty.

Organization of the present volume

In addition to this introduction, the present volume comprises 13 chapters that report on original L2 research motivated by Sociocultural Theory. Although all of the chapters are framed by Vygotsky's general dialectic approach to the study of mind, which, as we have said, necessarily encompasses his proposals on mediation, they do not approach it from the same perspective. Five of the chapters (Mahn; Haught and McCafferty; Poehner; Ableeva; and Erben *et al.*) address mediation within the Zone of Proximal Development. Of these, three – Poehner's, Ableeva's and Erben *et al.* – deal with a subdomain of the ZPD, Dynamic Assessment. The chapter by van Lier extends Poehner's discussion of learner reciprocity in ZPD interactions to the broader issue of learner agency in the L2 classroom and how this may be supported and developed. Five of the chapters (Negueruela; Ferreira and Lantolf; Lapkin *et al.*; Serrano-Lopez and Poehner; and Thorne *et al.*) are concerned with mediation and language-based scientific concepts in classroom instruction. All but one of these chapters deals with language instruction. The exception is the chapter by Erben *et al.*, who report on a study carried out in a teacher education program. The two remaining chapters, by Magnan and Grabois respectively, form a unity of their own. In challenging many of the practices of communicative language teaching, Magnan argues for moving systematic instruction beyond the walls of the classroom setting and into the target language community. Grabois, in turn, reports on a study which employed a service-learning approach to realize Magnan's proposal.

We would also like to point out that because of the integrated nature of SCT, it is difficult to attend to one aspect of the theory without bringing other aspects into the picture. Thus, while many of the chapters are included under a particular theoretical subheading, they also bring to bear principles that the chapters coalesced in the other subheading focus on. For instance, Negueruela's chapter is included among the chapters dealing with concept-based instruction, but it has much to say about the Zone of Proximal Development. At the same time, although the chapter by Poehner on Dynamic Assessment is included among the chapters that feature the ZPD, it also deals with concept-based instruction. Similarly, van Lier considers learner agency during dialogic interaction in the classroom while suggesting that agency itself is mediated. Additionally, many of the chapters also incorporate other principles of the theory that emerge from the general notion of mediation. Included among these are internalization, activity, participation and contribution, and the genetic method. Space does not permit us to address these topics here; however, they have been treated extensively in the general SCT literature (see Wertsch 1985) as well as in the L2 literature informed by SCT (see Lantolf and Thorne 2006). Moreover, the contributors also provide appropriate discussion of each concept as it relates to their particular project.

Of the empirically based chapters, ten focus on adult university-level language learners, while the chapter by Mahn deals with elementary and secondary school learners along with university level students and the chapter by van Lier draws data from a variety of adult (secondary and university) learners in the US as well as in the Netherlands. Finally, the chapters by Negueruela, Serrano-Lopez and Poehner and Grabois focus on Spanish as the object of learning and instruction, while the chapters by Poehner, Ableeva and Lapkin *et al.* are concerned with the teaching and learning of French. The remaining empirically-based chapters (Mahn; Haught and McCafferty; van Lier; Ferreira and Lantolf; Thorne *et al.*; and Erben *et al.*) deal with ESL or EFL settings.

Overview of the chapters

The first six chapters foreground the Zone of Proximal Development as a driving force behind the innovations they describe. The first three of these chapters form their own subgroup as they report on applications of Dynamic Assessment as a means of co-constructing ZPDs with learners in order to simultaneously perform teaching and assessment functions. Poehner's chapter, 'Both Sides of the Conversation: The Interplay between Mediation and Learner Reciprocity in Dynamic Assessment,' acknowledges the considerable attention in ZPD and DA research that has been devoted to elaborating the kinds of mediation that may successfully promote development but argues that this must be balanced by simultaneously focusing on learners' contributions. He identifies the construct of *learner reciprocity*, first proposed by Lidz (1991), as a way of interpreting learner behaviors during DA. His chapter develops reciprocity beyond its original conceptualization as an indicator of learners' receptiveness to mediation and he offers examples of L2 French learners who actively negotiate and even refuse mediation as they struggle to gain greater autonomy. Poehner concludes that just as the quality of mediation learners require reveals much about their abilities, analysis of their reciprocating behaviors completes the picture of their development. The implication for the classroom is that learner development from one interaction to the next may not result in improved performance or even in changes to the mediation learners require but might be apparent as they implicitly and explicitly seek, respond to, negotiate and refuse mediator support.

Ableeva's chapter 'The Effects of Dynamic Assessment on L2 Listening Comprehension' also reports on the use of DA in the context of an L2 French classroom, but unlike Poehner's study, hers compares the insights into learners' abilities gained through dynamic and non-dynamic procedures. Pointing to the current interest in listening comprehension assessment in the language testing literature, Ableeva carried out a small-scale pilot study in which she offered learners mediation as they listened to authentic French radio texts in order to ascertain whether a dynamic procedure uncovered features of their abilities not apparent from their solo performance. Her findings confirm Vygotsky's prediction that individuals whose independent performances are quite similar may have very different ZPDs. In fact, for some learners, comprehension of the aural text hinged on a single lexical item or on relevant cultural details. The non-dynamic procedure failed to detect these differences and indicated only whether learners could or could n   o   t

answer comprehension questions correctly. This finding leads Ableeva to argue in favor of the use of DA as both a diagnostic tool to uncover the causes of poor comprehension as well as an approach to supporting learners' development of their listening abilities.

In the third DA chapter, 'Changing Examination Structures within a College of Education: The Application of Dynamic Assessment in Pre-service ESOL Endorsement Courses in Florida,' Erben *et al.* expand DA principles beyond classroom interactions and describe its use at a programmatic level. Working to meet the state mandated ESOL endorsement requirement for teacher certification in Florida, Erben *et al.* reformulated a college of education's examination procedures in order to emphasize mediation and dialogic interaction, as called for by DA. This innovation is ongoing and has already met with success in the college's key ESOL methodology courses, as evidenced by instructors' and teacher-trainees' reflections on their experiences with DA. The chapter documents the initial institutional resistance to altering exam procedures as well as gradual acceptance of DA as faculty and students became better acquainted with Vygotskian developmental theory. As the authors point out, their application of DA on such a large scale not only helps university instructors to better understand and support teacher-trainees' developing abilities but it simultaneously is preparing a new generation of teachers who may employ DA in their own classrooms.

The next two chapters in this section underscore the importance of creativity and play in development. In his chapter 'A Dialogic Approach to Teaching L2 Writing' Mahn addresses the problem of helping ESL writing students express their intended meanings through the L2 by employing dialog journals as a mediating activity between the language and the students' internal systems of meaning. For Mahn, dialog journals represent a space and time of free experimentation in the ZPD, as learners 'play' with ideas and with language without the fear of correction or even ridicule that is often present during more formal writing exercises and face-to-face interactions. Citing students' own reflections of maintaining dialog journals, Mahn argues that the absence of a fear of correction enables students to focus on the meanings they wish to express and that while this may result, especially at first, in texts that are not acceptable in a traditional pedagogy (e.g., texts that contain many grammatical and lexical errors or that are written in more than one language), it nonetheless represents an important step in helping learners develop their own voice in the L2, a voice that is reflective of their lived experiences.

In the chapter by Haught and McCafferty 'Embodied Language Performance: Drama and the ZPD in the Second Language Classroom,' play in the ZPD is not concerned directly with students' lived experiences but rather with engaging them in the life and identity of another. These authors build directly on Vygotsky's analysis of role playing as a leading activity in child development to devise an ESL pedagogy around drama. While acknowledging that the value of drama in the classroom has been recognized for some time, Haught and McCafferty argue that through a process of careful modeling by the teacher, individual and class rehearsals and eventual performance, learners are guided into 'playing' beyond their current level of development. In other words, drama serves as a mediating activity to support learners' development as they act out the part of another in the L2. The power of drama-based pedagogy, according to Haught and McCafferty, is that rehearsal and performance involve not simply repeating lines or copying a model but *imitation* in the Vygotskian sense of transformative appropriation, or internalization, of ways of thinking and behaving. They also rely on Bakhtin's notion of ventriloquation to explicate the dynamics of learners' emergent and embodied performances, which went well beyond the teacher's modeling to include unique interpretations of characters, their feelings and motivations as communicated through facial expression, gesture, intonation and improvisation. In effect, the students created roles for themselves through the second language and culture.

In the final chapter of this section, 'Agency in the Classroom' van Lier argues that appropriately interpreting and mediating learners as they exercise agency in various ways is in fact more important for their development than the content matter and teaching materials. Just as Poehner's chapter introduces the notion of reciprocity to draw attention to learners' active negotiation of mediation during DA, van Lier similarly points out that Vygotskian theory compels us to understand agency not as a quality of an individual but as a contextually situated way of relating to the world that is shaped by our developmental history as well as our potential future. Agency, then, emerges as individuals, groups and communities interact with various affordances while engaging in goal-directed activity. The challenge for pedagogy is to design learning environments and activities in which students are optimally agentive in taking responsibility for their own – and indeed their classmates' – development. Van Lier illustrates some of the forms learner agency may take in the L2 classroom and suggests curricular approaches, such as project-based learning, that may be especially well suited to mediating agency.

The next section of the volume groups four chapters under the heading 'Concept-Based Instruction' where scientific understanding of the L2 is the focus of classroom learning. The initial chapter, authored by Negueruela and entitled 'Revolutionary Pedagogies: Learning that Leads (to) Second Language Development' serves to introduce this set of chapters as it outlines many of the principles of concept-based instruction as described in one of the two most important pedagogical interpreters of Vygotsky's theory, Piotr Gal'perin. Because it also questions some of the traditional assumptions associated with the ZPD, the chapter also bridges to the initial section. Negueruela argues for what the author calls a 'revolutionary pedagogy' based on the principle that in the ZPD learning and development form a dialectic unity in which each process promotes the other, unlike in a more traditional approach to instruction where it is assumed that effective learning depends on developmental readiness. Negueruela proposes that because neither the path nor the outcome of development is predictable (indeed, it is revolutionary) it is perhaps more appropriate to change the term Zone of Proximal Development, which the author argue carries implications of inevitability, to Zone of 'Potential' Development, which is more open-ended. The chapter then moves to a discussion of a portion of the data from a pedagogical study conducted by the author based on Gal'perin's concept-based approach to education. Drawing on his dissertation research (Negueruela 2003), Negueruela documents the process that one learner went through as she attempted to appropriate the concept of mood in Spanish through CBI principles. Here the author considers three sources of data: learner performance, verbalization of the concept and her reactions to the new pedagogical approach.

The next chapter in this subsection, by Lapkin, Swain and Knouzi, 'French as a Second Language University Students Learn the Grammatical Concept of Voice: Study Design, Materials Development and Pilot Data' reports on a study inspired by Negueruela's (2003) dissertation. The study focuses on only one aspect of CBI as implemented by Negueruela – the importance of verbalization of the concept as part of the internalization process. In addition to the SCT-informed work of Negueruela, Lapkin *et al.* also point out that empirical, atheoretical research in science and math education report positive effects when learners explained complex concepts to themselves aloud. In the study, the authors developed an explanation of the grammatical concept of voice in French. Intermediate-level university students of the language were trained to self-explain, exposed to a text with sentences in the active, passive and middle voices in the language and were asked to talk their way through an explanation of the concept. The researchers then administered an immediate and delayed posttest to the students. Interviews conducted with the students along with the pilot data suggest that learning occurred and that students perceived this approach to be an effective way to learn.

The chapter by Thorne, Reinhardt and Golombek, 'Mediation as Objectification in the Development of Professional Academic Discourse: A Corpus-informed Curricular Innovation' implements Concept-Based Instruction in an ESL International Teaching Assistant (ITA) Program at a large research university. The concern of the project is instruction in the pragmatic function of hedging in English, which according to the authors is an important function for ITAs when advising students during one-on-one office-hour sessions. The course of instruction designed by Thorne and his colleagues is situated within a perspective known as data-driven learning. To this end, the authors draw up the large corpus of academic English, MICASE, developed at the University of Michigan. They use this data to benchmark the performance of ITAs as well as to develop instructional materials. They then developed a series of systematic diagrams to present the concept of pragmatic hedging to the ITAs and to assist them in guiding their appropriate use of English when interacting with their American undergraduate students.

The fourth chapter that deals with Concept-based Instruction is by Ferreira and Lantolf, 'A Concept-based Approach to Teaching Writing through Genre Analysis.' It is, however, not based on Gal'perin's theory of instruction, but on the second important pedagogical interpreter of Vygotsky's theory, V. V. Davydov, who designed a more flexible model for educating students in scientific concepts. One of the differences between Davydov and Gal'perin is that Davydov asks students to draw their own models of the concept under study, whereas Gal'perin presents them with a finished model to follow. The idea here is that through self-generated modeling of the concept, learners come to a deeper understanding of the concept; in addition, their understanding is open to observation by the instructor, who can then interact with the learners in order to help them modify their understanding when necessary. The chapter reports on a 16-week university ESL writing course in which the guiding concept was the System-Functional concept of genre as developed in the work of James Martin and his colleagues working in Australia. The chapter traces the performance of a subset of the students who participated in the course in terms of the models they produced to represent their understanding of three concrete genres: invitations, job application letters and argumentative/expository texts. The authors then attempt to link changes in learners' understanding of the genre as reflected in their models with improvement in their writing performance as assessed by a team of independent raters.

The fifth and final chapter in this subsection by Serrano-Lopez and Poehner, 'Materializing Linguistic Concepts through 3-D Clay Modeling: A Tool-and-Result Approach to Mediating L2 Spanish Development,' discusses the results of a study which took a slightly different twist with regard to how the concept, in this case, locative prepositions in Spanish, are modeled. Instead of the instructor providing the model or asking the students to draw the model, students were encouraged to build their own 3-D clay models to illustrate the meaning of locative prepositions in the language. The argument the authors put forth to support the value of such an approach is based on Newman and Holzman's (1993) claim that effective instruction must allow learners to build their own mediation means (i.e., tool-and-result) rather than providing them with prepackaged materials (i.e., tools-for-result). This chapter resonates well with Negueruela's call for a revolutionary pedagogy, although the authors of this chapter take a different stance on how to concretize such a pedagogy from what is proposed by Negueruela. The study compared students who received instruction in the concept and then modeled it in clay with students who were given instruction in the concept only. Given that the modeling group outperformed the concept-only group of learners, the study confirms Vygotsky's argument that memorization of the definition of a concept alone does not result in genuine development. The definition must be connected to concrete activity.

The final two chapters in the volume form their own subsection entitled 'The Classroom-World Nexus.' They argue, on the basis of SCT principles, for the need to expand language instruction beyond the bounds of the formal classroom setting. In her chapter, 'The Unfulfilled Promise of Teaching for Communicative Competence: Insights from Sociocultural Theory' Magnan points out that pedagogies generally identified by the label Communicative Language Teaching (CLT), as inspired by Hymes' (1971) notion of communicative competence, need to broaden the scope of what counts as authentic communicative activity. To date, according to Magnan, CLT has emphasized group work, role play and the use of so-called authentic materials as a way of simulating everyday life in the target language community. She cautions, however, that the culturally and linguistically sheltered population of most foreign language classrooms means that while communication may take place in the L2, it is most likely to be anchored in the learners' native cultural concepts and discourse patterns. She goes on to consider the implications of Vygotskian principles, in particular Activity Theory, for CLT. Building on Wenger's (1998) notion of communities of practice, Magnan suggests how foreign language pedagogy can be reconceptualized to situate learning in communities wider than those afforded by most classroom contexts. Learners are thus given the opportunity to shape their evolving multilingual and multicultural identities through co-constructive relationships with other social groups.

Grabois's chapter 'Contribution and Language Learning: Service-learning from a Sociocultural Perspective' considers one possibility of concretizing Magnan's proposals to expand the boundaries of foreign language instructional programs into everyday communities where the target language is used. Grabois examines the reflections of students who participated in an advanced Spanish university service-learning course from the perspective of SCT. In particular it considers the concept of 'contribution' as described by Stetsenko and Arievitch (2004). These researchers suggest that contribution is a more useful way of considering Vygotsky's contention that internalization of cultural artifacts and concepts from a community has a flip side to it – externalization – or the giving back to the community what one may have appropriated and modified. This under-researched aspect of the developmental process derives its relevance according to Stetsenko and Arievitch from the fact that a contribution, as opposed to externalization, has a goal-directed aspect to it, which the latter notion does not. Grabois documents through the extensive commentary produced by the Spanish students who participated (here he brings in Sfard's (1998) study of the participation versus acquisition metaphor) in various activities with local Hispanic communities that learning through contributing to the well being of others can change student knowledge of and attitudes toward target communities, while elevating the meaningfulness of language learning activity to levels rarely attainable in the classroom. He further shows that situating language learning in relation to personal development and social consciousness also has significant influence on student motivation, attitudes, confidence and ability to successfully interact in the target language.

Notes

1. Edwards (2007: 99) speculates that the lack of influence may be due in part to the fact that Vygotsky, despite some arguments to the contrary (e.g., Rogoff 1995; Wells 1999), is not a social constructivist along the lines of Dewey, James and Mead, but is instead a realist who believed that the world is knowable through the application of scientific principles and procedures, especially those grounded in Marxist philosophy (see Bakhurst 2007).
2. There are of course differences between downwardly reductionist positions. At the extreme end of things are theories that propose that all mental knowledge, including linguistic as well as conceptual knowledge, is innately specified. Less extreme views hold that while knowledge itself is not innately given, the architecture which organizes and processes knowledge is genetically determined.
3. In using the term 'scientific' Vygotsky does not restrict abstract knowledge to the domain traditionally understood as constituting science (e.g., physics, chemistry, biology, etc.), but he also includes the social sciences and the humanities under the umbrella of scientific in this case. This is because for Vygotsky scientific is understood to include knowledge that results from systematic and principled observation of the object of interest. One can, for instance, develop scientific concepts relating to human behavior (social as well as psychological) as well as artistic undertakings, such as literature, visual art and music (see Vygotsky 1971).
4. The task employed the 'method of dual stimulation' in which participants are given two sets of stimuli. One set is the object of their activity (e.g., the forbidden colors) and the other is designed to help the participants carry out the activity (e.g., the forbidden color cards).

References

Acton, H. B. (1967) Dialectic materialism. In P. Edwards (ed.) *The Encyclopedia of Philosophy Vol. 2* 389–97. New York: Macmillan and the Free Press.

Bakhurst, D. (1991) *Consciousness and Revolution in Soviet Philosophy*. Cambridge: Cambridge University Press.

Bakhurst, D. (2007) Vygotsky's demons. In H. Daniels, M. Cole and J. V. Wertsch (eds) *The Cambridge Companion to Vygotsky* 50–76. Cambridge: Cambridge University Press.

Chaiklin, S. (2003) The zone of proximal development in Vygotsky's analysis of learning and instruction. In A. Kozulin, B. Gidnis, V. S. Ageyev and S. Miller (eds) *Vygotsky's Educational Theory in Cultural Context* 39–64. Cambridge: Cambridge University Press.

Clark, A. (1998) Magic words: how language augments human computation. In P. Carruthers and J. Boucher (eds) *Language and Thought: Interdisciplinary Themes*. Cambridge: Cambridge University Press.

Cole, M. (1996) *Cultural Psychology. A Once and Future Discipline*. New York: Bradford Books.

Daniels, H. (1993) *Charting the Agenda: Educational Activity after Vygotsky*. London: Routledge.

Daniels, H. (2001) *Vygotsky and Pedagogy*. London: Routledge/Falmer.

Davydov, V. V. (1984) Substantial generalization and the dialectic-materialistic theory of thinking. In M. Hedegaard, P. Hakkarainen and Y. Engstrm (eds) *Learning and Teaching on a Scientific Basis* 11–30. Aarhus, Denmark: Aarhus Universitet Press.

Davydov, V.V. (1988) *Problems of Developmental Teaching. The Experience of Theoretical and Experimental Psychological Research*. Excerpts (Part I). *Soviet Education* 30 (10): 3–77.

Davydov, V. V. and Radzikhovskii, L. A. (1985) Vygotsky theory and the activity-oriented approach in psychology. In J. V. Wertsch (ed.) *Culture, Communication, Cognition. Vygotskian Perspectives*. Cambridge: Cambridge University Press.

Edwards, A. (2007) An interesting resemblance. Vygotsky, Mead and American Pragmatism. In H. Daniels, M. Cole and J. V. Wertsch (eds.) *The Cambridge Companion to Vygotsky* 77–100. New York: Cambridge University Press.

Feuerstein, R., Rand, Y. and Rynders, J. E. (1988) *Don't Accept Me as I Am. Helping Retarded Performers Excel*. New York: Plenum.

Gal'perin, P. Ya. (1989) Study of the intellectual development of the child. *Soviet Psychology* 27: 26–44.

Gindis, P. (2003) Remediation through education: sociocultural theory and children with special needs. In A. Kozulin, B. Gindis, V. S. Ageyev and S. M. Miller (eds), *Vygotsky's Educational Theory in Cultural Context* 200–24. Cambridge: Cambridge University Press.

Haywood, H. C. and Lidz, C. S. (2007) *Dynamic Assessment: Clinical and Educational Applications*. Cambridge: Cambridge University Press.

Hedegaard, M. (1990) The zone of proximal development as basis for instruction. In L. C. Moll and J. B. Greenberg (eds) *Vygotsky and Education*, 349–371. Cambridge: Cambridge University Press.

Hedegaard, M. (1999) Activity theory and history teaching. In Y. Engström, R. Miettinen and R. L. Punamaki (eds) *Perspectives on Activity Theory* 282–97. Cambridge: Cambridge University Press.

Hedegaard, M., Chaiklin, S. and Pedraza, P. (2001) Culturally sensitive teaching within a Vygotskian perspective. In M. Hedegaard (ed.) *Learning in Classrooms: A Cultural Historical Approach* 121–43. Aarhus: Aarhus University Press.

Hymes, D. (1971) *On Communicative Competence*. Philadelphia, PA: University of Pennsylvania Press.

Ilyenkov, E. (1977) *Dialectic Logic*. Moscow: Progress Press.

Karpov, Y. V. (2003) Vygotsky's doctrine of scientific concepts. Its role in contemporary education. In A. Kozulin, B. Gindis, V. S. Ageye and S. M. Miller (eds) *Vygotsky's Educational Theory in Cultural Context* 65–82. Cambridge: Cambridge University Press.

Karpov, Y. B. and Haywood, H. C. (1998) Two ways to elaborate Vygotsky's concept of mediation: Implications for instruction. *American Psychologist* 53: 27–36.

Kozulin, A. (1995) The learning process: Vygotsky's theory in the mirror of its interpretations. *School Psychology International* 16: 117–29.

Kozulin, A. (1998) *Psychological Tools: A Sociocultural Approach to Education.* Cambridge, MA: Harvard University Press.

Kozulin, A. (2003) Psychological tools and mediated learning. In A. Kozulin, B. Gindis, V. S. Ageyev, S. M. Miller (eds) *Vygotsky's Educational Theory in Cultural Context* 15–38. Cambridge: Cambridge University Press.

Kozulin, A., Ageev, V. S., Miller, S. and Gindis, B. (eds) (2003) *Vygotsky's Theory of Education in Cultural Context* 117–29. Cambridge: Cambridge University Press.

Langford, P. (2005) *Vygotsky's Developmental and Educational Psychology.* East Sussex: Psychology Press.

Lantolf, J. P. (ed.) (2000) *Sociocultural Theory and Second Language Learning.* Oxford: Oxford University Press.

Lantolf, J. P. and Appel, G. (eds) (1994) *Vygotskian Approaches to Second Language Research.* Norwood, NJ: Ablex.

Lantolf, J. P. and Thorne, S. L. (2006) *Sociocultural Theory and the Genesis of Second Language Development.* Oxford: Oxford University Press.

Leont'ev, A. (1994) The development of voluntary attention in the child. In van der Veer, R. and J. Valsiner (eds) *The Vygotsky Reader* 289–312. Oxford: Blackwell.

Lidz, C. S. (1991) *Practitioner's Guide to Dynamic Assessment.* New York: Guilford.

Lompscher, J. (1984) Problems and results of experimental research on the formation of theoretical thinking through instruction. In M. Hedegaard, P. Hakkarainen and Y. Engstrom (eds) *Learning and Teaching on a Scientific Basis* 293–357. Aarhus: Aarhus Universitet.

Luria, A. R. (1961). Study of the abnormal child. *American Journal of Orthopsychiatry. A Journal of Human Behavior* 31: 1–16.

Luria, A. R. (1973) *The Working Brain.* New York: Basic Books.

Luria, A. R. (1976) *Cognitive Development. Its Cultural and Social Foundations.* Cambridge, MA: Harvard University Press.

Luria, A. R. (1982) *Language and Cognition.* New York: John Wiley and Sons.

Mercer, N. (1995) *The Guided Construction of Knowledge: Talk Amongst Teachers and Learners.* Clevedon: Multilingual Matters.

Mercer, N. (2000) *Words and Minds: How We Use Language to Think Together.* London: Routledge.

Moll, L. and González, N. (2005) *Fund of Knowledge: Theorizing Practices in Households, Communities and Classrooms.* Mahwah, NJ: Erlbaum.

Poehner, M.E. (2008) *Dynamic Assessment: A Vygotskian Approach to Understanding and Promoting Second Language Development.* Berlin: Springer Publishing.

Negueruela, E. (2003) Systemic-theoretical instruction and L2 development: A sociocultural approaching to teaching-learning and researching L2 learning. Unpublished doctoral dissertation, Pennsylvania State University. University Park, PA.

Ratner, C. (2006) *Cultural Psychology. A Perspective on Psychological Functioning and Social Reform.* Mahwah, NJ: Erlbaum.

Rogoff, B. (2001) *Learning Together: Children and Adults in a School Community.* Oxford: Oxford University Press.

Rogoff, B. (2003) *The Cultural Nature of Human Development.* Oxford: Oxford University Press.

Salomon, G. (ed.) (1993) *Distributed Cognitions. Psychological and Educational Considerations.* Cambridge: Cambridge University Press.

Sfard, A. (1998) On two metaphors for learning and the dangers of choosing just one. *Educational Researcher* 27: 4–13.

Stetsenko, A. and Arievitch, I. (2002) Teaching, learning and development: a post-Vygotskian perspective. In G. Wells and G. Claxton (eds) *Learning for Life in the 21st Century Sociocultural Perspectives on the Future of Education* 84–96. Oxford: Blackwell.

Stetsenko, A. and Arievitch, I. (2004) Vygotskian collaborative project of social transformation: history, politics and practice in knowledge construction. *Journal of Critical Psychology* 12: 58–60.

Tobach, E., Falmagne, R. J., Parlee, M. B., Martin, L. M. W. and Kapelman, A. S. (eds) (1997) *Mind and Social Practice. Selected Writings of Sylvia Scribner.* Cambridge: Cambridge University Press.

Tzuriel, D. (2001) *Dynamic Assessment of Young Children.* New York: Plenum Publishers.

Valsiner, J. and van der Veer, R. (2000) *The Social Mind. Construction of the Idea.* Cambridge: Cambridge University Press.

van der Veer, R. and Valsiner, J. (1991) *Understanding Vygotsky. A Quest for Synthesis.* Oxford: Blackwell.

van Lier, L. (2004) *The Ecology of Semiotics of Language Learning: A Sociocultural Perspective.* Boston: Kluwer.

Vocate, D. R. (1994) Self-talk and inner speech: understanding the uniquely human aspects of intrapersonal communication. In D. R. Vocate (ed.) *Intrapersonal Communication. Different Voices, Different Minds* 3-32. Hillsdale, NJ: Lawrence Erlbaum.

Vygotsky. L. S. (1933) Dinamika umstvennogo razvitija shkol'nika v svjazi s obucheniem. In L. S. Vygotsky (ed.) *Umstvennoe razvitie detej v processe obuchenija.* Moscow-Leningrad: Uchpedgiz.

Vygotsky, L. S. (1956) *Isbrannye psikhologicheskie issledovaniya* [Selected psychological investigations]. Moscow: Izdatel'stvo Akademii Pedagogischeskikh Nauk SSSR.

Vygotsky, L. S. (1971) *The Psychology of Art.* Cambridge, MA: MIT Press.

Vygotsky, L. S. (1978) *Mind in Society: The Development of Higher Psychological Processes.* Cambridge, MA: Harvard University Press.

Vygotsky, L. S. (1981) The instrumental method in psychology. In J. V. Wertsch (ed.) *The Concept of Activity in Soviet Psychology* 134–143. Armonk, NY: M. E. Sharpe.

Vygotsky, L. S. (1986) *Thought and Language. Newly revised and edited by A. Kozulin.* Cambridge, MA: MIT Press.

Vygotsky, L. S. (1987) *The Collected Works of L. S. Vygotsky. Volume 1. Problems in General Psychology. Including the Volume Thinking and Speech.* New York: Plenum.

Vygotsky, L. S. (1998) *Child Psychology. The Collected Works of L. S. Vygotsky: Vol. 5. Problems of the Theory and History of Psychology.* New York: Plenum.

Wells, G. (1999) *Dialogic Inquiry: Toward a Sociocultural Practice and Theory of Education.* Cambridge: Cambridge University Press.

Wenger, E. (1998) *Communities of Practice: Learning, Meaning and Identity.* Cambridge: Cambridge University Press.

Wertsch, J. V. (1985) *Vygotsky and the Social Formation of Mind.* Cambridge, MA: Harvard University Press.

Wertsch, J. V. (2007) Mediation. In H. Daniels, M. Cole and J. V. Wertsch (eds) *The Cambridge Companion to Vygotsky* 178–92. Cambridge: Cambridge University Press.

Part I

Mediation and the zone of proximal development

1 Both sides of the conversation: the interplay between mediation and learner reciprocity in dynamic assessment

Matthew E. Poehner

Introduction

> Like a gardener who in appraising species for yield would proceed incorrectly if he considered only the ripe fruit in the orchard and did not know how to evaluate the condition of the trees that had not yet produced mature fruit, the psychologist who is limited to ascertaining what has matured, leaving what is maturing aside, will never be able to obtain any kind of true and complete representation of the internal state of the whole development. (Vygotsky 1998: 200)

Analogies such as the one above were frequently used by Vygotsky and his colleagues as they became increasingly convinced that conventional testing methods did not reveal the full range of individuals' abilities (van der Veer and Valsiner 1991: 337). Their research pointed to the fact that individuals whose independent performance is quite similar may vary considerably when offered assistance in the form of hints, leading questions and demonstrations, an observation that led to Vygotsky's formulation of the Zone of Proximal Development (henceforth, ZPD; for discussion, see introduction, this volume).

Originally, Vygotsky discussed the ZPD as an alternative to conventional intelligence testing, but later he came to see it as a new way of organizing all educational activities, including both teaching and assessment, in order to optimally impact learners' development (see van der Veer and Valsiner 1991; Lantolf and Thorne 2006). This is a radical proposal when one considers that even in most educational systems today assessment and instruction remain distinct, and often conflicting, endeavors. The point comes into sharp relief when one considers that what are generally thought to be good teaching practices, such as helping students when they encounter problems, are proscribed during assessment activities. Similarly, many of the constraints imposed during assessment (e.g., isolating learners from one another, removing cultural artifacts such as calculators, computers and dictionaries, imposing time limits, etc.) are very unusual in non-assessment contexts and antithetical to learning.

The ZPD has been widely interpreted and reformulated by educational and psychological researchers, sometimes in contradictory ways (Chaiklin 2003; Valsiner and van der Veer 1993). The range of perspectives on the ZPD is nowhere more prevalent than in the field of Dynamic Assessment (henceforth, DA). DA researchers offer learners mediation that is sensitive to their maturing abilities and in so doing support their engagement in activities at a level beyond what they could achieve independently. Such interactions not only render visible the full range of learners' abilities – those that learners have gained full control over and those that they do not yet completely control – but they simultaneously take on a leading role in their development. A single DA procedure thus functions as both an assessment and an instructional session as these become a seamless activity concerned with understanding learners' abilities by promoting their development.

The varied interpretations of Vygotsky's writings have led DA proponents to pursue a number of approaches to constructing ZPDs with learners. Some DA methods adhere closely to traditional assessment procedures of standardization and the quantification and generalizability of results, while others are more flexible allowing for cooperative interaction between assessor and learner. Lantolf and Poehner (2004: 54) refer to these DA orientations as *interventionist* and *interactionist*, respectively. These authors explain that interventionist and interactionist DA can be distinguished according to the outcomes they wish to obtain, with the former generally following a more formal approach in order to determine learners' potential for future development and the latter abandoning psychometric concerns in order to help learners realize their potential. Thus, while both forms of DA are concerned with learners' potential development, which they maintain is not revealed during traditional assessments and both break with the traditional dichotomy between assessment and instruction, they differ with regard to the relative emphasis each gives to these functions.

For instance, Sternberg and Grigorenko (2002) classify intervention-ist approaches as following either a *sandwich* or *cake* format. In the *sandwich* format, learners are administered a test in a traditional, non-dynamic manner, after which they receive an intervention designed to help them with problems they experienced before repeating the initial test or a parallel version. The intervention stage varies among DA ap-proaches, with some adhering more closely to pre-determined media-tion scripts than others (see Haywood and Lidz 2007). The *cake* format embeds intervention in the test administration itself so that learners are offered mediation for each test item or task that they find difficult. In this case, mediation is usually very tightly scripted and often arranged as a menu of hints and prompts that must be followed in a pre-determined sequence, usually from most implicit to most explicit. Mediation continues until the learner either overcomes the problem or until the final hint is reached, which usually includes the solution to the problem and an explanation of how the solution was reached. This process begins anew with the next test item (see Lantolf and Poehner 2004: 56). In both its *sandwich* and *cake* formats, interventionist DA displays many of the characteristics of formal testing despite its focus on learner development.

In interactionist DA, mediation is not scripted beforehand as media-tors are given significant latitude in how they respond to learners. In fact, mediator-learner dialoging would likely appear to a casual ob-server to be about teaching rather than testing. Of course, as Reuven Feuerstein has repeatedly argued with regard to his own interactionist DA model, teaching and testing are inseparable since the purpose of the procedure is to bring about change in learners' abilities. The chal-lenge faced by mediators is to provide support that is neither too implicit and therefore ineffective, nor too explicit such that it threatens learner agency and self-regulation.

While the quality of mediation during ZPD interactions is crucial to understanding development, equally important are learners' attempts to become more autonomous. That is, interpretation of learners' abili-ties includes both the mediator's moves during DA as well as learners' contributions. Lidz and colleagues (Lidz 1991; Van der Aalsvoort and Lidz 2002) coined the term *learner reciprocity* to capture this aspect of DA and devised a scale to evaluate the quality of reciprocity (discussed below); to date, however, this important construct has not received the level of attention it deserves. The reason this is so important is that change in reciprocity over time is an indicator of learner development.

In this chapter I argue that learner reciprocity must be better understood if, as Poehner and Lantolf (2005) contend, interactionist DA is to ameliorate L2 classroom instruction and assessment by systematizing teacher-learner interactions. For DA to achieve its purpose of understanding and promoting development teachers must attune mediation to learners' changing needs and this requires sensitivity to learners' reciprocating acts during DA. Drawing on protocols of French L2 DA interactions, this chapter will illustrate facets of learner reciprocity and suggest how a focus on both sides of mediator-learner dialogs deepens our understanding of learner development. My goal here is not to propose a formula for constructing a ZPD nor to offer an exhaustive inventory of reciprocating acts. Rather, I intend to draw teachers' and researchers' attention to the often complex interactions that occur in DA while at the same time outlining principles for their systematic interpretation.

Interpreting mediator-learner interactions in DA

The focus of both interventionist and interactionist DA is not to simply help learners complete the task at hand but to support their development of cognitive abilities. However, interventionist and interactionist orientations differ not only in their approach to mediation but also in how they interpret learners' contributions. In interventionist DA learners are limited to responding to the forms of mediation offered and their responses are understood in a more or less dichotomous manner – they are either correct or incorrect and this indicates whether additional mediation is required. Thus, while non-dynamic forms of assessment (NDA) prohibit examiner–examinee interaction on the grounds that independent performance of assessment tasks indicates learners' underlying abilities, interventionist DA permits some interaction but does not implicate the mediator in the resulting performance. That is, both NDA and interventionist DA share an assumption that performance falls within the provenance of the learner. In the former the assessor is responsible for eliciting learner performance and in the latter the assessor offers clues and hints but the learner still takes on the lion's share of responsibility for the performance. Where DA – and this is equally true of interventionist and interactionist orientations – diverges sharply from the performance focus of NDA is that its explicit goal is to help learners stretch beyond their current capabilities, not for the sake of improving assessment performance or earning a better test score but to promote learner development (Haywood and Lidz 2007). Indeed, NDA procedures are commonly described as either *norm-referenced,* in which case learner performance is captured by a score that is interpreted according to the distribution of all scores, or *criterion-referenced,* when learner performance is compared to some benchmark or standard. Given that DA is about activity in the ZPD, it can perhaps best be understood as *development-referenced,* with mediator-learner interactions tracked over time for the purpose of ongoing diagnosis and intervention (see Poehner 2007).

The following procedure, developed by Ann Brown and her colleagues as part of their Graduated Prompt Approach to DA (see Brown and Ferrara 1985), is an excellent illustration of interventionist principles. Following a *cake* format, the Graduated Prompt Approach (GPA) allows assessors to mediate learners as problems arise by referring to an inventory of hints and clues. Importantly, these prompts are determined prior to administration, are standardized and ranked from most implicit to most explicit and must be followed from first to last or until the learner produces the correct response. No deviation from the procedure is permitted as this would jeopardize its psychometric attributes (for discussion of this approach, see Lantolf and Poehner 2004; Sternberg and Grigorenko 2002). The following example concerns inductive reasoning ability among normal and learning disabled school children (reported by Campione, Brown, Ferrara and Bryant 1984; Palinscar, Brown and Campione 1991).

The children were presented with a string of eight letters and asked to provide the next four letters in the series that would correctly complete the pattern. For instance, a sequence such as NGOHPIQJ... would require learners to discern that every other letter is sequenced alphabetically (that is, N, O, P, Q and G, H, I, J). In this case, the four empty spaces must be filled with RKSL to complete the pattern (Campione *et al.* 1984: 81). When learners fail to produce the correct answer they are offered a series of standardized hints as follows: After an initial unsuccessful attempt at the item, the assessor asks the child 'Is this problem like any other you have seen before?' If the child recalls another item that follows the same pattern, the child is then directed to re-attempt the problem. Otherwise, the assessor prompts the child to 'read the letters in the problem out loud' and then asks, 'Did you hear a pattern in the letters?' If the child still does not respond correctly, the assessor begins to help the child think through the solution by asking, 'Are there any letters written more than once in the problem? Which ones? Does this give you any ideas about how to continue?' If necessary, the assessor reveals the correct answer and explains the pattern to the child before they move on to the next item (Palinscar *et al.* 1991: 75–6).

The researchers explain that their aim was to determine 'how much input they [the learners] would need before they mastered certain sets of problems' (Campione *et al.* 1984: 79). They continue, 'the number of hints required for the attainment of the learning criterion' is taken to be a 'metric of learning efficiency' (Campione *et al.* 1984: 82). This description is revealing in several respects. GPA is only indirectly concerned with learners' abilities and the processes of their development; the primary focus of the procedure is to measure how quickly learners profit from mediation, as this is argued to signify how close they are to successful independent performance. In other words, counting the number of mediating moves learners need to complete problems (no mediation, the first prompt only, the first two prompts, etc.) is an indication of their ZPD.

GPA's commitment to standardization ignores the possibility that the sequence and content of scripted mediation may not be appropriate to an individual's needs. In effect, even if mediators judge that a learner can be more effectively helped by a suggestion or comment not included in the inventory, they cannot offer this to the learner but must instead proceed through the pre-established mediation hierarchy. There is some overlap with NDA, since it is incumbent upon learners to perform under the conditions laid out by the mediator. Furthermore, the dichotomous interpretation of learners' responses (producing a correct or incorrect response) does not allow mediators to pursue why learners answered as they did.[1] In other words, the goal of moving individuals to some 'learning criterion' narrows the ways in which development might manifest itself because it downplays or overlooks the possibility that, over time, learners' incorrect responses may represent different problems and processes.

Interactionist DA differs qualitatively from interventionist approaches because it places no constraints on the mediation that can be offered to help learners develop their abilities. Following Vygotsky, interactionist DA eschews standardization in favor of a dialogic relationship between mediator and learner in order to broaden the possibilities for understanding and intervening in learner development (Minick 1987: 137). Performance belongs neither to the mediator nor to the learner but comprises the interplay between them as they raise questions, debate ideas, brainstorm alternatives, offer explanations and jointly work out solutions to assessment tasks. In essence, the 'conventional attitude of neutrality' that characterizes NDA is 'replaced by an atmosphere of teaching and helping' whereby instruction and assessment are fused into a single activity (Sternberg and Grigorenko 2002: 29). Interest in learners' contributions to DA is not limited to whether they provide a correct answer but also includes their implicit and explicit acceptance of mediation and requests for additional support as well as their questioning of and refusal to accept mediator support.

To return to the GPA pattern completion activity, had this been carried out in an interactionist framework the focus would have shifted from measurement to cooperation, with mediator and learner 'bowed over the same task' (Feuerstein, Rand and Hoffmann 1979: 102). Vygotsky himself described interactions that create a ZPD as cooperation between mediator and learner, clearly implying a dialogic orientation (e.g., Vygotsky 1986, 1998; see also Minick 1987). Thus, a mediator might begin by asking learners to explain their initial response, regardless of whether it is correct or not. Their reasoning can provide important insights into their level of understanding of the underlying principles involved and also helps mediators to fine-tune their support. For instance, it becomes possible to differentiate learners whose errors result from guessing with the aim of getting a good score (see Duvall in progress), carelessness, misinterpreting the task directions, incorrect information or assumptions regarding the nature of the task, inefficient use of strategies, etc. Without understanding the reasons learners failed to solve the problem, the mediator cannot appropriately guide their development. In the case of guessing, the mediator might begin by helping to orient learners to the problem by reminding them that they should look for a pattern and perhaps provide an example of how letters can be arranged in various ways. With learners who think the pattern is repeating, the mediator could challenge them to provide evidence for this claim. The mediator could then guide their search for other patterns in the letters and might suggest a strategy such as focusing only on the first four letters before considering the others. A learner who is close to independent performance might be recommended to materialize the final stage in completing the pattern by writing out the alphabet in order to see which letters are needed.

With each of the learners, mediation would be negotiated as the mediator-learner dialog unfolded and this is why one cannot predict beforehand the direction that DA interactions will take. In fact, it is the unpredictable nature of development that renders the ZPD such an important concept. Through flexible dialog with learners, mediators alter the timing and content of their support to remain in step with learners' changing needs. In this way, the mediator endeavors at every moment to provide precisely the right mediation to support learner development, although of course mediators are not always successful (2008). To be sure, interactionist procedures demand a great deal of mediators, since success depends upon their ability to correctly interpret and respond to learners. Attention to learners' reciprocating acts is essential to this process.

Mediation and learner reciprocity

Successful collaboration in the ZPD is dependent upon both the quality of mediation and learner reciprocity. In effect, these are inseparable features of DA: for mediation to be appropriate (i.e., promote learner development) learners' reciprocating acts must be correctly interpreted. As explained earlier, mediators should offer the most implicit form of support to which learners respond and should only become more explicit when necessary, thereby ensuring that learners remain as agentive as possible. Aljaafreh and Lantolf (1994: 467) further elaborate that mediation must be *contingent* on learners' needs and removed when they shows signs of independent behavior, even if such behavior is not fully appropriate. This is an especially important point, as it highlights the dynamic quality of mediator-learner interactions. Unlike NDA, which assumes learners' abilities to be unchanging (see Poehner 2007), DA recognizes that learners' needs are in flux and mediation that is appropriate at one moment may not be at the next. It is therefore imperative to be attuned to learners' reciprocating acts.

Learner reciprocity includes not only how learners respond to mediation that has been offered, but also their requests for additional support or specific kinds of support as well as their refusal to accept mediation. Lidz (1991) initially proposed the concept of reciprocity after noting that DA researchers have extensively described the quality of mediation offered during their procedures but have yet to account for how individuals 'differ in the ways they respond to the adult's input' and the fact that they 'elicit different quantities and methods of help from that adult' (Van Der Aalsvoort and Lidz 2002: 115). Drawing on her own clinical experience with young children, Lidz argues that the crux of DA is 'the level of receptivity of the child to the mediational intentions of the adult. How open is the child to input from the mediator? How able or willing to "receive" or cooperate?' (Lidz 1991: 110).

Van Der Aalsvoort and Lidz (2002: 122) conducted a grounded analysis of DA protocols and devised a scale to capture the various dimensions of learner reciprocity, including, for example, individuals' *responsiveness to the mediator, self-regulation of attention and impulses, comprehension of activity demands* and *reaction to challenge.* These authors suggest that learner profiles generated from interactionist procedures should include observations and commentary for the above categories. It is not difficult to imagine the value for classroom teachers of documentation that a learner responds to mediation in a suspicious or even hostile manner or that an individual eagerly turns to the mediator for support but does so even when he is capable of functioning independently. Such insights clearly augment the picture of learners' developing abilities.

Caution should be taken however when adopting any such scale as a lens for interpreting mediator-learner interactions. Just as standardized mediation limits the possibility of co-constructing a ZPD, imposing a strict set of categories for interpreting learners' behavior during DA risks overlooking or misunderstanding their contributions. To be sure, Van Der Aalsvoort and Lidz's scale represents a substantial advancement in reporting and interpreting interactionist procedures, but the categories they suggest should be viewed only as potential manifestations of learners' abilities. A given DA interaction may not include examples of all the categories and may well comprise behaviors that do not neatly fit any of them. I now turn to a discussion of learner reciprocity in the context of L2 development.

L2 learner reciprocity

The protocols below are taken from an interactionist DA procedure involving L2 learners of French in which the learners orally composed narratives based on video clips from two Hollywood movies: *Nine Months* and *The Pianist. Nine Months* is a comedy involving the misadventures of two characters, Samuel and Rebecca, who learn unexpectedly that they are going to have a baby. The film contains several sequences of both action and dialog, providing ample material for learners' narratives. Moreover, its lighthearted tone helped to ease any anxiety learners may have had during the sessions. During the last DA session, these comedic scenes were replaced with a clip from *The Pianist* in which the title character narrowly escapes death in the Warsaw Ghetto at the hands of German soldiers during World War II. The clip contained no dialog but several disturbing images of war. In this regard, the session was intended to reveal learners' success at recontextualizing their abilities as they encountered new and more complex tasks (see Poehner 2007).

A recurring problem experienced by many of the learners was their ability to control verbal tense and aspect. Perfective aspect, realized in French as the *passé composé*, emphasizes events, actions and states of being as completed while imperfective aspect (in French, the *imparfait*) makes no reference to their completion. In what follows, I show how control over the *passé compose–imparfait* distinction lies within each of the learners' ZPD. Although none of the learners is able to perform completely independently, when one considers their reciprocating actions it becomes clear that in each case the linguistic features under consideration are in the process of ripening. I will focus my analysis on five forms of reciprocity labeled as follows: *negotiating mediation, use of mediator as a resource, creating opportunities to develop, seeking mediator approval and rejecting mediation.* It must be stressed that these by no means constitute an exhaustive inventory of learner reciprocity. Rather, they are examples of the complex ways in which learners' abilities are revealed through dialogic cooperation. As will become clear, this entails much more than whether learners are able to produce a correct response during mediational interaction.

Negotiating mediation

In a dialogic approach to DA, all forms of reciprocity involve negotiation as mediator and learner collaborate. However, an especially important form of negotiation occurs when learners realize the mediation that has been offered is not adequate but must be supplemented with further explanation or additional information and they attempt to elicit this from the mediator. In an interventionist framework, learners must simply respond according to the mediation that is available. In the dialogic approach under analysis here, mediators and learners negotiate the support that is needed. In the following example (1), Donna (D) and the mediator (M) discuss the correct formation of the past conditional. Note M's use of English to support D as she encounters problems. Dialoging in the L1 helped to ensure that learners fully understood the mediation they were offered and encouraged them to more freely negotiate it with M. We pick up the exchange as D is attempting to relate a scene from *Nine Months* in which Rebecca informs Samuel that she is pregnant and he reacts by losing control of the car and driving off the road.

(1)

1. D: *...elle ne ja elle ne (...) elle ne pouv pouvriait* jamais faire un-*
    ...she not she not (...) she couldn't wouldn't ever be able to
    do

2. M: oh *conditionnel?*

3. D: conditional past

4. M: right

5. D: *elle elle ne peux jamais faire*
    She she can't ever do

6. M: actually you would form the conditional in that case with the

7. auxiliary verb

8. D: *elle ne peux (...) est-ce qu'il y a un autre mot pour auxiliary*
    She can't (...) is there another word for auxiliary

    (laughing)?

9. M: yeah like you use *avoir* and *être* [when you're using the past
    tense

10. D: *je ne comprends pas ce mot*]
    I don't understand this word

11. M: you have *avoir* or *être* and then for example *je suis allé* okay
          to have or to be   I went

12. *suis* is the auxiliary verb

13. D: oh okay

In line 1 D produces the non-existent verb form, **pouvriait* and so M
begins the interaction by ascertaining the learner's intention. When D
explains that she is attempting to use the past conditional, M does not
immediately respond but instead allows her an opportunity to reformulate. D's second attempt, in line 5, is also unsuccessful as she switches
to the present indicative. M then provides a clue as to the correct formation of the past conditional, but his use of metalinguistic terminology,
in this case 'auxiliary verb,' further confuses D. Importantly, D does not
remain silent at this point nor does she begin to guess, both of which
are possible reactions when one does not have enough information
to overcome a problem. Instead, she recognizes that she needs

clarification of M's terminology. In lines 8 and 10 she requests that M explain the meaning of an auxiliary verb. After he offers examples using the verbs *avoir* and *être* to illustrate the concept, she immediately recognizes them. Of course, identifying auxiliary verbs was not sufficient for D to succeed in this case and it was only after additional interaction that she later produced the correct form, *aurait pu*. The importance of this exchange is that D prompts M to further elaborate the mediation he had offered. M was attempting to adjust mediation to the learner's abilities, but it was only through negotiation that the learner was appropriately supported. I will next consider a case whereby a learner assumes an even more active role using the mediator as a resource. Rather than 'fine-tuning' the mediation that has already been offered, learners here seek out specific forms of support while in the midst of performance.

Use of mediator as a resource

Assessments typically do not afford learners the opportunity to request assistance, as this would be considered cheating, but DA fosters a collaborative posturing that encourages learners to initiate such interactions. This form of reciprocity is important for two reasons. From a pedagogical perspective, learners' requests for specific types of support help the mediator to better attune his interactions with the learners' needs. In other words, the mediator's responsibility for interpreting a learner's behavior in order to provide appropriate mediation is distributed between the mediator and the learner. This leads to the second reason why this form of reciprocity is important – the fact that learners are taking on responsibility for determining the mediation they require reveals something of their underlying abilities. More specifically, using the mediator as a resource indicates that the learners understand the linguistic (i.e., syntactic, lexical, phonological, pragmatic) resources needed to express their intended meaning and that they are aware that they do not fully control these. In this case, learners are not yet fully autonomous but they are exercising a form of self-regulation: they know the mediation they require and they know that they are not able to provide it for themselves so they turn to the mediator as a knowledgeable interlocutor. In contrast to the above form of reciprocity (negotiating mediation), learners here do not respond to mediation that has been offered but initiate the discussion themselves and in so doing reveal features of their development that remain hidden during procedures that focus on solo performance.

The exchange below (2) illustrates how a learner may use the mediator as a resource in DA. Amanda (A) is recounting an argument from *Nine Months* during which the character of Samuel doubts Rebecca's claim that birth control is not a hundred percent effective.

(2)

1. A: ...*la contrôle de naissance n'est pas absolument effective et Samuel ne*
    ...birth control is not completely effective and Samuel

2. *n'a pas croit?* cru?*
    didn't believes believe

3. M: uh which tense?

4. A: *passé composé*

5. M: oh *croire* has *cru* for a past participle

6. A: uh

7. M: so what was it *it*?

8. A: *il ne lui ne lui* a pas cru?*
    He didn't believe it

9. M: except *lui* is an indirect object right?

10. A: yeah so it would be *il ne l'a pas cru? et Rebecca...*
     He didn't believe it? And Rebecca...

In line 2, A produces two ostensible past participles for the verb *croire* (to believe). However, *croit* is not a past participle but is in fact a present tense form. *Cru* is the correct irregular past participle. The problem is that A does not seem to know which of the forms is correct. Through rising intonation, she turns to M for assistance. Once M ascertains that the learner wishes to use the perfective aspect to portray Samuel's reaction, an acceptable choice in this context, he supplies the correct past participle. A does not proceed immediately with her narration because she realizes that something more is needed to convey the meaning she has in mind. In particular, she shifts her focus from the irregular past participle to determining the correct object pronoun ('Samuel did not believe it'). In line 8, A attempts to formulate the construction, but does so as a question to M. Once again, she seems aware that there is a problem but she is not confident in her linguistic knowledge to overcome it without help from M. A manages to produce the correct word order but fails to select the appropriate particle, which M points out in line 9. M does not need to provide the direct object pronoun as A produces this herself in line 10.

In contrast to the first example, in which D negotiated mediation she was offered, this interaction is initiated and largely controlled by the learner herself. In this type of reciprocity, the mediator does not intervene until assistance is elicited by the learner. However, one should not assume that the learner's more active role during the exchange necessarily implies a higher level of development. I will return to this point later in the chapter but will now consider a form of reciprocity in which learners seize upon a mediating move and take the dialog in a new direction. While all mediator–learner interactions in DA represent opportunities to develop, this form of reciprocity involves a complex response to mediation whereby learners stretch their knowledge and abilities and experiment with the language.

Creating opportunities to develop

As explained earlier, standardized approaches to DA focus on whether learners are able to succeed when mediation is offered. More open-ended approaches do not attempt to fit learners' responses to mediation into neat, pre-determined categories, but instead attempt to interpret unpredicted features of performance that emerge. For example, a mediator may intervene simply to request clarification or to ask the learner to repeat an utterance and this may yield unexpected results as learners use this interruption as an opportunity to reformulate and to try to improve their performance. Sometimes their experimentation does not succeed, but their self-initiated revisions shed light on their development and also show a drive toward greater autonomy.

This form of reciprocity is apparent in the following exchange (3) between Nancy (N) and the mediator. N is describing a scene from *Nine Months* where Samuel and Rebecca are waiting for a repair truck to arrive and assess the damage their car sustained when they drove off the road:

(3)

1. N: *il a fait un accident avec un camion et* um so *après* uh um *ils ils attendent*

he caused an accident with a truck and um so after uh um
they they wait

2. or um *ils ont attendé** uh oh *ils attendaient le service pour*
they waited they were waiting for the service for

3. M: using *imparfait* for *attendre?*

4. N: yeah

5. M: okay because?

6. N: uh (...)

7. M: because you were starting off with the other one

8. N: okay no I got a better one *pendant qu'ils attendaient* (laughs)
while they were waiting

9. *attendaient le* service pour fixer la voiture
were waiting for the service for fixing the car

10. M: *réparer*
to repair

11. N: *pour réparer la voiture ils parle ils ont parlé de um le situation*
For repairing the car they speak they spoke about um the
situation

In lines 1 and 2 N successfully mediates herself as she selects a form
of the verb *attendre* (to wait for) that is both temporally and aspectually
appropriate to the context. She begins with the present tense and then
switches to the *passé composé* and finally to the *imparfait*. When M
questions her choice in lines 5 and 7, N does not answer directly but
instead produces another, more complex construction, that situates the
act of waiting in relation to another event in the story, the characters'
discussion of their situation. Her recasting of the action clarifies for M
why she feels the verb *attendre* must be in the imperfect – because it
serves to foreground Samuel and Rebecca's conversation.

What is significant about this episode is that N could have simply
explained her reasoning in English, given that M had asked her in English why she selected the imperfect. However, her reciprocity in this
case is more sophisticated. In line 8, N appears to tell herself ('no') that
she is capable of better expressing herself in French. She introduces her
new construction with the preface 'I got a better one,' announcing that
her new formulation expresses her intended meaning even more clearly.

Indeed, her addition of '*pendant que*' makes the case for imperfect aspect much stronger. This episode provides strong evidence of DA's potential to more fully reveal learners' abilities than is usually possible in NDA. Without mediation, N's original utterance would have been deemed appropriate but this opportunity to understand the extent of her abilities would have been lost. The resulting evaluation would have likely underestimated N's level of development. I now turn to a form of reciprocity that occurs when learners' performance is nearly autonomous but they still require a mediator to play an evaluative role.

Seeking mediator approval

Following the work of Vygotsky's colleague, Piotr Gal'perin, Lantolf and Poehner (2007) argue that the ability to evaluate the appropriateness of one's acts is a crucial component of performance. According to Gal'perin, human action is composed of three phases: orientation, execution and control (for discussion see Talyzina 1981; Poehner 2008). During orientation individuals must plan their performance and take account of the various resources they will need. Execution is the stage of actually carrying out the activity and which is traditionally understood as performance. Control refers to the evaluation of the performance, determining whether it has been successful or needs to be re-attempted. Individuals may experience problems at any of these stages, but typically it is the execution stage that receives attention during assessments. Difficulties in planning and evaluating performance are not as easily detected and usually only become evident during mediator-learner dialoging. Consider the following interaction (4) between Jess (J) and the mediator, where the learner is narrating the same car-accident scene from *Nine Months* that D described in (1) above.

(4)

1. J: ...*Samuel il est il avait choqué* et il a fait un accident, uh alors* (laughs) *et*
    he is he had shocked and he had an accident, uh so and

2. *puis Rebecca a dit uh je divine que tu ne veux pas le bébé*then
    Rebecca said uh I guess that you do not want the baby

3. M: actually could you repeat that last part after the accident?

4. J: *après l'accident? Elle a dit je je divine que tu ne* wait *que tu ne veux pas le*

> after the accident? She said I I guess that you wait that you do not want the

5. bébé (...) okay et elle lui a demandé qu'il était* qu'il être* plus positif?
   > baby and she asked him that he was uh that he to be more positive?

6. *Est-ce que ça marche?*
   > does that work?

7. M: *uh elle lui a demandé?*
   > she asked him?

8. J: *elle lui a demandé s'il peut* wait *s'il pourrait pouvait être plus positif*
   > she asked him if he can wait if he would be able could be more positive

9. *pouvait être? Uh (...)*
   > could be? Uh

10. M: okay?

11. J: okay, um *en réponse il...*
    > in response he...

At two points in this exchange J turns to M to evaluate the performance. In line 6 J explicitly asks whether her construction with the verb *être* (to be) is correct. In fact, she oscillated between an imperfect and an infinitival construction, neither of which work in this case and she seems to be aware that there is some problem. When M does not answer but instead prompts her to repeat her utterance, J switches to the verb *pouvoir* (to be able to). Once again, she struggles with the verb form, beginning with the present indicative, then changing to the conditional and finally settling on the imperfect. This time her choice is appropriate, but her repetition of the construction with a questioning intonation in line 9 invites the mediator to provide an evaluation.

J was faced with a complex task, as she had to use an imperfect verb form ('*pouvait*') to express a conditional (whether the character Samuel could be more positive). She successfully considers various options and even uses English to regulate her own behavior by telling herself to stop ('wait') so that she can think through the problem. Interestingly, J produces the correct form without help from M, but she still needs him to determine the acceptability of her performance. In other words, J is not yet able to perform completely independently; M must play an evaluative role.

Rejecting mediation

Learners do not always accept a mediator's intervention during DA, but may choose to ignore or even contest it. Aljaafreh and Lantolf (1994) similarly remarked that learners in their study sometimes refused mediation because they felt confident they could perform independently. Of course, a learner may mistakenly disregard mediation. What is interesting about this form of reciprocity is not only whether learners succeed in functioning without mediator support but that they are striving to perform more autonomously and believe that they have developed sufficiently that they can self-regulate. Learners' efforts to 'stretch' their abilities in this way are an important indication of development.

In the following excerpt (5) from Sara's second DA session, she is describing the car accident from *Nine Months*. Sara (S) uses the verb *parler* (to speak) in the preterit, but then hesitates and switches to English, where she employs an imperfect:

(5)

1. S: ... *il a parlé de la situation* wait so they were speaking about
      he spoke about the situation

2. the pregnancy is that what I said?

3. M: uh yeah

4. S: *ils* (...)

5. M: *ils parlaient* they were speaking

6. S: (...) when something happened, you know I see *plus-que-*

7. *parfait* being used in this

8. M: *plus-que-parfait?*

9. S: because they were speaking about this when she said this,
      well I think

10. M: where would *plus-que-parfait* fit in? How's that?

11. S: before she said this this had happened

12. M: like you said –

13. S: they were talking about something when she said this or or

14. before she said this this had happened

15. M: oh, like they had had an accident?

16. S: they had had an accident before they had a conversation be-

17. fore they discussed this but I think what they're talking about a

18. certain situation at that moment yeah it should be *imparfait* there as well

19. M: okay, because remember a lot of it has to do with your timeline and how

20. you're how you want to [talk about

21. S: see it]

In line 4 S appears uncertain how to continue her narration and so M prompts her by supplying the appropriate imperfect form. S, however, does not accept this assistance but continues to reason aloud in English, considering various ways in which the event she is describing could be temporally positioned in relation to other events in the story. Her suggestion of the *plus-que-parfait*, or pluperfect, surprises M and in lines 16 through 18 she explains how alternative linguistic forms impact meaning. Ultimately, S returns to the imperfect aspect for the verb *parler*. The importance of this episode is that the learner did not simply accept the mediation she was offered, but thought through the problem herself and eventually made her own determination. It is unlikely that Sara's high level of autonomy would have been apparent in a procedure that was not dialogic.

Not all attempts by learners to perform without mediator coopera-tion are successful. In the exchange below (6), Amanda (A) is unable to produce a correct lexical item as she narrates a scene from *The Pianist*. Recall that this video clip differed from the others in both its violent content and absence of dialog. Here A is explaining the main character's escape from German soldiers via a hole in the wall of his apartment.

(6)

1. A: ...so *ont été déstruits*
       ...so were destroyed

2. M: right right

3. A: *par des Nazis et il a échappé par le tri*
        by some Nazis and he escaped by the 'tri'

4. M: *oui le trou le trou* [the hole
        yes the hole the hole

5. A: *le cercle] dans le mûr et il parti**
        the circle] in the wall and he leaves

A attempts to produce the correct term *trou* (hole) but instead utters 'trî' in line 3. M recognizes the error and simply offers the needed lexical item but A does not accept this, preferring instead the word *cercle* (circle). Indeed, her utterance of *cercle* follows M's provision of *trou* and overlaps with his translation of the word as 'hole.' It appears then that A is aware of the French equivalent of 'hole' but opts instead to circumlocute. Although the hole was in the shape of a circle, the word *trou* is clearly more appropriate and A should have accepted it. Of course, it is also possible that A was not refusing M's assistance outright but was simply not paying attention. However, even in this case the point remains that she had committed to overcoming the problem on her own by relying on her knowledge of the lexicon to identify a 'good enough' alternative to get past the difficulty and continue the narration. Thus, although A's choice is not completely appropriate, her reciprocating act reveals a desire to regulate her own use of the language.

Conclusion

In this chapter I have argued that greater attention needs to be paid to learners' contributions to interactions if the full range of their abilities are to be understood. Expanding the focus of assessment in this manner represents a major shift away from most conventional assessment practices, which interpret learners' abilities in dichotomous terms – correct or incorrect – with little consideration given to understanding the underlying sources of learners' difficulties and even less to their remediation. Even DA practitioners, emphasizing the importance of mediation, have often overlooked aspects of development by adopting a 'medical' view of mediator–learner interactions according to which mediation, as in traditional medical treatment, is administered to passive patients rather than to agents who actively participate in making appropriate decisions. As the interactions reported in this chapter have illustrated, a more useful analogy for classroom language teachers is to understand DA as a dance in which performance results from the active participation and cooperation of both mediator and learner. The dialogic nature of this dance means that one does not script mediation beforehand and indeed that it is difficult to imagine a complete inventory of possible mediating and reciprocating acts, since these are always emergent. That said, I would like to conclude this chapter with a cautionary remark that nonetheless points the way toward overcoming certain challenges to the implementation of interactionist DA in the L2 classroom. Specifically, I am referring to the need to contextualize mediating and reciprocating acts in order to appreciate what they reveal about learners' abilities.

It would certainly be convenient if we could devise an exhaustive list of all the possible mediating moves and reciprocating acts one can expect to find in L2 DA interactions. One might even arrange these moves hierarchically, as prompts are organized in interventionist DA so that interpreting mediator-learner interactions would be a simple matter of marking each move that is made and checking its corresponding significance. For example, a learner might request mediation, as Amanda did in example (2) above. Amanda's request for mediation revealed that although she was not yet able to perform completely independently she was aware of the linguistic resources she needed to complete the narration task and to formulate her intended meanings. It might therefore be tempting to assume that this always represents a high level of reciprocity indicating that the learner is close to independent performance. However, obvious problems result from this line of reasoning. Consider if Amanda had made this same request while searching for the past participle of a verb that was lexically inappropriate or if she had been committed to the *passé composé* when the *imparfait* was needed. Far from indicating that Amanda simply needed a specific linguistic resource to complete the task, these scenarios would suggest confusion of lexical items and lack of control over verbal aspects, respectively. Thus, the signification of a given reciprocating act such as requesting mediator assistance can only be appropriately interpreted by contextualizing it within the mediator-learner dialog.

Similarly, mediating moves should not be assumed to always contribute in the same ways to interactions. For instance, in example (2) Amanda searches for the correct past participle of the verb *croire* (to believe) and the mediator simply tells her which of the two forms she had produced was appropriate. If, on the other hand, he had provided a more implicit form of mediation, such as a hint that *croire* functions similarly to the irregular verb *voir* (to see), Amanda's response would have revealed more about her level of awareness of this class of French verbs. Of course, the level of explicitness of this hint would vary according to a number of factors, including the frequency of the verb *voir* (Is this a rare, archaic form or one that learners are introduced to at the earliest level of study?), previous mediator–learner discussions of regular and irregular past participles and the learner's attention to other demands of the task. Thus while scales of mediation such as the one developed by Aljaafreh and Lantolf (1994) serve as a useful point of reference for the various ways in which one might mediate learners, the degree of explicitness of each mediating move they contain is not absolute. The significance of reciprocating and mediating moves is tied to the context in which they appear.

Elsewhere (Poehner 2008) I argue that efforts to attribute meaning to mediating and reciprocating moves can be enriched by connecting them to the problematic aspects of performance that they address. In this regard, Gal'perin's model of human action, described earlier, is especially relevant. By expanding the notion of performance to include orientation, execution and control stages, it becomes possible to more precisely diagnose the sources of performance breakdowns. To return to the example of Amanda (2), her interaction with the mediator targeted the selection of the appropriate past participle of the verb *croire*. Although Amanda was unable to select the appropriate form without support from the mediator, she had clearly developed a plan for how she wished to express that the character could not believe something (in this case, the effectiveness of birth control) and was also aware of the necessary linguistic resources (lexical, grammatical, phonological, etc.). This contrasts with a scenario such as Jess's (4), in which the execution is successful but the learner is unable to evaluate it without turning to the mediator for help with the control phase. These are very different kinds of problems and while both might involve extensive dialoging with various mediating and reciprocating moves, the insights into development offered by such interactions can only be interpreted in relation to the problem they address. Contextualizing mediator–learner interactions in this way should prove especially important in the development of learner profiles that classroom teachers can use to fulfil the everyday assessment responsibilities they face, including record keeping, assigning grades and certifying learners for the next level of study.

Note

1. A noteworthy exception is an interventionist model referred to as *Testing-the-Limits* (Carlson and Weidl 1992; 2000) that prompts learners to verbalize their reasoning. In this case, the prompts themselves are standardized ('Can you explain how you arrived at the solution?') but learners' responses are included in a profile that also comprises counts of mediating moves and numbers of correct and incorrect answers. In this way, the profiles attempt to bring out not just performance but the processes that underlie it.

References

Aljaafreh, A. and Lantolf, J. P. (1994) Negative feedback as regulation and second language learning in the zone of proximal development. *The Modern Language Journal* 78: 465–83.

Brown, A. and Ferrara, R. A. (1985) Diagnosing zones of proximal development. In J. V. Wertsch (ed.) *Culture, Communication and Cognition. Vygotskian Perspectives* 273–305. Cambridge: Cambridge University Press.

Campione, J. C., Brown, A.L., Ferrera, R. A. and Bryant, N. R. (1984) The zone of proximal development: Implications for individual differences and learning. In B. Rogoff and J. V. Wertsch (eds) *Children's Learning in the 'Zone of Proximal Development'* 77–91. San Francisco, CA: Jossey-Bass.

Carlson, J. S. and Weidl, K. H. (1992) Principles of Dynamic Assessment: The application of a specific model. *Learning and Individual Differences* 4: 153–66.

Carlson, J. and Wiedl, K. H. (2000) The validity of Dynamic Assessment. In C. S. Lidz and J. G. Elliott (eds) *Dynamic Assessment: Prevailing Models and Applications* 681–712. Amsterdam: Elsevier.

Chaiklin, S. (2003) The zone of proximal development in Vygotsky's analysis of learning and instruction. In A. Kozulin, B. Gidnis, V. S. Ageyev and S. Miller (eds) *Vygotsky's Educational Theory in Cultural Context* 39–64. Cambridge: Cambridge University Press.

Duvall, E. (in progress) *No Secrets to Conceal: Dynamic Assessment and State Mandated, High Stakes Reading Assessments for Children with Learning Disabilities.* Unpublished doctoral dissertation. The Pennsylvania State University, University Park, PA.

Feuerstein, R., Rand, Y. and Hoffman, M. B. (1979) *The Dynamic Assessment of Retarded Performers: The Learning Potential Assessment Device, Theory, Instruments and Techniques.* Baltimore, MD: University Park Press.

Haywood, H. C. and Lidz, C. S. (2007) *Dynamic Assessment: Clinical and Educational Applications.* Cambridge: Cambridge University Press.

Lantolf, J. P. and Poehner, M. E. (2004) Dynamic Assessment: Bringing the past into the future. *Journal of Applied Linguistics* 1: 49–74.

Lantolf, J. P. and Poehner, M. E. (2007) *Dynamic Assessment in the Foreign Language Classroom: A Teacher's Guide.* Center for Advanced Language Proficiency Education and Research, The Pennsylvania State University, University Park, PA.

Lantolf, J. and Thorne, S. L. (2006) *Sociocultural Theory and the Genesis of Second Language Development.* Oxford: Oxford University Press.

Lidz, C. S. (1991) *Practitioner's Guide to Dynamic Assessment.* New York: The Guilford Press.

Minick, N. (1987) Implications of Vygotsky's theories for Dynamic Assessment. In C. S. Lidz (ed.) *Dynamic Assessment: An Interactive Approach to Evaluating Learning Potential* 116–40. New York: The Guilford Press.

Palincsar, A. S., Brown, A. L. and Campione, J. C. (1991) Dynamic Assessment. In H. L. Swanson (ed.) *Handbook on the Assessment of Learning Disabilities* 75–94. Austin, TX: Pro-Ed.

Poehner, M. E. (2007) Beyond the test: L2 Dynamic Assessment and the transcendence of mediated learning. *The Modern Language Journal* 91, 323–340.

Poehner, M.E. (2008) *Dynamic Assessment: A Vygotskian Approach to Understanding and Promoting Second Language Development.* Berlin: Springer Publishing.

Poehner, M. E. and Lantolf, J. P. (2005) Dynamic Assessment in the language classroom. *Language Teaching Research* 9: 1–33.

Sternberg, R. J. and Grigorenko, E. L. (2002) *Dynamic Testing. The Nature and Measurement of Learning Potential.* Cambridge: Cambridge University Press.

Talyzina, N. (1981) *The Psychology of Learning. Theories of Learning and Programmed Instruction.* Moscow: Progress Publishers.

Valsiner, J. and van der Veer, R. (1993) The encoding of distance: The concept of the zone of proximal development and its interpretations. In R. R. Cocking and K. A. Renninger, (eds) *The Development and Meaning of Psychological Distance* 35–62. Hillsdale, NJ: Lawrence Erlbaum.

van der Aalsvoort, G. M. and Lidz, C. S. (2002) Reciprocity in Dynamic Assessment in classrooms: Taking contextual influences on individual learning into account. In G. M. Van der Aalsvoort, W. C. M. Resing, & A. J. J. M. Ruijssenaars (eds) *Learning Potential Assessment and Cognitive Training* 7 111–44. Amsterdam: Elsevier.

Van der Veer, R. and Valsiner, J. (1991) *Understanding Vygotsky.* Oxford: Blackwell.

Vygotsky, L. S. (1986) *Thought and Language. Newly revised and edited by A. Kozulin.* Cambridge, MA: MIT Press.

Vygotsky, L. S. (1998) *Child Psychology. The Collected Works of L. S. Vygotsky: Vol. 5. Problems of the Theory and History of Psychology.* New York: Plenum.

2 The effects of dynamic assessment on L2 listening comprehension

Rumia Ableeva

Introduction

The development of listening proficiency is a crucial component of foreign language learning and teaching. However, as Omaggio-Hadley (2000: 184) remarks, research in the area of learners' listening comprehension is 'still in its infancy.' The few studies that have been conducted focus primarily on factors affecting the listening comprehension process (e.g. Rubin 1994; Vandergrift 1998) and only a small number consider the assessment of listening comprehension (e.g. Ur 1984; Flowerdew and Miller 2005; Buck 2003). In this regard, Alderson and Bachman (2003: x), the editors of the *Cambridge Language Assessment Series*, point out that 'the assessment of listening abilities is one of the least understood, least developed and yet one of the most important areas of language testing and assessment.'

Perhaps due to the lack of research into what might constitute good listening assessment practice, teachers typically follow a traditional approach to assessing listening comprehension (see for example Buck 2003; Flowerdew and Miller 2005; Omaggio-Hadley 2000). While discussing the purposes and the types of listening tests (e.g. achievement, placement tests), Buck (2003) articulates the acute need for the creation of new diagnostic listening assessments that will identify specific areas where learners need improvement and, in so doing, will better inform the instructional process regarding learners' listening abilities. He explains the current lack of good listening assessments as follows: 'we still do not fully understand what the important sub-skills of listening are; nor are we sure what information educators need to teach listening better' (Buck 2003: 97).

Recent L2 research has begun to examine the applications of dynamic assessment (DA), a new approach to assessment grounded in Vygotsky's socio-cultural theory (SCT) of mind and in particular in his concept of the Zone of Proximal Development (ZPD) (e.g. Antón 2003; Lantolf and Poehner 2004; Poehner 2005). This work helps to frame the present study, which follows a DA-based approach to assessing listening abilities of intermediate French L2 university students enrolled in a fourth-semester language course (the first semester beyond the mandatory foreign language requirement).

University language classes are often comprised of students whose experience with the target language varies widely. This is perhaps especially true at the intermediate level, where some students have passed through the university's basic language program but where others have been placed as a result of language study in secondary school or time spent in an environment where the L2 is spoken. For many students, comprehending authentic aural language, especially during traditional approaches to assessment, is one of the most frustrating and difficult aspects of their language learning experience. There is also evidence that traditional assessment, or what will be referred to here as non-dynamic assessment (NDA, henceforth), does not always allow L2 students to achieve sufficient understanding of texts. In order to enhance students' comprehension of authentic audio texts, the study described in this chapter applies a DA intervention to help students develop their L2 listening abilities. Therefore, the purpose of the study was to investigate the effects of DA on developing L2 students' listening abilities. The research questions to be addressed are:

1. To what extent can a DA procedure diagnose L2 learners' listening comprehension difficulties?

2. How effectively can a DA approach to L2 listening instruction support the development of students' listening abilities?

The six DA-based case studies discussed here demonstrate that, in fact, DA is a helpful diagnostic pedagogical tool which not only allows instructors to establish the actual level of learners' listening comprehension abilities but also, and more importantly, to reveal their potential abilities 'that are now in the state of coming into being, that are only ripening, or only developing' (Vygotsky 1956: 447–8, cited in Lantolf and Poehner 2004:51) and that are hidden during NDA.

Applications of DA

DA, grounded in the Vygotskian concept of the ZPD, was originally implemented in Russia with children with various kinds of learning disabilities. According to Kozulin and Garb (2002), the term DA was not used by Vygotsky himself but was introduced by his followers outside of Russia, after his death. However, Vygotsky did discuss 'the whole range of possible interactive interventions to be used during the ZPD assessment, such as asking leading questions, modeling, starting to solve the tasks and asking students to continue ...' (Kozulin and Garb 2002: 113). Vygotsky's work led to decades of DA research in Russia before it gained the attention of psychologists and educators in the West. Before turning to a discussion of more contemporary DA research, the tradition of DA procedures in Russia and in particular DA work with L2 learners, will be briefly described.

DA research in Russia

Since the 1950s, researchers in Russia have conducted a number of studies applying different DA techniques. According to Lidz and Gindis (2003), Russian DA studies can be divided into two areas: a 'diagnosis of learning aptitude,' which emphasizes the assessment of intellectual development, and a 'teaching/learning experiment,' with a focus on improving learners' understanding and knowledge of various school subjects. The proponents of the 'teaching/learning experiment' include five of Vygotsky's most well known students and colleagues: Gal'perin, El'konin and Davydov, A. A. Leont'ev, and Luria. On the basis of theoretical principles and experimental models proposed by these five scholars, a series of DA studies was carried out to determine students' aptitude for learning in specific content domains, including L1 Russian (Juykov 1971, 1979; Gal'perin, 1992; Gal'perin, Zaporojez and El'konin 1992), geometry and mathematics (Talyzina 1993), physics (Kalmykova 1981) and L2 English (Kalmykova 1981).

Kalmykova (1981) describes a large-scale project in the 'teaching/learning experiment' tradition that she and several colleagues conducted during the 1970s that focused on learning aptitude in specific school subjects, including L2 English.[1] In Kalmykova's approach, researchers provided hints in order to determine not only learners' zone of actual development (cognitive functions that have already matured) but also their zone of proximal development, which they identified as an indicator of learners' potential for future learning in a given content domain.

Kalmykova and colleagues did not impose time limits on their testing procedures and they emphasized the importance of ensuring at the outset that all learners have comparable task-relevant background knowledge as well as a positive attitude toward the assessment. In this way, testers can help to eliminate sources of variance that may disadvantage certain learners. Kalmykova's group further advocates the use of problem-solving activities that engage learners in observation of new phenomena and that encourage them to draw conclusions regarding the regularity of these phenomena, to formulate explanatory rules that underlie the phenomena and, apply, these rules to new problems in different contexts. It is worth noting that this approach to extending learning beyond the initial assessment tasks is also a hallmark of DA methods outside of Russia, namely Brown's Graduated Prompt Approach (e.g., Brown and Ferrara 1985) where it is referred to as *transfer* and in Feuerstein's Mediated Learning Experience (Feuerstein, Rand and Hoffman 1979) in which it is conceptualized as *transcendence*. Recently, Poehner (2007) has introduced this feature of DA into applied linguistics.

Saburova was the principle investigator in the portion of the project that targeted learners of L2 English. In one study (see Kalmykova 1981 for details) 11 school children, aged 12–13 years, were asked to formulate the rule for the formation of the *present continuous*. The children had already studied the *present simple*, had learned to conjugate the verb *'to be'* and to use it as a copula and had been exposed to some English analytic structures while using verbs in interrogative and negative forms. Nevertheless, the *present continuous* poses certain challenges to L1 Russian speakers because Russian does not distinguish it from the *present simple* in the way that English does. In addition, formation of the *present continuous* in English is relatively complicated, as the ending *–ing* is a constant element but the auxiliary verb (*to be*) has different forms depending on person and number of the subject.

Saburova's 'teaching/learning experiment' comprised three stages termed *preliminary, essential* and *additional*. The *preliminary stage* involved three kinds of activities. The first of these was intended to minimize lexical errors and involved vocabulary exercises containing lexical items used in subsequent stages. This was followed by a review of previously learned grammar points that are relevant to the formation of the *present continuous* (e.g., forms of the verb *to be*). Finally, the researcher explained the use of the *present continuous tense* to participants and engaged them in an activity to inductively teach the formation of the *present continuous*. Working individually, learners were given cards that contained English sentences using the *present continuous* and were asked to analyze the verb forms and to formulate the rule for the formation of the *present continuous*. Not all learners were able to do this independently and so guidance was offered learners as needed in order to be sure that at the end of this stage all participants understood how to form the *present continuous*.

During the *essential stage*, the children were given cards containing sentences in Russian. They were first asked to sort the cards according to whether they thought the sentences would be most appropriately rendered in English using the *present simple* or the *present continuous*. They were then directed to translate the sentences into English and to explain how they formulated the *present continuous* when they employed it. The children were allowed to cycle through this stage four times and it was noted that some learners were able to perform appropriately before others. Those learners who were still unsuccessful after four repetitions proceeded to the *additional stage*. This stage was devoted to the identification of learners' ZPDs, interpreted according to the amount of help needed for each learner in order to complete the task independently. Help during this stage consisted of four hints of increasing explicitness, with the last hint being a detailed explanation of *present continuous* formation.

Saburova's analysis noted the differences among learners that emerged at each of the three stages of the procedure. Differences pertaining to learners' ability to independently formulate the rules during the *preliminary stage* were particularly successful predictors of future L2 performance. In fact, the data obtained during the completion of this activity allowed Saburova to place learners into three groups, one that required little or no help to identify all formal features of the *present continuous* and to formulate the underlying rule, a second group that included four children who could partially identify the formal features but were not able to formulate the rule and a third group consisting of four learners who could not solve the problem independently at all. Saburova concluded that the process of independently formulating rules that underlie grammatical structures could be an important indicator of children's L2 learning aptitude.

DA research outside Russia

DA was first introduced to audiences outside the former Soviet Union by A. R. Luria (1961), one of Vygotsky's most influential colleagues. In the intervening decades, DA procedures have been developed for use with various populations around the world.[2] However, language educators have only recently turned their attention to DA. For example, Antón (2003) only mentions two L2 DA publications and Lantolf and Poehner (2004) refer to just five.[3] Following this work, DA is defined here as a procedure that:

> integrates assessment and instruction into a seamless, unified activity aimed at *promoting learner development* through appropriate forms of mediation that are sensitive to the individual's (or in some cases a group's) current abilities. In essence, DA is a procedure for simultaneously assessing and promoting development that takes account of the individual's (or group's) zone of proximal development. (Lantolf and Poehner 2004: 50, italics added)

In contrast to NDA which focuses on already matured abilities, 'DA promotes functions that are maturing' and 'foregrounds future development' (Lantolf and Poehner 2004: 54). Through interaction in the ZPD, DA allows instructors to diagnose/assess not only the actual level of students' language abilities but also their potential development, while at the same time promoting this development.

The effectiveness of a DA procedure is dependent upon the appropriateness of the mediation offered to learners because this must be sensitive to the dynamics of their maturing abilities. The goal of DA is to reveal learners' potential future development on the intermental plane and to help it develop on the intramental plane through mediator-learner interaction. DA proponents argue that this kind of assessment-with-mediation brings assessment and instruction together into an organic unity whereby learning is the result of mediation, which is then internalized and becomes accessible to be deployed later in other contexts.

According to Sternberg and Grigorenko (2002: 28–9), DA can be distinguished from NDA in three ways. In terms of assessment goals, NDA focuses on 'products formed as a result of preexisting skills.' At the level of assessment administration, the non-dynamic paradigm does not permit 'feedback from examiner to test-taker regarding quality of performance' during the test procedure. Finally, with regard to the examiner's orientation in NDA, it is important 'to be as neutral and as uninvolved as possible toward the examinee.'

DA contrasts sharply with NDA. In a dynamic approach, the focus is on learners' emergent (i.e., dynamic) abilities. The assessment is inseparable from instruction and the learners are continuously mediated during the procedure because 'the examiner functions as a mediator who reacts to learner's responsiveness and is more concerned with cognitive transformation than with performance efficiency' (Lantolf and Poehner 2004: 59). According to Lantolf and Poehner (ibid.), in DA the examiner and the examinee have the same goal and represent a functional system, a unit where all parts work together.

Dynamic assessment of second language listening: a pedagogical experience

In order to understand the potential contributions of DA to the listening comprehension assessment and instruction, a DA intervention was used with learners of L2 French at a large US public university during the spring semester of 2005. The students were recruited from two sections of a fourth semester French oral communication and reading comprehension course. At the beginning of the semester, students were given some basic information about the study and were asked to contact the researcher via email if they were interested in participating. Six students volunteered. They considered their participation as an opportunity to gain additional practice in listening comprehension. Before engaging in DA, all participants were asked to fill out a questionnaire concerning their L2 learning background. The questionnaire (Appendix 2.1) provided insights into participants' language learning experiences and enabled better organization of the intervention stage of the study.

Participants

Six undergraduate students, one male and five females, aged 18–20 years, participated in the study. They included one male participant, Dimitri and five females: Katya, Jenia, Alina, Sonia and Bertha (all names are pseudonyms). Five participants were English native speakers and one participant was a bilingual speaker of Spanish and English. The number of French courses the learners had taken at the university varied as some had studied the language in secondary school. However, all participants had taken a minimum of two semesters of French at the university. Participants' language learning backgrounds are summarized in Table 2.1.

Table 2.1. Language learning backgrounds

Participants	Years of secondary school level language study	Semesters of university level language study
1. Katya	4 years	2 semesters
2. Jenia	4 years	2 semesters
3. Alina	6 months	4 semesters
4. Sonia	4 years	3 semesters
5. Bertha	4 years	2 semesters
6. Dimitri	6 years	2 semesters

Study design

Although researchers have elaborated a number of approaches to DA (e.g. Dillon and Carlson 1978; Kalmykova 1981; Guthke, Beckmann and Stein 1995; Karpov and Gindis 2000), the study reported on in this chapter follows Poehner (2005). Poehner (ibid.) describes the incorporation of DA in an advanced French L2 university program. His study documents students' construction of past-tense narratives in French. Participants narrated video clips from two feature films and attempted to relate events using perfective and imperfective aspect, a distinction in French that commonly presents difficulties for L2 learners. Poehner's design included the following stages: 1) a dynamic and nondynamic pretest; 2) an L2 enrichment program; 3) a dynamic and non-dynamic posttest; and 4) two transfer assessment sessions. The enrichment program involved one-on-one tutoring sessions and was focused on learners' problem areas identified during the pretest stage. The posttest repeated the initial non-dynamic and dynamic assessments. Finally, in order to establish the extent to which participants could internalize and extend the mediation provided in the course of previous sessions, two transfer sessions were conducted. During the dynamic and transfer sessions, the mediator engaged in flexible interaction with the participants, offering hints, prompts, questions, suggestions and explanations. As noted by Poehner, the mediation used throughout the assessments and the enrichment program 'was not determined a priori and then applied to a given assessment but, rather, was dependent on the specific context of mediator-learner interactions' (Poehner 2005: 151). These suggestions underlie the design of the present study and were used during the stages that involved interaction between the researcher/mediator and the learners.

Procedure

All six sessions took place within a one-week period (15–20 February 2005) and were conducted on an individual basis. Each session lasted approximately 50/60 minutes and was audio recorded. Two cassette tape recorders were used: one for playing the selected text and the other for the simultaneous recording of sessions.

During the first ten minutes of each session participants were given instructions about the procedure. Participants were told that they would listen to the radio text and would be asked to identify the nature of the program. In addition, participants were informed that they could use French or English, or a mixture of both. During the remaining 45–50 minutes, the participants listened to the radio advertisement, answered basic comprehension questions and summarized the text.

The procedure included the following stages: 1) the pretest; 2) the mediation process stage (DA intervention); and 3) the retest. During the pretest stage, participants listened to the selected recording twice and answered a series of questions in writing. The pretest contained questions adapted from the textbooks currently used for teaching French as a foreign language at the intermediate university level (e.g. Bragger and Rice's *Du Tac au Tac* 2004). At the beginning of the DA intervention, it was emphasized that participants would be allowed to ask questions and the researcher would provide necessary hints, explanations and suggestions. Given that this stage involved interaction sensitive to specific linguistic problems experienced by learners, the number of listenings was not planned in advance and varied depending upon the learner. During the retest stage, participants were asked to summarize the text in order to verify their text comprehension. This stage also involved flexible mediator-learner interaction.

Listening materials

One radio advertisement recorded from a French radio station was used in this study. This advertisement was chosen with the intention to provide students with linguistic as well as with cultural information concerning the target speech community. The radio text (20 seconds in real time) advertises *Léon de Bruxelles*, a restaurant chain in France. The text is characterized by conventions typical of advertisements, including speaker intonation patterns, music and sound effects. A transcript of the text is given below accompanied by an English translation:

Léon de Bruxelles

Feminine voice: *Bientôt midi. C'est le moment d'aller déjeuner chez 'Léon de Bruxelles.' Moules et frites au menu.*

(Soon it will be noon. It is time to go to 'Léon de Bruxelles' and to have lunch. Mussels and fries on the menu.)

Masculine voice : *Des moules. Des frites. C'est belge. C'est 'Léon de Bruxelles.' – 'Léon de Bruxelles.' La brasserie belge.*

(Mussels. Fries. It's Belgian. It's 'Léon de Bruxelles.'– 'Léon de Bruxelles.' The Belgian pub.)

Data analysis

First stage: pretest

This stage proceeded non-dynamically, with participants listening to the text twice and preparing written responses to comprehension questions without mediation. Analysis of the pretest results indicates that although all six participants answered the proposed questions, their comprehension of the text was not complete. This is evident in the responses presented below (participants' answers contain their original spellings):

Text: *Léon de Bruxelles* (Leon of Brussels)
(1) *De quoi s'agit-il dans cette publicité ?*
          (What is the main idea of this advertisement?)

Katia: *Je ne sais pas*
          I don't know

Jenia: *Une femme et un homme parlent* pour Léon de Bruxelles.*[1]
          A woman and a man speak *for Leon De Bruxelles.

Alina: *Dans cette publicité il's'agit un*restaurante.*
          This advertisement is about a *restaurant.

Sonia: *petit *dejeuner*
          breakfast

Bertha: **la restaurant fast-food*
          fast food reastaurant

Dimitri: *C'est une publicité* pour les produits que Léon de Bruxelles *offrais *à les *écouters.*

    It is an advertisement * for the products that Leon de Bruxelles *offered to listeners.

(2) *Quel endroit est mentionné dans cette publicité ?*
    (What place is mentioned in this advertisement?)

Katia: *Pour les vacances un restaurant avec un menu des frites.*
    For vacation a restaurant with a menu of fries.

Jenia: *Je ne sais pas*
    I don't know

Alina: *Bruxelles, Belge est *mentionne dans cette publicité. (Leon de Belgique)*

    Brussels, Belgian is *mention in this advertisement. (Leon of Belgium)

Sonia: *Restaurant*
    Restaurant

Bertha: *des frites*
    fries

Dimitri: *Je ne sais pas*
    I don't know

(3) *Que peut-on manger dans l'endroit mentionné dans cette publicité ?*
    (What can we eat at the place mentioned in this advertisement?)

Katia: *Des frites*
    fries

Jenia: *On peut manger * les frites dans l'endroit mentionné dans cette publicité.*

    We can eat *the fries at the place mentioned in this advertisement.

Alina: *Dans l'endroit mentionné il peut manger *les frites.*
    At the mentioned place he can eat *the fries.

Sonia: *les frites.*
    the fries

Bertha: *des frites*
    fries

Dimitri: *les frites et *quelque autres ... je ne sais pas.*
    fries and some others ... I don't know

(4) *A quel moment de la journée peut-on manger des produits
    mentionnés dans cette publicité?*
    (At what moment of the day can we eat the food mentioned
    in this advertisement?)

Katia: *L'*apres-midi et le soir.*
    In the afternoon and in the evening.

Jenia: *L'après-midi on peut manger *les produits.*
    The afternoon we can eat products.

Alina: *Je pense à midi mais je ne sais pas.*
    I think at noon but I don't know.

Sonia: *je n'ai pas compris*
    I didn't understand.

Bertha: *la nuit*
    the night

Dimitri: *Pour le *dejeuner. Le midi*
    For the lunch. The noon

Participants' responses suggest that they understood certain parts
of the text but that this comprehension was rather vague. Even though
the formulation of questions contained some cues (e.g. *Léon de Bruxelles,
manger des produits* /to eat food/, etc.), none of the participants
could indicate that it was an advertisement for a restaurant named
'Léon de Bruxelles' offering mussels and fries, specialties of Belgian
cuisine.

Jenia and Dimitri's answers to the first two questions are vague and
do not indicate whether they understood the main idea of the advertisement or not; they only mentioned the name *Léon de Bruxelles*. Alina,
Bertha, Katia and Sonia understood that it was an advertisement for a
restaurant, although Bertha qualifies this restaurant as a 'fast food' establishment. Apparently the word *frites* /fries/ has an impact on Bertha's
interpretation which reflects her everyday knowledge connected to the
American cultural context, where fries are primarily associated with fast
food. None of the participants picked up on the word *belge*, although
this word was repeated twice in the advertisement and can be easily
understood by expert speakers of English with basic knowledge of
French (the French adjective *belge* being a cognate of English 'Belgian').

In response to question #3 all participants mentioned *frites*[5] (transfer from L1) but none included *moules*. The answers to question #4 suggest that Sonia and Bertha missed the word *midi* /noon/ and gave completely wrong answers. However, it would be doubtful that they, being intermediate students of French, do not know the word *midi* or *le déjeuner* /lunch/, which also can convey the idea of noon. In fact, Sonia's use of the word *petit déjeuner* /breakfast/ in her response to question #1 confirms that she knows this word but was unable to appropriately use her knowledge while responding to question #4. Presumably, attentional constraints or phonological coding of the text did not allow Sonia and Bertha to capture this word from the text. Katia, Jenia and Alina do not seem to be sure about their answer, but certainly they were able to detect the word *midi* from the string of words they heard. Only Dimitri's answer indicates that he picked up both *le déjeuner* and *midi*.

Apparently the impact of phonological processes, such as assimilation, unstressed words and varying speed of input (Rost 2002), coupled with the non-interactive nature of the NDA format, reduced participants' capacities to construct meaning from the text. Undoubtedly, their linguistic knowledge is much broader and permits them to comprehend more difficult texts containing more complicated sentence structures and vocabulary than the one under consideration here. The answers presented above suggest that the NDA format inhibits students' ability to perform according to their potential. In what follows, it will be demonstrated how appropriate support through DA enables learners to better apply and also to extend their linguistic and cultural knowledge. These DA interactions offers L2 teachers the possibility to identify the source of the problems that impede students' text comprehension, to establish their potential ability to understand an authentic audio text and to foster students' L2 listening abilities.

Second stage: the mediation process stage

During the mediation process, participants listened to the same audio text as many times as they needed and were offered mediation as problems arose. Mediation included leading questions, hints and prompts. Given that assessment, in a dynamic approach, is inseparable from instruction, participants were also offered linguistic and cultural explanations whenever necessary to aid text comprehension.

The mediation stage gave a fuller picture of the difficulties experienced by the participants while listening to the text. Two recurring problems were identified: 1) students could not recognize words they already knew and could use in oral production; and 2) students were unable to discern the meaning of new lexical items. The examples below document Sonia's and Bertha's previously acquired linguistic knowledge (the lexical item *midi* /noon/) which they could not apply during NDA. This knowledge surfaced only in the course of the dynamic interaction:

(1) Example from Bertha's data:

1.   R: *mais quand ... quand ... à quelle heure, à quelle heure nous pouvons ... ils disent*
    but when ... when ... at what time, at what time we can ... they say

2.   *bon, ok, venez ... come ... venez chez Léon de Bruxelles, vous pouvez manger des*
    well, ok, come to Leon de Bruxelles, you can eat

3.   *frites, des boules-des moules ... quand?*
    fries, bussles/mussels ... when

4.   B: *midi, déjeuner*
    noon, lunch

5.   R: *ok ... déjeuner, midi ... est-ce que tu as entendu le mot 'midi?'*
    ok ... lunch, midi ... did you hear the word 'noon?'

6.   B: did I hear it? *non mais déjeuner c'est midi*
    did I hear it? no but lunch it's noon

(2) Example from Sonia's data:

1.   R: *tu as entendu bientôt midi?*
    Did you hear 'soon it will be noon?'

2.   S: *midi::*
    noon

3.   R: *tu connais le mot 'midi?'*
    do you know the word 'noon?'

4.   S: *oui ... et bientôt?*
    yes ... and soon?

5. R: *bientôt? soon et midi c'est quoi? est-ce que tu peux dire en*
     'bientôt?' soon and 'midi' what's that? can you tell in

6. *anglais ... qu'est-ce que c'est midi ?*
     English ...what does it mean 'midi'?

7. S: *midday ... like ... noon*

8. R: *ça veut dire que ... à quel moment de la journée cette publicité*
     it means ... at what moment of the day this advertisement

9. *nous propose d'aller manger le déjeuner ?*
     proposes to us to eat lunch?

10. S: *à midi*
     at noon

The second major problem that occurred during this stage concerns unknown vocabulary. For example, while listening to the text *Léon de Bruxelles*, all participants had difficulties with the French word *moules* /mussels/. Interestingly, they all heard this word as 'boule.' This may be due to phonological effects:

> French [b] is fully voiced while English [b] is only partially voiced
> and tends to sound more as [p]. In order to make a fully voiced [b],
> American English speakers tend to prenasalize [b] producing a
> sound close to [mb]. Presumably in this study students perceived
> French [m] as very close to [b], hence the confusion of *boule* for
> *moule*. (B.Bullock, personal communication, spring 2005).

In (3) Bertha offers a response (line 10) that was typical for all participants:

(3)

1. R: *alors là, est-ce que tu peux dire de quoi s'agit-il dans ce texte,*
     en général?
     so, can you say: what is the main idea of this text, in
     general?

2. B: (silence)

3. R: *est-ce que tu peux dire ... en général=*
     can you say ... in general=

4. B: *=uhm ... en général...*
     =uhm ... in general ...

5. R: *quelle compagnie, quel produit ou quels services, qu'est-ce que nous pouvons faire avec ces produits ou ces services, en général ?*

    what company, what product or what services, what can we do with these products or these services, in general?

6. B: *j'ai entendu … uhm … Léon et Bru … Bruxelles …*

    I heard … uhm … Léon et Bru … Bruxelles

7. R: *ok, Léon et Bruxelles …*

    ok, Léon et Bruxelles

8. B: *oui … et des frites* (almost unaudible)

    yes … and fries

9. R: *des … des frites ?*

    fries?

10. B: *oui … et des … bou-les* (not sure)

    yes … and … bussels

11. R: *des boules? quelque chose comme 'boules?'*

    bussels? something like 'bussels?'

12. B: *oui*

    yes

Five of six participants did not know the word *moules*. This fact can be explained by the low frequency of this word. However, one participant, Alina, claimed she was familiar with the word but recognized its oral form (line 12) only after having received an explicit hint in the form of choice offered by R (line 11). (4) is an example from Alina's data:

(4)

1. R: *et qu'est-ce que nous pouvons manger dans ce restaurant ?…*

    and what can we eat at this restaurant?

2. A: *euh … les frites …*

    uhm … the fries

3. R: *et c'est tout ?*

    and that's all?

4. A: (laughter) *non … mais … c'était seulement la nourriture * que je comprends… il a*

    (laughter) no … but … it was the only food I understand … he

5. *dit que le menu ...*
       said that the menu ...

And later during the interaction:

6. A: *oui, je ne sais pas ... et ... manger... les boules ... et les frites*
       yes, I don't know ... and ... to eat ... the bussels ... and the fries

7. R: *les boules et les frites ? boules ?*
       the bussels ... and the fries? bussels?

8. A: *boules ...*
       bussels ...

9. R: *peut-être boules ... tu ne connais pas=*
       may be bussels ... do you know=

10. A: *= * je ne sais pas boules* (laughter)
       = i don't know bussels (laughter)

11. R: *peut-être boules, peut-être moules ?*
       may be bussels, may be mussles?

12. A: *ooh!!! moules !!!* mussles!!!

This example suggests that Alina knows the meaning of the word *moules* but was unable to recognize it without mediation. Clearly, in a non-dynamic procedure where the tester adopts a disinterested stance, she would not have received credit for her response '*frites et boules.*' The other five participants were provided with a necessary explanation (described below) in order to familiarize them with the word *moules,* which they had not previously encountered. The difficulty posed by the word *moules* is important because the underlying source of the problem was not the same for all learners. That is, Alina knew its meaning but simply did not recognize it in the stream of speech, indicating a phonological problem. For the other learners, *moules* presented not only a phonological challenge but a lexical one as well in that the term was unfamiliar to them. In this regard, it should be emphasized that the problem areas were revealed only on the basis of participants' performance throughout the DA stage, during which a flexible mediator-learner interaction was involved.

In addition, it should be noted that during the mediation stage, great care was taken not to overload students with unnecessary help.

However, given that DA is a procedure in which instruction and assessment go together and the mediator 'is more concerned with cognitive transformation than with performance efficiency' (Lantolf and Poehner 2004: 59), the researcher was required to use supplementary explanations in order to foster more detailed comprehension of the selected text. This is exemplified in (5) and (6) from Bertha's data.

In (5) the mediator's explanation (lines 7 and 9) to Bertha is quite typical of the explicit support that all participants required to appreciate the correct use of the adjective *belge* and the noun *la Belgique*:

(5)

1. B: *qu'est-ce que c'est belge ?*
    what does it mean 'belge'?

2. R: *belge ? Belgian … donc, Léon de Bruxelles … Bruxelles c'est la*
    Belgian … so, Léon de Bruxelles … Brussels is the capital of

3. *capitale de la Belgique ? Belgique*
    Belgium=

4. B: *=ah, ok=*

5. R: *=et c'est un restaurant… quel restaurant ? français ? canadien ?*
    and it's a restaurant … what kind of restaurant? French? Canadian?

6. B: Belgian

7. R: *Oui, belge … ok … euh … la Belgique c'est un pays … Belgium … en français on dit*
    yes, Belgian … ok … uhm … la Belgique it's a country … Belgium … in French they say

    la Belgique et l'adjectif c'est belge, par exemple, un restaurant belge …=
    'la Belgique' and the adjectif is belge, for example, a Belgian reataurant …=

8. B: *=oui..=*

9. R : *=mais le pays c'est la Belgique… il s'agit de quoi dans cette publicité ?*
    =but the country is la Belgique…it's about what this commercial?

10. B: *le restaurant belge et euh … la nourriture que … qu'il vend …
pour déjeuner…*

> the Belgian restaurant and uhm … the food that … that it sells
> … for lunch …

In (6) the mediator addresses another type of difficulty that impeded
accurate comprehension: learners' failure to understand cultural information embedded in the text. Given that text comprehension depends,
to a degree, on appreciating cultural references, mediator-learner interactions also included elaboration (in French) of the facts that mussels
and fries constitute a stereotype in Belgian cuisine and that *Léon de
Bruxelles* is a restaurant chain in France. The exchange in (6) is representative of the kind of cultural explanation offered to students:

(6)

> R: *c'est un restaurant belge et tu peux trouver ce restaurant dans
> … presque dans toutes les grandes villes françaises. Léon de
> Bruxelles c'est une chaîne it's a chain … bon … ok … des frites et
> des moules ça ces les spécialités de la cuisine belge mais ce res-
> taurant tu le trouves en France …*
>
> > it's a Belgian restaurant and you can find this restaurant in
> > …in almost every big French city. Léon de Bruxelles it's
> > a chain … well … ok … fries and mussels, these are specialties
> > of Belgian cuisine but this restaurant you can find it in
> > France…

Third stage: retest

During the retest stage participants summarized the audio text. The transcripts of the summaries include timed pauses (given parenthetically)
in order to portray the slow rate of students' speech. Alina's (7) and
Sonia's (8) summaries serve to illustrate the learners' performances and
interactions with the mediator during this stage.

(7)

1. A: *il est un *advertisment pour Léon de Bruxelles (0.2) il est *dans
Belgique et Léon*

> it's an *advertisment for Léon de Bruxelles (0.2) it's in
> Belgium and Léon

restaurant (0.3) uhm à *cette restaurant il y a des moules et des frites (0.2) et (0.1)uhm=

restaurant (0.3) uhm at this restaurant there are mussels and fries (0.2) and (0.1) uhm=

2. R: = et (0.1) à quel moment de la journée (0.1) à quelle heure nous pouvons manger=

    = and (0.1) at what moment of the day (0.1) at what time we can eat=

3. A: = à midi

    = at noon

4. R: à midi ok

    at noon ok

5. A: uhm (0.2) il est un homme et *un femme …

    ihm (0.20 it's a man and woman …

6. R: comment?

    say it again...

7. A: un homme et *un femme

    a man and woman …

8. R: aha un homme et une femme qui parlent?

    aha a man and a women speaking?

9. A: oui

    yes

10. R: et c'est un restaurant … tu as dit … qui propose quelle cuisine?

    and it's a restaurant … you said … that proposes what kind of cuisine?

11. A: uhm (0.2) des moules et (0.1) des frites …

    uhm (0.2) mussels and (0.1) fries …

12. R: et c'est la cuisine de quel pays?

    and it's the cuisine of what country?

13. A: umh (0.1) Belgique

    uhm (0.1) Belgium

14. R: c'est la cuisine belge (0.1) et quel est le nom de ce restaurant?

    it's Belgian cuisine (0.1) and what's the name of this restaurant?

15. A: *uhm (0.2) Léon de belge*
    uhm (0.2) Léon de belge

16. R: *de Bruxelles*
    of Brussels

17. A: *de Bruxelles oui*
    of Brussels yes

18. R: *et ce restaurant il se trouve où? en France ou en Belgique?*
    and this restaurant where is it located? in France or in Belgium?

19. A: *umh (0.5) en France*
    umh (0.5) in France

(8)

1. S: *Léon de Bruxelles est un restaurant *que je peux (0.2) aller (0.1) manger (0.2) *en midi ...*

    Léon de Bruxelles it's a restaurant *that I can (0.2) go (0.1) to eat (0.2) *in noon ... =

2. R: *= à midi uhu ...=*
    = at noon ... =

3. S: *= à midi à midi (0.2) et je peux (0.1) manger (0.3) des moules et des frites (0.3) uhm=*
    = at noon at noon (0.2) and I can (0.1) eat (0.3) mussels and fires (0.3) uhm=

4. R: *=et c'est un restaurant (0.1) c'est quel restaurant?*
    = and it's a restaurant (0.1) what kind of restaurant is it?

5. S: *uhm (0.1) belge*
    uhm (0.1) Belgian

6. R: *très bien!*
    very good!

It should be noted that the participants experienced significant difficulties summarizing the text in French. For example, they spoke very slowly, sometimes they could not recall the correct French words and their responses contained errors typical for intermediate-level university students (e.g. the incorrect use of noun gender: 'cette restaurant' instead of 'ce restaurant'; or the incorrect use of prepositions: 'en midi' instead of 'à midi'). For that reason, they were consistently given assistance by the researcher in the form of leading questions and prompts. Despite all the difficulties and efforts, the text summaries demonstrate that participants achieved a better understanding of the text *Léon de Bruxelles* and evidently, the DA-based procedure facilitated this process.

Follow-up data

Since the major focus of the study was to improve learners' listening ability through a DA interaction, limits were not placed on the number of times the audio text was played for learners. As indicated by Table 2.2, the number of listenings varied from three to five times for each learner. Of course, the primary form of intervention was not listening to the text multiple times but rather the quality of mediation offered to learners during the second stage. The number of listenings is therefore of interest because it indicates the extent of mediation required by individual learners.

These differences, although slight, can perhaps best be interpreted with reference to participants' language learning background as described earlier. For instance, Katya and Bertha, both of whom had completed four years of French study in secondary school and two semesters at the university, required five listenings to understand the text. Jenia, Sonia and Dimitri, who had almost the same L2 learning background (four to six years at school/two French courses at the university level), achieved the same understanding after hearing the text four times. It is surprising to note, then, that Alina, who had studied French for only six months at the secondary level and three semesters at the university, understood the text after only three listenings. However, a follow-up interview with Alina allowed the researcher to gain deeper

Table 2.2. Number of listenings per student

Students	Number of listenings
1. Katya	5 times
2. Jenia	4 times
3. Alina	3 times
4. Sonia	4 times
5. Bertha	5 times
6. Dimitri	4 times

insight into her L2 learning background. In the course of the interview, it was revealed that she had resided in a trilingual (French, Flemish, German) country. At the age of 13–14, she had spent two years with her family in Belgium where she was exposed to oral French while watching TV. Alina's comments during this interview were revealing:

(9)

1. A: ... and then when I was in Belgium like I didn't know any French because we were in Flemish part ... in Belgium and ... and the north is French and then the south is ... German and Dutch speaking ...

2. R: so ... they don't speak French ...

3. A: (well) they speak Flemish and it's a sort of ... like ... uhm ... combination of French and Dutch but you can still like ... on tv ... there are a lot of French things and we would like ... I mean you still have ... you have like English subtitles and we had like option I mean ... with subtitles ... but I think that ... I got accustomed to listening to a lot of French and we watch tv a lot =

4. R: = a lot? =

5. A: = because that ... i mean ... because there wasn't anything in English just English ... so it's all ... either you had French or then you had German stations ...

6. R: and your preference was ...

7. A: ... was the French stations ... 'cause ... their channels were better (laughter) ... that's what we all watched ... i mean ... my brother and sister we all watched it ... my little brother went to a French speaking school ... whenever he was there ... but ... the rest of us ... we didn't really speak French because we didn't know any French

Following a sociocultural perspective, it should be noted that Alina's case confirms the importance of A. A. Leontiev's claim concerning learners' previous (spontaneous) development and their educational environment. Leontiev (2001a) points out that instructors should always take into account learners' self-development, previous spontaneous (or everyday life) development as well as learners' educational environment that includes family, communication with friends, the mass media and is important for learners' learning development. Apparently,

Alina's previous history allowed her to comprehend the text in question better as opposed to other participants. Even though Alina resided in the Flemish part of the country during her sojourn in Belgium, an extensive exposure to Belgian everyday life explains why she knows specialties of Belgian cuisine such as mussels and fries. In addition, the fact that she was exposed to French TV might have had an impact on her capacity to understand spoken French faster than the other five participants.

Discussion

This pilot study has shown that all participants had difficulties understanding an authentic audio text and were only able to achieve a better comprehension with mediator guidance. The individual difficulties experienced by the participants necessitated different types and amounts of mediation. These differences, in turn, indicated that the learners had different unique ZPDs; that is, they were each developmentally different despite similarities in their pretest performances. The differences only emerged during the second stage of the study as participants interacted with the mediator. In fact, learners were not homogeneous even with regard to the features of the text they found problematic. Five students experienced phonological, lexical and cultural difficulties while listening to the text but one student (Alina) had problems mainly related to French phonology (bottom-up process: she was unable to appropriately discern L2 sounds) and partially to cultural information (top-down process: *Léon de Bruxelles* was absent from her knowledge). Moreover, even when two learners had problems in the same domain, such as phonology, this did not mean that they were at the same level of development. For example, neither Alina nor Dimitri was able to discriminate certain words (e.g. '*moules*') in the stream of speech, even when they were clearly familiar with the words. For both learners, it is fair to say that their L2 phonology is not fully developed and this led to auditory confusion between L1 and L2 sounds (e.g. the confusion of [m] and [b] sounds). However, Dimitri differed from Alina in both the lexical and cultural domains: unlike Alina, he did not know the word mussels and was totally unfamiliar with cultural references in the text (i.e. mussels and fries as a popular dish in Belgian cuisine).

While none of the participants can yet fully understand the text independently and, therefore, still require mediation, their responsiveness to assistance demonstrates that the capacity to comprehend such texts is in the process of ripening. In other words, it is anticipated that the learners are ready to respond effectively to appropriate instruction, but the instruction must take into account their developmental differences. Thus, even though the learners were enrolled in the same level course (i.e., intermediate French course, fourth semester), they were clearly not at the same level of ability with regard to comprehending the advertisement. This crucial fact, along with knowledge of the source of the problems unique to each learner was only brought to light as a result of DA.

Conclusion

This chapter has presented a pedagogical approach to developing students' L2 listening comprehension that is grounded in Vygotskian theory. The conceptual principle of this theory is that learning and intellectual development constitute the unity where learning promotes and thereby stimulates, development (Vygotsky 2003). Taking a SCT perspective on L2 learning and teaching, this pilot study has investigated one way of applying a DA procedure to L2 listening instruction. Although the findings obtained in this study are limited, they indicate that a DA approach can facilitate comprehension of authentic aural language when used with intermediate university students learning a foreign language. All the learners in this study arrived at a more complete understanding of the audio text through DA. This outcome is not all that surprising, given DA's commitment to flexible mediator–learner interaction in response to learners' needs.

The results of this study suggest that a DA approach to listening instruction enables teachers to more accurately evaluate learners' listening abilities, to identify the source of the linguistic problems impeding text comprehension and in so doing to promote learners' L2 development. It is important to emphasize, however, that this study represents only an initial attempt to deal with DA and the complex problem of the development of L2 listening ability and should, therefore, be considered an orientation point for future investigation.

As indicated by the above discussion, non-dynamic approaches to assessing listening comprehension are prominent in today's language classrooms. The study described here suggests that language pedagogy might benefit from further research into effective ways of implementing DA in the L2 classroom. The integration of dynamic forms of assessment with L2 listening instruction promises to offer insights into language learning as a developmental process while simultaneously creating opportunities for intervention to support learners' emergent abilities.

In his articles 'Pedagogy of common sense' (2001a) and 'Technology of developing education: some considerations' (2001b), A. A. Leontiev appeals to the proponents of SCT and calls for the integration of a SCT-based approach to teaching and learning, or at least of its elements, into the practices of the existent traditional educational system. The findings of the study presented in this chapter further reinforce the urgency of Leontiev's call.

Notes

1. The Kalmykova project was carried out at the Laboratory of Education and Intellectual Development. The director of the Laboratory, N. A. Menchinskaya (1905–84), was one of Vygotsky's students from 1927–30 and under Vygotsky's guidance defended a PhD dissertation devoted to the problem of teaching/learning arithmetic among elementary school children. The Laboratory was a unit in the Research Institute of Psychology and Pedagogy at the Academy of Pedagogy (in the former USSR). Its primary research responsibility was to create diagnostic methods that could determine various components of children's intellectual development. More specifically, the researchers of the Laboratory studied the relationship between the teaching/learning process and the intellectual development of school children. They developed and implemented methods that enabled them to identify strong and weak points of learners' thinking activity as well as their ZPDs. The diagnostic methods designed were intended to lead to interventions and much greater individualization of learning.
2. For instance, ethnic minorities (Dillon and Carlson 1978), children with speech and language impairments (Peña and Gillam 2000), children exposed to different educational experiences (Guthke, Heinrich and Caruso 1986), children with significant learning problems (Karpov and Gindis 2000), etc.
3. Antón (2003) refers to Schneider and Ganschow (2000) and Kozulin and Garb (2002), while Lantolf and Poehner (2004) refer to the following studies: Guthke, Heinrich and Caruso (1986), Peña and Gillam (2000), Kozulin and Garb (2002), Antón (2003) and Gibbons (2003).
4. Here and elsewhere asterisks (*) indicate an error occurred in participants' written and spoken discourse (see also Appendix 2.2: Abbreviations and Transcription Conventions).

5.   The use of the word *frites* could be also explained by the fact that *frites*, unlike *moules*, is a vocabulary item introduced in most first-year L2 French textbooks.

References

Alderson J. C. and Bachman L. F. (2003) Series editors preface. In G. Buck *Assessing Listening*, x –xi. Cambridge: Cambridge University Press.

Antón, M. (2003) Dynamic assessment of advanced foreign language learners. Paper presented at the American Association of Applied Linguistics, Washington, DC, March.

Auger, J. and Valdman, A. (1999) Letting French students hear the diverse voices of Francophony. *Modern Language Journal* 83: 403–12.

Bragger, J. and Rice, D. (2004) *Du Tac au Tac*. Boston: Heinle and Heinle Publishers.

Brown, A. and Ferrara, R. A. (1985) Diagnosing zones of proximal development. In J. V. Wertsch (ed.) Culture, Communication and Cognition. Vygotskian Perspectives, 273–305. Cambridge: Cambridge University Press.

Buck, G. (2003) *Assessing Listening*. Cambridge: Cambridge University Press.

Davydov, V. V. and Kudryavzev, V. T. (1997) Razvivayushee obrazovanie: Teoreticheskie osnovaniya pereemstvennosti doshkol'noi i nachal'noi schkol'noi stupenei [Developing education: Theoretical basis of preschool and elementary school stages continuity]. *Voprosy Psychologii* 1: 3–19.

Davydov, V. V. and Markova, A. K. (1992) Razvitie myshleniya v detskom vozraste [Development of thinking of school children]. In M. O. Suare (ed.) *Vozrastnaya i Pedagogicheskaya Psikhologiya: Teksty [Age and Pedagogical Psychology: Texts]*, 132–46. Moscow: Moscow State University Press.

Dillon, R. and Carlson, J. S. (1978) Testing for competence in three ethnic groups. *Educational and Psychological Measurement* 38: 438–43.

Feuerstein, R., Rand, Y. and Hoffman, M. B. (1979) *The Dynamic Assessment of Retarded Performers: The Learning Potential Assessment Device, Theory, Instruments, and Techniques*. Baltimore, MD: University Park Press.

Flowerdew, J. and Miller, L. (2005) *Second Language Listening: Theory and Practice*. Cambridge: Cambridge University Press.

Gal'perin, P. Ya. (1992) K issledovaniyu intellectual'nogo razvitiya rebyonka [On the research of the child intellectual development]. In M. O. Suare (ed.) *Vozrastnaya i Pedagogicheskaya Psikhologiya: Teksty. [Age and Pedagogical Psychology: Texts]*, 96–109. Moscow: Moscow State University Press.

Gal'perin, P. I., Zaporojez, A. V. and El'konin, B. D. (1992) Problemy formirivaniya znanii I umenii shkol'nikov i novye metody obucheniya v shkole [Problems of knowledge and abilities formation in school children and new methods of teaching at school]. In M. O. Suare (ed.) *Vozrastnaya i Pedagogicheskaya Psikhologiya: Teksty [Age and Pedagogical Psychology: Texts]*, 230–43. Moscow: Moscow State University Press.

Gibbons, P. (2003) Mediating language learning: Teacher interactions with ESL students in a content-based classroom. *TESOL Quarterly* 37: 247–73.

Guthke, J., Heinrich, A. and Caruso, M. (1986) The diagnostic program of 'syntactical rule and vocabulary acquisition' – A contribution to the psychodiagnosis of foreign language learning ability. In F. Klix and H. Hagendorf (eds) *Human Memory and Cognitive Capabilities. Mechanisms and Performances*, 903–11. Amsterdam: Elsevier.

Guthke J., Beckmann, J. F. and Stein, H. (1995) Recent research evidence on the validity of learning tests. *Advances in Cognition and Educational Practice* 3: 117–43.

Juykov, S. (1971) K probleme diagnostiki obychaemosti shkol'nikov [The diagnosis of children's learnability] *Voprosy Psykhologii* 5: 85–99.

Kalmykova, Z. (1981) *Prodyktivnoe Myshlenie Kak Osnova Obuchaemosti [Productive Thinking as the Basis of Learning Aptitude]*. Moscow: Pedagogika.

Karpov, Y. V. and Gindis, B. (2000) Dynamic Assessment of the level of internalization of elementary school children's problem-solving activity. In C. S. Lidz and J. G. Elliott (eds) *Dynamic Assessment: Prevailing Models and Applications*, 133–54. Amsterdam: Elsevier.

Kinginger, C. (2002) Defining the zone of proximal development in US foreign language education. *Applied Linguistics* 23: 240–61.

Kozulin, A. and E. Garb. (2002) Dynamic Assessment of EFL text comprehension of at-risk students. *School Psychology International* 23: 112–27.

Kramsch, C. (1993) *Context and Culture in Language Teaching*. Oxford: Oxford University Press.

Lantolf, J. P. and Poehner, M. E. (2004) Dynamic Assessment: Bringing the past into the future. *Journal of Applied Linguistics* 1: 49–74.

Leontiev, À. À. (2001a) Pedagogika zdravogo smysla [Pedagogy of common sense]. In A. A. Leontiev (ed.) *Yazyk I Rechevaya Deyatel'nost' v Obchej I Pedagogicheskoj Pyskhologii [Language and Speech Activity in General and Pedagogical Psychology]*, 343–365. Moscow: NPO 'MODEK'.

Leontiev, À. À. (2001b) Tekhnologia razvivaushego obuchenia: Nekotorye soobrajenia [Technology of developing education: Some considerations]. In A. A. Leontiev (ed.) *Yazyk I Rechevaya Deyatel'nost' v Obchej I Pedagogicheskoj Psykhologii [Language and Speech Activity in General and Pedagogical Psychology]*, 366–377. Moscow: NPO 'MODEK'.

Leontiev, A. A. (2003) *Osnovy Psykholingvistiki [Fundamentals of Psycholinguistics]*. Moscow: Smysl.

Lidz, C. S. and Gindis, B. (2003) Dynamic Assessment of the evolving cognitive functions in children. In A. Kozulin, B. Gindis, V. S. Ageyev and S. M. Miller (eds). *Vygotsky's Educational Theory in Cultural Context*, 96–116. Cambridge: Cambridge University Press.

Omaggio-Hadley, A. (2000) *Teaching Language in Context*, 2nd edition. Boston: Heinle and Heinle Publishers.

Peña, E. D. and Gillam, R. B. (2000) Dynamic assessment of children referred for speech and language evaluations. In C. S. Lidz and J. G. Elliot (eds) *Dynamic Assessment Prevailing Models and Applications*, 543–75. Amsterdam: Elsevier.

Poehner, M. E. (2005) Dynamic Assessment of Oral Proficiency among Advanced L2 Learners of French. Unpublished doctoral dissertation. The Pennsylvania State University.

Poehner, M. E. (2007) Beyond the test: L2 Dynamic Assessment and the transcendence of mediated learning. *The Modern Language Journal* 91: 323–340.

Poehner, M. E. and Lantolf, J. P. (2005) Dynamic Assessment in the language classroom. *Language Teaching Research*, 9: 1–33.

Rost, M. (2002) *Teaching and Researching Listening*. Longman: Pearson Education.

Rubin, J. (1994) A review of second language listening comprehension research. *The Modern Language Journal* 78: 199–211.

Sternberg, R. J. and Grigorenko, E. L. (2002) *Dynamic Testing. The Nature and Measurement of Learning Potential*. Cambridge: Cambridge University Press.

Talyzina, N. F. (1993) Teoriya planomernogo formirovaniya umstvennykh deistvii segodnya. [Theory of planned formation of intellectual actions today]. *Voprosy Psikhologii*, 1: 92–101.

Ur, P. (1984) *Teaching Listening Comprehension*. Cambridge: Cambridge University Press.

Vandergrift, L. (1998) Successful and less successful listeners in French: What are the strategy differences? *The French Review* 71: 370–95.

Van Lier, L. (1996) *Interaction in the Language Curriculum: Awareness, Autonomy and Authenticity*. London: Longman.

Vygotsky, L. S. (1978) *Mind in Society: The Development of Higher Psychological Processes*. Cambridge: Harvard University Press.

Vygotsky, L. S. (1987) *The Collected Works of L. S. Vygotsky: Vol. 1. Problems of General Psychology*. Including the volume *Thinking and Speech*. New York: Plenum.

Vygotsky, L. S. (1996) *Anthology of Humanistic Pedagogy*. Moscow: Smysl.

Vygotsky, L. S. (2003) *The Psychology of Human Development*. Moscow: Smysl.

Appendix 2.1. Questionnaire

1. Your name

2. Your major

3. How many years did you learn French at school/at High school?

4. Did you learn French at Penn State University (or other universities) before? How many semesters? What kind of courses did you take?

5. Have you ever been exposed to real French speech (e.g. native speakers, radio/TV programs, stays in France) before? If so, in what contexts?

6. Have you ever listened to authentic texts (e.g. real French radio or TV programs) before? What kind of? If so, in what contexts (classroom, on the Internet, in France)?

7. If you listened/watch/to French radio/TV programs in French classrooms before, how often were you exposed to French authentic texts (once, twice etc. a week, a month, a semester)? Is it difficult for you to understand real French? If so, what causes difficulties?

Appendix 2.2. Abbreviations and transcription conventions

I. Abbreviations

R = researcher, A = Alina, B = Bertha, S = Sonia

DA = dynamic assessment

NDA = non-dynamic assessment

L 1 = participants' native language

L 2 = participants' second (or foreign) language learned at an educational setting

SCT = Vygotsky's socio-cultural theory

II. Transcript Conventions

*   indicates an error

...   indicates a pause

=   indicates no interval between two adjacent utterances, the second occurred immediately after the first without overlapping it

3 Changing examination structures within a college of education: the application of dynamic assessment in pre-service ESOL endorsement courses in Florida

Tony Erben, Ruth Ban and Robert Summers

Introduction

Lorraine, Billig, Tavalin and Gibson (2000) describe a learning/adoption trajectory within an educational environment that models the diffusion of an innovation as a cyclical process in which teachers evolve from learners (teacher-trainees), to adopters of educational innovation, to co-learners/co-explorers with students in their own classrooms, to a reaffirmation/reflection and decision modality and then to a final stage, where teachers take the role as leaders and promoters of the innovation. This chapter employs Lorraine's framework to understand the processes of promotion, acceptance, use and spread of dynamic assessment (DA) amongst the ESOL faculty and pre-service teachers in a College of Education at a major research university in Florida.

This chapter is divided into three parts. In the first part we situate the study in the general literature on program innovation. Specifically, we seek to describe the characteristics of program innovation within the process of implementing an ESOL Endorsement program at a large metropolitan university in Florida. In the second part, we outline the process of introducing DA as a component of a mandated College-wide ESOL comprehensive exam. The third part details how faculty and pre-service teachers adjusted to the use of DA as a pedagogical innovation and reflected on its potential use as a tool in K-12 education settings.

ESOL endorsement in Florida

In accordance with a 1990 State of Florida Department of Education mandate, all educational institutions are required to educate pre-service teachers in ESOL methods in order to enable teachers to deliver comprehensible instruction to English Language Learners. Consequently, teacher-trainees in the areas of elementary, special and early childhood education, as well as secondary English and foreign languages are only allowed to graduate from state-accredited teacher education institutions if they attain an endorsement in ESOL to accompany their major. The Florida Department of Education has interpreted an endorsement in ESOL to mean that a student must complete the equivalent of 300 master plan points or 15 semester hours (five courses) in ESOL.

Shifting cultures and ESOL infusion at the University of South Florida

At the University of South Florida (henceforth, USF), students are required to complete not only ESOL courses but also non-ESOL courses that infuse ESOL concepts, methodologies and theories into their curriculum. Table 3.1 outlines the particular ESOL requirements for each program.

Table 3.1. ESOL endorsement requirements per degree

Degree program	# of ESOL courses	ESOL binder /folder	ESOL infused courses	Comprehensive exam and ESOL practicum
Undergraduate				
English, foreign language, special education	2	Extensive binder	Many	3 hr exam + 10 day practicum
Early childhood, elementary	3	Focused folder	Fewer	3 hr exam + 10 day practicum
Social studies, business, mathematics, science	1	None	none	none
Graduate				
MAT (Eng., FL, Spec. Ed., El., Early Ch.)	3	Focused folder	Fewer	3 hr exam + 10 day practicum

When first implemented, ESOL infusion was an innovative practice within Florida's Colleges of Education. Its diffusion, however, was neither smooth nor readily accepted by non-ESOL teacher-educators. Although innovations are frequently reported in the educational research literature it is not clear how they come to be adopted by classroom practitioners. Indeed, Frank, Zhao and Borman (2004: 148) admit that the processes of implementing new practices are not well understood. As they explain, 'The standard model of diffusion suggests that people change perceptions about the value of an innovation through communication and these perceptions then drive implementation.'

The process of implementing ESOL infusion across the university's curriculum has given rise to a number of issues which remain difficult to manage from both pedagogical and managerial/organizational perspectives. Specifically, implementation requires the following: 1) providing appropriate content-specific resources to faculty teaching infused courses; 2) offering professional development opportunities to help faculty better integrate ESOL-specific content with their own areas of expertise; 3) developing support mechanisms for students, instructors and the administration on ESOL issues and state mandates; 4) constructing appropriate assessment mechanisms across disciplines within a college of education that meet individual department needs and state comprehensive exit exam requirements; and 5) streamlining processes of ESOL accountability and teaching practices that fit comfortably with each departmental culture. Issues revolving around assessment procedures have been particularly problematic and it is to this that we now turn.

Changing a traditional assessment culture

When ESOL was first mandated for pre-service education programs in Florida, it was envisaged that a comprehensive exam would be administered as an exit requirement for the endorsement. Students who passed the comprehensive exam were said to have met numerous *standards* and *accomplished practices* that were aligned with the expectations of various bodies charged with accrediting American colleges and universities, including NCATE, SACs and the FLDOE.[1]

The decision to administer a one-off comprehensive ESOL exam was located within the College's existing historical practices. For example, at the end of most graduate programs in the College students must pass a three-hour comprehensive exam. Many in positions of authority within the College therefore thought it would be a simple transferal of existing exam practices if this custom were also applied to the ESOL endorsement program.

Even though the ESOL comprehensive exam was mandated and had the approval of the Dean's Office in the College of Education, it was met with resistance from various departments in the College. At the end of the day, the exam did not work because it was effectively rejected by faculty and students alike. There were numerous reasons for this. A primary difficulty with the exam procedure stemmed from the fact that the departments within the College operated on a cohort system. Consequently, while the ESOL classes comprised a mix of pre-service teachers working toward certification in various areas (elementary, secondary, early childhood and special education) and while the existing ESOL exam was written such that it was generic enough to be administered to all pre-service teachers regardless of their major, individual department chairs requested that the ESOL exam be rewritten for each of these areas of certification. The effect of this was that the sections of each ESOL course were reorganized along cohort lines and the content matter in each cohort section became far more major-specific. Thus, pre-service teachers specializing in elementary education had their own section of each ESOL course, as did those in other specialization areas. In addition, the initial generic ESOL comprehensive exam was rewritten into five content-specific assessments to cater to the differing majors.

Another area of resistance led by the various departments in the College of Education concerned the format of the ESOL exam. Again influenced by historical testing practices, students were more familiar with traditional multiple-choice test assessments in all their courses than with alternative assessment procedures. In addition, students complained vigorously that it was inequitable to have an exam at the end of the degree program which tested content delivered at the beginning of the program (sometimes numerous years earlier). Students voiced concerns when the ESOL instructors tried to administer the ESOL exam in a format other than a multiple-choice format (e.g., through a case study, applied essay, research project, task-based open-ended problem scenarios or oral exam). Consequently, ESOL instructors received lower scores on their course evaluations and departments complained about the format of the ESOL exam when it wasn't in a multiple choice format arguing that non-traditional ESOL exam formats were less rigorous, less reliable and less valid. Such testing practices were anchored in a psychometric paradigm and presupposed that a student's capabilities could be reliably evaluated only by a one-off test.

One way to conceive of such conflict is within notions of resistance. van Schoor (2003) explains how within institutions *change* implies *loss* and is associated with emotional responses such as *stress and anxiety*. Following the work of Carr (2001) and Elrod II and Tippett (2002), he likens the common emotional reaction to change to an experience of grief. In this regard, van Schoor concurs with Bovey and Hede (2001) that the process of change can be characterized by denial and resistance before exploring and committing to new options.

Trader-Leigh (2002) identifies other forms of institutional resistance that were also apparent to the instructors of ESOL within the College of Education. They were (explained in light of the context of this present study):

- *Self interest* of individual faculty who saw alternative forms of testing as neither valid nor reliable and therefore an inappropriate basis for making decisions about students. Some faculties were well known among colleagues as very resistant to change.

- *Psychological impact* of administering alternative forms of assessment and possible status loss of the College in the eyes of the FLDOE,

- *Tyranny of custom* in which any substantive change to a course syllabus (such as changing the format of a major exit exam) required the approval of institutional committees and where applications to use alternative assessment procedures were routinely rejected,

- The *redistributive factor* suggesting that students resisted change because through the administration of alternative assessment tasks they stood to lose some or all of their test-taking advantages,

- The *destabilization effect* created through the hiring of new ESOL faculty from 2000 onwards. The new faculty tended to take the lead in changing College ESOL practices. This may be due to the fact that the new faculties were not familiar with the culture and operations of the College of Education and therefore not constrained by tradition. The destabilization that accompanied such a change in faculty and their push for change was resisted strongly,

- *Culture incompatibility* between departments and the means by which the ESOL team wanted to implement the ESOL mandates set forth by the FLDOE Consent Decree,

- The *political effect* emanating from department faculty who were threatened by what they perceived as a loss of academic freedom because they were required to infuse their courses with ESOL content, attend ESOL in-service workshops and have their students' assignments graded by ESOL instructors to determine whether they met the ESOL standards and accomplished practices.

Obviously, in 2000, the ESOL team was faced with denial and resistance and had yet to discover a means to get the non-ESOL faculty to commit to new ways of assessment. van Schoor (2003) shows that resistance is very much a process-oriented phenomenon and not an event that can be dealt with in a one-off fashion.

In a business organization, Zwick (2002) argues that employees will be reluctant to invest their personal resources, such as time and skills, in a change event unless they are sure that their investment will realize an adequate return. After attempting to overcome such resistances, by 2003 the ESOL team decided on a different tack and invested time in coming to understand the dynamics of diffusion and innovation in order to apply them to ESOL in the College of Education.

Looking at the processes of diffusion and innovation more closely, we see a number of dynamics at work. Rogers (1995: 5) defines *diffusion* as 'the process by which an innovation is *communicated* through certain channels over time among members of a social system.' Rogers's representation comprises an individual's acquaintance with an innovation, formation of an attitude toward the innovation, decision to adopt or reject the innovation, implementation of the decision and a willingness to collaborate within the decision-making process.

Frank and colleagues refer to schools, such as the College of Education, as complex social organizations that typically draw on informal processes to implement innovations or reforms (Frank *et al.* 2004: 149). According to these authors, implementation of reforms potentially places competing demands on the social structure of the school. In their view, social capital plays a unique and very important part relative to the social structure and the specific mechanisms through which social structure affects implementation. They define social capital as the potential to access resources through social relations and they argue that the success of an innovative practice depends on an individual teacher's access and response to social capital within an institution.

From the perspective outlined by Frank and colleagues, members of an organization are likely to help and talk to one another because they share a common fate and they can exert social pressure on one another because they affiliate with a common social system. These authors explain, 'Help, talk and social pressure are not merely disjoint processes. Each plays off the other as organizational members generate and draw on, social capital' (Frank *et al.* 2004: 162). As a consequence, the ESOL team came to realize that while the effects of social capital may be moderate, it need not have dominating effects to be an important force for the implementation of innovations. In other words, social capital leverages expertise and social relations that are already in a system.

The ESOL team decided to change things from within, starting with the ESOL social system. Rather than give students an extended exam at the end of their program, it was decided to administer one section of the comprehensive exam per course, so that by the time students reached the end of their program they would only need to complete a more manageable one-hour test rather than an unwieldy three-hour exam. Organizationally, each of the three ESOL courses is situated respectively at the beginning, middle and end of students' programs. In this way, one of the major concerns with the original exam format expressed by students was resolved. In the next section, the discussion turns to a more radical change to the exam procedure.

The road to dynamic assessment

Students appreciated changing the three hour ESOL exam to three one-hour exams. Their positive reaction to this change filtered back to their respective department chairs and faculty. To further win approval of the faculty from other departments, the ESOL section exams were reconstructed only to reflect and test ESOL content delivered in the ESOL courses and not the ESOL infused courses located within departments. The non-ESOL faculty were further empowered through the handing back of responsibility and control to assess ESOL content within their own ESOL infused courses. Over time the faculty within the various departments became more favorably disposed to the ESOL program and less resistant to the ESOL team's initiatives, particularly with regard to assessment. DA was first trialed as a pedagogic initiative within ESOL 2.

The second of the three mandated ESOL endorsement courses, *ESOL 2: Second Language Literacy and Reading Development*, customarily has between 150–200 pre-service students enrolled each semester. As a function of the high number of students, the course is split into five or six sections each taught by a different instructor. In order that the course be taught uniformly across the five and six sections, regular instructor meetings are held to discuss, share and review topics, materials and assessment procedures.

It was within one of these regular meetings in 2004 that the issue of reformulating the ESOL 2 section of the ESOL endorsement comprehensive exam from a traditional multiple-choice assessment to a dynamic procedure was first introduced. While some of the faculty saw this as an exciting as well as a theoretically and pedagogically informed way to proceed, others were less sure; some were unfamiliar with DA and with SCT and therefore skeptical of the ability of a DA procedure to adequately assess emerging developmental level in terms of ESOL knowledge required for state certification. Others were simply reticent to proceed with an assessment that was out of synch with the rest of the College of Education and the other sections of the ESOL comprehensive exam. This was exacerbated by a sustained history of resistance to change within the College, as described earlier. It should be noted that only select ESOL instructors had decided at this point to infuse dynamic assessment into their curriculum.

Cyclical nature of the change process: adoption, implementation and institutionalization

Poehner and Lantolf (2005: 257) describe DA's goal as 'not simply to help learners to master a specific task but to help them to develop a principled understanding of the object of study that will enable them to transfer from the given activity to other activities.' They then go on to say that:

> this idea is central to the distinction between formative assessment and DA. In traditional formative assessment teacher and student interaction is targeted to helping the student to answer correctly and not necessarily the transfer of knowledge to novel situations. The task is the focus in formative assessment and not on the learner's future. (ibid.)

Table 3.2 illustrates the progressive introduction of DA into ESOL 2 classes beginning in Fall, 2004. Originally DA commenced in a graduate level section of ESOL 2 in one instructor's class. In order not to threaten the students (and therefore filter back to their respective department chairs), the DA procedure was administered to replace an existing multiple-choice quiz within the course. This was non-threatening to the students because it was a 'low-stakes' quiz. In the week prior to the DA quiz students were taught about the theory behind DA and the underlying pedagogical advantages of using this approach to assessment. The thrust of the main point to the students was that it was not to be perceived as a test per se but as a learning activity. After this initial DA experience, the students became very positive toward the innovation. Consequently, in the following semesters, DA was applied first to the mid-term and then to the final exam. In each instance, it has been received extremely positively within ESOL 2 classes (see data below).

During this same period a variety of strategies were employed to discover which DA technique best suited the students, the class and the now changing culture of the College. At present, we continue to experiment with and learn from, the implementation of a variety of DA exam formats. Gradually, the rest of the ESOL faculty came on board with the idea of using DA. All of the ESOL 2 faculty (six in all) have used DA in their classes at some time. Faculty in ESOL 1 (six faculty in six sections)

Table 3.2. Progressive introduction of DA into ESOL 2

ESOL 2: Second language literacy and reading development		*Summative procedure (e.g., quiz)*	*Midterm test*	*Final exam*
Fall 2004	Undergraduate			
	Graduate	✓ 1 section		
Spring 2005	Undergraduate			
	Graduate	✓ 1 section		
		✓ 3 sections		
		✓ 1 section		
Fall 2005	Undergraduate			
	Graduate	✓ 3 sections	✓ 1 section (a)	✓ 1 section (b)
		✓ 3 sections	✓ 3 sections	✓ 3 sections
Spring 2006	Undergraduate			
	Graduate	✓ 4 sections	✓ 4 sections	✓ 4 sections
		✓ 4 sections	✓ 4 sections	✓ 4 sections
Fall 2006	Undergraduate			
	Graduate	✓ 5 sections	✓ all sections	✓ 5 sections
		✓ all sections	✓ all sections	✓ all sections

and ESOL 3 (five faculty in five sections) are exploring its uses and learning about DA's theoretical underpinnings. Recalling Lorraine *et al*'s cyclical model of adopting educational innovations (Lorraine *et al.* 2000), we see that at this point in time ESOL faculty in the College of Education are in various stages of readiness to use, implement, experiment with and promote DA. ESOL 2 faculty are continuing to explore DA testing formats as well as reflecting on how DA could be used in other courses, aside from ESOL, that they teach. ESOL 1 and ESOL 3 faculty are currently in the 'trainee' and/or adoption stage.

In Spring 2006, the College of Education went through the process of NCATE, SACS and FLDOE re-accreditation. An external team that included academics, administrators and education officials visited the College and reviewed our academic operations. Included in this review was our use of DA as a section of the required state ESOL comprehensive exam as well as the identified core task in ESOL meeting a range of standards and accomplished practices. Our use of DA was very well received and this has further alleviated institutional resistance.

The DA format that is now used as the final exam for ESOL 2 tries to capture the beneficial effect derived from pair as well as group interactions. Collective group work has been cited numerous times in the literature as enabling students to open potential zones of proximal development (Donato 1988, 1994; Erben 2001, 2006). The current iteration of the ESOL 2 DA exam is shown in Table 3.3.

A study of diffusion and change among students and faculty concerning DA

To date, ESOL 2 instructors have adapted their instructional practices to include various forms of DA in their classrooms. In terms of Lorraine *et al*'s model of change (Lorraine *et al.* 2000), ESOL 2 instructors are still shifting between being learners, adopters and co-explorers of DA use in their courses. ESOL 1 and ESOL 3 instructors, on the other hand, are very much at the learning stage. As a group they are sitting on the sidelines as it were and 'learning from a distance' through the social networks of the ESOL faculty and the ESOL 2 instructors' recounting of their experiences of DA in their classes. While ESOL 2 instructors are actively using DA, ESOL 1 and ESOL 3 instructors have yet to commit to it on a permanent basis. In order to facilitate this process, regular formal ESOL meetings are held each semester where instructional issues such as DA are discussed.

Table 3.3. Outline of implementation of DA in an ESOL class

The ESOL 2 DA exam is formatted with multiple choice, case study, short answer, multiple answer, and fill in the blanks questions. Next to each question, space is provided for an *individual* answer, a *joint pair* answer, and a *group* answer. *Rather than writing multiple choice questions where there is a clear right and wrong answer, test questions are given that have more than one correct response. In the multiple choice test format, rather than a single correct answer, on the (a), (b), (c) and (d) choices there is a continuum of 'best' answers depending on the logic of how a question is argued. In a context where students have to justify their answers in DA, in our experience, this has prompted high levels of discussion among student pairs/groups.*

Step 1: The exam is completed one page at a time. First, students complete the first page of answers on their own.

Step 2: When everyone is finished, students are paired up and discuss each question. This time the students have to arrive at a joint answer. This joint answer may or may not be the same as students' individual answers.

Step 3: The students are put into groups of three or four. The answers are negotiated again and a collective answer is entered on the answer sheet.

Step 4: The class as a whole now goes over the answers. A discussion is held on each question. Students by this time are extremely willing to debate their answers based on their pair and group deliberations.

Step 5: The page of answers is graded. One point is given for each individual, pair and group answer. A student receives a possible score out of three for each question. After each stage students cannot go back and change their answers. In a class of 30, it is impossible for an instructor to police students' adherence to honesty. An honor system is used and students are reminded of professionalism and ethical standards in teaching.

Overview: at each stage, students are encouraged to interact with, deliberate and negotiate their answers with their peers. In order to encourage insightful debate so that quality interaction is encouraged, a rubric is provided to each student to peer-assess and guide their own as well as others' interactive contributions. Because of institutional requirements of assigning a final grade, students' accomplishments in DA are incorporated into their final grade for the course.

The present study sought to examine pre-service teachers' understanding of DA as a form of assessment, particularly in ESOL 2, within College of Education practices. In addition, ESOL 1 and ESOL 3 instructors' understanding of DA as an assessment process was examined. As educators and researchers, the ESOL team is interested in uncovering how individual cases of DA were described both by students who had experienced the process and instructors who had a limited understanding of DA.

Methodology

Following a case study methodology, evidence of the participants' understanding of DA use in their ESOL class was gathered from open-ended interviews with the participants in order to understand their perspectives on DA. All ESOL instructors were invited to participate, whether or not they employed DA in their classes. This bounded case study focused on instructors and students in the college of education.

In Spring 2005, students in four of the six sections of ESOL 2 were interviewed after completing requisite assessment procedures. Students in three of the participating sections had completed a DA final exam before the interview. Students in the remaining one section had completed a traditional multiple choice exam (see Figure 3.1 below).

Data collection

Four groups of ESOL 2 students, approximately 25 students per group who were taught by three instructors, were interviewed regarding their

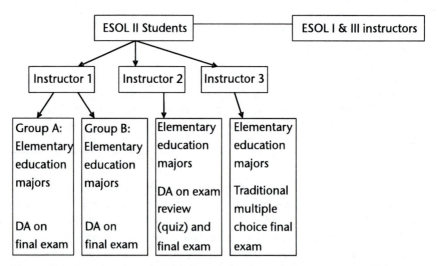

Figure 3.1. Examination of ESOL 2 students through DA in Spring 2005

experiences with the ESOL 2 final exam. Data were collected from the three DA groups through a written interview protocol; one group had a focus group interview with the classmates they had worked with in the DA process in addition to the written interview. All interviews were conducted by the course instructors, who were well qualified to carry out qualitative research. In the interview, ESOL students were asked how confident they felt in the exam, how they studied for the exam, the tools they used to prepare and how they interacted with their classmates during the DA process.

Additionally, three ESOL 2 instructors and nine ESOL 1 and 3 instructors were interviewed regarding their conceptualization of and professional opinions regarding DA as an assessment process. One of the interview participants was the ESOL co-coordinator, who is responsible for the administrative functioning of the college-wide program as well as serving as an instructor of both ESOL 1 and 3. These participants were chosen based on their willingness to participate in the interview as well as their interest in DA as an assessment tool. Two of the ESOL 2 instructors were researchers in this study.

Semi-structured interviews (Berg 2004) took place at the College of Education in a meeting room at the instructors' convenience; two interviewers asked six initial questions based on a predetermined protocol. Based on the instructors' responses and/or questions posed to the interviewers, additional probes were made into their understanding of DA. The interviews ranged between 20 and 55 minutes in length, depending on both the interview process and the willingness of the instructor to discuss his or her assessment procedures.

First and third semester ESOL instructors were asked what they felt the role of assessment was in the learning process, how pre-service ESOL teachers learn best, and whether they had used/proposed any alternative assessment procedures in their ESOL courses. After listening to a prepared explanation of DA by one of the researchers, the instructors were asked for their professional opinion regarding this type of assessment (see Appendix 3.1).

Data analysis: students

All data collected through interviews and focus groups were transcribed and coded by two of the researchers on this project. Individual researcher coding was then triangulated. Through the use of NVIVO (QSR International Pty Ltd, 2002), coded data were displayed to facilitate researcher understanding of the participants' explanations. The following subsections report students' responses to particular issues raised during the interview about their experience with the DA ESOL examination, Table 3.4 illustrates themes derived from student interview data.

Student Descriptions of Final Exam Preparation (Traditional Format)

This question sought to understand exam preparation practices among the students who did not participate in DA. These learners reported using class notes, relevant book chapters and power point presentations posted to the course management system as tools to prepare for their final exam. Some were guided by an in-class review (termed a 'power' review by the instructor) provided before the exam.

The majority of the respondents in the traditional assessment group did not study more than approximately two hours for their final exam, although some studied more than one day. One student explained, 'I have been studying throughout [*sic*] the course, but last night and this morning probably three hours.' One student described her study time by saying, 'an hour before exam time and reviewed a little here and there during the weeks before the exam.' Still another stated, 'past weekend, I have taken out at least 25–35 minutes a day to look over my

Table 3.4. Themes deriving from interview data with students

How students prepared for exam	• Use of course materials • Instructor provide in-class review • Small group study
When they studied for the final exam	• No specific study time • One day previous to exam • Before exam day
Confidence in their own knowledge	• Studied but felt lack of confidence • Confident they were prepared
Group mediation	• Group mediation increased confidence • Uneasy with shared responsibility for grade
Mediational processes	• Different behavior with known and unknown classmates • Student diversity
Pedagogical applications as teachers	• Use in future classrooms

notes. It was probably 4 or 5 days that I did that.' This quote illustrates that this particular student spent a total of about 2.5 hours studying in the days prior to the final assessment.

When asked about how much they had studied, various students who did not participate in DA commented that they felt that their class attendance and note-taking process prepared them sufficiently for the exam. One stated, 'I did not study for this exam I have a pretty good feeling most of the stuff I picked up in class would be enough to help me pass the exam.' Another said, 'I looked over my review notes for about ten min. I did not feel that more preparation was necessary.'

All of the students who responded, including those who took DA and those who did not, expressed an understanding that ongoing study, reading and preparation throughout the course and/or condensed study was necessary for the final exam. In spite of this realization, many students described feelings of heightened nervousness, anxiety or apprehension before the exam. One stated, 'leading up to [*sic*] I was a little uneasy and worried I have my doubts' while another admitted, 'I still felt nervous and scared as I do for every test but I also felt there was so much info between class and the two books it was a little overwhelming.' This statement speaks to this particular student's feelings regarding the traditional assessment process. In other words, this student's experience reveals that a course that covers a good deal of material is stressful due to the eventual accountability, which amounts to little more than a test of memorization ability. Still another student said, 'leading up to the exam my feelings were that of anxiety. Not knowing exactly what to study I felt unprepared to take this exam.' Other students explained that their initial feelings of anxiety decreased throughout the examination process. One stated, 'My feelings prior to the exam were unsure if I was prepared enough but during the exam I felt very confident that the majority of my studying aligned with the exam.' These students' comments evidence their negative experiences with formalized testing in the ESOL courses. In spite of feelings of being prepared, they remained anxious about the testing process and their resulting final score on the multiple choice exam.

In the same group, those who were not in a class where DA was used, four students specifically described engaging in mediation in small groups outside the classroom to prepare for the final exam. One student commented, 'I studied with a group of girls from other ESOL classes. Each of us brought the study guide we received for this test and we all shared and talked about it together.' Another commented, 'Then I met with a group to go over the notes At this time we looked back in the book for anything we were unsure of'. Yet another described specific tools the group used, 'I studied with friends. We made an outline during the last class meeting. We filled in with more detail discussed and questioned each other.' In other words, these students developed their own mediational strategies in the absence of DA. However, as we argue below, the systematic, theoretically-motivated forms of mediation inherent in DA offer certain advantages over the strategies students generally formulate when left to their own devices.

Student confidence in their knowledge (learners participating in DA)

Conversely, students who participated in DA reported greater confidence in their content knowledge. It is important to note that this increased confidence may or may not be due to the fact that student participated in DA. Certain students felt confident before the assessment process. They explained their feelings by stating, 'I was pretty confident in the material that would be presented in the class and on the test.' One student commented, 'I had studied and listened so I felt good.' Similar feelings were expressed by yet another student, 'Pretty confident. I have a relatively strong base that I built on beginning about a year and a half ago.' One participant responded, 'Very confident.' From this statement one could infer that participating in DA leads to feelings of increased confidence. Indeed, several students made references to the fact that they felt the DA exam was as much a learning activity as it was a test. One student commented, 'Doing it DA style, well I guess I feel I know more because the stuff we learned during the DA exam stuck.'

The group that had experienced DA on the review for the quiz pointed out that they had mixed feelings in spite of their previous experience with the DA process. One said, 'I thought it was pretty self-explanatory. It was short, it was easy. I thought this was a piece of cake.' Another student stated, 'I liked it better that it was sort of open-ended ... like I'm more comfortable.' The same student reflected on how she studied by saying 'you know, I didn't take super great notes [notes from class lectures], I didn't even study really and I thought I was fine with everything by just showing up and listening.' This student comment could well be interpreted as a negative statement and indeed, while the theoretical rationale of DA is explained to the students in terms of reaching potential learning limits, some students still view it as an occasion 'to talk to one's neighbor about the answers during the test.' This was not true for all students. The vast majority perceived doing DA as a way of pushing their understanding of the content matter further. For example, one student expresses this view particularly well:

> It's like, I get the chance to talk through my reasoning for an answer with my peers … it is so much less stressful. Think of it like a mathematics problem … in our DA test we are given the chance to explain our logic for each answer and sometimes our answer might not be correct but we still get a point if our reasoning is sound. That would never show up in a normal multiple-choice test.

Interestingly, whereas previous cohorts of students in ESOL 2 expressed that they felt disadvantaged by assessments that were not in a multiple-choice format, the learners who experienced DA came to recognize advantages of other assessment procedures. This suggests that the crucial issue to the students may not be whether one opts for a traditional assessment instrument such as a multiple-choice test or an alternative approach (e.g., portfolios, projects, presentations), but whether one follows a dynamic or non-dynamic method for administering the assessment.

Student perception of their own knowledge

Students who participated in DA were asked about their perceived knowledge as they began the mediational process. They were asked how they felt about their knowledge. On this point, the overall reaction was mixed among the participants. Whereas some felt support from the group, others felt uneasy with the shared responsibility for the final grade. One student expressed it as follows: 'it's good to have someone else you can talk to about it, but I'm just saying I don't wanna be responsible for other people.' This viewpoint is hardly surprising given the American culture's emphasis on the individual, individual achievement and competition. Another student explained how it made her more confident by stating:

> Actually, it gave me confidence though. It really did, cause if I thought of one answer and the majority of the group had my same thought process that means that if I didn't know and I was solely basing it on the class discussion or something, it kind of gave me more confidence.

Mediational processes

Group interaction was described as a mediational process by one of the students. She said:

> It was more like we would say what the answers were and who-
> ever had different answers, we would go to the first person and go
> 'why did you put this answer?' Talk to the other person, 'why did
> you put this answer?' 'Here's why we put this answer' and then we
> would talk about why we had the answers, but ... I don't know ...
> my group is good! Like nobody gets rowdy or anything.

This student's explanation reflects her definition of a 'good' group as one with few dissenting opinions. This suggests the need for further research into how students view dissent in the DA process. Within the other ESOL 2 classes, group interaction was seen differently. The participants pointed to both the similarities and differences they felt with their classmates as well as how well they knew their group members. One student mentioned, 'With the classmates that I knew I felt more confident and with the classmates that I don't know I was a little discomforted, but I enjoyed it because I learned from them too. We learned to listen to each other's arguments.' Another student pointed to the advantages of having diversity in the classroom, 'I had a very diverse class and it made my class more interesting. I learned a great deal from people who were not the same background as mine.' This quote is particularly illuminating given contemporary Western education's focus on multicultural education. Moreover, attempting to understand another's situational definition (Werstch 1984) is paramount in the achievement of intersubjectivity.

One participant expressed concerns about how others perceived him as well as the difference between working with people he or she knew and those who he or she did not know. This participant stated:

> Those I knew well. We quickly checked to see which ones we
> disagreed on only looked to discussed [*sic*] those questions. With
> the students I wasn't familiar with I carefully slowed down.
> Considering each question allowing them the opportunity to state
> their answers and opinions first I'm very well aware of coming of
> [*sic*] [off?] as a know it all and I don't want to offend. Test taking is
> stressful enough as it is.

Reflecting on pedagogical applications

Within the focus group interviews, students expressed an unexpected interest in the DA process. They asked their instructor in the interview if there was any problem using this approach to assess in their own future classrooms. When probed further, they discussed the advantages they had experienced and related them to their personal experiences as teachers. One participant said:

> I learned more. Even though I thought it might have been a long
> answer, by you explaining to me why that wasn't right and why
> the one she put was, I learned it and it's gonna stick in my head.

Another student reflected, 'I would definitely use this in my classroom. I mean you have to trust the kids though. A little more maybe.'
Many in the focus group agreed on the benefits of using DA with school-
aged children. Some, however, were more critical. The following student's
comment shows perhaps a lack of complete understanding of what DA
tries to achieve:

> I don't think you could use this with younger kids though. You'd
> have to use it with older kids that are used to taking tests. It
> wouldn't work very well on anything but multiple choice. I don't
> know, unless there are other forms of dynamic assessment ... like
> how would you do it with fill-in-the-blank?

When asked why not with younger kids, she said that they would
get too rowdy and cheat. More probing during the interview showed
that this particular student was critical of DA in terms of test
administrability and manageability issues rather than for theoretical or
pedagogical reasons.

Data analysis: instructors

The ESOL instructors, including those who did and did not use DA,
were interviewed to discuss their understanding of the existing assessment process as well as the use (or potential use) of DA in their courses
(see Table 3.5). Two ESOL 2 instructors and six ESOL 1 and 3 instructors were interviewed. Of the two ESOL 2 instructors, one was familiar
with the principles underlying DA and sociocultural theory, while for
the other instructor DA was completely new. None of the six instructors
of ESOL 1 and 3 had prior experience with either DA or sociocultural
theory. In the terms of Lorraine *et al*'s learning/adoption trajectory
model of innovation and change in education (Lorraine *et al.* 2000), the
ESOL 1 and 3 instructors were clearly still in the 'learning phase' of DA
use. None had yet decided to adopt the innovation formally, though
they were trying it out in their classes. Their perspective was, on the
whole, positive toward DA. The two ESOL 2 instructors were at what
Lorraine and colleagues refer to as the co-exploration stage. Both were
committed to using DA and more importantly, both were reflecting on
ways to better administer and format DA tests within their classes.

Table 3.5. Themes deriving from interview data with instructors

	Theme	
Role of assessment	• Formal and informal processes • Shows how much students have learned • Prepare students for content • Learning tool • Big stick: motivation for grade	
Thoughts on alternative assessment	Yes • Because of stress • I have proposed changes; they were accepted • Would like to see a technology based assessment	No • I am new here • It works, why change
How pre-service teachers learn	• Involved • Hands on • Teaching and assessing at the same time • Activities for reinforcement • Doing something with the input	
DA use	Positive • Better than the static exam • You can see them mediating answers • Allows a lot of learning to take place • Instructor choice – we are encouraged to work collaboratively	Limitations • If we had another major area or another type of exam • Time consuming to prepare for individual students

The ESOL 1 and 3 instructors learned about DA in various ways. For instance, their knowledge of DA was mediated through informal discussions about assessment with their colleagues. Also, some instructors of DA participated in an informal workshop that outlined the theoretical underpinnings of DA as well as its implementation. Lastly, the curriculum of ESOL 1, which includes a section on assessment, was modified by two different instructors to include a section on DA. In turn, these instructors were invited to discuss DA in other sections of ESOL 1.

What is assessment?

When asked what assessment was, instructors in the ESOL courses described assessment in their ESOL classes as a combination of formal and informal criterion referenced assessment processes designed to determine whether or not a student achieved certain standards of learning. Specifically, they mentioned informal assessment tools such as in-class activities and discussion of readings, checking for comprehension and problem solving scenarios. The participants mentioned quizzes, projects and midterm and final exams as aspects of formal assessment.

Role of assessment

All of the ESOL instructors defined assessment as part of the learning process. They suggested that assessment is the tool they use to determine whether the student has learned or not. More than one ESOL instructor stated that assessment serves to push the students to learn as well as guide their teaching process. One instructor commented, 'The results of your teaching. Based on the results you can improve your teaching.' This quote illustrates the cyclical relationship between teaching and assessment that is characteristic of formative assessment. It is important to note that formative assessment presupposes the separation of assessment and instruction (Lantolf and Poehner 2004), whereas DA views assessment and instruction as indivisible, 'existing in synergistic union' (Summers forthcoming: 76). Concerning assessment, another instructor explained:

> I need to [be] assured that my students leave my class with a
> particular knowledge base. I want to know they absorbed the
> material. Was it mastered? Did they understand it? Have they
> processed it? Are they able to use it in some kind of way?

Within their discussion of their concept of assessment, they referred to the fact that their students were motivated by the final grade in the assessment process. One instructor conceptualized the relationship between instruction, practical application, assessment and motivation in this way:

> I think that when students are explicitly instructed what exactly
> they'll be assessed on, that will increase their instrumental motiva-
> tion. Especially if they are … this instruction extends to the topic
> how this will not be on the test, this particular skill or area of
> knowledge will not only be assessed in class but how this will be
> instrumental to their performance as teachers in the classroom that
> will even increase higher their motivation for learning.

Another instructor reflected on the role of the final exam as the one aspect of formal assessment when he said, 'twenty percent of the final grade it is that formal assessment which the state requires but a student can get an A in the course without passing the final.' This separation of the final grade from the final comprehensive examination recognizes the concerns for high stake traditional assessment, but does not offer any alternative to the assessment process. This contradiction between the final grade and the final exam is resolved by allowing students multiple attempts to meet the state standards on the comprehensive exam.

How ESOL students learn best

The ESOL instructors agreed that the pre-services teachers learned best by presenting the content and then using games, activities, worksheets and other practical applications to reinforce their learning. One instructor explained:

> They don't learn by just oral explanations, I use a lot of animations and diagrams and power points, a lot of work sheets, a lot of chunking where I give them a little bit of content and then lets' [*sic*] do something to apply it. See how this plays out in the real world. They need a lot of variety, their palette is not developed to just listen and learn. Multi mode.

One of the participants viewed these practical applications of the content as a way to assess the students' understanding of the content. She stated, 'It's not a test given after but it's how the activity is carried out.' This comment suggests an understanding of DA as an investigation into a dialogic process rather than an attempt to capture a product or end-state to be represented by a numerical score.

Options for DA in the ESOL courses

Despite an overall positive attitude toward DA, ESOL 1 and 3 instructors had some reservations about adopting it. Concern for state-mandated standards was mentioned as one factor that limited the assessment process. One instructor ventured an explanation that the College of Education was limited in their assessment processes by NCATE guidelines. As a result, she offered her opinion that 'to introduce a new teaching strategy or even a dynamic assessment into a classroom this can't be decided by the individual teacher, right? You also need to get approval from the program director or something.' Another instructor pointed to the state requirements by saying, 'the final exam for ESOL 1 and ESOL 2 need to address what the state requires in terms of their exam and demonstrating that our students have met the requirements for certification.'

This hesitancy on the part of this instructor points to Trader-Leigh's (2002) description of resistance to change. Here the instructor's self-interest is reflected in not changing the assessment process. This instructor's lack of understanding of the DA process does not permit him to visualize the use of DA to meet state mandated standards. A majority of the instructors spoke favorably of implementing DA within their ESOL courses. However, once again, their understanding of the DA process consisted primarily of having the students engage in group work. One instructor explained:

> We're strongly encouraged to provide feedback to incorporate into our teaching collaborated work and small group activities and create student centered environment which are all elements of dynamic assessment and is moving from one point of knowledge to another through social interaction.

During the interview process, the participants were given a short explanation about how DA is applied in the assessment process in ESOL 2 classes. This brief description, as well as instructors' participation in a DA training workshop, informal discussions with their colleagues and through invited presentation in their classes, provided the basis of most instructors' knowledge, although limited, about DA. Upon hearing the explanation in the interview, most instructors were generally favorable, but expressed apprehension regarding the time factor, amount of additional work for the individual teachers and implementation of the DA process. One instructor expressed concern that having to create individual assessments for each student and mediate their learning would become unwieldy along with her other responsibilities.

One of the ESOL 2 instructors who has been experimenting with DA for a few semesters, but did not use it in the semester that this study was conducted, summarized the current stage of DA diffusion as:

> It seems to me that the ESOL 1 and ESOL 3 instructors need a little push to feel comfortable with using DA ... perhaps some workshops given by the ESOL 2 folks or reading up on it more or talking to some of the students who have done their final exam through DA ... they always have very positive comments and favorably disposed to DA once they have experienced it. I think the ESOL 1 and 3 instructors are where the ESOL 2 folks were 2 years ago ... I mean in their learning curve ... *some* are also not as pedagogically adventuresome.

Discussion

The student interviews suggest that there was no noticeable difference in the way the DA and non-DA students prepared for their exam. Some students reported use of mediation to facilitate their developmental process, although they did not use that terminology. The students who participated in the DA process reported higher levels of confidence in their own knowledge before the examination process. Some students who used DA expressed traditional concerns about final grades. These students specifically stated that they did not like the idea of shared responsibility for each other's grades. The vast majority of students thought they had actually learned during their DA compared to taking other types of tests and many expressed achieving a better test grade because of it. Finally, there was a common misunderstanding about the mediational process among the student participants. Commonly, students preferred groups where there was no dissonance in the process. Here they failed to realize how conflict or contradictions can enrich the mediational process and result in further development.

The instructor interviews uniformly suggest a lack of knowledge regarding DA and its relationship to the development process. This was to be expected in part because the ESOL 1 and 3 had as yet only minimal opportunity to learn about DA and its underlying principles. Their elementary understanding of DA is apparent when they conflate DA with other collaborative classroom activities as well as when they fail to distinguish formative assessment from DA. The instructors shared the opinion that pre-service ESOL teachers need to be active in their learning process; however this activity was described as pair or group work along with a constructivist approach to teaching *prior* to the administration a formal 'static' test. Although the instructors stated that they were in favor of alternative types of assessment, all were concerned with meeting state mandated standards. They could not visualize how this could be possible using DA. The final instructor concern was that each student must be mediated individually. This reveals their belief that mediation must occur between an expert and a novice. As a result, instructors in this study expressed concerns that planning and implementation would become an enormous task.

Since the 1960s, the diffusion of an innovation was very much conceived of as a linear process with the decision to adopt within any given context occurring through a series of actions and choices over time. The data collected through this study has made obvious the fact that to a degree the same process has emerged in the diffusion and adoption of DA by the ESOL faculty within the College of Education. Both students and ESOL faculty are still weighing the relative advantages of using DA, the compatibility of DA within their own personal teaching and assessment philosophies, its complexity, its feasibility as well as its transparency. The latter is of special import as social and/or educational capital frame how an innovation such as DA takes shape within an institution as it relates to individual concerns, pedagogic concerns and programmatic concerns.

What we have found is that DA use among the ESOL faculty and indeed among the pre-service teachers considering whether it is an assessment tool they want to use in their future classrooms boils down to individuals deciding whether or not DA is manageable for them. What this means is whether DA contributes to their self-efficacy as teachers and whether it is ultimately worth their time and effort. Students who readily saw themselves learning through their participation in the actual DA procedure expressed positive attitudes toward adopting its use in their own classrooms. Ultimately, whether a teacher considers DA from a test administrability perspective or a curricular perspective to enhance learning, what is important is the social and institutional support that the individual receives that will help decide if DA as an educational innovation becomes embedded in a teacher's classroom practice.

Conclusion

The process of legitimatizing DA within the College of Education has not yet reached its conclusion. In order to hasten DA's acceptance, the onus will be on the ESOL 2 instructors to provide public as well as private in-service workshops on DA for individuals and groups of ESOL 1 and ESOL 3 instructors and to assist colleagues to troubleshoot especially when they are trying to construct, administer, or grade a DA procedure. At a programmatic level it could be possible to have the program coordinator prescribe its use in all ESOL 1, 2 and 3 sections and then construct template quizzes and test formats so that they can be administered dynamically. However, considering the residual history of the institution, the power of social capital and the gains made in the diffusion of DA via a bottom-up approach of building capacity such a strategy would be counter-productive.

This exploratory case study has raised the inevitable need for more research. In particular, our work brings to the fore questions relating to the pedagogical impact of using different types of DA. Currently, DA is administered primarily through a multiple choice format in quizzes and as a final exam. Future work will explore applications of other assessment formats in the context of our ESOL program. These may include task-based assessments, case studies, problem scenarios, webquests and/or interview protocols. Additional research is also needed to better understand issues involved in pair, group and whole class formats of DA. Finally, we have questions relating to more practical implications of DA, namely how students and faculty might usefully be oriented to DA, especially its implementation and the interpretation of DA outcomes. In this context, we are talking about exploring different approaches to introducing DA principles, such as through workshops, presentations, guidebooks and coursework.

In closing, we feel that our case of how DA has been and is continuing to be infused in the ESOL program merits further closer investigation. While promising and more dynamic models of activity within social networks exist (Schein 1996; Havelock and Zlotolow 1997; Senge 1990), Engström (1996) provides a social mediational model of activity that can shed further light on the dynamics of how an innovation such as DA comes to be adopted within educational contexts. It will be Activity Theory that we will use next as a lens through which we will further try to make sense of the viability of DA in a large teacher-education institution.

Note

1. National Council for Accreditation of Teacher Education, Southern Association of Colleges and Schools, Florida Department of Education.

References

Berg, B. L. (2004) *Qualitative Research Methods for the Social Sciences*. Thousand Oaks, CA: Sage.

Bovey, W. H. and Hede, A. (2001) Resistance to organizational change: The role of defence mechanisms. *Journal of Managerial Psychology* 16: 534–48.

Carr, A. (2001) Understanding emotion and emotionality in the process of change. *Journal of Organizational Change Management* 14(5): 421–36.

Donato, R. (1988) Beyond Group: A Psycholinguistic Rationale for Collective Activity in Second Language Learning. Unpublished doctoral dissertation. The University of Delaware.

Donato, R. (1994) Collective scaffolding in second language learning. In J. P. Lantolf and G. Appel (eds) *Vygotskyan Approaches to Second Language Acquisition* 33–56. Norwood, NJ: Ablex.

Elliott, J. G. (2000) Dynamic assessment in educational contexts: purpose and promise. In C. S. Lidz and J. G. Elliott (eds) *Dynamic Assessment: Prevailing Models and Applications* 713–40. Amsterdam: Elsevier.

Elrod II, P. D. and Tippett, D. D. (2002) The 'death valley' of change. *Journal of Organisational Change Management* 15: 273–29.

Engström, Y. (1996) Interobjectivity, ideality and dialectics. *Mind, Culture and Activity* 3: 259–65.

Erben, T. (2001) The Construction of Sociolinguistic Knowledge within a Teacher Education Degree Program Delivered through Language Immersion. Unpublished doctoral dissertation. University of Lancaster, UK.

Erben, T. (2006) In-service education mediated through curriculum development: An issues-based study. *Journal of In-service Education* 32: 451–76.

Frank, K. A., Zhao, Y. and Borman, K. (2004) Social capital and the diffusion of innovations within organizations: The case of computer technology in schools. *Sociology of Education* 77: 148–71.

Havelock, R. and Zlotolow, S. (1997) Who's on first, what's on second: Change process and the roles we play. Presentation at the Association for Educational Communication and Technology, Albuqerque, NM.

Lantolf, J. P. and Poehner, M. E. (2004) Dynamic Assessment: Bringing the past into the future. *Journal of Applied Linguistics* 1: 49–74.

Lorraine, S. , Billig, S., Tavalin , F. and Gibson, D. (2000) New insights on technology adoption in community of learners. Proceedings, Society for Information Technology & Teacher Education International Conference SITE.

Minick, N. (1987) Implications of Vygotsky's theories for Dynamic Assessment. In C. S. Lidz (ed.) *Dynamic Assessment: An Interactive Approach to Evaluating Learning Potential* 116–40. New York: The Guilford Press.

Poehner, M. E. and Lantolf, J. P. (2005) Dynamic Assessment in the language classroom. *Language Teaching Research* 9: 1–33.

Rogers, E. M. (1962) *Diffusion of Innovations*. New York: The Free Press.

Rogers, E.M. (1995) *Diffusion of Innovations* 4th Edition. New York: The Free Press.

Schein, E.H. (1996) Three cultures of management: The key to organizational learning in the 21st Century. Available online at http://learning.mit.edu/res/wp/10011.html

Senge, P. (1990) *The Fifth Discipline*. New York: Doubleday.

Summers, R. (forthcoming) Dynamic Assessment: Toward a Model of Computer-mediated Dialogic Engagement. Unpublished doctoral dissertation. University of South Florida.

Trader-Leigh, K. E. (2002) Case study: Identifying resistance in managing change. *Journal of Organizational Change Management* 15: 138–55.

van Schoor, A. (2003) Learning to overcome resistance to change in higher education: the role of Transformational Intelligence in the process. Annual conference proceedings of HERDSA (Higher Education Research and Development Society of Australasia Inc.) July 2003, Christchurch, New Zealand. Retrieved on 3 August 2006 from http://surveys.canterbury.ac.nz/herdsa03/pdfsref/Y1189

Wertsch, J. V. (1984) The zone of proximal development: Some conceptual issues. In B. Rogoff and J. V. Wertsch (eds) *Children's Learning in the Zone of Proximal Development* 45–64. San Francisco, CA: Jossey-Bass.

Zwick, T. (2002) Employee resistance against innovations. *International Journal of Manpower* 23: 542–52.

Appendix 3.1. Prompted instructor interview questions

What is the role of assessment for you?

Does assessment contribute to the learning process? How?

How do you think ESOL students best learn? How does the assessment process work in this learning process?

How is this played out in the ESOL class you teach?

Is this assessment an indicator of learning? Why?

If you had half a chance, would you do another type of learning? Why?

What would it look like? What advantages would it have?

Have you proposed alternative assessment in (ESOL) meetings? Why/Why not?

What is your concept of DA?

Do you know what DA is? [We describe] What is your professional reaction to that? Describe how you can or cannot see it being used in the ESOL classes. [How? Why?]

4 A dialogic approach to teaching L2 writing

Holbrook Mahn

Introduction

> I realized that journal really help me to write down my idea
> without any blocking into my elbow. When I have idea in my head
> and I start to make it go down my arm to the paper, if I think about
> grammar, structure my idea blocks into my elbow and never goes
> to the paper. (Trang, Viet Nam)[1]

Trang echoes the experiences of many second language writers who become frustrated when they cannot adequately convey their thoughts in written English. In describing the disconnect between her thinking and composing processes, Trang, a student in a first year ESL university writing class, relates what can happen when students focus on correctness and form rather than meaning. Using Vygotsky's (1987, 1978) writings on meaning, verbal thinking, inner speech and the zone of proximal development (ZPD),[2] this chapter examines problems that English language learners (ELLs) encounter when writing in English. It then describes the use of dialog journals to teach L2 writing and analyzes student reflections to understand the influence journals had on their motivation and confidence. Since theory should be used both to guide and to assess instructional practice, this chapter uses Vygotsky's work to establish a theoretical foundation for an analysis of the development of the cognitive processes ELLs use to learn to write in English. This foundation then provides the framework for students' reflections on the efficacy of this dialogic approach.[3]

Vygotsky's broader theory of psychological development and his analysis of *meaning making* as central to that process provide the basis for his concept of the zone of proximal development. He describes his theory of development most succinctly in the 'Problem of Age' (Vygotsky

1998); his analysis of meaning making is most fully articulated in his last and best-known major work, *Thinking and Speech* (Vygotsky 1987) in which he analyzes the essential role that meaning plays in verbal thinking and inner speech. Vygotsky's writings make clear that when he uses *znacheniye slova* to describe *meaning* his denotation of the word *slovo* is that the meaning, about which he is writing, has it origins in social language use. Regarding Vygotsky's use of *slovo* (word), Kozulin argues that 'more often than not "word" is used as a synecdoche [a part *word* is being used for a whole *language*] and stands for any form of verbal discourse' (Kozulin 1990: 151). However, English translations of the Russian *znacheniye slova* as 'word meaning' have led to a focus on the external meanings of words and the appropriation of those meanings, without analyzing how the internalization of meaning creates internal mental structures in a *system* of meaning.[4] Therefore, I briefly present Vygotsky's (1978, 1987, 1997a) analysis of the development of the internal system of meaning and how this system of meaning contributes to the development of writing before describing the dialogic approach to teaching L2 writing.

Over the last 20 years, I have used dialog journals with English language learners – kindergarteners through university students, from beginning English writers to those on the cusp of fluency. Since journals have been used in multiple ways, I make explicit the technical and philosophic considerations that shape my use of dialog journals. Using voices of students like Trang, I explore the journals' influences on: 1) their making of meaning through writing; 2) their attitudes toward writing in English; 3) their confidence in themselves as writers; 4) their fears and anxieties with writing; 5) themselves as reflective writers (Verity 2000); 6) other writing they do in school; and 7) their ZPDs.

Meaning and the Zone of Proximal Development

The concept of the zone of proximal development, for which Vygotsky is best known, is often used to describe an individual learning a specific skill in a concrete situation, but it loses its explanatory power when it is isolated from Vygotsky's work as a whole. Chaiklin (2003) argues persuasively that Vygotsky used the concept of the ZPD to explain qualitative changes in a child's development, transformations that Vygotsky called critical periods (Mahn 2003; Vygotsky 1998). These periods, such as the times when children acquire speech, when they enter school and are exposed to broader systems of knowledge, and when adolescents begin to use abstract, conceptual thinking as their main mode of thought, are all marked by fundamental changes in the relationship between mental functions. These changes, in turn, precipitate the creation of new psychological structures that give the new period its character. For example, during the critical period when a child is three, all mental functions and the interrelationships of those functions are affected by the acquisition of language. The analysis of the changes in these interrelationships has been called 'functional systems analysis' (John-Steiner, Meehan and Mahn 1998; Vygotsky 1999).

Chaiklin (2003: 48–9) ties the concept of the ZPD to these critical periods and describes two of its purposes:

> One purpose is to identify the kinds of maturing psychological
> functions (and the social interactions associated with them)
> needed for transition from one age period to the next. The other is
> to identify the child's current state in relation to developing these
> functions needed for that transition.

The cognitive processes that lead to conceptual thinking in a second language described in this chapter are the 'maturing psychological functions' in what Chaiklin calls the *objective* ZPD. The *state* of the individual in the objective ZPD, affected by a great number of general and particular factors that influence individuals, constitutes the *subjective* ZPD.

Some general, broad factors present in the objective ZPD, from birth to death, include – social situations of development, cultural ways of knowing, oral and written language used in social interaction to make and construct systems of meaning and emotional/psychological responses to experiences (*perezhivanie*) (Vygotsky 1994). Students' subjective ZPDs at any particular time are affected by many different positive and negative factors: 1) physical and emotional – hunger, anxiety, fear, confidence, among many; 2) consequences of living in a loving home as opposed to not; 3) recent interactions with peers; and 4) the way that interactions in sociocultural environments are appropriated and internalized. The degree to which students gain control over these influencing factors, by becoming consciously aware of their thinking processes and using conceptual thinking to guide activity, determines whether the subjective ZPD expands or narrows – a process that can be facilitated by effective pedagogy (see Chapters 1 and 2, this volume).

Vygotsky and the system of meaning

The dialogic approach explored in this chapter builds on Vygotsky's examination of the cognitive processes through which children learn to make meaning and communicate. Vygotsky felt that the mind could only be fully studied as part of a constantly emerging system of interrelationships between different mental functions and psychological processes in interaction with social, cultural, linguistic and historical systems. He conceived of the mind as consisting of a complex of interconnected systems of meaning, systems that reflect different mental processes – visual, aural, tactile, emotional, linguistic, mathematical, artistic, musical, among others – through which humans perceive and experience their environments. His ultimate goal was to explain the systemic character of the mind as a whole, in essence to explain consciousness. While he recognized that there were many systems of meaning, he focused on how children create meaning as they acquire and develop language, both spoken and written, in their specific sociocultural environments (Vygotsky 1987, 1994).

Vygotsky succinctly defined *meaning* as 'the internal structure of the sign operation' (Vygotsky 1997b: 133) – *sign operation* referring to the unique human capacity to use symbolic representation. In examining human symbol use Vygotsky explored how generalization, key to symbolic representation, came into existence and how a structure of generalization developed. 'The signifying structure (i.e., the function associated with the active use of signs) is the law that is common to the constructions of all the higher forms of behavior' (Vygotsky 1987: 133). The term 'structure' has been used in different ways in psychology to describe concrete and abstract representations and can imply an anatomical formation. While Vygotsky recognized the material base of the mind – the physical brain and all its electrical and chemical systems – his focus was on how the human mind came into being, how consciousness emerged from the material brain. Even though Vygotsky refers to meaning as the internal **structure** of the sign operation, I examine meaning as the internal **system** of the sign operation because of Vygotsky's use of a functional systems approach to study the mind. Vygotsky used the term 'meaning' in two different but related ways. One refers to the sociocultural meaning that is in existence when an individual is born into a particular social situation. This is tied to the dictionary meaning. His other use of **meaning** refers to the internal system developed through signs, symbolic representation through language. It is within this system that an individual sense develops. Unless otherwise specified, the term 'system of meaning' refers to meaning that results from the unification of thinking and speaking processes into a new unity, what Vygotsky called **verbal thinking**. (In describing language use in general, Vygotsky includes writing/written language when he uses **speaking/speech**.)

The description of the origin and development of this system of meaning is the focus of Vygotsky's major work, *Thinking and Speech* (1987), in which he describes the unification of the distinct processes of thinking and speaking that occurs when children acquire language. He calls this unification verbal thinking and examines it by analyzing the origins and course of development of the system of meaning as the essential core of verbal thinking. Meaning is constructed through the children's mental capacity to generalize, developed through social interaction. The development of generalization is the foundation for the system of meaning and for the cognitive processes involved in learning to write.

In exploring the origins of the structure of generalization Vygotsky examined children's first words. Through interaction with caretakers, children come to attach a particular sound with a fused image of their visual field. Although the word includes more than the object or action to which the caretakers refer, its use indicates that the child is developing the ability to generalize, to use a symbol to stand for something. The ability to generalize is the foundation upon which the child's system of meaning arises. Through ongoing social interaction representations begin to coincide more and more with those of the adult members of the child's speech community. Vygotsky studied the constant interplay between the internal system of meaning an individual constructs and the external sociocultural meaning system in that individual's environment. The children's systems of meaning continue to expand as they discover relationships between objects and begin to use categories by making generalizations of generalizations (rose – flower, chair – furniture). A qualitative change in the system occurs when children realize that everything has a name and that words have their own existence and are not a part of the object they represent. This brings about a rapid expansion of the child's vocabulary and facilitates further communication, central to the growth of the internal system of meaning.

In *Thinking and Speech* Vygotsky describes in detail the development of the system of meaning, focusing on the times when children acquire language, when children start school and are exposed to academic concepts that are part of broader systems of knowledge, and when adolescents become aware of their own thinking, developing abstract, conceptual thinking. He also analyzes the differences between acquiring a first language and a second language, comparing and contrasting first and second language acquisition with learning to write. An important component in the ZPDs of English language learners (ELLs) is the system of meaning constructed through their first language. When learning a second language, learners draw on the system of meaning constructed through their native language and incorporate the new language into their developing system of meanings (see Lantolf and Thorne 2006). In order for them to communicate their thoughts in English, ELLs need to connect their conceptual thinking to composing processes that include developing ideas and conveying them in written language. For the most part, my students had already made the transition to conceptual thinking that Vygotsky (1998, 1994) describes as central to the critical period of adolescence, but they revisited the process when learning to write in a second language. As Trang and other students describe, this process can be quite frustrating, but an approach that helps them expand their ZPDs as they draw on verbal thinking and their systems of meaning results in greater competency, fluency and confidence.

Students have had unique meaning-making experiences and have created unique systems of meaning before they come to our classrooms. The phrase 'meaning making' appears regularly in educational literature, but the cognitive processes through which children create and develop meaning often remain unexplored. To understand and appreciate each child's system, it is important to understand how children learn to use language to make meaning of experiences in their sociocultural contexts. This system changes qualitatively when children come to school and are exposed to a number of different academic concepts and systems of knowledge – linguistic, mathematical, scientific and social, among others. Throughout schooling there is interplay between the students' system of meanings and the dominant sociocultural meanings that the educational institution in a particular sociocultural context is trying to convey. The interaction that takes place between individuals and their environment, broadly conceived to include social relationships and the way that this interaction influences the individual's cognitive processes were central foci for Vygotsky's work.

Vygotsky (1987) emphasizes that the internalization of experiences is essential in developing the internal sense (*smysl*) individuals have as an important plane in their internal systems of meaning. The way that children internalize meanings is strongly influenced by their prior experiences and the circumstances surrounding the appropriation of meaning. In children's systems of meaning there is an ongoing dialectical relationship between sense and sociocultural meaning. This relationship is also very important in the learning and teaching of writing, especially for second language writers, who are developing sense and meaning in a new language. Sense is not just tied to individual words but also includes broader concepts and theories that develop through everyday interactions (everyday or spontaneous concepts) and through interactions in formal academic settings (systematic or scientific concepts) (Lantolf and Thorne 2006) that are part of a constantly developing system of meaning. In his analysis of the internalization of meaning, Vygotsky focuses on inner speech's role in children acquiring and producing written and spoken language.

Inner speech

Adults helping children solve problems, such as completing a puzzle, use speech to direct children's actions, thus helping them learn to use speech to regulate their own actions. Initially, children verbalize this speech, but over time truncate the vocalization and internalize it. '[I]nner speech is an internal plane of verbal thinking which mediates the dynamic relationship between thought and word' (Vygotsky 1987: 279). Vygotsky investigated the way socially elaborated symbol systems are appropriated by children as a critical aspect of their learning-driven development. 'This appropriation of symbol systems was a central focus of Vygotsky's work, particularly as applied to educational pedagogy and led to his most fully elaborated application of the concept of internalization – the transformation of communicative language into inner speech and further into verbal thinking' (John-Steiner and Mahn 1996: 196). Vygotsky (1987: 279-280) viewed inner speech as 'an internal plane of verbal thinking' and as 'a dynamic, unstable, fluid phenomenon that appears momentarily between the more clearly formed and stable poles of verbal thinking, that is, between word and thought.' He traced the internalization of meaning from external speech to the innermost plane – the affective/volitional plane that lies behind and motivates thought. He also described the reverse process of externalization which moves 'from the motive that gives birth to thought, to the formation of thought itself, to its mediation in the internal word, to the meanings of external words and finally to the words themselves. However, it would be a mistake to imagine that this single path from thought to word is always realized' (Vygotsky 1987: 283). It is along this path that Trang experienced her blocking in her elbow, as she could not express her conceptual thought in writing.

When students focus on meaning and are relieved of the pressure of producing error-free writing, they increasingly rely on inner speech and verbal thinking, both central components of conceptual thinking. A dialogic approach allows students to build upon their socially and culturally shaped meaning-making processes and personal histories, which 'affect the way they write. For writing touches the heart of a student's identity, drawing its voice and strength and meaning from the way the student understands the world' (Fox 1994: *xiii*). Vygotsky (1978: 106) relying on his genetic approach, which looks at origins and history of development, argued that it is necessary to examine 'the entire history of sign development in the child and the place of writing in it' to understand the relationship between the thinking and writing processes.

Written language and the system of meaning

In the early development of writing, children utilize processes that they used in the acquisition of speech – directing voluntary attention, abstracting and isolating features of objects, as well as synthesizing and symbolizing. 'The processes that occur in effective oral language learning can occur in reading and writing as well, if reading and writing are understood as fundamentally dialogic' (Peyton and Staton 1991: xv). Another important component in the acquisition of oral language – making hypotheses and testing them in practice – plays an important role in the acquisition of literacy (Snow 1986). Dialog journals give students a vehicle that allows risk-taking and hypothesis testing in a safe setting.

The examination of the similarities and differences between oral and written language constitutes an important part of Vygotsky's theory of writing, which starts with the premise that contemporary psychology 'does not have a cogent view of the development of written language as a historical process, as a unified process of development' (Vygotsky 1978: 107). He examines the formation of the foundation for writing during pre-school years as children use symbolic representation for communication. Infants' hand and arm movements are given intentionality by adults and become gestures, symbols for something – pointing at what is wanted. Vygotsky (1987: 107) holds that an infant's gesture 'is the initial visual sign that contains the child's future writing as an acorn contains a future oak. Gestures, it has been correctly said, are writing in air and written signs frequently are simply gestures that have been fixed.'

In children's development, there are two other domains in which gestures are linked to the origins of written language – the first is in scribbling and the dramatizations that often accompany it; the second is in the area of symbolic play, during which children assign meaning to an object through gesture. A child's initial scribbling is often a gesture written down, such as dots representing running. Vygotsky illustrates symbolic play through an example of children using broomsticks as horses, because they can receive the appropriate bodily gesture. 'It is terribly difficult for a child to sever thought (the meaning of a word) from object. Play is a transitional stage in this direction. At that critical moment when a stick – i.e., an object – becomes a pivot for severing the meaning of horse from a real horse, one of the basic psychological structures determining the child's relationship to reality is radically altered' (Vygotsky 1933). The second-order symbolism developed in make-believe play is 'a major contributor to the development of written language' (Vygotsky 1978: 110).

Vygotsky showed that children's systems of meaning developed in oral language acquisition provide the foundation for written symbolic representation, but he also emphasized the differences between learning to speak and learning to write. Children achieve a high level of abstraction in the process of language acquisition; however, for writing there is yet another level of abstraction – a child must abstract 'from the sensual aspect of speech itself. He must move to abstracted speech, to speech that uses representations of words rather than the words themselves ... The abstract nature of written speech – the fact that it is thought rather than pronounced – represents one of the greatest difficulties encountered by the child in his mastery of speech' (Vygotsky 1987: 202). Vygotsky adds that an additional layer of abstraction is involved in writing since an interlocutor is not present in writing. The dialog in the journal allows the teacher to take on features of the interlocutor and helps in the creation of an environment in which students can grow as writers. A challenge for all writing teachers, but particularly for those educating linguistically and culturally diverse students, is to create environments in which students can expand their ZPDs in their writing by more freely drawing on their systems of meaning and verbal thinking.

Dialog journals and the system of meaning

Dialog journals have been used at all age and proficiency levels providing opportunities for native language and second language writers alike to write in a stress-free environment with an emphasis on communication, to write within their zones of proximal development. The dialogic character of language and learning (Bakhtin 1981, 1986) and the instrumental role of social interaction in the development of thought and language (Vygotsky 1978, 1987) provide the theoretical basis for journals. Drawing on their systems of meaning when writing in English presents a major challenge for ELLs. Trang felt that writing in dialog journals helped her to meet this challenge. Through her dialog journal she became aware of her writing/thinking processes and was able to draw on her system of meaning in developing and conveying ideas in written English.

Dialog journals have been used in a number of different ways, but if they are merely plugged into a traditional classroom, there is a danger that they will become just another writing exercise. Effective use of dialog journals entails 'three equally important components: (1) the written communication itself, (2) the dialogic conversation and (3) the responsive relationship between a literacy learner and a more competent member of a literate culture' (Peyton and Staton 1991: xvii). An additional component is the attitude that teachers take toward dialog journals. '[S]uccess in using dialog journals seems to require from teachers a low need to control their students' actions and a high need to find out and use their students' knowledge and experiences for learning – what Freire calls an "attitude of dialog"' (Peyton and Staton 1991: xxiv).

Effective dialog requires trust between the student and teacher, trust that can be engendered through the initial presentation of the journals and the way that the teacher responds to the journals (Staton, Shuy, Peyton and Reed 1988). When I introduce journals, I explain that making mistakes is a natural part of the learning process, especially when students are trying new words or are trying to convey a complex idea or concept. To take their minds off correctness, I have students write in ink to eliminate the tendency to erase. Students become motivated to produce more standard usage as they realize that it facilitates effective communication. Dialog journals help indicate what aspects of writing need to be addressed in mini-lessons or in student conferences about other writing assignments. Because students write about whatever they want, dialog journals offer them the opportunity to share their personal narratives and to write about things that are important to them. They come to see writing both as an authentic means of communication and as a way to reflect on personal growth and development. The dialog in the journals is facilitated when students understand that their lives have meaning and that their life experiences are of interest to others.

While there are different methods of responding to journals, narratives at the end of their contributions help students appreciate the dialogic nature of the journals and alter the traditional teacher role of evaluation. A statement of praise in the response helps the students gain confidence and shows them that their writing is meaningful. I try to make praise as concrete as possible. 'I really like the way that you described ...' Also, I relate my own experiences to something about which they have written and usually try to ask a question or two to help them deepen their thinking on a topic or to give them some material to consider for further journal entries. While the focus in responses is on meaningful communication rather than mechanics or correctness (I feel journals should not be corrected), teachers can model proper usage in their responses. Students receive instruction in adherence to certain norms and conventions in other assigned writing so that they become aware of different ways to effectively communicate their meaning.

When students are reluctant to write, teachers can initiate a conversation asking some general questions and when they hit upon something of interest, a more extended conversation can ensue. After a few minutes, teachers can then suggest, 'Why don't you just write that down?' Students write on a wide variety of topics as they create narratives of their choice and through their journals they make meaning of their lives, experiences and aspirations. '[O]ne of the significant ways through which individuals make sense of and give meaning to their experiences is to organize them in a narrative form' (Mishler 1986: 118).

When students feel comfortable sharing their thoughts, struggles and growth, teachers come to understand them more profoundly as writers and human beings with different experiences, interests, learning styles, systems of meaning and ZPDs and can, therefore, help them succeed academically and socially. It is important to assure students that their journals are confidential but also to let them know that teachers have an ethical and legal responsibility to refer them for help if they write about being abused or if they are contemplating hurting themselves or others.

In using dialog journals with English language learners, it is important to ascertain whether students are literate in their native language. If they are not and if it is possible, given their grade level and the programs available at the school, they should be introduced to literacy through their first language (Brisk and Harrington 2000; Freeman and Freeman 1996). It is easier for them to draw on their systems of meaning and their more extensive vocabulary in their native language and they are more likely to have the '*ah ha* moment' Vygotsky (1997a, 1978) describes in which they recognize that written symbols have meaning. This affords them a considerably broader ZPD. If they are already literate in their first language, but are at the very beginning of learning English, they can start writing their journal in their native language. In such cases, if the teacher does not know the native language, she can rely on other teachers, siblings or community members to help with the translation. As students transition to English, they can use words from their own language if they do not know them in English. While I have students in my teacher education courses dialog with students from elementary and secondary classes, the students whose voices are heard below were high school and university ELLs in my classes who were literate in their own language and who were intermediate to advanced writers in English. I use these voices to comment on a dialogic approach to teaching/learning to write in English through the use of dialog journals.

Student perspectives on dialog journals

> The level of ideas go downward as the problem of English. We have to choose simple word to express the abstract and beautiful feeling which appear in my Chinese thinking. It, of course, is impossible. The thinking level decreases and then the original mood and idea cannot continue. And I need to struggle with the sentences construction, the grammar, the tense and the vocabulary. (Pi Lan, China)

The students' perspectives on dialog journals to be considered in this section come from dialog journals, written reflections, questionnaires and interviews as they describe: 1) how they make meaning through writing in their journals; 2) how journals influence their attitudes toward writing in English, their confidence in themselves as writers, their fears and anxiety with writing; and 3), how journals help them develop conceptual thinking. The influence of all of the above on their ZPDs is also explored (Mahn 1992, 1997). The student's pseudonym and country of origin are given the first time that a student's perspective is given.

Many students echo Trang's description of the disconnect in their writing and thinking processes, the subsequent loss of confidence and the attendant fear if they focus on grammar and correctness. Doing so interrupts the meaning they intend to communicate and, at the same time, inhibits them from developing fluency. Conversely, dialog journals facilitate using writing to develop and convey meaning. '[T]he journals allowed me to expand my thoughts and get my message across without interrupting myself thinking about what words to use or what the correct grammer should be (all the things that can be done later)' (Andre, France). 'I still have a lot of mistakes, but now I can express my ideas clear' (Masha, Russia). Once she took her focus off grammar, Trang was surprised by her own ideas: 'after reading the journal I think I have many good ideas written down that I haven't noticed it.'

When they are concerned primarily with form and/or mechanics – whether vocabulary, spelling, usage, punctuation or agreement – students cannot clearly explain their ideas. An emphasis on grammar and error correction is similarly inhibiting to language learners attempting to make meaning in oral speech. Masha indicates that she had to stretch her vocabulary and take risks – she was able to expand her ZPD – because, 'If I use just the right words I can't explain anything clear.' When students focus on communicating ideas, they draw on verbal thinking in the move to written speech. 'Journals helped me to think first; to think about ideas of writing instead of thinking of the grammar errors that I might make' (Jabar, Palestine). Making this connection to their systems of meaning significantly changes and expands their ZPDs. On the other hand, an overdependence on correctness blocks other mechanisms, including those responsible for native language acquisition – risk taking, hypothesis testing, communicating with intentionality, responsive dialog, scaffolding and practice – with a consequent narrowing of the ZPD.

Fear

A dialogic approach is designed to help reduce the fear of making mistakes. Mike Rose (1989: 1) captures this fear in the words of Laura, an ELL student from Tijuana. '[A]s soon as we start writing, I freeze up. I'm a crummy writer, I know it. I know I'm gonna make lots of mistakes and look stupid. I panic'. Rose (1989: 1–2) then offers this haunting description:

> The Middle Ages envisioned the goddess of grammar,
> Grammatica, as an old woman. In one later incarnation, she is
> depicted as severe, with a scalpel and a large pair of pincers ...
> [T]he scalpel, the pincers, are reminders to the teacher to be
> vigilant for error, to cut it out with the coldest tool. Laura has never
> seen the obscure book that holds my illustration of Grammatica,

> but she knows the goddess intimately, the squinting figure who
> breathes up to her side whenever she sits down to write.

Jabar, expresses similar fears: 'the grammar ghost was present in every sentence and between the lines.' This fear, which also haunts basic writers of English, can be exacerbated by insensitivity. 'When I was in regular English, I felt out of place. Because everybody in the class could easily converse in english and I couldn't. If I said something wrong 1 or 2 students used to laugh. I really felt humiliated at that moment' (Raj, India). 'I was always afraid everybody would laugh if I read my writing' (Illyich, Croatia).

Unfortunately, teachers' negative attitudes contribute to ELL students' fear and lack of confidence. 'Like our ESL 101 teacher last semester gave me the idea, he gave everybody the idea that they were so bad in English' (Karin, Norway). 'My first composition I turned in at high school my teacher give it back and say she understand nothing. I feel terrible because I made a big effort to write it' (Shu-Tse, Taiwan). This sort of teacher response contributes to the frustration students feel when they are not able to develop a thought and then convey it in their writing. It certainly narrows their ZPDs.

Confidence

Dialog journals help students overcome their fears, develop their fluency through meaningful communication and gain self-confidence as English writers. Jabar eloquently expresses this sentiment: 'For the first time in my life I see English teacher who want his student to be released from the verbs and tenses prison and to wake up from the grammar nightmare. It was a relief.' Other students echo his sense of relief, 'I write whatever I want. No pressure for writing. I don't need to worry about grammar, structure and detail' (Jung, China). In addition to being bolstered by not having to worry about grammar, interactions between student and the teacher can play an important role in developing confidence through genuine responses, which expand a student's ZPD. 'When you writing me back it makes me feel that you understand what I am talking about (even if I have a lot of mistakes). I start to use more new words which I never used before because I was afraid of mistakes. So my writting is more interesting now. All that make me feel better and I want to write. I start to enjoy it' (Masha).

Helping students become aware of their reading and writing processes and then using this knowledge to more effectively communicate their meaning is central to a dialogic approach as it gives them confidence. 'Once I had everything I wanted on the paper, I could go and fix the grammar later. This was a huge step for me because I noticed that a lot of my fears toward writing were gone' (Ana, Mexico). 'I allowed myself to take risks (vocabulary I wasn't sure about, grammar structures …) without having to pay for it (Bad grades, shame …)' (Andre). 'Journal makes me more confidence in writing because it is my first time that I write journal and my first time have to write it in English. I can see that I first write with simple sentence then, the more I write, the more complex thought I want to express. And whenever I can express my complex thought, the more confident I have' (Lan, Viet Nam). These students all reveal a metacognitive awareness of their own thinking and composing processes.

Conscious awareness

Vygotsky (1978) writes about students being consciously aware of learning to read and write. However, if their conscious awareness is primarily focused on grammar and correctness, it can have a deleterious affect. In examining students' awareness of and reflections on their thinking and writing processes, it is important to recognize that a tremendous amount of the mental activity that goes into the production of language occurs at a subconscious level. 'I'm not good with rules so I have to trust my intuition' (Karin). 'I worry much less about the proper use of imperfect and plusquamperfect (or how that thing was called), actually, I don't worry at all about that. I go a lot with what sounds or "feels" right' (Helga, Germany). While students are gaining conscious awareness of their thinking and writing processes, they are also acquiring knowledge on a subconscious level. 'When we are learning something, we do not notice that we are getting more and more knowledge' (Pancha, Mexico). 'As I write, I start sometimes to remember some words I never used before, but I just tried to write it and then next time I remember it. Some words like I took from friends, native speakers and as they tell me something, I thought it was a neat sentence. I never used it. But I try to use it in journal and if the teacher understands that means I use it right, so I can use it next time' (Michi, Japan).

Motive

In contrasting oral and written speech, Vygotsky (1978, 1997a) notes that an infant's motivation to speak is stronger than a child's motivation to write. While L2 writing approaches that primarily focus on structure and grammar can induce anxiety and diminish motivation, journals help motivate students because of the authentic and meaningful communication with another person. 'Communication is not always possible in a verbal way. Journals helps us to communicate our real feelings' (Moises, El Salvador). 'Writing Journal to me is just like communicate with other. So, not only it help me to express my feeling by writing, but also help me to practice to communicate in English' (Lan). Motivation also increases when students receive a response that shows that their communicative intent has been realized or their experiments using new words or expressions are successful. 'Everytime when I wrote journals and you write comments back I feel that I can express what I want to say. It change my confidence because I am not afraid anymore that people is not going to understand what I say. Now I think that I can write whatever I want, even if I have a lot of mistakes' (Pancha).

Affective factors such as motive, fear, frustration and confidence influence students' motives to write and can expand or constrict their ZPDs. The most common motive for writing in academic settings is the grade. Not having to worry about grades in the journals changed students' motives for writing and allowed them to set their own goals. 'Instead, I can write more freely and maybe enjoy it and not really have to worry about making mistakes for the grade' (Tina, Taiwan). Even when students know that the stress of receiving a grade is eliminated, if a teacher highlights errors in any way, students will focus more on correctness and the uninhibited element of journal writing will be diminished. They will be less likely to write freely and concentrate on expressing their meaning. 'These journals worked more to express yourself through writing than to achieve the desired goal in writing set by the teacher' (Jae Min, Korea).

Thinking and writing processes

> When I got each idea for a paper, the process I took was a
> Japanese thinking way. I don't think I can easily change my
> thinking process to an American style. My brain has naturally been
> influenced by Japanese culture and language. Twenty three years

experiences since I was a second year old is like a big trunk of a tree inside me and its a main stream of my every process. So, I guess it may be impossible to change my process completely, but I can add a new way as a branch of the tree since I'm learning a new way through my experience. (Mich)

Vygotsky (1987), drawing on Goethe, wrote that learning a second language helps in the development of a more systematic understanding of the first language – the metalinguistic awareness which Michi displays above. Dat (Viet Nam) shows a similar awareness: 'Writing in journals has built my confidence in writing and I found that writing helps me understand something deeper.' Ho Chong (Korea) describes how overcoming fear helped her access her thoughts: 'I am not afraid to put down something more "deep" or philosophic in a paper' but Jung wrote that 'everytime I thought I had wrote or describe emotion (happiness or sadness for example) but after I read what I wrote, it always seemed not as deep as I wanted.' This reflects the gap that exists between the student's ability to use English to express meanings and the student's understandings of those meanings in their native language,

If teachers respond to their meaning in writing, students are often motivated to rely on their conceptual thinking to write on a deeper level. Michi and Karin used an interesting metaphor to describe this process: 'Not like the other teachers who gave us a topic and just grade our papers, your first emphasis was letting us float any ideas in our brains and then you asked us to write them.' 'The English words pretty much just float out.' Once 'floated,' students felt an urgency to get their words down on paper. 'Those journals in the class helped me to bring down my thoughts on the paper as quickly as possible' (Ilyich). 'I transferred my thought processes into writing without lifting the pen as fast as I could' (Cesar, Guatamala). Doing so helped them connect to their systems of meaning and expand their ZPDs.

When writing, students usually have time to think and reflect on what they are going to say. During this time ESL students often perform a grammar check, breaking the connection between inner speech and external speech resulting in the loss of their ideas. And when they do begin to write, the sentence unfolding on paper is a reminder of their lack of mechanical skill, further disrupting their composing processes (Shaughnessey 1977). Dialog journals help students overcome the disconnect between thinking and composing as they write more quickly: 'The good strategy that really helped was writing without stopping and always having my brain and my hand connected with each other' (Ali, Saudi Arabia). A number of students wrote about the connection between their writing and thinking processes: 'My hand and mind work without thinking about it' (Carlos, Nicaragua); 'Learning to write as I'm thinking' (Abdul, Afghanistan), 'The journal makes my thinking flow' (Sharin, Thailand); and 'Writing in journal helps my idea run smoother' (Dat). These comments are illustrative of Vygotsky's (1987: 202–3) statement that '[Written speech] is a conversation with a white sheet of paper, with an imagined or conceptualized interlocutor.' In this conversation, students felt that their ideas flowed to the paper more readily.

Connecting thinking and writing helped students generate ideas. 'Writing in journals has been helpful by helping me develop ideas quickly when needed. My ideas developed as I wrote. When I was in need of what to write, I would brainstorm to find it. My ideas developed well because of the writing in journals' (Jose, United States). The recursive process – writing engendering thinking and thinking engendering writing – is central to a dialogic approach. 'With the journal you have one idea and start writing about it and everything else just comes up' (Karin). Through the written dialog students not only generate ideas, but also begin to incorporate understandings of the structure of English. In her study of L2 learners of French, Merrill Swain (2000: 13) concludes that 'collaborative dialog is problem-solving and, hence, knowledge-building dialog.' Journals also help students generate ideas for other kinds of writing. 'I go back and read it, I think there are some ideas that I never think about and that ideas I can expand to an essay' (Trang). Trang, in recognizing that she can use journals as an artifact to support other writing activities beyond corresponding to me, expanded her ZPD.

Capturing thoughts as completely as possible in written language presents a challenge for all writers, but especially for those writing in a second language. 'My thoughts about this trip very interesting in russian but in English … Sorry I'll think about it and write you better next time' (Masha). In trying to find the 'correct' words and syntax to express ideas, students' thought processes become diminished, undermining the recursive process and constricting the ZPD 'The thinking process will be cut off if I am worried about grammar mistakes' (Dat). '[P]utting down on paper right away what is on my mind, instead of worrying about how to word it, because some other thoughts would be gone' (Tina). 'They seemed to help me focus on what I was writing in the sense that I let the words just flow and form by themselves' (Gertrudis, Philippines). 'The journals we did in our class were useful to me because it help me form my thoughts' (Channary, Cambodia). Karin describes how dialog journals provided the antidote to losing ideas, 'You learn to write as you think instead of thinking and then writing and then stopping.

You just think and you write and maybe things come to mind as you write and you write them down. Maybe wait 3 sentences, but you still have it in your mind and you get it down.' Karin again illustrates Vygotsky's notion of conversing with a sheet of paper. Instead of losing ideas, not only could Karin write down her ideas, she could hold them in her mind for a period of time. The ability to store and retrieve ideas using inner speech and verbal thinking significantly expanded her ZPD by giving her greater access to her system of meaning.

The confidence to write without anxiety contributed to students' fluency. 'When I wrote the journals in class, I didn't think that it would help, but now when I looked back, I think I can write more fluently than before and can just write about everything that comes to mind' (Hui Fen, China). 'They helped me write fluently; helped me phrase things in my mind while I'm writing' (Claudia, Guatemala). Part of the process of gaining fluency is developing the ability to use subvocal planning based on verbal thinking and inner speech – to compose and produce their writing, to hold their thoughts as Karin describes. Developing automaticity in writing helps students connect to their thoughts, to their system of meaning and to convey their thinking in meaningful, dialogic communication with an authentic, encouraging responder. They also are motivated to develop their mastery of the structure and grammar of written language when they see how it facilitates meaningful communication. In their responses teachers can model correct spelling and structure and ask students to expand on a point, to think about it more deeply and to express it in a different way, but most of the overt writing instruction is done outside of the journals. That knowledge was often used by students to communicate more effectively in their journals. Not so motivated are those students whose main exposure to grammar is in completing meaningless, isolated, exercises in a non-communicative context and in being on the receiving end of the red pen highlighting their inadequacies.

Dialog journals and other writing

Students had a number of interesting insights that could be used to answer the question: Does a ZPD expanded through students' ability to draw on verbal/conceptual thinking and inner speech in journal writing carry over to other school writing? '[J]ournal helped us to understand the difference between informal writing and essays. While writing essay you have to connect everything so that it makes sense. In journal writing you don't have to connect each and every idea of yours' (Raj). 'Writing in my Journal certainly improve my ability of composing sentences in english and thinking in english, which is very usefull when I write essays in other classes' (Andre). 'For a long answer in the tests, I can start writing my answers down at the same time I think them in my head' (Michi). 'When I have to answer some essay questions on the test for Chem, I feel very confidence to write down my answer without worrying that I can't explain clearly' (Trang).

Some of the strategies students developed writing in dialog journals carried over to other types of writing. 'I think that writing in journals helped me to use techniques and strategies in other writing such as taking notes, short answer test questions, essay questions and research' (Ana). 'Journals give me an idea of how to start writing anything such an essay, a letter, notes' (Pancha). 'I pretend to be sitting in class and writing a Journal' (Ali). 'From the journals I have learned and applied good ideas to the papers. I now make good ideas my first priority in writing a paper without considering the grammar, because otherwise if I think about the grammar the most I will write a poor paper in both ideas and grammar' (Jabar).

Conclusion

In an era in which the effectiveness of pedagogical approaches is reduced to scores on standardized tests, the need to listen to students' perspectives is magnified. The voices heard in this chapter testify to the important insights that students can offer about how teaching approaches affect their learning. This volume is organized around the notion that the true test of an educational theoretical framework is whether it can be applied in concrete contexts and whether it improves learning/teaching in the classroom. The students' persuasive voices certainly affirm that Vygotsky's theory cannot only help explain how the cognitive processes involved in writing work, but also can help explain why a particular pedagogical approach is effective. While the application of Vygotsky's theory to classroom practice has been written about extensively (John-Steiner, Panofsky and Smith 1994; Kozulin, Gindis, Ageyev and Miller 2003; Moll 1990; Wells and Claxton 2002) there are areas that remain unexplored, such as the concept of the internal system of meaning. This chapter has attempted to show that this concept can provide an important guide for teachers in developing both efficacious pedagogy and a means for assessing its implementation.

Dialog journals, the centerpiece of the approach described here, help ELLs develop their literacy competency, especially the ability to write fluently, as they focus on the meaning they want to convey and not on whether a particular grammatical construction is correct. In focusing on what is meaningful to them, students draw on their own life experiences, sociocultural environments and their meaning-making processes as resources for their writing. Journals provide them space and time within their ZPDs to explore and develop their own written voices – authentic voices that speak from their lives and their experiences, ones that are not diminished or silenced by approaches that focus primarily on correctness and that feature assigned writing with little room for authenticity. These voices are answered in an ongoing, meaningful dialog.

These voices give us insights into how journals help English language learners solve the problem Trang poses at the beginning of this chapter: How to avoid the disconnect between their verbal thinking and writing processes? They also describe how dialog journals help students draw on their systems of meaning when the focus is taken off of correctness and placed on meaningful communication. Students' ZPDs are expanded as they draw on their systems of meaning and gain a metacognitive awareness of making meaning through written communication. Their voices describe the struggles that adolescent and young adult ELLs have capturing ideas that come from conceptual thinking and conveying them in written English. ELL students who have made the transition using conceptual thinking in their own language revisit it when faced with communicating complex ideas in written English. As they become aware of their thinking and composing processes, ELLs use this awareness to shape their writing; in a way similar to the process through which they became aware of their own thinking processes and used this awareness to shape their thinking.

Dialog journals help ELLs of all ages gain self-confidence as they use writing to problem solve, to focus their thoughts and to convey ideas as clearly as possible in dialog with another whose language skills enhance the expansion of the student's ZPD. Through the expansion of their ZPD students develop new strategies to effectively communicate their meaning in written language. The genuine development of the ZPD was evidenced by students who commented on using their journals as artifacts to support other kinds of writing and also by students who developed a deeper understanding of what writing in any language including L1 by writing in their journals and reflecting on their experience. The adult responders also learn from and about their students, their lives and experiences and their needs, but most importantly, they learn what happens when they give their journal partner something all teachers should give to all students – the gift of confidence (Mahn and John-Steiner 2002).

Notes

1.   Student writing reproduced here is unchanged. Pseudonyms have been used and the first time a student's writing is used, his or her country of origin is listed to give the reader a feel for students' linguistic and cultural diversity.
2.   As the editors of this book indicate there are different interpretations of the concept of the zone of proximal development, which Vygotsky (1978, p. 86) described as 'the distance between the actual developmental level as determined by independent problem solving and the level of potential development as determined through problem solving under adult guidance or in collaboration with more capable peers.'
3.   While Vygotsky did not have a fully elaborated theory of second language acquisition, his writings on first language acquisition, on literacy acquisition and on the relationship between first and second language acquisition and between learning to write and learning a second language (Vygotsky 1978, 1987, 1997b) provide a comprehensive foundation on which to explore second language literacy.
4.   A translation of *znacheniye slova* that more accurately reflects Vygotsky's emphasis on meaning would be 'meaning through language' or 'verbal meaning.'

References

Bakhtin, M. M. (1981) *The Dialogic Imagination: Four Essays by M. M. Bakhtin* (M. Holquist (ed.) and C. Emerson and M. Holquist (trans.)). Austin, TX: University of Texas Press.

Bakhtin, M. M. (1986) *Speech Genres and Other Late Essays* (C. Emerson and M. Holquist (eds) and V. W. McGee (trans.)). Austin, TX: University of Texas Press.

Brisk, M. E. and Harrington, M. M. (2000) *Literacy and Bilingualism: A Handbook for All Teachers*. Mahwah, NJ: Lawrence Erlbaum Associates.

Chaiklin, S. (2003) The zone of proximal development in Vygotsky's analysis of learning and instruction. In A. Kozulin, B. Gidnis, V. S. Ageyev and S. Miller (eds) *Vygotsky's Educational Theory in Cultural Context* 39-64. Cambridge: Cambridge University Press.

Fox, H. (1994) *Listening to the World: Cultural Issues in Academic Writing*. Urbana, IL: NCTE.

Freeman, Y. S. and Freeman, D. E. (1996) *Teaching Reading and Writing in Spanish in the Bilingual Classroom.* Portsmouth, NH: Heinemann.

John-Steiner, V. and Mahn, H. (1996) Sociocultural approaches to learning and development: A Vygotskian framework. *Educational Psychologist* 31: 191–206.

John-Steiner, V., Meehan, T. and Mahn, H. (1998) A functional systems approach to concept development. *Mind, Culture, & Activity* 5: 127-134.

John-Steiner, V., Panofsky, C. P. and Smith, L. W. (1994) *Sociocultural Approaches to Language and Literacy: An Interactionist Perspective.* New York: Cambridge University Press.

Kozulin, A. (1990) *Vygotsky's Psychology: A Biography of Ideas.* Brighton: Harvester Wheatsheaf.

Kozulin, A., Gindis, B., Ageyev, V. S. and Miller, S. (eds) (2000) *Vygotsky's Educational Theory in Cultural Context.* Cambridge: Cambridge University Press.

Lantolf, J. (ed.) (2000) *Sociocultural Theory and Second Language Learning.* Oxford: Oxford University Press.

Lantolf, J. and Thorne, S. L. (2006) *Sociocultural Theory and the Genesis of Second Language Development.* Oxford: Oxford University Press.

Mahn, H. (1992) ESL Students and the Reading and Writing Processes: An Attitudinal Profile. Unpublished master's thesis, California State University, Los Angeles, CA.

Mahn, H. (1997) Dialog Journals: Perspectives of Second Language Learners in a Vygotskian Theoretical Framework. Unpublished doctoral dissertation, University of New Mexico, Albuquerque.

Mahn, H. (2003) Periods in child development: Vygotsky's perspective. In A. Kozulin, B. Gidnis, V. S. Ageyev and S. Miller (eds.) *Vygotsky's Educational Theory in Cultural Context* 119–37. Cambridge: Cambridge University Press.

Mahn, H. and John-Steiner, V. (2002) The gift of confidence: A Vygotskian view of emotions. In G. Wells and G. Claxton (eds) *Learning for Life in the 21st Century: Sociocultural Perspectives on the Future of Education* 46–58. Oxford: Blackwell Publishing.

Mishler, E. (1986) *Research Interviewing: Context and Narrative.* Cambridge, MA: Harvard University Press.

Moll, L. C. (1990) *Vygotsky and Education: Instructional Implications of Sociohistorical Psychology.* New York: Cambridge University Press.

Peyton, J. K. and Reed, L. (1990) *Dialog Journal Writing with Nonnative English Speakers: A Handbook for Teachers.* Alexandria, VA: TESOL.

Peyton, J. K. and Staton, J. (1991) *Writing our Lives: Reflections on Dialog Journal Writing.* Englewood Cliffs, NJ: Prentice Hall Regents.

Peyton, J. K. and Staton, J. (1993) *Dialog Journals in the Multilingual Classroom: Building Language Fluency and Writing Skills through Written Interaction.* Norwood, NJ: Ablex.

Rose, M. (1989) *Lives on the Boundary.* New York: Penguin.

Shaughnessy, M. P. (1977) *Errors and Expectations: A Guide for the Teacher of Basic Writing.* New York: Oxford University Press.

Snow, C. (1986) Conversations with children. In P. Fletcher and M. Garman (eds) *Language Acquisition: Studies in First Language Development* 69–89. Cambridge: Cambridge University Press.

Staton, J., Shuy, R., Peyton, J. K. and Reed, L. (1988) *Dialog Journal Communication: Classroom, Linguistic, Social and Cognitive Views.* Norwood, NJ: Ablex.

Swain, M. (2000) The output hypothesis and beyond: Mediating acquisition through collaborative dialog. In J. Lantolf (ed.) *Sociocultural Theory and Second Language Learning* 97–114. Oxford: Oxford University Press.

Verity, D. (2000) Side effects: The strategic development of professional satisfaction. In J. Lantolf (ed.) *Sociocultural Theory and Second Language Learning* 179–98. New York: Oxford University Press.

Vygotsky, L. S. (1933) Play and its role in the mental development of the child. Retrieved 26 June 2006 from http://www.marxists.org/archive/vygotsky/works/1933/play.htm [Reprinted in *Soviet Psychology* 5: 6-8]

Vygotsky, L. S. (1978) *Mind in Society: The Development of Higher Psychological Processes.* Cambridge, MA: Harvard University Press.

Vygotsky, L. S. (1987) *The Collected Works of L. S. Vygotsky: Vol. 1. Problems of General Psychology.* Including the volume *Thinking and Speech.* New York: Plenum.

Vygotsky, L. S. (1994) The problem of the environment. In R. van der Veer and J. Vlasiner (eds) *The Vygotsky Reader* 338–54. Cambridge, MA: Blackwell.

Vygotsky, L. S. (1997a) *The History of the Development of Higher Mental Functions. The Collected Works of L. S. Vygotsky: Vol. 4. Problems of the Theory and History of Psychology.* New York: Plenum.

Vygotsky, L. S. (1997b) *Problems of the theory and history of psychology. The Collected Works of L. S. Vygotsky: Vol. 3. Problems of the Theory and History of Psychology.* New York: Plenum.

Vygotsky, L. S. (1998) *Child Psychology. The Collected Works of L. S. Vygotsky: Vol. 5. Problems of the Theory and History of Psychology.* New York: Plenum.

Vygotsky, L. S. (1999) *Scientific Legacy. The Collected Works of L. S. Vygotsky: Vol. 6. Problems of the Theory and History of Psychology.* New York: Plenum.

Wells, G. and Claxton, G. (eds) (2002) *Learning for Life in the 21st Century: Sociocultural Perspectives on the Future of Education.* Oxford: Blackwell Publishing.

5   Embodied language performance: drama and the ZPD in the second language classroom

John R. Haught and Steven G. McCafferty

Introduction

This chapter argues that language is not a separate domain from communication, that language in use is necessarily an embodied phenomenon that includes mimetic properties that are part and parcel of the language culture mix, such as facial expressions, gestures, posture, body language and so forth; and that body, language and mind are unified in the engendering of a thought and its production in linguistic and imagistic form through speech and gesture. Moreover, we believe that L2 teaching and learning benefits from utilizing embodied contexts of activity.

Vygotsky (1978) discussed the critical role of play in child development, basically contending that through play a child is able to creatively formulate her coming of age intellectually by behaving and thinking in ways that are beyond her current state of development. When children, for example, imitate those they will become (mother, father, older sibling) they are engaging in the process of learning-leading-development, one of the principle constructs of Vygotsky's theory of mind. Pretend play is also a matter of *performing*, which in Newman and Holzman's (1993) sense means creating new roles for ourselves in the Zone of Proximal Development (ZPD).

Drama is a form of play through the taking on of another identity in activities such as reading a script in character, improvization, rehearsal and performance. It provides the opportunity for L2 learners to embody language and culture. Furthermore, such contexts afford recursive practice, with students coming to understand the form and meaning of language and nonverbal communication over time. Although the potential for drama in the second language classroom has been recognized for some time, to date comparatively little research has been conducted in the area (to be reviewed below).

SCT and the embodied mind

Vygotsky, following Spinoza, his favorite philosopher (Van Der Veer and Valsiner 1991), rejected dualistic accounts of mind and body, a philosophical disposition still very much with us today. From an SCT perspective, people are always participating within frames of sociocultural activity and on both the material and ideal planes. Indeed, from a material dialectical perspective as established by Marx, words in the mind are the mental echo of material actions in the world. From an SCT viewpoint, then, mind is directly related to the materiality of existence. This is well illustrated in the work of Luria and Vygotsky, who, for example, found that if they laid strips of paper on the floor in a straight line that Parkinson's patients could to some degree gain control over their tremors and walk with more facility than they had been able to do prior to the intervention. Eventually the researchers were able to remove the strips of paper entirely, the patients having internalized the mediational means (see Homskaya 2001: 22). In this case, mind and body are clearly unified as a functional system. There are those, of course, who would claim that this has little to do with language acquisition. But we believe, as we propose to show, that it does.

Embodied language learning

At least one theory of formal linguistics privileges language as an innate human biological endowment, the proper study of which focuses on the supposed underlying abstract rules and principles that govern language acquisition – or in Chomskian terms: competence not performance[1]. Moreover, the emphasis of this approach has been on studying the emergence of syntactic structures as a result of input to the Language Acquisition Device (LAD), or in more recent terminology, Universal Grammar (UG). From this perspective mind is disembodied to an almost absolute degree – there is no consideration of human agency nor do contexts exert any influence on language development, outside of supplying the LAD with input or triggers.

Another prominent theory of language acquisition stems from information processing research in cognitive psychology, which examines the acquisition of finite-state grammars (laboratory languages) in an attempt to reveal the inner workings of the brain/mind. However, processing approaches as applied to SLA and thus the acquisition of natural languages, take much the same general tack (see Sanz 2005 for a recent volume on this perspective). Also, like formal linguistics, this viewpoint reduces language to an atomic level (linguistic structure) and again, as with formal linguistics, the emphasis has largely been on how language is acquired through input, although in this case, as a result of cognitive operations as opposed to engaging underlying abstract, genetically programmed principles.

This approach also has found its way into the classroom, primarily through Van Patten's (2004) Processing Instruction, which centers on the idea that we are limited capacity processors of information, so that in classrooms we need to attempt to enhance learners' intake through an explicit focus on form. Once again, outside of enhancing input, the particulars of engagement – who is talking to whom and for what purpose (meaning) as well as how interlocutors engage one another through facial expressions, gestures and other means of communication receives little consideration (see Harris 1998 on the importance of including these and other forms of meaning making as part of linguistic analysis).

Additionally, UG leaves no room for conscious learning to take place (the underlying rules and principles of competence cannot be consciously accessed) and information processing-inspired SLA is currently in a heated debate as to the role of implicit and explicit learning/knowledge, whether one can become the other and under what circumstances and what role each has in the acquisition process. SCT, as indicated above, is a theoretical perspective that explores the consequences of avoiding such dualisms and considers psychological and linguistic processes in a holistic way. Thus, Vygotsky focused on the development of conceptual knowledge as the foundation of learning-leading-development. As such, conceptual knowledge takes a central role in teaching and learning as demonstrated by Gal'perin's pedagogy, Systemic-Theoretical Instruction, which provides students with a material basis for understanding concepts (Lantolf and Thorne 2006: 302). This approach was applied to the language classroom by Negueruela (2003 and Chapter 7 this volume), who developed a schema for advanced learners in the form of a flow chart for making decisions as to the correct form for tense and aspect in Spanish. However, unlike other such mediational means, Negueruela grounded his schema, conceptually, in the process of making meaning in the L2, resulting in a far more effective tool than the decontextualized rules of thumb that the students in the study had internalized over the years as part of previous classroom learning.

Indeed, SCT is not a competing theory of language acquisition, but a theory of mind, or perhaps more accurately, a theory of person, which argues that in conjunction with our biology we are shaped through cultural-historical contexts by our interacting with one another and with cultural artifacts within the cultural-historical activity structures that make up our lived experience (going to school, conversing at the family dinner table, going online), although this activity also includes all that actually happens within any concrete activity frame as well as being an abstract template (embodiment in the larger sense). Human activity, from this point of view, then, has a direct impact on how language learning/acquisition unfolds.

In line with this reasoning, Johnson (2004: 171–2), called for replacing the acquisition metaphor for SLA altogether, preferring a participation metaphor instead, stating that 'Vygotsky's and Bakhtin's theories restore "dignity" and value to the neglected part of human language – language performance.' She further argued that 'a dialectical interaction between the interpersonal and the intrapersonal planes leads to the merging of language performance and language competence.' On this view, language performance cannot be separated from language learning.[2]

Furthermore, SCT explicitly views semiotics (meaning making through signs), which of course includes language, as embodied activity. For example, Bakhtin (1981) emphasized the history of words, noting that our voices are never entirely our own, but come from the voices of others as we *ventriloquate* and *appropriate* utterances from specific individuals within specific contexts (a view that has been empirically demonstrated with L1 acquisition by Tomasello 2003). Ultimately, every utterance from Bakhtin's view is both heteroglossic, containing the many voices of our experience and dialogic, in concert with and responding to others' voices.

Moreover, Donald (2001: 265) argued that mimesis, or mime at its most basic level, is foundational to making meaning and central to tribal identity (culture), for example, the way we look at each other when we talk, how we stand and walk and particularly how we emote. Ontogenetically, mimesis starts at an early age. For example, Donald cites Linda Acredolo, who found that a nine-month-old child puckered her mouth to represent a fish. Donald speculated that in the evolution of language it is possible that after earlier, simpler forms of mimesis, gestures may have been combined to produce rudimentary forms of grammar, something that was found to apply to a naturalistic L2 speaker, who relied heavily on gesture to make meaning in the face of difficulties with the language (McCafferty 2008).

Additionally, in an extention of Vygotsky's theorizing on the interface of thinking and speaking, McNeill (1992, 2005) held that gesticulations (the gestures that accompany speech) form a dialectic with speech in the unfolding of thought, speech providing the linear, analytic (linguistic) elements of thought and gesture the imagistic, holistic and synthetic aspects. Moreover, McNeill (2005) contended that sign is not to be seen as isolated from contexts, so that his theoretical unit of analysis for the coming together of thought, speech and gesture, the Growth Point, is part of both the interpsychic and intrapsychic psychological planes at once.

Furthermore, gesture has proven integral to the study of language and cognitive development (see Goldin-Meadow 2003 for an overview of this work) and has found developmental application to L2 learning as well. For example, McCafferty (2006) found that an intermediate ESL student, although engaged with another person, synchronized beat gestures (typically the up-and-down movement of the hand) with the parsing of his words into syllables, apparently utilizing gesture to help himself gain control over the rhythmic pulse of the L2. It was suggested that this occurred through both his mapping of gesture onto linguistic structure, thus creating a conceptual foundation through materialization and through motor imagery from the movement of the hands in conjunction with his speech. These findings indicate that gesture, like speech, can serve as a 'private' mediational means for individual learners, which in turn, may help in the development of L2 proficiency.

Drama (play) and the ZPD

Vygotsky always had a keen interest in theater and he is known to have met the famous director of the Moscow Theatre, Konstantin Stanislavsky as well as film-maker Sergei Eisenstein. As a young teacher, Vygotsky directed theater groups in his school in Gomel in Belorussia and wrote a paper entitled 'On the Problem of the Psychology of the Actor's Creative Work' in 1932 (Vygotsky 1987). Vygotsky believed that dramatic activity is highly related to play and that it has a direct connection to his concept of the ZPD. For Vygotsky (1978), play is the optimal context for young children to develop, providing a foundation for the future. However, he argued that play is not totally free and unstructured activity but is bound within constraints and rules. It is in the recognition of these rules and the motivation to abide by them that young children first develop the ability to regulate their behavior.

As clearly observable, imitation within families is a highly productive feature of interaction and furthermore, imitation itself is central to creating ZPDs. Vygotsky (1978: 88) argued that 'a person can imitate only that which is within her developmental level' and Newman and Holzman (1993: 151) stated 'To Vygotsky imitation is what makes it possible for the child's capacities to develop by virtue of doing what she/he cannot yet do' (the future in the making). Moreover, Vygotsky (1978: 211–12) goes on to state that imitation is 'the source of instruction's influence on development' and that 'instruction is possible only where there is a potential for imitation' (as cited in Newman and Holzman 1993: 150).

Imitation is quintessentially embodied activity – it involves the appropriation and then, according to Vygotskian theory, *internalization* of aspects of another person – *what* she says and does and *how* she says and does it. It is important to point out that although imitation is linked by Tomasello (1999) to joint attention, which is fundamental to a child's coming to understand the intentions of others, in the case of naturalistically exposed L2 learners, imitation may not result from joint attention but instead, because of unfamiliarity with the language and culture, the true intention of a utterance or action may not be realized until some later point in time when greater exposure leads to greater understanding, at which point the learner may choose to accept or reject what was imitated earlier. Imitation, on this view, then, serves as a vital step in the process of becoming and is not an end in-and-of itself.

However, development, according to Vygotsky, is not a linear process – if one only imitated the actions of another for instrumentalist purposes, that is, only to be able to perform a specific action, then imitation would remain a tool *for* result. To be sure, transmission by imitation is a necessary part of doing things on an assembly line, where if one does not do exactly the same operation at a given station then all subsequent work on the particular widget would be in jeopardy. However, development, from Vygotsky's perspective, is associated with transformation. In its transformative sense, imitation is *revolutionary activity* in Newman and Holzman's (1993) words.

For example, in relation to language learning, DaSilva Iddings and McCafferty (2005) found that two elementary school children, each speaking a different L1 (Spanish and Brazilian Portuguese) and with no real competence in the L2 (English), when asked by their teacher to interact regarding a shared picture book on spiders with only minimal text in English, created an imaginative narrative concerning a picture of a tarantula, during which they imitated each other's L1 and turned the spider into something else – a form of play – calling the spider *Branca de Neve*, in Portuguese (Snow White) and *Blanca de Nieve* in Spanish (Vygotsky 1978 called an artifact used to shift activity to an imaginary plane in play a 'pivot'). The students of course recognized cross-linguistic similarities between their respective languages (English was not used at all). Moreover, when speaking Portuguese, the Brazilian participant tried to overlay it with what she perceived as Spanish intonation patterns, perhaps both an attempt to make herself better understood to her interlocutor and to create a heightened sense of shared positive affect.

Overall, the authors concluded that on entering each other's linguistic worlds, the two children were both using and inventing sign at the same time. This was characterized as a 'tool and result' (Vygotsky 1978: 65 as quoted in Newman and Holzman 1993: 34) formulation of learning as opposed to the instrumentalist (tool *for* result) example above. In their interaction the students were creating ZPDs, possibly transforming their metalinguistic awareness and knowledge and perhaps even gaining insights into the very nature of sign/symbol relationships. Also, and the authors consider this crucial, this example indicates the unpredictable, creative path that learning-leading-development in the ZPD, particularly with regard to play, can take.

Another aspect of imaginary play is performance. Newman and Holzman (1993: 102–3) contended that on an everyday basis we *act* out our predetermined societal roles, such as being parents, but that when a child pretends to be her mother, she is in fact performing, that is, she is 'self-consciously creating new roles' for herself. Therefore, in the case of L2 learners in naturalistic contexts, engaging in drama activities involves performing not only other characters but also a new language and culture. In these circumstances learners are potentially developmentally ahead of themselves (learning-leading-development in the ZPD), performing themselves as L2 speakers.

Keeping the creative, transformative role of the ZPD in mind, Engeström (1987), building on Vygotsky, brings attention to the fact that the multiplicity of perspectives inherent to interaction often leads to contradictions and breakdowns (whether internal or external), which in turn, can give rise to invention and transformation (something he termed Expansive Learning). Engeström (2002) further characterized the ZPD as a collective process by which fundamentally new, revolutionary activity emerges through cooperative action. Moreover, he theorized that Expansive Learning begins with the perception of helplessness in the face of a double bind situation in the course of everyday actions, one that cannot be resolved through individual action alone. This of course typifies what learners in naturalistic contexts often face in second language encounters both inside and outside the classroom (as in the example of the two children in the DaSilva Iddings, Haught and McCafferty (2005) study mentioned above).

In another, and particularly compelling, example of this process in action, DaSilva Iddings, Haught and Devlin (2005) reported on how two girls in the same elementary school classroom, who shared no common language, enlisted a number of semiotic means to mediate their friendship. Of particular interest, the students appropriated (imitated) aspects of each other's drawings, incorporating both objects and the artistic style in which they were drawn, that is, performing cultural historical aspects of one another on paper.

Also, in a longitudinal study of a Taiwanese student after he had first arrived in the US, McCafferty (2002) found that gesture proved to have a transformational impact on learning in the ZPD, particularly in regard to imitation. Once a week the student interacted with an American graduate student, a former teacher of English as a Foreign Language (EFL), mostly concerning topics of mutual interest. Over the course of their meetings, both participants imitated each other's gestures, which proved to become a significant part of the meaning-making process. Moreover, following McNeill's view of the interconnection between thought, language and gesture, McCafferty found evidence for the contention that gesture also played a part in the L2 participant's efforts to gain self-regulation in both developing and conveying his thoughts in the L2. Furthermore, by imitating the gestures of the American, the L2 participant was learning to use an important symbolic means of the new language culture (or 'languaculture' as Agar (1994) terms it), which also resulted in a sense of shared activity and interpersonal rapport. Additionally, as suggested above, the Taiwanese participant may also have been in the process of performing himself in the L2, both *renting* his interlocutor's gestures (to use Bakhtin's term) as a part of this process in its initial stages and then appropriating and internalizing them as well.

Also in regard to SCT, performance and the ZPD, Kramsch (2000), in her study of semiotic mediation with L2 writers, noted how the students constructed rhetorical roles through both spoken and written mediums which allowed them to experience themselves as private individual, as well as public, social sign makers. She argued that personality is composed of the myriad different roles that get played out in dialogic interactions and that making L2 students aware of such roles enhances their ability to engage in a greater variety of discursive situations (also see Moro 1999 for a similar account).

Furthermore, DaSilva Iddings and McCafferty (2007) suggested that at times L2 children have a need to transform the institutional activity of schooling through imagination in order to re-create meaningful contexts for continued participation. Drawing upon Bakhtin's (1984) conceptualization of *carnival*, the authors found that the two kindergarten children studied appeared, to an observer, to be off-task or just playing with regard to a story-retelling assignment. However, the researchers argue that because the students were bored, could not do the task as assigned, or for whatever reason, they engaged in the playful, irreverent, dialogic and discursive world of carnival. They found renewal through the sense of liberation afforded them by turning the task upside down, creating and performing their own highly spontaneous, contingent and comic activity while adhering to aspects of the assigned genre and in English despite sharing the same L1. Although a transfiguration, this activity allowed the students to continue to participate in the class instead of disrupting others or simply doing and saying nothing, which unfortunately is the plight of many L2 students in mainstream classrooms.

Drama, SCT and the L2 classroom

Drama is a Greek word meaning action. Although there is a tendency to equate drama with theater, there are important differences between the two. Theater is a collaborative enterprise between actors, writers, designers, technicians and others, all working together for a period of rehearsal and creative exploration toward the common goal of performance. Drama, on the other hand, has the ability to allow us to momentarily be another person or to encounter a situation outside of our everyday experience. Moreover, drama does not necessarily lead to a formal performance. Indeed, some forms are completely improvisational, one-time events highly akin to creative play.

Drama activities of many types have been used in the L2 classroom. However, unlike the Drama in Education and Creative Drama communities, language teachers originally embraced a performance product. One of the earliest pioneers of drama-based language teaching, Via (1976), a theater professional, went to China and found himself teaching EFL. Using a product-based approach, his students performed plays in English. Sharing both approach and era, Hines (1973) saw the value in scripted performance as well, publishing a collection of skits specifically for the L2 classroom. However, Via was the first to argue that learning a language cannot be separated from acquiring culture, although in accordance with his times, he focused on how language learners need to resemble idealized native speakers, to learn how they 'hold their bodies, how far they stand apart, where they look when they talk' (Via 1976: xiv). Via saw performance as a way for students both to understand and practice embodied social norms.

In the 1980s the first and most influential SCT-based approach to drama in the L2 classroom appeared with Di Pietro's (1987) monograph, *Strategic Interaction* (SI). He stated his overarching view of language learning as 'To speak is to be human and to learn how to speak a new language is to find new ways in which to express that same humanity' (Di Pietro 1987: 12, as found in Lantolf 1993). In describing the intellectual influences on Di Pietro (the book itself does not go into any depth with regard to its academic influences, belonging more to the methods genre), Lantolf (1993: 3) suggested that Di Pietro was fundamentally interested in 'helping learners develop ... [a] linguistically configured self in a second language,' and that he drew on Bakhtin's notions of dialogism to understand how self is created discursively. Di Pietro recognized that language in use constructs a particular voice that is inseparable from its contexts of meaning, that this promotes learning a language as part of one's identity and not as a decontextualized set of grammatical structures.

Di Pietro, through adopting a dialogic framework, also built into the method the possibility or likelihood of forming ZPDs for L2 learning, the players creating circumstances, for example, where one provides help to the other through added elaboration or where both players play off of one another in a creative and contingent manner. Indeed, the immediate goal of the scenario is for the students to utilize creativity and resourcefulness in the face of potential communication breakdowns. Moreover, as Lantolf (1993: 19) suggests, by design two of the three stages in the approach provide contexts for constructing ZPDs. During the rehearsal phase, which is a collaborative process whereby the learners develop aspects of the scenario, the instructor is expected to allow the students to interact with as little intervention as possible; and the third stage, debriefing, provides the opportunity for the instructor to help students find their own voices through discussing what they did in the scenario both with regard to language and content. Furthermore, Di Pietro purposefully has the instructor interject a conflict into the scenario once it is underway in an attempt to get students to collectively resolve the difficulty through interaction, which allows further opportunities for the creation of ZPDs.

Di Pietro's work has influenced a number of second language researchers and/or practioners. Artigal (1993), when teaching kindergarten children, had the teacher first create through mimesis a shared semiotic space, a kitchen in a house, for example, by pantomiming actions that become recognizable to the students as belonging to the activity of a kitchen and then proceeding to enact a narrative, taking a cookie from a cookie jar, for instance. The students are expected to verbalize the teacher's actions – tell the story in the L2, although they continue to receive support from the teacher, who at the same time, interacts with them, listening to what they say, but employing only non-verbal means of communication.

Additionally, drawing upon both the process approach of Di Pietro (1987) and the product approach of Via (1976), ESL instructor and researcher Miccoli (2003) led her students through a three-phase program that began with theater games, improvisations and SI scenarios. The students then engaged in more formal theater training, which culminated in the performance of short plays. Miccoli also had the students reflect on their drama experience, putting their written responses in their portfolios. She cited some of these reflections as evidence of the power of drama to both engage learners and improve their language skills.

Moreover, Wagner (2002) argued that Educational Drama is the perfect medium for engaging L2 learners in the ZPD, suggesting that in role playing activities learners assumed not only the language but the entire personae of others, which catapulted them to a developmental level above their actual level and in a more engaging and motivating manner than through use of the L2 in a decontextualized forum. Also, Liu (2002) contended that SI allows students to recognize the power of language, although he envisioned a more complex model than SI, involving a series of episodes to be improvised or composed and rehearsed over time, allowing for greater exploration and elaboration through recursive practice. Also, SI has been incorporated into the rapidly emerging world of Computer Assisted Language Learning. Colburn (1998), for example, has adapted all three stages to an internet relay chat format.

Although not specifically tied to SCT, another aspect of research on drama in the L2 classroom that has relevance to the present study comes from Fels and McGivern (2002), who found that drama activities such as improvisation, role playing and writing in role (an exercise in which the student writes from the perspective of the character she is playing) opened up possibilities for intercultural conversations and explorations beyond what is found in more traditional classrooms. Part of this, they suggested, stems from the embodied, multimodal form of learning that takes place through drama, which involves the comprehension and production of affective and bodily/kinesthetic states as well as listening and speaking. Furthermore, they found that drama allows learners to formulate in-depth questions about explorations of L2 languaculture (a process they termed 'Performative Inquiry').

The study

Participants

The study involved six adult ESL students, several of whom were enrolled in a university English Language Institute at a large southwestern university in the US. All had agreed to participate in a voluntary semester-long workshop entitled 'English through Drama.' The participants, all women, were from Japan, Korea, Russia and Belarus. The Russian-speaking women (H and M) had each been in the United States for a year and a half and were good friends. Both considered themselves to be beginning speakers of English and reported that they had had little opportunity to speak the language. One of the two Korean learners (A) was in her second year of study and had had the benefit of living in a dormitory the previous year. She was better acquainted with American culture than the others, but still had difficulty with spoken English. The other participants were all recent arrivals. A Japanese student (C) was forced to withdraw midway through the study. The remaining students, W and N, had studied English in their native countries, Korea and Japan, respectively, but felt that their listening and speaking skills were weak.

All of the participants had fairly strong decoding skills, but had trouble comprehending what they read. They all reported being drawn to the workshops in order to improve their spoken English. Though the workshops began as one group, after four weeks, students split into two groups due to scheduling problems. Group One consisted of H, M and C (until C was forced to withdraw) and asked to meet twice weekly. Group Two consisted of W, A and N and wanted to meet once a week. John, (the principle author of the chapter), an experienced theater professional and a drama and language teacher, was a participant observer, serving as both researcher and workshop leader.

Setting

The 90-minute workshops were held in a university classroom, which contained several long tables and chairs. This set-up permitted the participants to clear an open space for the activities, but there was no stage or performance space. Also, two video cameras were in the room.

Classroom practices and materials

The students engaged in theater games, improvisations, tongue twisters and the rehearsal of written dramatic scripts. The workshops entailed no homework, though students often took notes on their scripts and sometimes re-wrote their dialogs. Though the students participated in both warm-up activities and theater games, they were less comfortable with improvisation, claiming that their limited vocabulary made it difficult to communicate effectively. Instead, the students demonstrated a strong preference for working with written scripts and reported that they felt they learned vocabulary and lexical phrases from the short scenes selected. The scripts came from a book of rehearsal scenes targeted for student actors and a series of ten-minute one-act plays. The scripts were chosen to reflect contemporary spoken American English.

The students took turns playing the different roles and John assumed different roles as well if a participant was absent. In addition, John often directed the participants to play the scenes but would change the relationships from, for example, mother and child to doctor and patient or teacher and student. The short comedic scenes also gave rise to a number of interesting conversations centering on the characters and their different personalities and points of view. These interactions became, at times, a source of instructional focus.

Data collection

Typically the two video cameras were mounted on tripods and remained on for the entire session for each of the workshops unless one was being used for the students to view their performances as a television monitor. This arrangement allowed students' reactions to themselves and their interactions while viewing their performances to be recorded. Additionally, the notes the students took and the changes that they made to their scripts were collected at the end of the workshop for analysis.

Analysis

For this chapter, we chose to focus on the participants' rehearsals of two scripts, examining the use of modeling and imitation, which proved to be important and frequent activities in the workshops in relation to creating ZPDs.

Modeling and imitation

Although unanticipated by the researcher, participants in both groups in their attempts to decode a script for both meaning and form, asked John to model pronunciation and prosodic features they had questions about, after which they would imitate him and sometimes discuss the features in question. The students also noticed that John used gestures and other nonverbal means of communication when modeling and these too became a focus as they both imitated and discussed them.

Subsequent rehearsals often brought new questions about meaning and form, which resulted in another round of discussion, modeling and imitation. This pattern of recursion provided multiple opportunities for the participants to collectively deepen their understanding of the scripts on multiple levels and to increase both their verbal and nonverbal fluency when rehearsing the scenes as well.

Prosody and intonation

The two students in group one (H and M), being aware that cadence and intonation differ cross-linguistically for Russian and English, asked John to model some lines from the script for them, which in choral format they imitated:

Examples

(1) (see appendix for transcription conventions)

/ __ __ __ / /   _____ /*

J   *You have the audacity to call them that?*

/ __ __ __ / /   _____ /*

H&M *You have the audacity to call them that?* (in unison)

__ __ / /   \ _____   \ _____ \

J   *That's what they are. High school students. Nothing more.*

__ __   / /   \ _____   \ _____ \

H&M *That's what they are. High school students. Nothing more.*

M   [marking her script, recording in her own way how J said the line] This is nice.

H   [quietly repeating the line a second time]

__ __   / /   \ _____   \ _____ \

That's what they are. High school students. Nothing more.

J   [resuming modeling]

____ \   _____ \ *\ __ __ _ __   / / \   __ _   / \

That's like saying a great white shark is just a fish and nothing more.

H   [sub rosa]

____ \ _____\ *\ ____ ___ _ ___ / / \   ____ _ / \

That's like saying a great white shark is just a fish and nothing more.

M   [as H reads she moves her right hand like a conductor] (Excited)
You see it is all the time. Ahh, I'm trying to follow you like a
[Russian], I don't know how, [Russian], an orchestra ... [Looking
to H for help with finding the word in English for conductor].

After a few sessions, the students in both groups began with a new
script, again by having John model so that they could imitate him. In the
following example, W had heard John model the line 'I can't do this!
How can I do this?' for the first time at the beginning of the session and
when it came her turn to play the role of the character who speaks the
line, W, although still uncertain as to the meaning and a half an hour
having passed since imitating John, repeated the line with almost the
same exact intonation pattern modeled by him:

(2)

　　* \ ＿＿＿ /* ＿/ ＿＿ / /*

J   I can't do this! How can I do this?

　　* \ ＿＿ /* ＿/ ＿ / /*

W I can't do this! How can I do this?

Apparently, the referent for the demonstrative pronoun, 'this,' was
not transparent to W until she repeated it a second time ('this' refers to
the fact that W's character is nervously waiting to see if the coin their
roommate is flipping will land on heads or tails, which will determine
whether she or her other roommate is to try and take advantage of the
rich awkward young man knocking at the door). Evidently, at some
point, W must have grasped how her character was torn and conflicted
about what she was doing (perhaps through the intonation she employed), for at the end of the scene she laughed and with a sense of
incredulity, uttered 'Oh my God! They choose!' Two weeks later the
students again worked with the same script, but by this point they had
read through it numerous times and their readings had begun to exhibit
subtleties of expression with regard to prosodic elements and a fluency
nearing that of spontaneous speech.

Mimesis and gesture

The recursive process of gaining increased understanding of the texts
through the pedagogical practices in the workshops also included the use
of gesture, proxemics, gaze and posture, all mimetic/embodied aspects

of the unity of language and culture in communication. As with aspects of verbal production, the students often imitated nonverbal elements of John's production when modeling lines in the script or when providing explanations of the meaning of phrases or individual lexical items. Most of the gestures modeled by John were iconic/metaphoric gestures (concrete representations) that accompanied speech and provided an imagistic dimension to the verbal channel as found in the example to follow. Additionally, beat gestures (typically the sharp up-and-down movement of the hand, head or foot) were used by John to indicate emphasis and were imitated by the students as well. The following excerpt is from a scripted rehearsal.

(3)

J   *Dump him!*

W   *Dump him!* [Self corrects to imitate J's reading] *Dump him!* [imitates John's dismissive gesture – right hand, palm facing chest, sweeping laterally away until arm is fully extended, palm facing outward] Margaret, *dump him!* [Looking N directly in the face with an appropriate 'demanding' facial expression and leaning in close to her]

N   *Is this a joke, or what?*

W   *Call it off!* [Emphatic, said quickly, with a downward chopping movement, hand held vertically fingers together] Cancel!? [W turns to J to verify the meaning of the phrase, pointing towards the script]

W had appropriated the dismissive gesture J had used earlier with the same line (*dump him!*) with his explanation of its meaning. However, she also used a novel gesture, the chopping gesture, which was consistent with the verbal expression it accompanied (*call it off!*). Moreover, it helped her illustrate or expand on the meaning of the phrase, providing the metaphoric image of severing, which was materialized further through the gesture's articulation, that is, the hand shape, the extent of the gesture in space, hand speed and so forth. Also, W used proxemics, leaning in close to the other actress, apparently to establish a sense of her character as persuasive or controlling, thus demonstrating her new-found understanding of the character through both speech and mannerisms and in a novel way not initiated by John.

Over time the participants began to incorporate many more gestures, such as emphatic up-down 'beats,' which were performed with both the hand and with nodding of the head. Though they were still holding their scripts and thus were limited from full dramatic physicality, they engaged each other through gaze and proxemics, often leaning toward or away from the other person during verbal contests. By the time this came about they had largely given up asking for clarification of the script.

We believe that this transformation was, at least in part, an effort by the students to adhere to their workshop experience concerning drama – that actors portray characters through gesture and other nonverbal means as well as speech and that the two need to go together coherently. This interpretation gains further support from the fact that there were several recorded instances where a student would silently mirror a gesture being performed by one of the other students in the class while that student was reading. In all cases, however, these were gestures that had first been modeled by John. This happened with the following utterances: 'about this high,' 'she squeezes me!' and 'cross my heart.' Also, one participant engaged in this mirroring behavior while watching herself on the monitor. All of these forms of production constituted private rehearsal.

Moreover, on several occasions participants demonstrated their growing understanding of the script through the use of gestures previously modeled by John but used with different utterances, demonstrating a possible internalization of a gesture and its meaning. The example below is from a later session. The excerpt is the same part of the script as in Example 3 with W taking the same part as well. In this example we also see the use of emblems, or gestures that have a relatively fixed lexical meaning, for instance, in American languaculture the waving of the hand to greet or take leave.

(4)

W   *Dump him!* [shaking head from side-to-side ('no')]

A   *Is this a joke, or what?*

W   *Call it off!* [Head nodding up-and-down emphatically ('yes')]

A   *I'm in love!*

W   You were in love last year. [hand beat on *love* and a dismissive gesture on *last year* (as found in the excerpt above)]

A   *That was different.* [leans back and away from W]

W   *Six times!* [Chin beat on *times*]

A   *Okay, six times.*

W   *And three weeks ago you went out with someone else.* [hand beats on each word of *three weeks ago*. Repeats dismissive gesture on *out*, ending with hand beat on *else*.]

Discussion and conclusion

The analysis of the data supports the notion that imitation proved to be a transforming aspect of teaching and learning in relation to the use of drama in the classroom for all participants. First of all, the students created a collective ZPD by having John model his interpretation of how the lines of the scripts might be said and put into an embodied presentation in accordance with expectations for the production of drama. This allowed them to ventriloquate, appropriate and finally internalize aspects of his presentation through imitation. This process was one that the students seemingly found useful because it was first initiated by them and then became a regular pedagogical practice that they relied on. Moreover, because of the recursive nature of how this took place (in a spiraling manner, repeatedly returning to lines and nonverbal forms) the students were able to deepen their knowledge and understanding of the items they selected to concentrate on, which in turn increased their comprehension of the texts as a whole.

At the individual level, students were able to ask John to model those forms that each wanted to work on, providing the circumstance for each to realize her potential within the ZPD to the degree that she was able. Furthermore, this was a dialogic process, of course. As such, the students had to participate through use of the target language, asking questions that they truly wanted answered. However, as the students were not filmed in other settings, particularly while interacting with others in naturalistic conversations, we do not know to what extent they utilized what they had internalized outside of the classroom. This is an issue for future research. Nonetheless, during the time they attended the workshops each student showed evidence of having gained fluency.

With further regard to the ZPD, the highly contextualized and social nature of the scripts provided a setting in which the students could perform themselves as fluent speakers of the L2, something none of them were. Indeed, such circumstances are characteristic of 'developmental performance – the ongoing collective activity of creating new kinds of environments where people can be active performers of their lives' (Holzman 1999: 14). Moreover, the way that dramatic practices were undertaken in the L2 classroom engendered learning-leading-development – a process that is key to Vygotsky's theorizing concerning the ZPD.

This is not to say that the students expected to realize the goal of living in the US as native speakers, yet, it is reasonable to assume that their trajectory included being able to operate with an increased degree of facility within the cultural-historical context that they inhabited, especially as all had enrolled in the class voluntarily. However, the students unfortunately felt they lacked proficiency in the L2 and so did not attempt to take performing to the level that Di Pietro (1987) felt most significant – creating identity through performing improvisational, culturally relevant scenarios. We believe that this activity would almost certainly enhance what can be accomplished through the use of drama in the L2 classroom and could prove highly transformational in relation to the ZPD. We believe this constitutes an important area for future research.

We also argue that a critical aspect of the act of becoming in a second languaculture concerns embodiment. Again, although no attempt prior to instruction was made to incorporate imitation as an explicit aspect of teaching, all of the participants chose to imitate the nonverbal forms that John at first unwittingly modeled for them as part of his rendering of the lines of the scripts. We find it particularly striking that the students also imitated one another's gestures (although only those previously modeled by John) while watching themselves on the monitor. This form of private rehearsal is clear evidence of the importance they accorded this part of their performance. Also, it is worth noting that one of the students (W) used a spontaneous metaphoric gesture with speech (gesticulation) with the line *call it off*, providing her own imagistic interpretation (severing with a cut of the hand). This use of gesture demonstrates that she had understood the illocutionary force of the idiom within the contexts of the script, as indeed the function in this case was to exhort one of the other characters to end a relationship. Gestures, proximics, facial expressions, posture and other mimetic features of interaction are a part of how meaning is encoded in an L2 and obviously deserve further attention.

In closing, we support the efficacy of drama in the L2 classroom. Language learning through dramatic explorations leads to the possibility for language learners to become active participants in their own language learning through engaging in physical, cognitive and affective activity. Using drama in the L2 classroom allows the complexities of language learning to be framed within the affordances of dramatic play, giving rise to ZPDs. Play can be a serious business and the L2 classroom should expand to include this multimodal form of teaching and learning.

Notes

1. For a critique of this approach as it relates to SLA, see Lantolf (2006)
2. For a similar view arrived at independently see Lantolf and Johnson (2007).

References

Agar, M. (1994) *Language Shock. Understanding the Culture of Conversation.* New York: Quill.

Artigal, J. M. (1993) The L2 kindergarten teacher as a territory maker. In J. E. Alatis (ed.) *Georgetown University Round Table on Languages and Linguistics 1993, Strategic Interaction and Language Acquisition: Theory, Practice, and Research* (452–468). Washington, DC: Georgetown University Press.

Bakhtin, M. M. (1981) *The Dialogic Imagination, Four Essays.* Austin, TX: University of Texas.

Bakhtin, M. M. (1984) *Rabelais and his World* (H. Iswolsky, Trans.). Bloomington, IN: Indiana University Press.

Colburn, C. M. (1998) Online strategic interaction: ESL role-playing via internet relay chat. *The Internet TESL Journal IV: 6.*

DaSiva Iddings, A. C. and McCafferty, S. G. (2005) Creating zones of proximal development in a third-grade multilingual classroom. In A. E. Tyler, M. Takada, Y. Kim and D. Marinova (eds.) *Language in Use: Cognitive and Discourse Perspectives on Language and Language Learning 112–23.* Washington, DC: Georgetown University Press.

DaSilva Iddings, A. C. and McCafferty, S. G. (2007) Carnival in a mainstream kindergarten classroom: A Bakhtinian analysis of second language learners' off-task behaviors. *The Modern Language Journal 91.1: 31–44.*

DaSilva Iddings, A. C., Haught, J. and Devlin, R. (2005) Multi-modal representations of self and meaning for second language learners in English dominant classrooms. In J. K. Hall, G. Vitanova and L. Marchnkova (eds) *Dialogue with Bakhtin on Second and Foreign Language Learning* 33–53. Mahwah, NJ: Erlbaum.

Di Pietro, R. J. (1987) *Strategic Interaction: New Directions in Language Teaching.* Cambridge, UK: University of Cambridge.

Donald, M. (2001) *A Mind So Rare.* New York: Norton.

Engeström, Y. (1987) *Learning by Expanding: An Activity-Theoretical Approach to Developing Research.* Helsinki: Orienta-Konsultit.

Engeström, Y. (2002) A video interview with Yrjo Engestrom. Retrieved on 2 September 2006 from http://csalt.lancs.ac.uk/alt/engstrom/

Fels, L. and McGivern, L. (2002) Intercultural recognitions through performative inquiry. In G. Brauer (ed.) *Body and Language: Intercultural Learning through Drama:* 19–36. Westport, CT: Ablex.

Gal'perin, P. (1989) Mental actions as a basis for the formation of thoughts and images. *Soviet Psychology* 27 (3): 45–64.

Goldin-Meadow, S. (2003) *Hearing Gesture: How our Hands Help us Think.* Cambridge, MA: Harvard University Press.

Harris, R. (1998) *Introduction to Integrational Linguistics.* Oxford: Pergamon.

Hines, M. E. (1973) *Skits in English as a Second Language.* New York: Regents Publishing.

Holzman, L. (1999) Introduction. In Holzman (ed.) *Performing Psychology* 5–32. New York: Routledge.

Homskaya, E. D. (2001) *Alexander Romanovich Luria. A Scientific Biography.* New York: Kluwer/Plenum.

Johnson, M. (2004) *A Philosophy of Second Language Acquisition.* New Haven, CT: Yale University Press.

Kramsch, C. (2000) Social discursive constructions of self in L2 learning. In J. Lantolf (ed.) *Sociocultural Theory and Second Language Learning* (133–54). Oxford: Oxford University Press.

Lantolf, J. P. (1993) Sociocultural theory and the second language classroom: the lesson of strategic interaction. In J. A. Alatis (ed.) *Georgetown University Round Table on Languages and Linguistics 1993. Strategic Interaction and Language Acquisition: Theory, Practice, and Research* (220–233). Washington, DC: Georgetown University Press.

Lantolf, J. P. (2006) Re(de)fining language proficiency in light of the concept of 'languaculture.' In H. Byrnes (ed.) *Advanced Language Learning. The Contributions of Halliday and Vygotsky* 72–91. London: Continuum.

Lantolf, J. P. and Johnson, K. E. (2007) Extending Firth & Wagner's ontological perspective to L2 classroom praxis and teacher education. In B. Lafford (ed.) *The Modern Language Journal* 91 (Focus Issue, Second Language Acquisition Reconceptualized ? The Impact of Firth and Wagner (1997)): 877–892. Oxford: Blackwell.

Lantolf, J. P. and Thorne, S. L. (2006) *Sociocultural Theory and the Genesis of Second Language Development.* New York, NY: Oxford University Press.

Liu, J. (2002) Process drama in second- and foreign-language classrooms. In G. Brauer (ed.) *Body and Language: Intercultural Learning through Drama* 51–70. Westport, CT: Ablex.

McCafferty, S. G. (2002) Gesture and creating zones of proximal development for second language learning. *The Modern Language Journal* 86 (2): 192–203.

McCafferty, S. G. (2006) Gesture and the materialization of second language prosody. Special Issue, Gullberg, M. (Guest Editor), *International Review of Applied Linguistics* 44 (4): 195–207.

McCafferty, S. G. (2008) Material foundations for second language learning: gesture, metaphor and internalization. In S. G. McCafferty and G. Stam (eds) *Gesture: Second Language Acquisition and Classroom Research*. Mahwah, NJ: Lawrence Erlbaum, 47–65.

McNeill, D. (1992) *Hand and Mind: What Gestures Reveal about Thought*. Chicago, IL: University of Chicago Press.

McNeill, D. (2005) *Gesture and Thought*. Chicago, IL: University of Chicago Press.

Miccoli, L. (2003) English through drama for oral skills development. *ELT Journal* 57 (2): 122–9.

Moro, Y. (1999) The expanded dialogic sphere: Writing activity and authoring of self in Japanese classrooms. In Y. Engestrom, R. Miettinen and R. Punamaki (eds) *Perspectives on Activity Theory* 165–82. Cambridge, UK: Cambridge University Press.

Negueruela, E. (2003) *A Sociocultural Approach to the Teaching and Learning of Second Languages: Systemic-theoretical Instruction and L2 Development. PhD dissertation. Pennsylvania State University, University Park, PA.*

Newman, F. and Holzman, L. (1993) *Lev Vygotsky: Revolutionary Scientist*. New York: Routledge.

Sanz, C. (ed.) (2005) *Mind and Context in Adult Second Language Acquisition*. Washington, DC: Georgetown University Press.

Tomasello, M. (1999) *The Cultural Origins of Human Cognition*. Cambridge, MA: Harvard University Press.

Tomasello, M. (2003) *Constructing a Language: A Usage-Based Theory of Language Acquisition*. Cambridge, MA: Harvard University Press.

Van Der Veer, R. and Valsiner, J. (1991) *Understanding Vygotsky*. Cambridge, MA: Blackwell.

Van Patten, B. (2004) Input processing in SLA. In B. Van Patten (ed.) *Processing Instruction: Theory, Research and Commentary* 5–31. Mahwah, NJ: Lawrence Erlbaum.

Via, R. (1976) *English in Three Acts*. Hong Kong: University Press of Hawaii.

Vygotsky, L. S. (1978) *Mind and Society: The Development of Higher Psychological Processes*. Cambridge, MA: Harvard University Press.

Vygotsky, L. S. (1987) *The Collected Works of L. S. Vygotsky Volume 6. Scientific Legacy*. R. W. Rieber and A. S. Carton (eds) New York: Plenum Press.

Wagner, B. J. (2002) Understanding drama-based education. In G. Brauer (ed.) *Body and Language: Intercultural Learning through Drama* 3–18. Westport, CT: Ablex Publishing.

Appendix. Transcription conventions

Symbol

Meaning

J

Teacher/researcher

W,N,H

Participants

[ ]

Researcher's comments

CAPS

Emphatic or strongly stressed utterance

sub

sub rosa, barely audible private rehearsal of word or phrase

..

Short pause

...

Medium pause, up to 5 seconds

/

Rising intonation (whether a question or not)

\

Falling intonation

/\ \/

Rise-fall and fall-rise pitch

—

Flat or continuing intonation

*

High pitched voice

6 Agency in the classroom

Leo van Lier

Introduction

This chapter is about the notion of agency and its role in classroom language learning. The main principle involved is that learning depends on the activity and the initiative of the learner, more so than on any 'inputs' that are transmitted to the learner by a teacher or a textbook. This does not, of course, diminish the need for texts and teachers, since they fulfill a crucial mediating function, but it places the emphasis on action, interaction and affordances, rather then on the texts and contents themselves. Although this is nothing new if we take seriously the writings of Comenius, Vygotsky, Montessori, Dewey and many other educational thinkers over the centuries, it is good to remind ourselves of the wisdom of this fundamental pedagogical principle.

Agency can be defined in a 'bare bones' way as 'the socioculturally mediated capacity to act' (Ahearn 2001: 112). This definition begs the question (acknowledged by Ahearn) of what kinds of sociocultural mediation might be involved or, indeed, what we mean by sociocultural mediation. In another analysis, Duranti (2004: 453) provides a 'working definition' of agency that includes three basic properties: 1) control over one's own behavior; 2) producing actions that affect other entities as well as self; 3) producing actions that are the object of evaluation. Although this definition is more detailed than Ahearn's, it does not elucidate the notion of sociocultural mediation.

According to Wertsch, Tulviste and Hagstrom (1993: 336), Western theories about agency assume that agency is a property of the individual. In contrast, these same authors argue that agency, from a sociocultural perspective (following Vygotsky) is 'intermental' as well as 'intramental' (ibid.: 337). More plainly put, agency is not simply an individual character trait or activity, but a contextually enacted way of being in the world.

It follows that agency is always a social event that does not take place in a void or in an empty wilderness. Even when an unsolicited individual act is agentive, it is socially interpreted (as well as often socially motivated). Lantolf and Thorne (2006: 143) argue that agency 'is about more than voluntary control over behavior.' They explain that agency also 'entails the ability to assign relevance and significance to things and events.' From a sociocultural perspective, agency is shaped by our historical and cultural trajectories, hence Ahearn's notion that agency is socioculturally mediated. Lantolf and Thorne also point out that agency can be exercised by individuals as well as by communities (ibid). In a classroom, for example, learners can act individually as well as in groups, or indeed as a whole class (as when a whole class negotiates workload or deadline issues with the teacher). Thus, students can speak from an 'I' as well as from a 'we' perspective.

The aim of this chapter is to examine the notion of agency and its dynamics in language classrooms. A better understanding of agency can help us find ways of creating learning environments favorable to its emergence and development. A related aim is to note some difficulties and possibilities in investigating agency from the classroom perspective, through reflective teaching, action research and classroom interaction analysis. In the process we will examine some notions that have been researched before and that may seem to be related to agency, such as control, initiative, autonomy and motivation.

Locating agency: when and where?

In this section I will present some extracts from diverse classrooms to examine some of the problems and possibilities involved in the analytical search for agency. It will become apparent that locating agency is by no means an easy or straightforward matter and, like other complex, mulifaceted constructs (*motivation* comes to mind), we know that it is important but it may be difficult to observe and analyze in natural instances of its occurrence.

We will look at six extracts that I place roughly in an ascending order of agency, in a largely intuitive way. When I discuss each one in turn, some of the problems and ambiguities will be brought out and some of the difficulties of assigning agency in actual classroom activity will become apparent.

(1) (Forman 2005)

An EFL class in Thailand:
T: Would you be afraid of moving to a foreign country?
(pause)
T: Yes or no?
(pause)
T: Uh?
S: Yes.
T: Yes. Why?
(pause)
T: Why?
(pause)
T: Why?
(pause)
T: Mm?
(pause)
T: Why?
(pause)
T: Who would like to answer the question?
(pause)
T: Now, if you cannot answer the question and if you don't want to answer the question,
Okay, move further.

(2) (van Lier 2003):

In a project-based ESL class in the US, the teacher is going round the class assisting the learners who are working on constructing simple websites:
T: warmer .. warmer .. it is warmer – that means more warm ... so maybe what you need to dooooo let's see is – it's double u a, double u a .. r m.... ... ... there you go and then you say replace...... ... ... done ...

(3) (van Lier, author's data):

A CLIL[1] class (geography) in a secondary school in the Netherlands:
T: Is there anyone who knows subduction?
S: If one plate moves under another.
T: Yes.

(4) (van Lier, author's data):

The same CLIL class:
S: Why are some lava thick and fast and other...
T: ... I don't know ... probably ... (continues in Dutch)
S: How can you measure when a volcano will erupt?
T: ...Well, it's mostly unpredictable ...

---

(5) (van Lier 2003):

Two learners working together in the same project-based ESL class as extract (2), later on in the semester:
L2 (XXX) link?
L1. You want?
L2 Yes
L1 Oh so you just link ... so now I teach you how to link
L2 Link ..
L1 Ya link ... link list is an addres in you::r ... in your disk
L2 uhuh
L1 So. First we mark.... ...
L2 yah.
L1 uhuh ... and click ... ahh... right .. yah
L2   uhuh
L1 (XXX) right and copy ... ... copy? and then ... ... we go to ... you:r web ... file ... graphic
L2   hmm   uhuh
L1 and then ... we link .. ya link
L2   link
L1 click right ... and [pest ... pest (=paste)] ... and okay ... okay
L2. okay
L1 you got it!
L2 Thank you

---

(6) (QTEL, WestEd 2005[2])

L is reading from a poster tacked on the blackboard containing the first part of a letter about language she is in the process of writing:
L: I fou-uhhh ... I found from my research that animal communication is not a language. Animal communication is different from the human communication because in case of dolphins they communicate through ultrasonic pulses that cannot be heard by the human ear. I don't think that there are languages better than other. This is about

it, because I do not have enough time. But I appreciate that you teach me these things and I consider you the best teacher that I ever had in my life.

T: Amen, very nice job

(All): (Clap, laugh)

J (to L): Animal communication is not a language ... it IS a language, that's what I think. Because they are communicating with each other.

L: But they do not speak

(Lots of talking)

J: (You can have) everything in a language; you can have words, sounds and everything ...

L: But they don't have words. They don't say 'Mama.'

J: it is a characteristic and in animal language some of the characteristics that YOU [pointing to T] said ... it IS a language.

T: Juan is arguing very strongly that animal communication is a form of – is language, Lara is saying its not. What do you think is ... would be a way to help them resolve that argument in their writing?

L: I mean they have sound, both of them. Because we have sound and they have sound.

(All): (Lots of talking! Discussing)

T: do we need sound? Do we need sound...?

Girl: I heard people say that animals they understanding everything ... but they don't speak themselves ...

Boy: If you wanna say 'excuse me'... 'ahun-uhn' [clearing throat demonstratively]

L: They don't say 'excuse me'

Boy: Same thing

A: But I think we don't need a sound because people who can't talk they use signs ...

T: All right, all right. Now hold on, hold on. Amelia has a comment.

A: (xxx) cause they don't talk, but they they – they communicate by doing signs [gesturing the making of a sign] so they don't need to speak to communicate to others. So I think ...

J: It IS a language [Emphatically pointing a finger at L]

T: A lot is going to depend on how you define language. O.K.? You can define it in such a way as to exclude what animals do; you can define it in a very broad way, as a system of communication that includes everything.

As mentioned, I placed these extracts in a suggested ascending order of agency, so that (1) displays the least and (6) displays the greatest degree of agency. However, I am only doing so to initiate a discussion about what agency in the classroom is really about and to invite the reader to think about the various ingredients that may indicate more or less agency. It may well be, for instance, that some readers disagree with the ordering and consider the relative placement of one or more extracts rather arbitrary or even wrong. By analyzing the diverse reasons why one might disagree about the relative level(s) of agency displayed by learners, we may hope to gain a clearer idea of what the construct means and what its value in practical classroom terms might be. We are thus engaged in an exploratory exercise, aimed at an improved understanding of practice.

I will first give a straightforward (but not necessarily complete or accurate) gloss for each of the extracts, with an indication of sorts as to why they are placed in this order. The reader may provisionally go along at this point, or note doubts or disagreements. After the six glosses, we will attempt to work toward a deeper understanding.

Extract (1) takes place in an EFL class in Thailand. On the surface it clearly fails to engage the agency of the students. The teacher attempts to get a discussion going about moving to a foreign country but, in spite of repeated IRF-style questions, only manages to extract one contribution from a student, a single-word 'Yes.'

Extract (2) takes place in a project-based multimedia classroom where ESL learners are learning to produce simple websites. Here the teacher is giving simple instructions that are carried out by the learner. One might say that agency is more in evidence here than in (1), since the learner is carrying out actions by moving her mouse and cursor on the screen, clicking and replacing one thing with another thing (mediated by the teacher's instructions), whereas in (1) the learners were simply not responding overtly at all, with one small exception.

Extract (3) (from a secondary school CLIL class in the Netherlands) is a straightforward example of an IRF exchange, where the learner gives a response to a teacher's question and this response is positively evaluated. This can be seen as another step up in agency, since the learner now has to formulate and articulate a thought. It is reasonable to argue that other learners may also be formulating and articulating thoughts, even if they do not express them verbally and that these inner-speech articulations are equally valid linguistic responses (Lantolf 2007). However, in this instance the learner has to employ some additional level of initiative, since the teacher does not nominate him specifically, but rather makes a general solicit (van Lier 1988) to which this learner *chooses* to respond publicly.

Extract (4) takes another step up the agentive ladder, in that here a learner asks a self-initiated question, followed by a teacher explanation (part of which is omitted here), followed by another question from the same learner. The learner employs a significant amount of self-initiated agency in asking these open-ended content-oriented questions.

Extract (5) L1's higher sense of agency consists of the fact that she volunteers to teach her neighbor how to make links on a web page and she proceeds to lead her fellow student step by step through the process. This is an instructional initiative that requires a strong sense of autonomy. However, we can also look at the event as one that exhibits a strong level of joint (collaborative) agency, since not only does L1 offer to teach, but also L2 requests to be instructed. In this sense the event manifests a quality that transcends the individual learner and that characterizes the joint activity of collaborative teaching/learning. Thus, we can see agency as not only an expression of individual volition, but also as a feature that can characterize a collaborative, co-constructed enterprise.

Finally, *Extract* (6) shows high levels of agency in a number of learners during a spirited discussion about the nature of language. Here learners are directly debating with one another, without having been prompted by the teacher and they are contributing to the debate because they feel they have something to say and they have a strong opinion about it. As in extract (5), we can attribute agency to individual learners as well as to the entire speech event. Indeed, we might want to postulate two types of agency: *individual* and *collaborative*, where the second could be argued to be of a higher level in terms of classroom quality, since it would draw together the creative energies and symbolic capacities of a larger number of learners. Especially in extract (6), one can argue that the entire class is energized by the spirited discussion about animal communication and language (see Lantolf 2007 about the enhanced symbolic resources that become available in dialogical activity).

Summing up, the six extracts can be categorized in terms of agency in the following manner:

(1) Learners are unresponsive or minimally responsive

(2) Learners carry out instructions given by the teacher

(3) Learners volunteer answers to teachers' questions

(4) Learners voluntarily ask questions

(5) Learners volunteer to assist or instruct other learners and create a collaborative agency event

(6) Learners voluntarily enter into a debate with one another and create a collaborative agency event.

I suggest that it is indeed the case that, on the surface at least (in terms of overt, observable behavior), we have here an ascending scale or continuum of agency. Notice that I put the notion of 'volition' in (3)–(6), but not in (1) and (2). One might argue, of course that in (1) learners are purposely unresponsive, or that they are physically unresponsive, but mentally active and so on and that in (2) the learner merely 'goes through the motions' but does not in effect have a clue what she is doing or why.

There are many other observations one can make about any and all of the extracts. Nevertheless, I submit that the order given has a certain degree of intuitive (if not incontrovertible) plausibility.

There are other things a casual observer might note, subjectively, upon observing these six events; the observer might say something like (for Extract 1), 'The learners were passive.' Let's list a representative adjective for each one, realizing that behind each adjective there may lie a host of assumptions based on perceived learner behaviors and presumed learner attributes (whether they be of the *state* or *trait* variety):

(1) passive

(2) obedient

(3) participatory

(4) inquisitive

(5) autonomous

(6) committed

This brief look at classroom interaction from the perspective of agency has raised a number of questions about the attributes of agency as well as some of the ways in which it can be observably manifested in the classroom by individual learners and groups of learners (as in extracts (5) and (6)). We will now relate this initial analysis to various learner characteristics and properties of the learning environment that have been discussed in the applied linguistics and general educational literature.

Problematizing agency: active, passive and other dichotomies

> Victor Borge, the late Danish pianist and comedian, said that he
> had learned to speak Japanese by putting a tape recorder under
> his pillow and playing tapes while he slept. As a result he noted
> that he was quite fluent in Japanese, but unfortunately he could
> only speak it when he was fast asleep.

On the basis of the classroom extracts looked at above, we can say that agency is situated in a particular context and that it is something that learners *do*, rather than something that learners *possess*, i.e., it is behavior rather than property. This is in line with sociocultural perspectives such as those of Lantolf and Thorne (2006) and Wertsch *et al.* (1993), as noted above. Ahearn's (2001: 111) definition of agency as 'the socioculturally mediated ability to act' also goes in this direction, if *ability* is not equated with *competence* (as an individual possession), but rather is seen as *action potential*, mediated by social, interactional, cultural, institutional and other contextual factors.

Agency can be related to issues such as volition, intentionality, initiative, intrinsic motivation and autonomy, all of which have been extensively studied in educational research (a good overview, using autonomy as the umbrella term, is Benson 2001). It is my view that these terms in practice refer to very similar phenomena and if we use agency as an umbrella term, they may all fall under that umbrella, indeed they may be regarded as synonyms – differing shades of meaning, connotation and pedigree notwithstanding. If agency is the family name, then all the other terms mentioned are family members, sharing strong resemblances (following Wittgenstein 1958).

There is always a strong tendency to look at complex constructs in terms of dichotomies, or binary oppositions. The most obvious one that comes to mind in this case is *active-passive*. Learners can be active or passive, the former being conducive and the latter being detrimental to learning. The problem that this binary view raises is that there may be many ways and degrees of being active or passive. In addition, we cannot rule out the possibility that some forms of being active may not appear to be all that propitious in terms of learning (see e.g., Allwright's 'Igor,' who participated eagerly and frequently, yet did not seem to make progress at all; Allwright 1980). Conversely, some forms of what we might perceive as passivity may not be quite as devoid of learning potential as casual observers might assume. Verbosity and overt participation have been unquestioningly associated with positive learning potential and the quiet student has often been ignored and regarded as a weaker student, even though no evidence exists to support such a view (see Ohta 2001).

There are other dichotomies in our field and they may be too numerous to mention. However, a few of them must be looked at in order to put the construct of agency on a more solid footing. Table 6.1 summarizes some of the major dichotomies and we will briefly examine how they influence the language learning field.

The comparative table allows us to get a clearer idea about what we may mean by agency in the classroom. It allows us to relate the definitions that we started out with to terms that are already familiar from classroom research and applied linguistics. I suggest that on the basis of this analysis we can propose three core features of agency which are broadly compatible with the definitions of Ahearn (2001); Duranti (2004); Lantolf and Thorne (2006) and Wertsch *et al.* (1993):

1) Agency involves initiative or self-regulation by the learner (or group)

2) Agency is interdependent, that is, it mediates and is mediated by the sociocultural context

3) Agency includes an awareness of the responsibility for one's own actions *vis-à-vis* the environment, including affected others.

With this ground clearing in mind, we will now look at some central classroom issues that relate to agency. These issues, while not being in any way exhaustive, will bring us closer to establishing an empirical construct that can facilitate research and inform curriculum design and pedagogy. They include initiative, perception, identity and contingency. This will then be followed by recommendations for an agency-based (or action-based) approach to language education.

Initiative in interaction

Earl Stevick (1980: 19) defines initiative as 'choices about who says what, to whom and when.' Learners' initiative does not necessarily conflict with a teacher's control in terms of structuring the work and managing the classroom. Rather, a teacher's control in this sense in fact enhances the possibilities for initiative to emerge.

For practical purposes I will use initiative as essentially synonymous with autonomy, self-regulation and self-determination (Deci and Ryan 1985; Williams and Burden 1997). I will, however, place it in an

Table 6.1. Some dichotomies and their relation to agency

Dichotomy	Description	Relation to agency
Deliberate – incidental learning	Incidental learning occurs when something (say, language) is learned while being engaged in activity that is not learning-focused. Deliberate learning (or 'studying') involves an explicit learning goal.	This may not be relevant to agency, since both deliberate and incidental learning occurs in activities that may be initiated by a learner or conducted at the behest of others.
Declarative – procedural knowledge/ memory	Declarative refers to explicit, and procedural to 'how to' knowledge/ memory. The originator of the distinction, John Andersen (1983) originally claimed all knowledge starts out being declarative and gradually becomes procedural (automatized). This has since been qualified (1990 and later) and the unidirectionality has been questioned.	As with the above dichotomy, no clear judgments on agency can be made on the basis of this distinction. Both declaratively and procedurally based actions can exhibit various degrees of agency.
Autonomy – dependence	Autonomy can be defined as 'the capacity to take control over one's own learning' (Benson 2001: 2). Kohonen (1992: 19) emphasizes that it includes interdependence, i.e. the exercise of responsibility within the social context. Dependence means that one's actions are under the control of others.	This dichotomy relates closely to agency, since it depends on actions carried out of one's own accord within a socioculturally relevant context. Interdependence also suggests the notion of engagement.
Intrinsic–extrinsic motivation	Intrinsic motivation is in evidence when the agency manifested derives from an interest in and for the activity itself. In the case of extrinsic motivation, the interest comes from	This distinction is in many ways related to agency, but it will be very difficult to pinpoint or measure. Most complex activities, including those related to learning, evidence a complex mix of

Dichotomy	Description	Relation to agency
	external sources, such as reward or punishment (Deci and Ryan 1985).	intrinsic and extrinsic motivational factors (van Lier 1996).
Self-regulated – other-regulated	These terms derive from Vygotsky's developmental theory. Vygotsky showed that in developmental settings there are intricate relations between self-and other-regulated activity.	Self-regulated activity expresses agency. However, other-regulation plays a crucial role in achieving higher functional levels through interaction in the ZPD.
Self-initiated – controlled	These terms are very similar to the ones directly above. I used them in van Lier (1988), following Stevick (1980).	Activity that shows initiative is a clear indicator of agency. As in the ZPD above, controlling (or structuring) activity may be aimed at fostering agency – or not, of course. Indeed, one might argue that fostering agency is a defining feature of the ZPD.

interactional and dialogical context, that is, a context of interaction among learners in the classroom. The question asked here is therefore, how is initiative demonstrated and enacted in classroom interaction?

The idea of initiative can be related to long-established questions in language teaching, such as responsive teaching (Bowers and Flinders 1990), autonomy-supporting versus controlling teaching behavior (Deci 1995), active participation and so on. We may also relate it to the crucial defining feature of handover/takeover in scaffolding (van Lier 2004), which ties scaffolding to the learner departing from a set script or ritual and introducing something new. What we are talking about is thus a learner who makes some effort, however small and seemingly insignificant, to be original, say something new and different, set off in an unpredicted direction. Within sociocultural theory and Bruner's original notion of scaffolding, this departure, let's call it initiative-taking, is a pedagogical moment, a teaching opportunity and a learning promise.

How do we empirically capture this notion of initiative and tie it to agency? An obvious way to do so is by studying learner contributions in their context, i.e. in classroom interaction. How can we tell – unambiguously – from a transcript whether one contribution exhibits more initiative than another one?

To exemplify a measure that tries to get at *both* amount and *type* of initiative, I want briefly to revisit a coding and quantifying scheme I developed in my classroom interaction study (van Lier 1988). In this study, I allocated initiative in four areas:

1) Topic work

2) Selection to speak

3) Allocation of speaker(s) or activity

4) Sequencing the talk or activity.

Each of these categories was further subdivided into turn types, so that instances of initiative could be noted and tabulated. Thus, a variety of calculations can be carried out to show levels of participation and initiative for individual learners, groups, or types of activities or discussions (see also Kinginger 1994).

This level of analysis addresses aspects of the voluntary initiation of verbal behavior in social-interactive contexts. The advantage of this procedure is that evidence of initiative (as one constituent aspect of agency) is located in the interaction itself (following conversational–analytical conventions), so that prior theoretical biases or agendas do not read into the data subjective notions that may or may not in fact be valid. However, there is more to agency than overt interactive behavior.

As mentioned in the introduction, Lantolf and Thorne (2006: 143) claim that agency also includes 'the ability to assign relevance and significance to things and events.' Similarly, in their model of 'multi-factor' interaction, Novick and Sutton (1997) include (in addition to choice of task and choice of speaker, which are similar to the focus of my scheme described above), also choice of *outcome*, i.e., a purposeful pursuit of a particular goal. In addition, Duranti's model (1993) includes consideration of the possible effect of activity on others and oneself, as well as the realization that one's actions are one's own responsibility and thus will be subject to evaluation (including approval as well as possible censure, criticism and so forth).

It is clear that this second level of analysis of agency that takes it beyond the interactional analysis of initiative will require a different research methodology, since evidence of such things as desired outcome, knowledge of potential impact and the critical dimensions of one's actions may not be unambiguously locatable in the interaction (following ethnomethodological principles of context-free analysis), but may depend on features of the socio-cultural-historical context that are not immediately visible in the interaction but nevertheless influence, steer, or even determine it in subtle ways (Ratner 2006).

The difficulty for the researcher is to get at these influences, assignations of significance and awareness of consequences, without bringing to the data our own presuppositions and arguments, without clear evidence that they are actually there. We must always be cognizant of the fact that conversation analysis was developed precisely to avoid reading into data more than is actually given in the data. Harvey Sacks used to say, 'If it's a phenomenon, it must be in the interaction.' This is a prudent bit of advice and we are well-advised to take care not to read into the interactional data more than is strictly warranted by those data. Likewise, Aristotle already admonished the researcher to 'let the data lead the way.' But therein lies the rub: How can we address the other important factors mentioned without making unwarranted assumptions from the interactional data?

To address this problem I propose to add to the analysis of interaction a second level of analysis, namely analysis of narrative, introspective and dialogical data. Ethnographic and sociolinguistic interviewing can add an important level of depth to interactional analysis (Silverman 2001; Potter and Wetherell 1987).

In sum, then, the notion of initiative can be analyzed through interactional data, but in order to get at issues of content, purpose and higher levels of awareness (of possibilities, dangers and consequences) further methodological tools are needed in order to triangulate the complexities of the multiplex notion of agency. Some of these will be addressed below.

Perception and action

In an ecological perspective, perception goes hand in hand with action (Gibson 1979; van Lier 2004). Indeed, perceiving is a form of action. Information is not passively received by the learner (as is input in some versions of SLA), rather affordances are actively picked up by a learner in the pursuit of some meaningful activity. An important facet of agency is the active process of perceptual learning, which is multisensory and takes place in the context of real work in the real world. That means that perceptual learning is not a matter of increasingly sophisticated mental processing of basically fragmentary sense data (as it is usually regarded in brain-based cognitive models), but instead it is a matter of increasingly sophisticated ways of perceiving real features in the environment.

Language learning, in this view, is the process of finding one's way in the linguistic world, which is part of the semiotic world (i.e., the world of sign making and using) and taking an increasingly active role in developing one's own constitutive role in it (cf. Lantolf's (2007) notion of Enhanced Symbolic Capacity). How this aspect of agency is to be researched is a relatively unexamined issue in learning contexts. There will be physical indicators such as body orientation, gaze and pointing (Goodwin 2000; Norris 2004) and there will also be indicators to perceptual awareness and reactions in the verbal interactions during pedagogical work. Part of what we perceive will be influenced by first-language and first-culture experiences. However, following Gibson (1979) we also perceive directly (that is, perception is immediate as well as mediated, see van Lier 2004). Moreover, it may well be that perceptual agency involves learning to perceive from a third-space perspective (Bhabha 1994).

Perceptual learning does not occur while being strapped in a chair in a psychological laboratory, or while being bombarded with input stimuli. It occurs during meaningful and relevant activity in pursuit of a worthwhile goal in an ecologically valid environment (van Lier 2004). Thus, project-based learning is a natural vehicle for the promotion of such learning (Beckett and Miller 2006).

Voice and identity

In accordance with the ecological theory of perception, to perceive something is always also to co-perceive oneself (Gibson 1979). Thus, while learning to perceive, the learner not only learns about the linguistic environment (of the target language, in the case of language learning), but at the same time also learns about himself or herself, that is, every perception of the target language is simultaneously an act of self-perception. Learning an L2 and becoming engaged in a new culture thus involves adjusting one's sense of self and creating new identities to connect the known to the new. Depending on the prior languaculture (Agar 1994), learners may have very different (initial) perceptions of the new languaculture. Shaping new identities requires ongoing struggles and reconciliations and these can reflect resistance as well accommodation.

The learner perceives the language (a linguistic expression in context) as it relates to him or her and at the same time re-examines his or her sense of identity in the light of the meanings perceived. Whatever is perceived of the target language thus casts an echo back to the self and may contain a transformative message for the emergence of a linguistically expanding self, perhaps toward a third space in Bhabha's sense (1994) as noted above.

Voice (in Bakhtin's (1981) sense of the word) refers to infusing one's words with one's own feelings, thoughts and identity, that is, investing oneself in one's words. This can only be done if a close connection exists between the words and the self and its emerging L2 identity(ies). There should thus not be a separation between the person and the word and the notion of person here includes action, emotion, mind, body and purpose. The learner thus would comment, 'I said this because I WANTED to say this' (rather than because someone asked him or her to (re)produce, repeat, display or manufacture a linguistic piece for the sake of demonstrating proficiency). The claim here is that the notion of agency requires that the learner invest physical, mental and emotional energy in the language produced. The more important claim behind this is, of course, that this agency enhances second language development in demonstrable and durable ways. In many ways, L2 development is the development of agency through the L2 (or the enactment of an L2 identity).

Intersubjectivity, engagement and contingency

Language is a tool to relate to the world and to others. Human social life begins with intersubjectivity between baby and caregiver (Trevarthen 1998). As I have argued elsewhere (van Lier 2004), there are at least three phases of intersubjectivity: first, face-to-face engagement, during the first 9 months or so of life, next, the phase of joint attention – or triadic interaction, to use Reed's term (1996) – when the child realizes that she and her interlocutor are both focusing on the same object (see also Tomasello 1999) and third, symbolic intersubjectivity, when grammaticalized language permits the sharing of ideas, plans, goals and beliefs. In first-language development these three phases of intersubjectivity unfold over the space of four years or so, but in subsequent language learning they present themselves all at once, thus making the learning of a new language a very different and highly complex task. Engagement is clearly a central part of agency. Its opposite would be disengagement, or at a pathological level, anomie. However, somewhat paradoxically, some forms of withdrawal or aloofness, such as indications of a lack of willingness to communicate with others in some L2 contexts could be seen as an expression of agency.

I have written before about the notion of contingency (e.g., van Lier 1996) and a number of others in the field have picked up on it and explored it empirically (Kobayashi 2004; Young and He 1998). I have described it as having a Janus-faced *character*: a contingent utterance is linked in terms of content and sequential organization to (a) previous utterance(s) and at the same time it predicts, presages, or foreshadows other utterances to come. In addition, of course, every utterance is in some way anchored in the world. Thus, contingency is at least three-dimensional: *backward*, *forward* and *outward*. In light of what we said earlier about self-perception, I am inclined now to add *inward* as a fourth dimension.

This is also part of agency: the constant, conscious and overt work of situating one's linguistic acts in time, space and the socio-cognitive sphere. In some ways this relates to the interactional and sequential aspects of the initiative scheme I outlined above (van Lier 1988), but it also goes beyond that: we constantly have to work to place our words and actions within a recognizable chronotope (Bakhtin 1981) or time-space configuration. Of course, conversely, agency may also be expressed forcefully by a deliberate refusal to do so, so that simple descriptors of agency are by no means easy to find in this respect. This raises complex questions about 'degree' or 'quality' of agency. As I have suggested before (e.g., in the case of Allwright's (1980) 'Igor'), the most 'active' learner is not by any means always the most agentive (or successful) one. Not all enactments of agency are automatically conducive of learning, since the orientation of particular agentive behaviors must be aligned with the learning goals. Nor should we make the mistake of viewing agency through a window of conformity with established classroom practices and rejecting forms of resistance (however subtle) as expressing lack of agency.

Cognition and emotion: whole-body learning

Vygotsky (1987) already made an explicit link between cognition and emotion and this connection has been confirmed in recent years by neurological and brain research (e.g., Damasio 1999), psycholinguistic research (Rommetveit 1998) and research on language and mind. Goodman (1978: 8) puts the issue succinctly as follows: 'Feeling without understanding is blind and understanding without feeling is empty.'

Learning of any kind is not primarily a matter of making changes to the workings of the brain (through information processing), rather, it is a whole-person, body and mind, socially situated process. This holistic picture of learning is confirmed by neurological research as well as research into language development (Tomasello 1999; Tomasello and Slobin 2005). Descartes' 'I think therefore I am' might be appropriately replaced by 'I act therefore I am,' bearing in mind that thoughts and words are forms of action too (in a similar vein, Vygotsky (1987: 294) cites Goethe's *Faust* as declaring that 'In the beginning was the deed'). Language learning is physical as well as cognitive, individual and social, multisensory and situated in activity. Mental structures go hand in hand with participation structures (Sfard 1998). Indeed, there is increasing evidence that language is not stored separately in the brain, but as part of 'polymodal' experiential representations that include motor patterns as well as auditory and visual information (Kuhl, 1998). In this context, recent research on gesture in L2 learning is highly relevant. For example, Haught and McCafferty (Chapter 5, this volume) argue that gesture, body language and intonation are all a part of the learning process in a drama-based approach to ESL instruction (see, e.g., research in 'haptics' in education, Minogue and Jones 2006).

Whole-body learning was a central part of John Dewey's reform movement and in recent years educators have once again begun to pay attention to multisensory aspects of education. In language learning, action-based approaches such as project-based learning are currently receiving a great deal of attention (Lantolf 2007). These approaches highlight the role of whole-person involvement in learning (Lakoff and Johnson 1999; Beckett and Miller 2006). In the next section of this chapter I will address some curricular and practical classroom aspect of action-based learning.

The action-based curriculum

An approach to language teaching and learning that puts agency at the center, in all the ways that have been described above – i.e., action-based teaching and learning – will require paying attention to specific ways, kinds and levels of acting and interacting in the classroom. In many classrooms the focus is on language, either as *input*, the language that is presented for learning, or *production* (output), the language that learners produce in answers to teacher questions, in drills and exercises and sometimes in tasks.

In approaches that incorporate learner–learner interaction in tasks (for an overview, see Gass 1997), the focus is usually on negotiation sequences, episodes of focus on form (preemptive or reactive, see Ellis, Basturkmen and Loewen 2002; language-related episodes [LRE], Swain and Lapkin 1998), or uptake of particular forms that appear in the input (Slimani 1989). The actual phenomenon of agency in its various shapes or forms is not usually part of the analysis (though see Swain 2007). Indeed, it is not clear at this point in time (beyond the preliminary efforts in van Lier 1988 and Kinginger 1994) how agency would be or might be identified and how its diverse manifestations could be linked to success in language learning (however 'success' is defined by teachers, institutions and learners themselves).

An early study that focused on agency in some form was Seliger's (1977) study of High Input Generators (HIGS, which he contrasted with LIGS, or Low Input Generators). This research has often been linked in later years to extroversion, however, no reliable results exist that show an unequivocal advantage for gregarious learners. Indeed, some classroom studies, such as Allwright (1980) show that the most vocal learners in a classroom (e.g., his example of 'Igor') are by no means always the most proficient or successful ones (see also Varvel 1979, which showed that a reticent learner turned out to be the most proficient student of the class).

More recently the concepts of motivation and autonomy have been proposed as containing powerful ingredients for success. In terms of motivation, especially intrinsic motivation (which is activity-centered, see Deci 1995; van Lier 1996) and Willingness To Communicate (WTC, see Williams and Burden 1997), have been hypothesized as favoring language learning. In terms of autonomy (which, as I have argued, can be seen as virtually synonymous with motivation, van Lier 1996), a number of different models and conceptualizations have been proposed. In a comprehensive overview of autonomy in language learning, Benson (2001: 189) concludes that 'there is a pressing need for empirical research on the relationship between the development of autonomy and the acquisition of language proficiency.' So far, as Benson notes, advocacy of autonomy has largely been based on theoretical arguments or small-scale action research or case study projects.

Two examples of such research are Coughlan and Duff (1994) and Spence-Brown (2001). Coughlan and Duff studied learners' interactions as they engaged in picture-description tasks. They found that the same tasks can produce widely differing activities depending on learners' goals, interpretations and contextual variables. Spence-Brown

examined project-based learning and assessment and found that learners' framing of the task and their goals and motivations affected the task
outcomes significantly. In particular, those learners who focused on the
assessment goal of the task achieved higher scores on the test than
those who focused on the learning potential and intrinsic value of the
task. This finding illustrates the conflict that may arise between exter-
nally driven accountability purposes and autonomy in learning.

In general, there are few if any conclusive and incontrovertible findings from empirical research that establish the relative superiority of
action-based (or autonomous) language learning. In this respect the
topic under discussion is no different than any other topic in SLA or
applied linguistics: motivation, metalinguistic knowledge, strategy training, error feedback and so on. As mentioned above, a triangulated
approach combining interactional and various other sources of data
(interview, diary, stimulated recall, etc.) might be the best way to move
ahead in this research area.

As we saw above, Stevick (1980) notes that choice is a key determi-
nant of initiative. In addition, Duranti (2004) claims that agency
incorporates consideration of the effect of one's actions on others and
on oneself, as well as the knowledge that one's actions are open to
evaluation. Learners may weigh the alternatives (such as 'good grades'
versus 'rich learning') in different ways and obtain different results.
Lantolf and Thorne (2006) add that agency involves the assignment of
relevance and significance. From an active learner's perspective, agency
may be primarily the notion of speaking because 'of having something
to say,' 'because it is important to say such and such,' 'because of wishing to have one's opinion heard,' and so on. These kinds of remarks,
many of which can be located in the interaction, or will appear in journals or interviews, fairly unambiguously address aspects of agency such
as those mentioned. But what are the classroom circumstances that allow or encourage such expressions of agency? Or indeed, what are the
classroom circumstances that engender dissent or refusal to speak?

An action-based curriculum that promotes agency in the various ways
proposed, may be project-based, task-based, content-based, or any of a
number of 'hyphen-based' approaches. However, whether or not true
agency is actually promoted depends on the factors mentioned earlier:
choice, giving learners the right to speak and the responsibility for their
actions, stimulating debate and so on. These factors are by no means a
guaranteed or automatic consequence of doing project-based, content-
based (etc.) language teaching. The extracts provided at the beginning
of this chapter should make this clear.

Conclusion

The notion of agency in language learning has emerged as a central construct in sociocultural and other situated approaches to second and foreign language development. In this chapter I have linked it to related research into motivation, autonomy, identity, initiative and participation. From a curriculum design perspective, agency appears to favor a variety of 'hyphenated' approaches that incorporate agency as a central feature, e.g. project-based, task-based, content-based and theme-based learning, as well as the currently popular implementations of CLIL.

In this chapter I have tried to problematize the notion of 'agency,' and raise a number of questions about what the name may imply and what it might promise. I have also connected it to a number of issues in language learning and teaching research that appear to address *related* ideas: intrinsic motivation, autonomy, identity, engagement and initiative, among others. I have pointed out some of the possibilities and pitfalls of researching agency and briefly commented on six different extracts of classroom talk, illustrating different kinds and levels of agency. The challenge is to devise research studies that carefully and adequately address the multifaceted notion of agency and then find a way to link it to increased success, efficiency and proficiency.

Notes

1. CLIL refers to *Content and Language Integrated Learning*, a recent movement in Europe to teach school subjects, foreign language and intercultural understanding in content-based secondary and elementary classes where a foreign language is the medium of instruction.
2. I am grateful to the QTEL Program (Quality Teaching for English Learners) of WestEd (http://www.wested.org/cs/tqip/print/docs/qt/home.htm) for permission to use this extract, which is based on a class in linguistics taught at the International High School in New York, by Mr Anthony DeFazio (for some background, see DeFazio 1997).

References

Agar, M. (1994) *Language Shock: Understanding the Culture of Conversation*. New York: William Morrow.

Ahearn, L. M. (2001) Language and agency. *Annual Review of Anthropology* 30: 109–37.

Allwright, D. (1980) Turns, topics and tasks: Patterns of participation in language learning and teaching. In D. Larsen-Freeman (ed.) *Discourse Analysis in Second Language Acquisition Research* 165–87. Rowley, MA: Newbury House.

Anderson, J. R. (1983) *The Architecture of Cognition.* Cambridge, MA: Harvard University Press.

Anderson, J. R. (1990) *The Adaptive Character of Thought.* Hillsdale, NJ: Erlbaum.

Bakhtin, M. (1981) *The Dialogical Imagination.* Austin, TX: University of Texas Press.

Beckett, G. H. and Miller, P. C. (eds) (2006) *Project-Based Second and Foreign Language Education: Past, Present and Future.* Greenwich, CT: Information Age Publishing.

Benson, P. (2001) *Autonomy in Language Learning.* Harlow: Longman.

Bhabha, H. (1994) *The Location of Culture.* London: Routledge.

Bowers, C. A. and Flinders, D. J. (1990) *Responsive Teaching: An Ecological Approach to Classroom Patterns of Language, Culture and Thought.* New York: Teachers College Press.

Coughlan, P. and Duff, P. (1994) Same task, different activities: Analysis of a second language acquisition task from an activity theory perspective. In J. Lantolf and G. Appel (eds) *Vygotskyan Approaches to Second Language Research* 173–94. Norwood, NJ: Ablex.

Damasio, A. (1999) *The Feeling of What Happens: Body and Emotion in the Making of Consciousness.* New York: Harcourt Brace.

Deci, E., with Flaste, R. (1995) *Why We Do What We Do: The Dynamics of Personal Autonomy.* New York: Putnam's Sons.

Deci, E. L. and Ryan, R. M. (1985) *Intrinsic Motivation and Self-determination in Human Behavior.* New York: Plenum Press.

DeFazio, A. J. (1997) Language awareness at the International High School. In L. van Lier and D. Corson (eds) *Knowledge about Language. Volume 6 of the Encyclopedia of Language and Education* 99–107. Dordrecht: Kluwer Academic.

Duranti, A. (2004) Agency in language. In A. Duranti (ed.) *A Companion to Linguistic Anthropology* 451–73. Malden, MA: Blackwell.

Ellis, R., Basturkmen, H. and Loewen, S. (2001) Pre-emptive focus on form in the ESL classroom. *TESOL Quarterly* 35: 407–32.

Forman, R. (2005) *Teaching EFL in Thailand: a bilingual study.* Unpublished PhD thesis. University of Technology, Sydney, Australia.

Gass, S. (1997) *Input, Interaction and the Second Language Learner.* Mahwah, NJ: Lawrence Erlbaum.

Gibson, J. J. (1979) *The Ecological Approach to Visual Perception.* Hillsdale, NJ: Erlbaum.

Goodman, N. (1978) *Ways of Worldmaking.* Indianapolis, IN: Hackett Publishing Company, Inc.

Goodwin, C. (2000) Action and embodiment within situated human interaction. *Journal of Pragmatics* 32: 1489–522.

Kinginger, C. (1994) Learner initiative in conversation management: An application of van Lier's pilot coding scheme. *The Modern Language Journal* 78: 29–40.

Kobayashi, M. (2004) A Sociocultural Study of Second Language Tasks: Activity, Agency and Language Socialization. Unpublished doctoral dissertation, University of British Columbia, Vancouver.

Kohonen, V. (1992) Experiential language learning: second language learning as cooperative learner education. In D. Nunan (ed.) *Collaborative Language Learning and Teaching* 14–39. Cambridge: Cambridge University Press.

Kuhl, P. (1998) Language, culture and intersubjectivity: The creation of shared perception. In S. Bråten (ed.) *Intersubjective Communication and Emotion in Early Ontogeny* (pp. 297–315). Cambridge: Cambridge University Press.

Lakoff, G. and Johnson, M. (1999) *Philosophy in the Flesh*. New York: Basic Books.

Lantolf, J. P. (2007) *Dialectics and L2 proficiency. Paper presented at the Symposium on Sociocognitive Approaches to Second Language Learning and Teaching.* University of Auckland. 11 April.

Lantolf, J. P. and Thorne, S. L. (2006) *Sociocultural Theory and the Genesis of Second Language Development*. Oxford: Oxford University Press.

Minogue, J. and Jones, M. G. (2006) Haptics in education: Exploring an untapped sensory modality. *Review of Educational Research* 76: 317–48.

Norris, S. (2004) *Analyzing Multimodal Interaction: A Methodological Framework*. New York: Routledge.

Novick, D. and Sutton, S. (1997) *What is mixed-initiative interaction?* Papers from the 1997 AAAI Spring Symposium on Computational Models for Mixed Initiative Interaction, Stanford University, 24-26 March, Technical Report SS-97-04, AAAI Press. http://www.cs.utep.edu/novick/papers/mi.aaai.html

Ohta, A. S. (2001) *Second Language Acquisition Processes in the Classroom: Learning Japanese*. Mahwah, NJ: Erlbaum.

Potter, J. and Wetherell, M. (1987) *Discourse and Social Psychology: Beyond Attitudes and Behaviour*. London: Sage Publications.

Ratner, C. (2006) *Cultural Psychology: Theory and Method*. Mahwah, NJ: Erlbaum.

Reed, E. S. (1996) *Encountering the World: Toward an Ecological Psychology*. New York: Oxford University Press.

Rommetveit, R. (1998) Intersubjective attunement and linguistically mediated meaning in discourse. In S. Bråten (ed.) *Intersubjective Communication and Emotion in Early Ontogeny* 354–71. Cambridge: Cambridge University Press.

David Silverman (2001) *Interpreting Qualitative Data: Methods for Analysing Talk, Text and Interaction* (Second edition). London: Sage.

Seliger, H. W. (1977) Does practice make perfect? A study of interaction patterns and L2 competence. *Language Learning* 27: 263–78.

Sfard, A. (1998) On two metaphors for learning and the dangers of choosing just one. *Educational Researcher* 27: 4–13.

Slimani, Assia (1989) The role of topicalization in classroom language learning. *System* 17: 223–34.

Spence-Brown, R. (2001) The eyes of the beholder: Authenticity in an embedded assessment task. *Language Testing* 18: 463–81.

Stevick, E. (1980). *Teaching Languages: A Way and Ways.* Rowley, MA: Newbury House.

Swain, M. (2007) Languaging, agency and collaboration in advanced second language learning. In H. Byrnes (ed.) *Advanced Language Learning: The Contributions of Halliday and Vygotsky* 95–108. London, UK: Continuum.

Swain, M. and Lapkin, S. (1998) Interaction and second language learning: Two adolescent French immersion students working together. *The Modern Language Journal* 82: 320–37.

Tomasello, M. (1999) *The Cultural Conditions of Human Cognition.* Cambridge, MA: Harvard University Press.

Tomasello, M. and Slobin, D. I. (eds) (2005) *Beyond Nature-Nurture: Essays in Honor of Elizabeth Bates.* Mahwah, NJ: Erlbaum.

Trevarthen, C. (1998) The concept and foundations of infant intersubjectivity. In S. Bråten (ed.) *Intersubjective Communication and Emotion in Early Ontogeny* 15–46. Cambridge: Cambridge University Press.

van Lier, L. (1988) *The Classroom and the Language Learner: Ethnography and Second-Language Classroom Research.* Harlow: Longman.

van Lier, L. (1996) *Interaction in the Language Curriculum: Awareness, Autonomy and Authenticity.* Harlow: Longman.

van Lier, L. (2003) A tale of two computer classrooms: the ecology of project-based language learning. In J. van Dam and J. Leather (eds) *The Ecology of Language Acquisition* 49–64. Dordrecht: Kluwer Academic.

van Lier, L. (2004) *The Ecology of Language Learning: A Sociocultural Perspective.* Boston, MA: Kluwer.

Varvel, T. (1979) The silent way: Panacea or pipedream ? *TESOL Quarterly* 13: 483–94.

Vygotsky, L. S. (1987) *The Collected Works of L. S. Vygotsky. Volume 1. Problems of General Psychology Including the Volume Thinking and Speech.* New York: Plenum Press.

Wertsch, J. V. Tulviste, P. and Hagstrom, F. (1993) A sociocultural approach to agency. In E. A. Forman, N. Minick and C. A. Stone (eds), *Contexts for Learning: Sociocultural Dynamics in Children's Development* 336–56. New York: Oxford University Press.

Williams, M. and Burden, R. L. (1997) *Psychology for Language Teachers.* Cambridge: Cambridge University Press.

Wittgenstein, L. (1958) *Philosophical Investigations* (second edition). Oxford: Blackwell.

Young, R. and He, A. W. (eds) (1998) *Talking and Testing: Discourse Approaches to the Assessment of Oral Proficiency.* Amsterdam/Philadelphia, PA: John Benjamins Publishing Company.

Part II
Concept-based instruction

7 Revolutionary pedagogies: learning that leads (to) second language development[1]

Eduardo Negueruela

Introduction

The changing of words is not a guarantee for the changing of worlds. Indeed, what Freire (1970) calls empty verbalism in education is precisely one of the challenges of the theorizing and philosophizing that pervades academia and especially the humanities – the quintessential arena for the study of words. Freire's term 'mindless activism' (i.e., adopting new practices without much reflection) is also a challenge for teachers, who are often confronted with the task of adopting new practices without having much time for reflection. In the end, we in the teaching profession often maintain sedimented practices but adopt more fashionable and sophisticated discourse to explicate them. To avoid such a disconnect, in what follows I will be maximally theoretical and maximally practical, since it is the connection of the abstract theoretical and the concrete practical which allows for the particular, in this case, the emergence of a truly revolutionary/meaningful approach to second language (L2, henceforth) teaching.[2]

In this chapter, I explore the connection of a specific theoretical proposal with concrete pedagogical practices. Through applying sociocultural principles to the L2 classroom, I offer an alternative pedagogical approach to L2 teachers based on the notion of conceptual mediation. A conceptual approach to L2 development illuminates and makes available to L2 teachers a different array of pedagogical practices that have a revolutionary rather than an evolutionary outlook. The proposals I develop in this chapter are revolutionary in three senses: first, L2 development is conceived of as a non-linear process that can be shaped by properly organized instruction; second, learning and development are distinct processes but they are dialectically united; third, the revolution that is L2 development is semantic rather than formal in nature; in other words it is not based on morphology, or processing procedures, or even form to meaning mappings, but on conceptual categories.

The chapter has two main parts. The first, more theoretical in nature, explores the notion of revolutionary pedagogy in a Vygotskian framework. It then analyzes the importance of conceptual categories as central in the process of mediation to be able to define L2 development as a conceptual process. A reconceptualization of development based on the centrality of meaning allows us to explore the revolutionary quality of development. By modifying the Vygotskian notion of the zone of proximal development (ZPD) into the zone of potential development (ZPOD), I highlight the revolutionary nature of the process of L2 development. In this way, I emphasize the emergent nature of L2 development based more on potentialities than on proximities. In the second part of the chapter, the notion of mediation and the dialectics of learning and development are concretized into four basic principles, which form the basis of a concept-based pedagogy: minimal unit of instruction, materialization, verbalization and curricular articulation. These principles are exemplified through the teaching of Spanish grammar, specifically the Spanish indicative/subjunctive contrast. Data from Negueruela (2003) are used to illustrate the effects of a concept-based pedagogy applied to L2 teaching.

Revolutionary activity in the L2 classroom: tool-*and*-result and tool-*for*-result

The starting point for a revolutionary pedagogy is to understand development and learning as integrated components of a dialectic in which the mind is mediated by symbolic tools. The learning-development dialectic challenges an evolutionary – progressive building blocks – view of learning and development and allow both teachers and researchers to reframe their respective activities. Revolutionary pedagogical activity is centered on the activity of learners constructing meaning-making tools in a L2 and in the process, changing both the circumstances of their language development and who they are as learners. In a revolutionary process of teaching-learning, we become aware of our own change through meaning-making and we are able to orient to the change. In a sense, we become historical, that is, we are liberated from the here and now and we become aware of our own change – our own history. We open futures and understand our pasts through being aware of our own tool-mediated activity and this allows us to relate to the world around us, before us and after us. In the end, we transcend the here-and-now and explore the there-and-then. As Lotman (1990) would put it, we travel through the semiosphere, or the all-encompassing semiotic space of a culture.

As Newman and Holzman (1993) argue, the activity of making meaning is a fundamental expression of revolutionary activity. A critical step to understand the notion of revolutionary activity from a pedagogical point of view is Newman and Holzman's (1993) distinction between tool-for-result and tool-and-result. The notion of tool-and-result originates in the following quote from Vygotsky (1978: 65):

> The search for method becomes one of the most important
> problems of the entire enterprise of understanding the uniquely
> human forms of psychological activity. In this case the method is
> simultaneously prerequisite and product, the tool and the result of
> the study.

What Vygotsky is challenging here is thought about thought, the fundamental epistemological and ontological categories of Cartesian views of cognition. The very categories we use to think, do research, or teach, determine not only the methodology but also the results of our efforts.

In Vygotskian thinking, humans create tools in order to attain a particular goal and without these tools the goal would either be difficult or completely impossible to attain. Human tools are functional and material. Some are exclusively material: hammers, computers or power saws, while other tools, mainly semiotic in nature, become ideal and are internalized, achieving psychological status: concepts, schemas, graphs or formulas. The importance of material and ideal tools is not their objective quality but their functionality.

As Newman and Holzman (1993) argue in making the distinction between tools-for-results and tools-and-results, tools-for-results are tools that are constructed with a specific purpose and functionality in mind – the goal of the tool meets the reason for doing something. For instance, I have a hammer to hammer nails with the ultimate goal of building artifacts; or I give a quiz to compel my students to study the vocabulary covered in a particular lesson with the ultimate goal of helping them to learn a language in order to achieve particular communicative (spoken and written) goals. Tools-and-results are tools that are constructed and used as part of the results. The tool maker's tools are both tools and the results of tool making. This point is even clearer with ideal tools such as concepts where they are both the content and the tool of thinking. Concepts allows us to think through them, (i.e., verbal thinking) and are also part of what we think about; that is, the very content of thinking.

This theoretical distinction is critical to understanding the internalization of concepts in the process of L2 development. For instance, my understanding of Spanish modality is not only the content of my thinking, which I may or may not be able to verbalize in concrete terms, but it is also connected to my use of the language, that is, thinking through the language when I deploy a given grammatical mood marked by indicative/subjunctive morphology in concrete utterances.[3] This is not only critical for grammatical concepts, but for lexical, pragmatic and discourse conceptualizations that orient – but do not determine – our communicative practices. However, the connection between concepts and functionality in communication cannot be understood through simple causality, the a-for-b explanatory mechanism that emerges from pragmatism's tool-for-result approaches to explaining L2 development. It can only be approached and understood from an emergent meaning-making a-and-b, tool-and-result, revolutionary activity.

Mediation through concepts: the key to an ontological revolution

As teachers, there are activities that we can use as tool-for-result (a test/quiz that we utilize to determine whether our students know/do something) and as tool-and-result (a test itself might become a learning experience, as in the case of Dynamic Assessment, see Poehner, Chapter 1, this volume). This distinction is also fluid, that is, some of the tools we utilize for assessment might be constructed as tool-for-result or tool-and-result. For instance, portfolio assessment may either be a tool-for-result activity, as when students compile a portfolio to showcase their learning, or it may be constructed as a tool-and-result activity: the very process of creating a portfolio (tool for learning) is also the result of the learning experience (tool and learning).

Other conceptual tools in the L2 classroom, such as L2 grammatical rules of thumb presented in textbooks are well-intentioned and simplified explanations of grammatical features and hence are created to achieve a result, but as often happens, they do not meet their expected outcomes. As Seliger (1979) shows, grammatical rules of thumb seem to have little effect on language performance. Spontaneous and incomplete conceptualizations are not theoretically functional in a developmental sense, because they do not provide the complete basis of understanding, awareness, control and creativity. Along the lines of the present discussion, it could be argued that L2 grammatical rules of thumb are constructed as tool-for-result, but fail to promote conceptual understanding, since conceptual development is fostered through tool-and-result activity. From the present perspective, the proper tools to promote L2 development are theoretical concepts.

L2 concepts need to become a tool-for-result in the L2 classroom and this requires that instructional activity be organized according to revolutionary tool-and-result principles. That is, the content of thinking and explicit understanding of a concept and its functionality – the result of thinking through the concept – need to meet in pedagogical activity. Hence, the development of concepts cannot be taught through explanations that attempt to promote understanding of just concepts (i.e., the content) or through practicing just forms (i.e., the result).

Concepts cannot be systematically developed through some implicit approach where forms are processed so that they might be connected to some diffused implicit category of meaning. A revolutionary approach to L2 conceptual development is based on the internalization through application of conceptual categories to specific tasks – the connection of conceptual content and conceptual functionality – tool-and-result pedagogy. To be sure, the very activity of conceptual reflection constitutes the tool for learning and the result of development.

In what follows, I exemplify this approach through verbalization activities, a fundamentally tool-and-result approach to revolutionize L2 development. As we will see, the very tool that students used to help them internalize the concept of modality in a Spanish L2 classroom, talking to themselves to explain their own use of the concept, is indeed the result of development since as a result of applying the concept, the concept develops. This is the powerful ontological-dialectical implication derived from a Vygotskian understanding of development. L2 teaching methodology needs to understand this seemingly abstract distinction to be able to articulate a pedagogy that supports conceptual development.

A sociocultural approach to the study of learning and development

The Sociocultural Theory of Mind (SCT-M) pioneered by Vygotsky represents a synthesis of the sociogenetic scholarly traditions of the turn of the twentieth century and is grounded in philosophical bases which are incommensurable with most current paradigms in SLA. Indeed SCT-M offers a profoundly different understanding of basic categories such as mind, language and the processes of learning and development. Vygotsky's uniqueness is founded in his proposal that the notion of mediation overcomes the Cartesian dualism that split psychology into rationalist and empiricist camps. That is, the sociohistorical quality of human activity is mediated by semiotic tools, which gives rise to higher forms of human cognition in the process of internalization – the transformation of quantity into quality. SCT-M brings to light the uniquely human emergence of higher mental functions through the utilization of tools of the mind in the process of semiotic mediation – that is, the essence of participating in human sociocultural activities (see Cole 1996; Tomasello 1999; and Valsiner 2000, among many others).

The language-mediated mind is not about computation and information processing but about mediation through symbolization. Learning and development are not identical, although they are unified in learning activity through the dialectics of being and becoming. All of these theoretical proposals have critical implications for research in SLA (see also Lantolf and Thorne (2006) for a review of SCT-M applied to L2 development). From the present perspective, the concretization of a socioculturally-informed pedagogy in the L2 classroom is based on focusing mediation through implementing a conceptual approach to teaching.

The goal of L2 development: awareness about awareness through concepts

Elsewhere (Negueruela 2003) I have proposed that L2 development is a conceptual process where the emergence of meaningful consciousness, that is, conscious awareness through categories of meaning – i.e. concepts – leads to control. This conscious awareness is created through utilizing tools of the mind when participating in socio-historically situated activities. In other words, communicative development involves not only opportunities to communicate orally and in writing but also conceptual understanding of the L2, even if this occurs through the L1.[4] Conscious awareness is critical to the development of communicative abilities. The notion of internalization and mediation are at the center of understanding the role of conscious awareness in L2 development.[5] Development is normative in this approach. There are preferred outcomes: conscious awareness – awareness about awareness – that leads to self-regulation. But these outcomes are open rather than aimed at a specific and final end point.

The dialectical nature of learning and development through internalization is captured through the emergence of tools of the mind. As explained above, the core theoretical argument emerging in the last 80 years of sociocultural research on the nature of the human mind is that individual cognition emerges through socioculturally mediated activity. The process of internalization, the in-growing of cognitive tools is not direct, but mediated. The negation of immediacy implies an anti-causality stance, which also has critical implications both for L2 researchers and teachers. Models that attempt to explain L2 development through a direct cause-effect mechanism are not coherent with the understanding that the human mind is mediated (see also Cole 1996).

Defining the dialectics of learning and development

Internalization emerges from mediation, specifically mediation through psychological tools, which fosters development. All development occurs as part of learning activity and of course often times outside of formal settings (see Lave and Wenger 1991). However, not all learning activity leads to development. The learning/development distinction is neither a dichotomy nor an identity. Although the two processes are not identical, if and when instruction is properly organized, both processes form a dialectical unity where one promotes the other in an unending cycles of thesis, antithesis, synthesis, which is at the heart of all dialectical relationships.

Learning is fundamentally about internalization of knowledge and abilities which can potentially, not always, create new tools for regulation. Development is the internalization of tools of the mind with the function of orientation (awareness and control) through participating in socially mediated activity, that is, the re-structuring of higher mental functions (intentional memory, voluntary attention, abstract thinking, planning and imagination). Hence, if learning emerges through participating in mediated human activity, but not all learning leads to development, the critical question then becomes what types of learning activities, in formal and non-formal settings, foster development? Furthermore, are there learning activities that are detrimental to conceptual development?

Vygotsky (1978) articulates a fourth position where learning and development are related in the following way: both processes originate in socially mediated activity. In humans, they are mediated by psychological and material tools. Developmental processes are transformative. This transformative stance has epistemological consequences since it underscores the unpredictable nature of development such that an individual's future development cannot be adequately predicted solely on the basis of past development. In this fourth position, there is an ontological distinction in which learning and development are two different processes united through semiotically-mediated activity.

As Vygotsky (1978: 90) argues: 'the most essential feature of our hypothesis is the notion that developmental processes do not coincide with learning processes. Rather, the developmental process lags behind the learning process; this sequence results in the zone of proximal development.' On the one hand, development is then defined as the internalization of psychological tools resulting in the restructuring of psychological functions to achieve self-regulation in the process of participating in human activity. On the other, learning is defined as the activity of intentionally appropriating knowledge and abilities, which do not necessarily involve the internalization of new psychological tools and the re-structuring of psychological functions. Indeed one may participate in learning activity and not develop new conceptual categories with psychological functionality. As Kozulin (2003: 25) argues: 'the process of appropriation of psychological tools differs from the process of content learning. This difference reflects the fact that whereas content material often reproduces empirical realities with which students become acquainted in everyday life, psychological tools can be acquired in the course of special activities.' Kozulin exemplifies this distinction with learning geographical knowledge, such as Rome is the capital of Italy and understanding a map as a symbolic tool that helps learners find a city even if the place is unknown.

This same distinction is critical for understanding L2 development and L2 learning. It is one thing to understand and learn that the morpheme – s marks plurality in Spanish, or that articles specify reference in a noun, or that count and mass nouns are semantically different, but it is another to internalize the concept of definiteness and partitiveness such that the learner begins to think through these notions, not simply about them, when constructing utterances in a L2.

Development and learning in the L2 classroom

L2 development as a conceptual process is the internalization of new orienting tools for inter/intra personal communication. Consequently, the goal of L2 teaching is not communicative competence but communicative development.[6] The shift from competence to development has critical implications for research and teaching. Communicative development is the process of constructing meaning for others and for the self.

There is no development without activity, but not all activities lead to development. In other words, we can develop in many different ways:

1) Development in learning: The participation of humans in any activity, especially learning activity, may potentially foster some type of conceptual development depending on the history of the person. This development is unorganized from the perspective of educational instruction. This is what Vygotsky's means by everyday spontaneous development (see Vygotsky 1986). It is also present in classrooms that focus on 'doing,' as in constructivist approaches to teaching, etc.

2) Learning in development: Learning depending on the development of new psychological tools, that is, waiting for development to happen, typically when instruction is organized in a linear fashion and the basis for the assumption that there are developmental stages in L2 acquisition. This instruction separates content knowledge from procedural abilities. L2 instruction that falls into this category either focuses on practicing communication or on presenting content to learners. The methodological possibilities in this approach are many, as many as the different approaches and methodologies that we have in the field of L2 instruction. However, despite their vast differences, all maintain the theoretical and practical disconnection between content and procedures.

3) Learning-and-development as a revolutionary pedagogy: The organization of properly articulated pedagogical activity that centers on conceptual development promotes both development and learning. Furthermore, development facilitates and leads the learning process, while at the same time, learning feeds and leads development. In this scenario, the dialectical nature of the learning-development relationship is created with one feeding the

other. This is what Vygotsky calls the zone of proximal development (ZPD, henceforth) in the context of children's cognitive development and what I call the zone of potential development (ZPOD) in the field of L2 development.

Revolutionary pedagogies: from the Zone of Proximal Development (ZPD) to the Zone of Potential Development (ZPOD)

To emphasize that the ZPD is a potentiality that may be realized in many different directions depending on the tools and the activities in which the learners are engaged, I propose to utilize the notion of zone of potential development (ZPOD) instead of the conventional zone of proximal development for the field of SLA. It is motivated by three main reasons:

1) Field of study: As Chaiklin (2003) comments, the zone of proximal development is a construct that appears in a very specific domain, that is, as part of the general study of child development, framed under very specific theoretical and research considerations. Moreover, it was proposed by Vygotky to address a very specific set of questions. Here I concur with Chaiklin when he argues that the term ZPD should be utilized to refer to the phenomenon Vygotsky was writing about. Considering this, utilizing the notion of ZPOD seems more appropriate to frame the complexities of L2 development.

2) Terminology: Vygotsky (1978) defines the ZPD as the difference between independent performance, or the zone of actual development and assisted performance, or the zone of proximal development. However, the concrete articulation of the ZPD is a challenging task. Specific examples in Vygotsky's writing are scarce (see Chaiklin 2003). Furthermore, Vygotsky's own understanding of the ZPD changed overtime as evidenced in his writings and consequently, different interpretations of the ZPD abound. Since I do not claim to have the correct interpretation of Vygotsky's writing, nor do I find myself especially qualified to provide it, I find that the notion of ZPOD allows me to explore the potentialities of development in SLA with more intellectual freedom.

3) Development and not learning: As Chaiklin (2003: 43) also men-
    tions, the ZPD is not about learning but about development. 'In
    short, zone of proximal development is not concerned with the
    development of skill of any particular task, but must be related
    to development.' Here I continue this line of theorizing based on
    Vygotsky, where there is a unity but not an identity of these two
    processes. Through the ZPOD, I also emphasize that I focus not
    on L2 learning as ability or knowledge but on L2 development as
    a conceptual process.

The notion of ZPOD finds its revolutionary quality in overcoming
present stages of development through the 'cultural other,' not just as a
more expert peer that provides assistance, but as a cultural embodied
versatile being who fosters expertise through utilizing tools of the mind
in concrete meaningful human activity. Of course, tool-sharing by a
more expert peer does not automatically lead to internalization. The
fact that the learner is able to solve a task through help from an expert
does not mean that he/she has developed; it simply means that the
potentiality is there. In this sense, the notion of 'proximal' may be misleading and it may lead to interpretations of the ZPOD based on either
simple causality or a constructivist view of development where it is
assumed that we eventually develop in a certain 'proximal' way. It does
not have to be the case for adults learning a second language. If the
help a learner receives is not adequate, he/she may simply learn to
solve the task but the help may not promote new conceptual understandings and thus no genuine development.

Three considerations to situate the ZPOD as a revolutionary unit

There are three main issues that need to be explored in shifting our
focus from proximity to potentiality: 1) metamediation: the quality of
human mediation for internalizing psychological mediation; 2) the dialectics of concept development: concepts are always developing tools
that are not handed to learners as finished products; and 3) the dynamics of imitation: establishing the zone of potential development through
imitation. The full and complete exploration of these three principles
would require a lengthy theoretical explanation. Here, I will outline the
issues succinctly so we can appreciate their relevance for the claims
about L2 development made in this chapter. Constructing a revolutionary approach to teaching based on a conceptual pedagogy where the

potentiality of the ZPOD is fulfilled is not a question of methodological recipes, or about providing students with verbal or schematic accounts of a particular concept. Creating functional categories of meaning requires understanding the type of mediational interaction that learners will need to begin growing dynamic categories of meanings through the process of creative imitation.

A first step in this direction is the issue of metamediation: understanding the dynamic quality of instruction and interaction that mediates the internalization of the new orienting concepts that learners are internalizing. Kozulin (2003: 20) distinguishes between human mediation and psychological mediation. The former is based, according to Kozulin, on different types of mediation (approval, encouragement, structuration, organization, etc.) and techniques of mediation (heuristics, steps, reminders, writing techniques, etc.) provided to learners by instructors. The latter, psychological mediation, comprises a variety of higher-order psychological tools such as signs, symbols, graphs, formulae, etc. Below I define concepts as essential psychological mediators in L2 development. Methodologically, exploring these two basic types of mediators is a pedagogical imperative for teachers and researchers interested in promoting L2 conceptual development.

Furthermore, human mediation interacts with psychological tools which are deliberate, systematic and generalizable. Neither of these types of mediation functions in isolation from the other in formal instructional settings: 'Symbolic tools have a rich educational potential, but they remain ineffective if there is no human mediator to facilitate their appropriation by the learner. By the same token, human mediation that does not involve sophisticated symbolic tools would not help the learner master more complex forms of reasoning and problem solving' (Kozulin 2003: 35). This is a methodological issue and teachers may organize their classroom interaction in a variety of ways that foster meaningful and coherent learning activity through concept-based pedagogy.

Furthermore, the issue of helping learning in a broad sense (explaining, feedback, correcting) becomes critical since too much 'help' does not serve development (see also Lantolf and Ahmed 1989). In a sense, the dynamic mediation provided to learners while helping them internalize new concepts is also critical in the very internalization of concepts. Metamediation, or 'mediation for the mediation,' is indeed a critical pedagogical step to articulate a revolutionary approach to conceptual teaching in the L2 classroom. Insights emerging from the work on Dynamic Assessment may prove critical in this domain (see Poehner, Chapter 1, this volume).

A second key principle is to understand concepts as psychological mediators, which are not handed to learners as finished products. Defining the essence of concepts and devising pedagogical sequences that allow learners to create their own conceptualizations through guided imitation is essential. Research on pedagogical techniques to help learners in developing conceptuali-zations might show that it is more productive from a developmental point of view to guide learners in creating conceptual tools that can be applied in verbalization tasks than it is to hand them models of ready-made concepts. This is in itself a project for L2 researchers interested in concept-based teaching. Suffice it to say here, that concepts, which are basically semantic substance, are not internalized in ready-made form. They indeed interact with other concepts. On one hand, to become functional, conceptualizations need to grow from the point of view of content, that is, they need to become more semantic, general, abstract and systematic (see Negueruela 2003). On the other hand, concepts need to become abbreviated from the point of view of procedural functionality. This is what we might term the dialectics of conceptual development. Content and procedural functionality develop in opposite directions but with complimentary trajectories. For a concept to become a functional tool, it needs to become semantically heavy but procedurally light. At the beginning of instruction, concepts are semantically light and procedurally heavy, that is, semantically; concepts are isolated, not specific in their reference and not coherently and systematically connected to other concepts. From the point of view of procedural functionality, at the beginning of conceptual development the application of a concept is overt, it does not have the automaticity and the abbreviation necessary to be utilized as a tool for orienting activity. Development of concepts needs to allow for these two opposing trajectories to grow. The concretization of all these insights into specific pedagogical practices is in itself a research task.

Finally, once we have understood the developing quality of concepts, a third principle is to establish the ZPOD through imitation. The notion of imitation – defined as transformative process, provides a window into the potentialities of development. Learners can only imitate what is in their ZPODs. Indeed Vygotsky (1978: 87) emphasizes that: 'a full understanding of the concept of proximal development must result in reevaluation of the role of imitation in learning.' Vygotsky's understanding of imitation can be traced to Baldwin's understanding of imitation (Valsiner and van der Veer 2000), as meaningful copying where the learner understands the goals and the means of utilizing the language as a tool for both communication and understanding. As Vygotsky (1978: 88) argues: 'psychologists have shown that a person can imitate only that which is within her developmental level.' However, imitation only offers a window for realizing potentialities. The affordances provided by different tools of the mind, mainly concepts and participation in concrete activities will foster the emergence of L2 development which will enable learning. How to create dynamics that are able to assess the potentialities of imitation for learners is also a pedagogical and research task.

To summarize, the ZPOD emerges when the teaching-learning process is 'properly' organized. To be more specific, when the dynamics of interaction created in specific contexts allow for the emergence of the dynamics of imitation, where there are proper conceptual tools (i.e. developing categories of meaning) at the disposal of learners and where learning activity mediated by others is perceived as meaningful by the participants. The ZPOD is a revolutionary unity that finds its most fundamental realization in the development of categories of meaning that are utilized as developing tools for understanding in concrete tasks. Thus, the ZPOD, as revolutionary activity, is impossible to define as a proximal zone, construed as a process where one step in development is followed by the next in an inexorable movement toward a known end point. It is rather a potentiality to be realized through participation in concept-based humanly mediated meaningful instructed activity.

Pedagogical practices: L2 grammatical development in the L2 classroom

In the remainder of the chapter, I will discuss the ZPOD as it relates to concept-based instruction implemented in a university Spanish-as-a-foreign-language course. The data considered below are taken from one of 12 students who participated in the course conducted at a North American research university. The study, reported on in full in Negueruela (2003), was carried out over a 16-week period. The participants were enrolled in one section of a multi-section fourth-semester course that focused on writing and grammar instruction. The course followed the standard syllabus but integrated activities from a concept-based approach to teaching. The researcher, Negueruela, also served as course instructor.

Based on the work of one of Vyogotsky's most important pedagogical interpreters, Piotr Gal'perin (see Gal'perin 1969, 1989, 1992; Haenen 1996, 2001 and Arievitch and Stetsenko 2000), the course was framed by four basic principles of Gal'perin's approach to teaching: 1) concepts form the minimal unit of instruction in the L2 classroom; 2) concepts must be materialized as didactic tools that can be assigned psychological status; 3) concepts must be verbalized: speaking to oneself utilizing concepts as tools for understanding to explain the deployment of meaning in communication; and 4) categories of meaning must be connected to other categories of meaning, that is, a curricular articulation of categories of meaning.[7] These four principles, if properly integrated into a meaningful communicative classroom, allow for the emergence of learners' ZPODs through tool-and-result pedagogies.

The development of grammatical concepts in systematic ways in the L2 classroom allows us to concretize the theoretical principles presented in this chapter. Grammatical meanings have the potential to ignite the cognitive revolution that leads to L2 development by serving as the catalyst for the emergence of forms in L2 communication. However, as I will discuss below, it requires that we shift our understanding of pedagogical grammar from form to meaning. The internalization of concepts as tools of the mind should promote a more coherent and systematic emergence of forms. What I propose is that concepts, even those traditionally considered to be complex and therefore reserved for more advanced levels of instruction, can and should be taught to novice learners. This is not an easy task, since concept internalization is related to the functionality of concepts; that is, the ability to automatically utilize these concepts as tools for orientation. The functionality of concepts is precisely the theoretical solution that overcomes the limitations of the competence/performance dichotomy. Competence and performance are related here through the notion of development. The ideal (Ilyenkov 1977), called competence in a dichotomous world, emerges through the use of concepts as tools for understanding. From this theoretical abstraction a powerful practical application emerges: teachers should promote activities where concepts are used as tools for understanding and guiding communicative activity, not as the objects of instruction in themselves. This is done through self-explaining activities where learners utilize the concepts to make sense of utterances. As we will see, using concept-based reasoning to understand communicative episodes is indeed a developmental activity. Understanding is then created in the activity of explaining and applying concepts to specific instances.

Concepts as a minimal unit of instruction in the second language classroom

In L2 learning, adult learners have a long history as first language users, but the systematicity of the learners' understanding of language and the functionality of this understanding in promoting language development is questionable. Learners have spontaneous knowledge of grammatical concepts in their first language. My argument, although admittedly controversial in light of certain CLT practices, is that in the L2 classroom instruction must be grounded in, and guided by, explicit conceptual understandings that are internalized with the intent of developing functional concepts –that is concepts that orient communication.

However, not everything a learner needs to master to communicate in a language and to become literate is conceptual, at least not in the sense I am using the notion here. There are formal properties of the language, what Kozulin (2003) calls content learning, that need to be mastered automatically. That is, understanding that Spanish verb morphology marks subjecthood, tense, aspect or mood, for example and automatizing the utilization of that morphology is not a conceptual but a procedural challenge. However, developing a conceptual understanding of the semantic implications of tense, aspect and modality in concrete communicative utterances is a conceptual matter. Interestingly enough, many of the grammatical issues that are challenging for L1 adult English learners of Spanish in formal settings can be connected to conceptual categories: ser/estar, preterit/imperfect, prepositions, indicative/subjunctive, verbal tense, adjective placement, 'gustar' type-verbs, among other grammatical features.

Slobin's (1996) notion of thinking for speaking, as the quality that thinking takes on when one speaks (or writes) a language, is illuminating and allows us to more precisely frame the connections between communicating and thinking and is compatible with Vygotsky's proposals on thinking and speaking (see Vygotsky 1986, 2004). Grammatical categories such as verbal tense, modality, aspect, or motion are typologically different in different languages. These concepts, as meaning based categories, are not taught in the language classroom from a semantic point of view. They are taught from a morphological and rules-of-thumb approach. In the revolutionary approach I espouse here, concepts should be taught from the earliest stages of instruction (see Figure 7.1).

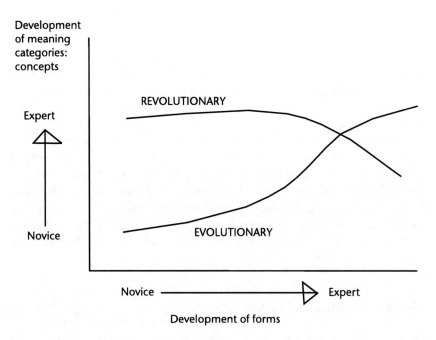

Figure 7.1. Revolution in meanings before evolution in forms.

Figure 7.1 simplifies the connection between forms and meanings in the development of expertise in a second language as it unfolds in the language classroom. In an evolutionary form-based approach to teaching, forms are learned and meanings are developed implicitly or through explicit rules of thumb. That is the evolutionary trajectory. In a revolutionary trajectory, meanings are conceptually taught from the beginning so that they foster the emergence of forms. The argument I am making is not that the goal of instruction should be the teaching and learning of lengthy grammatical explanations. It is however that the goal of teaching language from the novice to the advanced level is communicative development both in written and oral genres guided by coherent conceptual understandings. Recent proposals on literacy-based approaches to L2 instruction have already pointed out the importance of situating language use by connecting language learning and language use to the production of texts by readers and writers in specific cultural settings from novice to advanced courses (see for instance Kern 2000). At the same time, as proposed in this chapter, L2 development is about conceptual development. How to carry out this task in a coherent and meaningful fashion is indeed a pedagogical and methodological challenge for teachers and researchers.

A critical point in understanding a concept-based approach to L2 teaching is recognizing that concepts are not presented for their own sake. The challange to present the concept as a tool that can be utilized by learners in specific concrete communicative tasks. However, even before one designs pedagogical activities that foster the emergence of the functionality of conceptualizations, the quality of explanations is a critical first step. I have already discussed elsewhere the limiting effects of grammatical rules of thumb (see Negueruela 2003; Negueruela and Lantolf 2006). Rules of thumb, well-intentioned but simplistic explanations of grammar, promote inconsistent understanding of the meaning deployed by grammatical forms. In the following section I exemplify the issue of simplified grammatical rules of thumb with the grammatical concept of modality in Spanish and English.

Modality in Spanish and English

With the advent of communicative language teaching researchers and teachers have too often overlooked the quality of the grammatical explanations we present to learners (see Whitley 2002). The early contributions of William Bull (1984) and Dwight Bolinger (1991) to Spanish pedagogical linguistics were instrumental in formulating explanations that were coherent, systematic, sophisticated and teachable. Their approach to explaining language was based on directly relating intentionality and categories of meaning – what people mean when they say something – with structures and forms (see also Negueruela and Lantolf 2006 on teaching the concept of aspect).

Spanish verbal mood, the indicative/subjunctive distinction, has been traditionally viewed as one of the real challenges for English-speaking Spanish L2 students. Whitley (2002: 120) comments how some treatments of the subjunctive/indicative distinction incorporate as many as 34 separate rules. As Bolinger (1991) argues, the Spanish indicative/subjunctive distinction cannot be captured by rules, but by semantic tendencies: 'it is a mistake, says William Haas, to present as rules what are in fact concurrent semantic tendencies,' adding that 'however strong a semantic tendency may be, what happens "as a rule" is not to be stated by a rule' (Bolinger 1991: 256).

For Bolinger (1991: 256) 'the glue that holds the elements together into a speech act is the semantic intentions of the speaker.' He argues that speakers choose subjunctive morphemes as a direct reflection of meaning and not because of some clue found in the grammar. To make a long and fascinating story short, according to Bolinger (1991) indicative is the mode of 'intelligence': asserting new information that the speaker feels is new and true for the listener, whereas subjunctive is the mode of volitional involvement: commenting on an event from the perspective of the speaker. As Bolinger (1991: 263) concludes: 'the traditional view of the Spanish modes was correct: their significance is semantic; they represented two ways of looking at reality, one intellectual, the other, attitudinal.'[8]

One of the most interesting cases that reveal the constraining effect of rules of thumb for Spanish modality relates to the so-called verbs of emotion. Most current Spanish textbooks teach that the use of these verbs (e.g., '*alegrarse*' to be happy about something or '*lamentar*' to be sorry about something) in the main clause requires the verb in the subordinate clause to be marked for subjunctive regardless of the context. Examples such as '*Me alegro de que tengas el dinero*' (I am happy you have the money); '*Lamento que no hayas podido asistir*' (I am sorry you could not come); and '*Siento que estés enfermo*' (I am sorry you are sick) are usually given as the only possible options.

As Bolinger (1991) notes, however, the indicative options are also possible in exclamatory sentences introduced with verbs of emotion as in '*¡Me alegro de que tienes dinero!*' (I am happy to see that you have money), '*¡Lamento que no has podido asistir!*' (I am sorry to find out now that you could not go), '*¡Siento que estás enfermo!*' (It seems to me that you are sick). All of these examples convey 'intelligence' in Bolinger's sense (asserting new information that the speaker feels is new and true for the listener). Some Spanish speakers may feel that these uses are more marked, but the point is that subjunctive/indicative choice is based on the meaning the speaker wants to express and not on cues and rules that mechanically trigger the choice of mood. This can be seen even more clearly in adjectival and adverbial clauses. Compare for example the adverbial construction in (1) and (2):

(1) *Cuando vengas, comemos* (Whenever you get here, we eat)
(2) *Cuando vienes, comemos* (When you get here, we eat)

A very interesting and related grammatical issue in English concerns the use of gerunds and infinitives as complements after main verbs, which can also be related to the grammatical concept of modality. As Spanish teachers, we tend to say when we teach Spanish indicative/ subjunctive there is no counterpart in English, which has no subjunctive morphology except in a few – not always used – instances (e.g. 'It is important that she be told before it is too late'). This leads language teachers to state that the subjunctive is almost non-existent in English. At first glance, this might be a coherent assertion if we understand grammar through morphosyntax. However, if we understand that meaning-making, basically the semantic-pragmatic component, is the core of language, English needs to have linguistic resources that convey modality as a central semantic category even when it is not morphology marked. Logically, modality is expressed in English through a variety of other communicative resources: some morphological but mainly through intonation, gesture, modal verbs and also, it seems in the infinitive-gerund alternation (see examples below).

The issue of English verbs taking infinitive or gerund is usually presented in the L2 classroom through long lists of verbs that take only infinitive (aim, dare, expect, hope), verbs that take gerunds (admit, appreciate, defend, deny) and verbs that can take both (begin, continue, forget, hate). L2 learners are then asked to memorize these lists, basically learning to utilize the verb with an infinitive or gerund complement through rote memorization. Other treatments of the -ing or infinitive alternations (see Swan 1980) offer as many as ten different rules and explanations depending on the meaning of the verb. Bolinger (1968) offers a semantic explanation based on the concept of modality. Verbs that take an infinitive tend to go with events that the speaker asserts. Verbs that take a gerund tend to go with events that are commented on by the speaker, where there is volitional involvement. In the end, it is the intention of the speaker through the very meaning of the verb that determines whether an infinitive or a gerund complement is selected.

In English therefore, it is coherent to utter: 'I hope to go', that is, the event is asserted (new and true information), whereas 'I hope going' seems to be incoherent from a semantic point of view. Consider examples (3) and (4) below:

(3) Lou tried to go
(4) Lou tried going

Larsen-Freeman (2003) illustrates this difference, based on Bolinger's (1968) analysis as follows:

> (3a) Lou did not succeed in going
> (4a) He did indeed go but left for some reason.

Larsen-Freeman's example, however, fails to take account of verbal tense, which is also critical in constructing the intended meaning. Compare (3) and (4) to (5) and (6) below:

> (5) He tries to buy apples
> (6) He tries buying apples.

Example (5) is an assertion where the information in both 'try' and 'buy' is new. Example (6) is a metacomment where the important meaning is the act of 'trying' rather than the 'buying.' This is indeed a subtle, but crucial, distinction based on the concept of modality. And there are contexts where this distinction is meaningful for the speaker. Although it is true that it is a marked distinction, it is the same one found between indicative/subjunctive in Spanish morphology with verbs of emotion. For instance, consider in English:

> (7) I hate to dance with other people
> (8) I hate dancing with other people

This distinction, between (7) and (8), is one of assertion (7) versus volitional involvement (8). The parallelism with Spanish indicative/subjunctive is striking. Interestingly enough, in Spanish since only the infinitive can function as a noun, this contrast is not possible. However, there is a similar contrast through subordinate nominal phrases involving two subjects.

> (9) *Odio que bailas* [indicative] *con otros* (I hate that you dance with other guys)
> (10) *Odio que bailes* [subjunctive] *con otros* (I hate when you dance with other guys)

Some speakers, especially language teachers who have internalized textbook rules of thumb, may argue that (9) is not an acceptable sentence. However, the distinction parallels the one found in (7) and (8). Sentence (9) like (7) is an assertion where the speaker both asserts the feeling and presents the fact of dancing with other guys as something that he hates. Example (10) is a metacomment parallel to (8).

To conclude this discussion, the first step in a revolutionary pedagogy is to formulate conceptual/semantic explanations of language that allow learners to understand that the speaker's intent is central to making meaning. Developing adequate conceptual explanations that help learners to develop a coherent and systematic understanding of communication constitutes only a first research task for applied linguists and teachers. The work of Bolinger (1991) in English and Spanish is very illuminating in this respect. Work in cognitive linguistics (see for

instance Langacker 1987, or Tomasello 2001), where scholars understand language as symbolization and where language forms are
explained based on categories of meaning, is also compatible with the
present proposals.

The conceptual consequences of simplified cultural artifacts

Simplified grammatical explanations, despite their good intentions, become very problematic conceptual tools because they depict a constrained view of language as a sedimented entity that seems to have a
life of its own independent of human users (see also Agar 1994 and
Lantolf 2006). Once internalized, these kinds of understandings of grammar – and of language in general – are difficult to overcome. For SCT-M,
that is the reflective power of the tool, in this case, the grammatical
rule, created to explain language for L2 learners and to help L2 teachers
teach, yet leading to unintended constraints on how learners – and
even teachers – understand and use language. The simplified nature of
grammatical explanation points to the importance for both L1 and L2
speakers to develop theoretical semantically-based and functional
conceptualizations of grammar, if one really desires to control the language, instead of being controlled by rules of thumb.

   Direct approaches to L2 learning would contend that one does not
need to learn all grammatical or pragmatic concepts (verbal tense, aspect, verbal mood, etc.) to be able to use the L2. After all, we tend to
assume that there are plenty of people who learn to use the L2 with
sufficient time without explicitly studying too much grammar. Ultimately,
one could pose the question as follows: why should one bother developing the conceptual understanding of L2 learners, since many advanced
L2 speakers are after all functional in the language and can communicate effectively? From a Vygotskian perspective, this question can be
answered from different stances. First, from a grammatical point of view,
the understanding of grammar advocated in a conceptual approach is
not metalinguistic or structural but semantic and functional (see also
Lantolf 2006; Karpov 2003 and Kozulin 2003). The importance of understanding concepts is not based on knowing metalinguistic information,
but on constructing understanding that has a direct reflection on written and oral communicative development. This is a theoretical and
research challenge that is at the crux of the arguments presented here.
Second, from a developmental perspective, unless L2 learners – and L1
learners – become aware of the conceptual meanings behind notions

such as verbal mood, or aspect, they are unlikely to fully appreciate the ways in which they can manipulate the language to serve their communicative needs rather than being manipulated by it. More often than not, it is assumed that L2 learners develop without conscious attempts to understand and master the language. The fact that one does not receive formal instruction does not mean that as an adult one is not constructing *ad hoc* conceptualizations of how language works and how it is used to construct meanings. This is definitely an empirical question. From the present perspective, instructors should create the teaching-learning conditions for the development of grammatical concepts that are functional and make L2 learners aware of all the meanings implied by their linguistic choices. In the following sections, I explain two basic pedagogical steps for promoting internalization of categories of meaning: materialization and verbalization.

Materialization of concepts as didactic tools that can acquire psychological status

Once we find a suitable explanation of a grammatical concept, verbal mood in this case, teachers need to be able to construct a didactic model that can serve as a psychological tool. Learners need to utilize the model to help construct a semantic understanding of the concept that is abstract, coherent and as complete as possible. The value of abstract nature of the model is that it allows learners to generalize their use of mood across different communicative circumstances. Figure 7.2 is an example of a didactic aid designed by Negueruela (2003) to help learners internalize the concept of modality in Spanish. The development of these pedagogical materials is a research task and the option presented below is one among many possibilities.

Verbalization of concepts as tools for meaning making

In Negueruela (2003) I define verbalization as the intentional use of concepts as tools for understanding grammar. In this sense, verbalization activities are more than just self-explaining. They have to be self-explaining using the concept as a tool for understanding and not just verbalizing the concept aloud, but verbalizing the concept so as to explain the meanings a speaker/writer wishes to express, i.e. applying the concept consciously to concrete communicative utterances. Verbalizations are activities where learners talk through the concept and not about the concept.

In Negueruela (2003) each learner had to use the grammatical concepts as tools for explaining the grammatical features to himself/

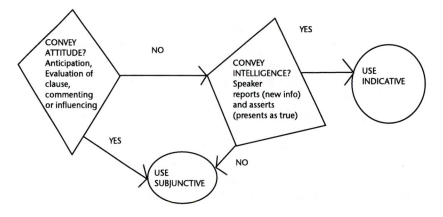

Figure 7.2. Didactic model for mood selection in Spanish (based on Whitley 2002).

herself. I also designed in-class tasks where students could explain to each other (and at the same time to themselves) a particular grammatical point using the conceptual charts. However, after observing students, I realized that these in-class explanations were not systematic and consistent. There were two main factors that were not conducive to verbalization: classroom time constraints and the private quality of verbalization clashing with the social environment of the classroom.

The first factor that seemed to negatively impact the quality of verbalizations was that students tended to abbreviate and simplify their verbalized explanations to peers in order to complete activities within the time limits for each class session. Each session lasted 50 minutes, but the realities of classroom management generally allow much less time for each activity. Second, the role of verbalization as explaining grammatical concepts for the self with the function of internalizing them was not fully met in social and peer verbalization activities. Considering the social environment and how learners are used to working in groups, students tried to finish tasks as quickly as possible instead of really reflecting on issues and fully verbalizing all explanations. Hence, learners tended not to talk aloud and fully explain the relevant concept for themselves and their peers.

Considering these issues, I designed verbalization tasks for homework where students could explain to themselves specific grammatical points using grammatical concepts as tools for understanding while doing exercises in a relaxed and private atmosphere. Figure 7.3 provides an example of a verbalization activity:

LEARNING ABSTRACT GRAMMATICAL NOTIONS IN SPANISH

STEP 1: A perfect Thanksgiving

Write an email to one of your Spanish friends where you describe and explain to him/her what they should do to have a perfect Thanksgiving. Use both the indicative and subjunctive structures.

STEP 2: VERBALIZATION: The concept of modality

Record explaining to yourself – using the flow chart – [See Figure 7.2 above] why you utilized each mood: indicative/subjunctive. Use SEMANTIC AND ABSTRACT reasons based on meaning and based on what you want to say. For instance: 'I am using indicative because I want to assert the event, that is, present the event as new information for my interlocutor, and something that I present as accurate.' Do not use mechanical rules such as: an expression like 'Pienso que ... requires indicative.'

Figure 7.3. Verbalization task adapted from Negueruela (2003)

To ensure that students fully verbalized their explanations, they were asked to tape record themselves while so doing. Interestingly, despite being asked to provide verbal explanations, students had difficulties using the semantic reasoning provided in the chart to explain modality in Spanish.

Conceptual development and communicative performance

In this section I present sample data from one of the students who took part in the study, referred to as participant 7. The data are of two types: excerpts from written performance and examples of conceptual verbalization. The participant was 19 years old at the time she participated in the course. She was double majoring in Spanish and Business. Before conceptual instruction, she had previously taken several courses in Spanish: Spanish 1 to 5 in High School and two courses at University: Spanish 3 (one semester: four hours a week) and Spanish 100 (one semester: three hours a week). She was a very committed student, who was eager to learn the language, as is evidenced in her initial statement explaining her reasons for pursuing a course of study in Spanish. The statement is given here:

First and foremost, Spanish is one of my majors, so obviously it is a
vital part to my education here at Penn State. More importantly,
however, is the fact that I want to become a fluent speaker of this
language. It has become part of my life and I hope to continue
studying the language and culture of those who speak it for years
to come. I traveled to Spain with my high school for ten days. I
wasn't able to actually study there, but I was observing the culture,
the way people spoke and conversed, the art and the history of
Spain. I hope to live abroad for a couple of years after graduation,
in a Spanish speaking country. If not, I hope to find a job that
requires a bilingual applicant; therefore I will be using the Spanish
I've learned here. I plan to continue to study Spanish throughout
college, taking at least one class each semester, also taking classes
about the culture and history of Spanish speaking countries. I've
been studying Spanish since 7th grade. I studied through the AP
level Spanish 5 in high school and took Spanish 003 and 100 in
college. My skills are in listening and understanding the language,
rather than reading and writing it. Therefore, it was very important
to me that my teachers spoke the language consistently. I feel that
once emerged [*sic*] in the language, it is much easier to pick up on
it. I often find myself leaving Spanish class and speaking Spanish
to my friends in the next class, which proves that once surrounded
by a foreign language, one thinks in that language. I expect, more
than anything, to become more comfortable with the language. I
hope to speak and write daily, as well as learn the grammar. I also
hope to apply the grammar that we've learned, which is the most
difficult task, into speaking. I've found that it is very difficult for
me to speak to native Spanish speakers (unless it is a professor). I
get very nervous and flustered and many times it is difficult for me
to even understand them. Professors usually speak a bit more
slowly for us and when in a foreign country, they don't realize that
I don't understand what they're saying.

Despite the fact that participant 7 had studied grammatical topics
such as aspect and mood in her previous courses, she was not able to
deploy the appropriate morphology in free written and oral discourse
with consistency nor did she have a coherent understanding of the aforementioned grammatical categories Following three self-verbalization
tasks during concept-based instruction, she evidenced marked improvement both in her grammatical performance and in the systematicity and
coherence of her conceptual understanding of modality in Spanish.

Written performance

The development of communicative functionality of concepts needs to be reflected in improvement in open performance. Below, I reproduce some instances of performance from one of the written diagnostics administered during week 1 and week 16 of the semester. Performance data allow us to investigate concepts in their orienting executive plane. If L2 learners develop more sophisticated semantic understandings of grammatical concepts in the Vygotskian sense – both in orientation and execution – we should observe improvement in the learners' spontaneous use of the relevant grammatical features in open written and oral tasks. To be clear, if theoretical concepts are indeed tools for L2 development and they have a genuine orienting function in communicative activity, the improvement in semantic understandings as evidenced in verbalization and definition data should be paralleled by an improvement in discourse performance manifested as a richer use of grammatical features connected to the grammatical concepts under study. Development of genuine theoretical concepts should be reflected in performance but there are other issues involved in L2 learning, among them, mastery of morphology and automaticity in communicative performance.

The written diagnostic asked students to write a one-hundred-word composition advising others on what it is necessary to do to have a successful surprise party for one of their friends. They were asked to incorporate phrases that may be used with indicative or subjunctive morphology. The following instances illustrate the type of examples deployed by participant 7 at time 1 in written performance:

WRITTEN DIAGNOSTIC: Week 1

(11a) *Sugeres que su amigo no tiene nada hacer durante el dia de la fiesta*
You suggest that your friend does not have nothing to do during the day of the party

(11b) *Hablas con sus padres entonces estos saben todo de la fiesta*
You talk with their parents then they know all about the party

(11c) *Ser importante que **invites** muchos otros amigos*
To be important that you invite other friends

(11d) *Es necesario que todas las personas que **invites** saben que es una fiesta sorprendidas*

It is necessary that all the people you invite know that it is a
surprising party

(11e) *Y esperas que nadie <u>habla</u> con su amigo*
And you hope that nobody talks to your friend

(11f) *<u>Necesitas muchos personas</u> a esta fiesta*
You need many people at this party

(11g) *Entonces cuando el **venga** pueden decir* [..]
Then when he may come you can decide

What is particularly surprising in the above example is that the learner
had studied Spanish subjunctive morphology for many years, she is
majoring in the language, she has a strong orientation to learn but she
still does not use Spanish subjunctive morphology appropriately. Only
in three instances, verbs in bold in 11.c, 11.d and 11.g, does she even
use subjunctive (two of the same token) and in all the underlined verbs
she uses the morphology incoherently. Consider the utterances from
week 16:

WRITTEN DIAGNOSTIC: Week 16

(12a) *Es necesario que **hables** con la familia*
It is necessary that you speak with the family

(12b) *Esto es porque **necesita** tener un plan*
This is because he needs to have a plan

(12c) *Es importante que muchas personas <u>saben</u> sobre la fiesta*
It is important that many people know about the party

(12d) *Recomiendo que **tengas** invitaciones*
I recommend that you have an invitation

(12e) *Es importante porque **necesitas** tener a todos en el cuarto*
It is important because you need to have everyone in the room

(12f) *Recomiendo que <u>tener</u> comida para las personas y bebidas*
I recommend having food for the people and drink

(12g) *Espero que **tengas** un buen tiempo durante su fiesta*
I hope you have a good time during your party

Although at the end of the course, 7's use of indicative/subjunctive
morphology is still not completely consistent, the improvement is very
marked. After conceptual instruction and even when it has been four
weeks after the last verbalization on subjunctive, which was in week

12, she begins to manifest consistency in her use of appropriate morphology. Only in examples (12c and 12f) are there problems. There is an improvement in the sophistication of her utterances and in the coherent utilization of subjunctive morphology. The learner may not know the irregular subjunctive form of the verb *saber* (*sepan*) as we can see in 12c, but she realizes that it is necessary to use subjunctive morphology in this case to express the appropriate modality. In 12f, she uses an infinitive form where she should have utilized the subjunctive '*tengas*.' Since she uses the correct form in 12g, it is reasonable to assume that the learner knows the morphology but she decides to utilize an infinitive, *tener*. It is difficult to speculate why she makes the mistake since she seems to know the correct form. The utterance would be coherent without the '*que*,' as in *es importante tener* 'it is important to have'; therefore this may be the source of the infelicity. At any rate, concepts orient performance but do not determine it. Another interesting example occurs in 12e where the learner utilizes an indicative form, which is coherent, although the construction is more marked than the subjunctive option: *Es importante que tengas*. Her option is grammatical and coherent with the conjunction *porque*. Data on 7's verbalizations and her final reflections presented in the next section illuminates the significance of the performance data.

Verbalizations and reflections

The first time participant 7 recorded herself, week 4 of the semester, she used perceptual rather than semantic criteria to explain why the subjunctive is used. This is illustrated in protocol (13):

> (13) *Ellos desean asistir a la reunión, pero es probable que tengan otro compromiso* [They wish to attend the meeting, but it is probable that they have other engagements]. *Cuando usa 'es probable' necesita el subjuntivo porque* it's a phrase that you always use the subjunctive with [when it uses 'it's probable' it needs subjunctive because it is a phrase that you always use the subjunctive with]

Participant 7 initiates her explanation in Spanish and then switches to English. In (13), the learner does not explain the meaning behind the use of the grammatical feature, but simply provides a perceptual reason seen in the phrase '*es importante*' requires the subjunctive. The fact that she was not able to follow the task instructions, that is, 'explain to yourself using the concept of verbal mood the meaning of your response,' evidences that perceptual reasoning is the basis for understanding in- dicative/subjunctive use. The student cannot imitate, in the sense of transformative application. Her previous history as a learner in classes where grammar was taught in a more conventional, form-based rule of thumb approach, is coming through in her explanation.

The second time, week 7, participant 7 begins to use more functional understandings to explain her use of grammatical features:

> (14) *No creo que <u>venga</u> mucha gente a la boda. No creo es un verbo de duda y cuando tienes duda necesitas subjuntivo para el segundo verbo.* [I don't think that many people will come to the wedding. I don't think is a verb of doubt and when you have 'doubt' you need subjunctive for the second verb].

She again chooses to explain the meaning of the sentence in Spanish and provides a functional/perceptual understanding of *dudar* as a verb that requires the subjunctive. Once again, she does not explain the meaning of the use of the subjunctive. She simply states that is used to express doubt.

Finally, at time 3, week 11, participant 7 was able to switch to a more semantic understanding of mood. She begins to utilize the chart (see Figure 7.2). Interestingly her attempt to provide an abstract semantic explanation occurs in English, which points to the fact that when she really attempts to reflect on the meaning of language, her L1 is logically the necessary tool to be used, since it is through this language that her deep conceptual meanings are constructed (see Lantolf and Thorne 2006 for a full discussion of the use of L1 and L2 for thinking):

> (15) *Es importante que tengamos mucha comida para todos.* [It is important that we have a lot of food for everyone] Subjunctive … I think from what the chart says just what the speaker thinks that the subordinate clause is true. I also add a reason that 'es importante' whenever I see that I always think subjunctive, even though I realize that that's not an abstract way to look at it.

Example 15 still does not reflect a fully coherent reason for use of subjunctive mood. First, the chart does not indicate that subjunctive is used to report or assert. In fact, indicative is the mood that emerges from this line of reasoning. Furthermore, the learner is struggling with concrete perceptual reasoning and she comments that she stills thinks that '*es importante*' is used with the subjunctive, most likely a reflection of her earlier history as a Spanish student. However, she does realize that this is not an abstract way of looking at things and there is finally a clear emergence of significance: 'what the speaker thinks.'

In example 16 below, also at time 3, participant 7 is able to use semantic reasoning to explain subjunctive based on Bolinger's (1968) notion of conveying attitude. More importantly, through the very process of reflection the learner discovers that she had used indicative morphology to convey a meaning that is better expressed by the subjunctive.

> (16) *Durante el día de gracias quiero que <u>miramos</u> fútbol americano por televisión.* [During the day of thanks (Thanksgiving) I want that we watch American football on TV] This ... [silence] I had this in indicative, but I think that it could be subjunctive. [Reaffirming tone] I think that actually would be subjunctive because it's conveying an attitude of something. Like I want that we watch TV during the day. I think that should be in the subjunctive, because it's saying it like for request, the same idea.

Participant 7 is beginning to show L2 development of the grammatical concept of mood. Certainly, the process is far from complete and rules of thumb and functional explanations are likely to continue to appear in the future, since her reasoning does not seem to be fully consolidated. At any rate, only three verbalization tasks (20 minutes each) allowed the learner to ascend from perceptual reasoning to the beginnings of conceptual understanding of grammar. It is in the activity of explaining through semantic reasons that learners develop semantic understanding of grammatical concepts in a L2.

Below I reproduce three of the final reflections that capture the importance of verbalization activities. Participant 7 comments on how the recordings were a bit awkward at the beginning:

> (17) Although sometimes recording myself speak was a bit awkward, I think it was overall extremely helpful. It made me more comfortable speaking and improvising and it forced me to truly think about the grammar. Plus, since you never had any negative comments about our recordings, I always felt very comfortable speaking, knowing you weren't going to penalize us for anything we did wrong, I knew I could just do my best to speak Spanish and I never felt bad about messing up.

The key to verbalization activities for participant 7 is that 'it forced [her] to truly think about the grammar.' This 'truly thinking' means thinking through concepts, that is, tool-and-result pedagogy that fosters the emergence of genuine conceptual understanding of grammar and not just thinking about grammar.

Interestingly enough, participant 7 also reports that it was beneficial for her to explain things to others and to herself even when her roommate did not understand anything at all:

> (18) Now that I think about it though, I made my roommate (who isn't a Spanish major, mind you, so she had no idea what I was talking about) listen to me explain when you use which pronoun, etc. Again, I always have found it helpful to explain to someone else (or a machine for that matter) the information.

The early nineteenth century German writer Heinrich von Kleist, in a short piece entitled *On the Gradual Working Out of One's Thoughts in the Process of Speaking*, quoted in Appel and Lantolf (1994, p. 438), nicely illustrates the importance of speaking for understanding:

> If you want to understand something and can't figure it out by pondering, I would advise you, my dear ingenious friend, to speak of it to the next acquaintance who happens by. It certainly doesn't have to be a bright fellow; that's hardly what I have in mind. You're not supposed to ask him about the matter. No, quite the contrary; you are first of all to tell him about it yourself.

In this case, participant 7 found both a friend who did not know anything about Spanish and a machine – a tape recorder – to understand complex grammatical notions. Finally, participant 7, comments on the importance of reasoning and avoidance of short cuts to generating the correct form, when she also reports how she has overcome grammatical rules of thumb in response to question 1 of the final reflections:

> (19) In past classes, we have studied every part of grammar that we studied in this course. The difference is this: throughout Spanish 200, we were taught a different way of looking at the material. Yes, we reviewed it and realized our previous mistakes, but we also learned how to look at the grammar abstractly. It's not longer, 'use subjunctive when you say "es importante,"' etc., now we can look at the meaning of the sentence and realize indirect reasons for using the subjunctive, for example.

This comment reveals the simplified understandings that emerge from rules of thumb traditionally used in most language classrooms. Students are supposed to use subjunctive morphology, not because they want to express a certain meaning or intentionality, but because they are using the phrase 'es *importante.*' And this is the critical issue at play here: to understand the conceptual meanings of grammar allows learners to function as agents in their new language rather than as followers of rules. L2 students are used to thinking about rules that determine their use of language, when in reality it is the speaker who decides what language to use to achieve specific communicative goals.

Connecting meanings to meaning: a curricular articulation of categories of meaning

One of the issues that we have not fully explored in the L2 classroom is how our understandings of language – framed through the way the curriculum is articulated – are passed on to and internalized by learners. Often times, our understandings about language and their reflection on the curriculum are funneled through textbooks; that is the power of the written word. The more traditional structural curriculum and textbook articulation (e.g. first, teach present tense, then past and then complex syntactical structures) has been replaced – to a certain extent in the language classroom – by a communicative curriculum constructed around themes (e.g. university life, technology, pastimes) and communicative functions (e.g. such as describing, narrating, expressing hypothesis). In any case most curricula and textbooks, are considerably eclectic in how they construct language learning.

One of the critical steps in articulating a concept based pedagogical approach is constructing a language curriculum that considers the conceptual implications of teaching language following certain sequences. That is, if learners learn about language through bits and pieces (vocabulary words as labels, one tense first and then the next, simple sentences and then complex sentences) and then they are expected to construct the whole activity of communication from these bits, it is logical to expect a certain sequence of development to emerge from a step-by-step articulation of curricula. The pedagogical challenge is captured through the cliché: 'the whole is greater than the sum of its parts' or at the very least, it takes a long time to construct a whole from these parts.

Pedagogically and from a conceptual point of view, the above challenge can be framed under the following paradox: to learn a concept you need to learn all concepts. For instance, the concept of modality does not function isolated from other concepts such as verbal tense, the concept of syntax, or any lexical concept, since they all intertwine in situated communicative utterances and texts. A possible solution to such a curricular challenge is found in the work of Davydov (1988) and his strategy of teaching from the abstract to the concrete (see Ferreira and Lantolf, Chapter 10, this volume). The work of Markova (1991) is also revealing in this respect. What scholars such Davydov and Markova propose is that curricula should be articulated starting from abstract concepts such as communication, utterance and then progress to more concrete conceptualizations. We cannot expect our students to develop coherent conceptualizations of modality and aspect if they do not understand the concept of utterance, text, pragmatic intention, or the grammatical concept of verbal tense. And certainly, most if not all, language classrooms do not work on systematically internalizing the semantic complexities of concepts in concrete communicative activities.

Final pedagogical considerations

After making the argument for conceptual grammar and conscious understanding of its functionality, it is important to highlight once more that the focus of the language classroom is still on the teaching of oral as well as written communication. Here we owe a debt to the CLT movement. For instance, practical pedagogical recommendations have emerged from CLT: contextualized activities, primacy of meaning, importance of creativity, the learners as the source of activities, utilization of authentic texts and group dynamics and interactions as learning sources are some of the well known recommendations. Approaches such as Di Pietro's (1987) *Strategic Interaction* are insightful methodological proposals that help teachers to transform language teaching into the teaching of communication. More recently, literacy approaches have been critical in reminding us about the situated and cultural nature of texts and the centrality of writing as a developmental activity. Principles emerging from a literacy approach to L2 teaching communication (Kern 2000) are also compatible as general pedagogical frameworks.

The proposals I have presented above attempt to continue our search for ways of teaching communication as a complex situated activity that requires sophisticated teaching practices. Below I summarize the proposals I have outlined in the present chapter:

1) L2 development is a conceptual process. Learning a language is not only about acquiring a code, or even internalizing a

communicative repertoire. It is indeed the development of new semiotic tools for orientation in concrete communicative activity.

2) L2 development, as a conceptual process – is about conscious awareness – 'height development' – the essence of the mediated mind. That is, through the use of tools, we become aware of the very activity we are engaged in. So we become an agent of change through changing ourselves. It is a personal revolution – a cognitive one – with a social origin.

3) To master one concept you need to master all concepts, this is a critical issue in curriculum design. Novice learners should internalize concepts such as text, utterance, mood, aspect, syntax, motion, etc. from the very first weeks of instruction. How to properly articulate this in an engaging and meaningful communicative classroom is the methodological challenge that we confront; but confront it we must.

4) The critical moment in conceptual development is the use of concepts as tools for understanding. The pedagogical issue is twofold: (i) what is the human mediation learners need; and (ii) to utilize the psychological mediation, concepts as tools of the mind, provided by teachers.

5) Tool-and-result revolutionary pedagogies can be instantiated in the classroom through articulating activities such as verbalization tasks that center on reflecting on meaning making, by talking/writing through concepts and not about them.

Conclusion

In this chapter I have proposed that a revolutionary pedagogy approach is feasible in the L2 classroom. This revolution, that inverts the relationship between learning and development – i.e. we do not need to wait for students to be ready, but conceptually-mediated learning activity not only prepares the way for development to occur but at the same time promotes development itself. This approach is not based on the teaching of morphology, syntax or just communication, but on meaningfully integrating the teaching of concepts as categories of meaning in the communicative language classroom. If as a matter of fact the learning of morphology, complex syntactic structures and processing procedures were to follow a linear stage-by-stage approach – a topic that itself still needs considerable research – I argue that the semantic-pragmatics of L2 development is revolutionary in two senses: first, concepts can be internalized through properly organized teaching from beginning levels; and two, their internalization may change the route and rates of learning. That is, if and when, learning leads development. The actual concretization of this revolutionary proposal is a research and practical challenge. Obviously, the teaching of concepts is not a question of presentation and controlled practice, but a question of designing classroom activities and even communication dynamics, that promote the use of concepts as tools of the mind. From the point of view of L2 teaching methodologies, there is many ways in which the above principles and ideas concretized.

The learning and development dialectic unified through the notion of mediation allows us to overcome the competence/performance dichotomy so as to explore different pedagogical practices. Four basic practical principles are proposed: 1) the concept as the unit of instruction; 2) materialization of categories of meaning in materials that can be used as tools of the mind; 3) verbalization: use of the concepts as tool for understanding; and 4) a proper organization of the curriculum. At this point, there is evidence (see Negueruela 2003, Negueruela and Lantolf 2006, Lapkin, Swain and Knouzi, Chapter 8, this volume) suggesting that proper articulation of these proposals are a very powerful and revolutionary pedagogy.

Notes

1. I would like to acknowledge the feedback received on this chapter from Jim Lantolf and Matt Poehner. The ideas originally outlined in this chapter have been considerably enhanced by their comments.
2. The extent to which new theories and new constructs are important in shaping our teaching practices is a topic of research in itself and is greatly illuminated by the study of teacher cognition (see Johnson 1999 among others).
3. Frawley (1992: 386) distinguishes between modality, a semantic phenomenon that 'reflects the speaker's attitude or state of knowledge about a proposition' and grammatical mood whereby specific inflectional morphology is affixed to verb form to express 'a subset of modal denotations.' Throughout the chapter, my concern is with the semantic feature of modality rather than with the grammatical property of mood. Mastering indicative and subjunctive morphology is not all that difficult for learners of Spanish; rather the challenge they face is to understand the subtleties of modality.

4. Like communicative approaches to language teaching, SCT-M also supports the use of the target language in the L2 classroom, but not because of input flooding, or because acquisition is subconscious, but because development is about participation in meaningful activities. However, the first language has an important role in meta-reflection.

5. For a theoretical discussion on the differences between the present proposals and the work on explicit instruction by N. Ellis or Schmidt among others, see Lantolf and Thorne (2006).

6. A thorough analysis of the inadequacies of communicative competence and its implications for L2 teaching is beyond the scope of the chapter (see Magnan, this volume). Suffice to say here that the notion of communicative competence is based on an understanding of mind that disconnects knowing from doing.

7. This is not the only way in which Gal'perin's approach has been interpreted. Haenen, Schrijnemakers and Stufkens (2003: 254) formulates three practical solutions for the teaching of historical concepts based on Gal'perin's proposals: orientation to the task, use of models and educational dialog. In my work, I propose four main principles.

8. For alternative explanations of Spanish modality see Whitley (2002).

References

Agar, M. (1994) *Language Shock. Understanding the Culture of Conversation.* New York: William Morrow.

Appel, G. and Lantolf, J. P. (1994) Speaking as mediation: A study of L1 and L2 text recall tasks. *The Modern Language Journal* 78: 437–52.

Arievitch, I. and Stetsenko, A. (2000) The quality of cultural tools and cognitive development: Galp'perin's perspective and its implications. *Human Development* 43: 69–92.

Bull, W. E. (1984/1965) *Spanish for Teachers.* Malabar, FL: Robert E. Krieger Publishing Company, Inc.

Chaiklin, S. (2003) The zone of proximal development in Vygotsky's analysis of learning and instruction. In A. Kozulin, B. Gindis, V. S. Ageyev and S. M. Miller (eds) *Vygotsky's Educational Theory in Cultural Context.* (39–64). Cambridge: Cambridge University Press.

Cole, M. (1996) *Cultural Psychology. A Once and Future Discipline.* Cambridge, MA: Belknap Press.

Bolinger, D. (1968) Entailment and the meaning of structures. *Glossa* 2: 119–27.

Bolinger, D. (1991) *Essays on Spanish: Words and Grammar.* Newark, DE: Juan de la Cuesta.

Davydov, V. V. (1988) The concept of theoretical generalization and problems of educational psychology. *Studies in Soviet Thought* 36: 169–202.

Di Pietro, R. (1987) *Strategic Interaction.* Cambridge: Cambridge University Press.

Frawley, W. (1992) *Linguistic Semantics.* Hillsdale, NJ: Erlbaum.

Freire, P. (1970) *Pedagogy of the Oppressed.* New York: Seabury.

Gal'perin, P. I. (1969) Stages in the development of mental acts. In M. Cole and I. Maltzman (eds) *A Handbook of Contemporary Soviet Psychology* 249–73. New York: Basic Books.

Gal'perin, P. I. (1989) Organization of mental activity and the effectiveness of learning. *Soviet Psychology* 27: 65–82.

Gal'perin, P. I. (1992) Stage-by-stage formation as a method of psychological investigation. *Journal of Russian and East European Psychology* 30: 60-79.

Haenen, J. (1996) *Piotr Gal'perin: Psychologist in Vygotsky's Footsteps.* New York: Nova Science Publishers.

Haenen, J. (2001) Outlining the teaching-learning process: Piotr Gal'perin's contribution. *Learning and Instruction* 11: 151–70.

Haenen, J. H. Schrijnemakers and J. Stufkens (2003) Sociocultural theory and the practice of teaching historical concepts. In A. Kozulin, B. Gindis, V. S. Ageyev and S. M. Miller (eds) *Vygotsky's Educational Theory in Cultural Contexts* 246–66. Cambridge: Cambridge University Press.

Ilyenkov, E. V. (1977) *The Concept of the Ideal. In Philosophy in the USSR: Problems of Dialectical Materialism.* Moscow: Progress Press.

Johnson, K. (1999) *Understanding Language Teaching. Reasoning in Action.* Boston, MA: Thomson-Heinle.

Karpov, Y. (2003) Vygotsky's doctrine of scientific concepts: its role for contemporary education. In A. Kozulin, B. Gindis, V. S. Ageyev and S. M. Miller (eds) *Vygotsky's Educational Theory in Cultural Contexts* 138–55. Cambridge: Cambridge University Press.

Kern, R. G. (2000) *Literacy and Language Teaching.* Oxford: Oxford University Press.

Kozulin, A. (2003) Psychological tools and mediated learning. In A. Kozulin, B. Gindis, V. S. Ageyev and S. M. Miller (eds) *Vygotsky's Educational Theory in Cultural Contexts* 15–38. Cambridge: Cambridge University Press.

Krashen, S. D. (1985) *The Input Hypothesis: Issues and Implications.* New York: Longman.

Langacker, R. W. (1987) *Foundations of Cognitive Grammar: Theoretical Perspectives.* Stanford, CA: Stanford University Press.

Lantolf, J. P. (2006) Re(de)fining language proficiency in light of the concept of 'languaculture'. In H. Byrnes (ed.) *Advanced Language Learning: The Contribution of Halliday and Vygotsky* 72–94. London: Continuum.

Lantolf, J. P. and Ahmed, M. K. (1989) Psycholinguistic perspectives on interlanguage variation: a Vygotskian analysis. In S. Gass, C. Madden, D. Preston and L. Selinker (eds) *Variation in Second Language Acquisition: Psycholinguistic Issues* 93–108. Clevedon: Multilingual Matters.

Lantolf, J. P. and Thorne, S. L. (2006) *Sociocultural Theory and the Genesis of Second Language Development.* Oxford: Oxford University Press.

Lave, J. and E. Wenger. (1991) *Legitimate Peripheral Participation. Learning through Communities of Practice.* Cambridge: Cambridge University Press.

Lotman, Y. M. (1990) *Universe of Mind: A Semiotic Theory of Mind.* Bloomington, IN: Indiana University Press.

Dunn, W. E. and Lantolf, J. P. (1998) Vygotsky's zone of proximal development and Krashen's i + 1: incommensurable constructs; incommensurable theories. *Language Learning* 48: 411–42.

Larsen-Freeman, D. (2003) *Teaching Language. From Grammar to Grammaring.* Boston, MA: Thomson-Heinle.

Markova, A. K. (1979) *The Teaching and Mastery of Language.* New York: M. E. Sharpe.

Negueruela, E. (2003) Systemic-Theoretical Instruction and L2 Development: A Sociocultural Approach to Teaching-Learning and Researching L2 Learning. Unpublished Doctoral Dissertation: The Pennsylvania State University, University Park, PA.

Negueruela, E. and Lantolf, J. P. (2006) Concept-based pedagogy and the acquisition of L2 Spanish. In R. M Salaberry and B. A. Lafford (eds) *The Art of Teaching Spanish: Second Language Acquisition from Research to Praxis* 79–102. Washington DC: Georgetown University Press.

Newman, F. and Holzman, L. (1993) *Lev Vygotsky: Revolutionary Scientist.* New York: Routledge.

Mitchell, F. and Myles, R. (1996) *Second Language Learning Theories.* London: Arnold.

Seliger, H. W. (1979) On the nature and function of language rules in language teaching. *TESOL Quarterly* 12: 359–70.

Slobin, D. (1996) From 'thought and language' to 'thinking-for-speaking'. In S. Gumperz and S. Levinson (eds) *Rethinking Linguistic Relativity* 70–96. Cambridge. Cambridge University Press.

Swan, M. (1980) *Practical English Usage.* Oxford: Oxford University Press.

Tomasello, M. (ed.) (2001) *The New Psychology of Language. Cognitive and Functional Approaches to Language Structure.* Mahwah, NJ: Lawrence Erlbaum.

Valsiner, J. (2000) *Culture and Human Development.* London: Sage Publications.

Valsiner, J. and van der Veer, R. (2000) *The Social Mind. Construction of the Idea.* Cambridge: Cambridge University Press.

van Lier, L. (2000) From input to affordance: Social-interactive learning from an ecological perspective. In J. P. Lantolf (ed.) *Sociocultural Theory and Second Language Learning* 245–60. Oxford: Oxford University Press.

Vygotsky, L. S. (1978) *Mind in Society: The Development of Higher Mental Processes.* Cambridge, MA: Harvard University Press.

Vygotsky, L. S. (1986) *Thought and Language.* Cambridge, MA: MIT Press.

Vygotsky, L. S. (2004) Thought and word. In Robert W. Rieber and David K. Robinson (eds) *The Essential Vygotsky* 65–110. New York: Kluwer Academic and Plenum Press Publishers.

Whitley, M. S. (2002) *Spanish/English Contrasts. A Course in Spanish Linguistics.* Washington, DC: Georgetown University Press.

8 French as a second language university students learn the grammatical concept of voice: study design, materials development and pilot data[1]

Sharon Lapkin, Merrill Swain and Ibtissem Knouzi

Introduction

Swain (2006) has argued that producing language, or 'languaging,' is an activity that mediates cognition and therefore is 'an agent in the making of meaning' (p. 96). The act of producing spoken or written language is thinking in progress and is key to our understanding of complex concepts. We reach those understandings through interacting with social and cultural contexts – through our interactions with other individuals and artifacts, such as the texts we read as well as information presented visually through charts and diagrams.

Although her research is framed in cognitive psychological rather than sociocultural theoretical terms, Chi (2000) demonstrated that languaging on the part of learners results in enhanced learning. Chi (2000: 169) focused on a process she calls 'self-explaining,' a 'process that the learner uses to help himself or herself understand external inputs that can be instantiated in any medium (e.g., text or video).'

Chi, De Leeuw, Chiu and Lavancher (1994: 442) conducted a study to explore what they termed the 'self-explanation effect' in learning about the human circulatory system. They were seeking evidence that 'the activity of generating self-explanations' that encourages 'declarative understanding of concepts' (p. 443) promotes learning, regardless of the ability level of the learner. Their study was unique in using an expository text taken from a secondary school biology textbook. Grade eight students 'talked their way through' a written expository text about the human circulatory system. These students read aloud and self-explained (a type of languaging) each sentence of a lengthy exposition (101 sentences) and arrived at a much more in-depth understanding of the text than that reached by a comparison group of students who simply read the text twice. Moreover, within the self-explanation group, those who generated more explanations and inferences achieved a more sophisticated understanding of the circulatory system than students who generated a more modest number of explanations or who simply repeated the sentences without trying to relate ideas to each other or without relating the information presented in the text to their previous knowledge.

Having conducted several such studies, Chi (2000) finds that: 'self-explaining can be conceived of also as processes of revising one's existing mental model of the learning materials' (p. 196) and that 'self-explaining is a process that students engage in for the purpose of customizing inferences to their own need' (p. 196). A Vygotskian socio-cultural perspective on this same phenomenon would suggest that through languaging, the learners 'articulated and transformed their thinking into an artifactual form and as such it became available as a source of further reflection' (Swain 2006: 106).

The studies Chi (2000) reviews relate to domains other than language. But language itself is amenable to examination, self-explanation and reflection. Negueruela and Lantolf (2006) argued for the role of self-explanation in learning grammatical concepts and propose an instructional approach that is predicated on the Vygotskian theoretical principle of Concept Based Instruction (CBI) (Vygotsky 1978, 1986; Gal'perin 1967). Negueruela and Lantolf (2006) reported the components and positive outcomes of an L2 Spanish syllabus implemented by Negueruela (2003), in which one component involved the teaching of aspect in Spanish. Students self-explained the concept in the presence of a tape recorder as part of their homework. Although aspect was taught in class explicitly, Negueruela and Lantolf distanced themselves from previous research and empirical studies that advocated the explicit teaching of grammar because previous researchers had equated 'explicit' with the overt teaching of formal aspects of the language. Those formal aspects, as Negueruela and Lantolf saw it, consisted mainly of morphological rules of thumb that are incoherent, fragmented, misleading and ultimately fail to promote learner development. Negueruela and Lantolf's argument is that the *quality* of the explicit knowledge matters and to date has been overlooked in most of the SLA research focused on grammar teaching (Lantolf, personal communication, November, 2006).

Negueruela (2003) adopted the CBI approach and designed a syllabus that respects three foundational principles of STI:

1) A coherent and theoretical conceptual unit. He re-introduced his students to the concept of aspect as an abstract, systematic, functional meaning-making resource offered by the language. The focus of the unit was to help the students exercise their linguistic agency as they came to understand the impact for meaning of selecting one aspect rather than another in describing events, actions and states of being.

2) Materialization through didactic models. Following Gal'perin, Negueruela used a concept diagram as a material form of mediation to help the learners represent the structural, procedural, functional and content properties of 'aspect' in Spanish, which resulted in a deeper understanding of the concept.

3) Verbalization of concept-based explanations. Self-explanations were an integral part of the instructional unit. These were aimed at fostering understanding and internalization of the concept and were founded on the idea (advocated by Vygotsky) that (private) speech serves to organize and control our mental processes.

Negueruela (2003) reported that the students found the concept diagram and the verbalizations to be effective mediators of learning that helped them progress in their zone of proximal development (ZPD). He also noticed some resistance from students who did the activities as instructed but eventually resorted to rules of thumb during subsequent writing tasks. It is not clear whether the mixed results in Negueruela (2003) are due to the students' 'resistance' to a new representation that challenges the rule-based approach that they are accustomed to or are rather the students' attempt to integrate two conflicting orientations to the problem of selecting aspect (the rule-based versus the concept-based orientations). His goal was to demonstrate that language instruction (be it in the L1 or L2) should aim at promoting the cognitive development and empowerment of the learners through a full and deep understanding of coherent concepts, not the rote-learning of decontextualized rules.

Negueruela's approach entails the development of pedagogical materials that present coherent concepts of grammatical systems. It seems to go beyond what has been characterized as pedagogical grammar:

Odlin (1994) defined pedagogical grammar as 'the types of grammatical analysis and instruction designed for the needs of second language students' (p. 1) and as 'a practically oriented hybrid drawing on work in several fields' (p. 11). Thus any textbook designed for a target audience studying the grammar of a second language is on some level a pedagogical grammar, along with what the teacher adds to its presentation. As we will see, few textbooks present grammatical concepts or systems in a way that is consistent with the principles of concept-based pedagogy.

Purpose of the study

The study served as a pilot study to Swain, Lapkin, Knouzi, Suzuki and Brooks (submitted), which investigates the effect of self-explanation on learners' understanding of the concept of voice in French. It specifically addresses the question: Does verbalization (languaging) of the grammatical concept of voice lead intermediate postsecondary students to a deeper understanding of that concept?

Participants

We recruited six pilot students at a major university in southern Ontario, from a course designed for intermediate learners of French. The course emphasizes the development of communicative performance; and limited observation and consultation with an instructor of the multi-sectioned course suggested that there is also regular instruction in grammar.

Table 8.1 lists the pseudonyms of the pilot participants along with their program and language background information. We included only English dominant students and asked them to verbalize in their strongest language; as a result all the verbalization was in English. The population of the university is highly diverse and students taking the intermediate French course have a variety of program backgrounds in elementary and secondary school.

Study design overview

In this section we present an overview of the study design. This is followed by a more detailed description of the stages we went through to

Table 8.1. Participants in the pilot study: pseudonyms and background information

Pseudonym	Program background/language info
P1	Core French grades 2–12; 5-week summer immersion in 2004
P2	Core French grades 1–5; immersion grades 6–9; International Baccalaureate grades 10–11 (standard Level 6); New Brunswick Certificate of Oral Prof. (Intermed. Plus)
P3	Lived in Belgium for 2 years when 10 years old; came to Canada at 14; took 2 years of Core French in grades 9–10
P4	5 years of core French in middle and high schools; English-dominant
P5	4 years of core French in elementary and 4 years in high school; English-dominant (young on arrival in Canada); L1 is Cantonese
P6	8 years of Core French in elementary and secondary; science major

finalize the design, with a particular focus on the development of the pedagogical material and the procedures used for data collection.

The study design is presented in Table 8.2. Data collection was distributed over two sessions, the first having several components and lasting 80 minutes including a short break. The second, the delayed posttest, lasted 20 minutes on average. To acquaint the participants with the procedure to be used (column 1 in the table), we developed a short explanation of French determiners. The explanation was presented, sentence by sentence, on cards with large typeface. The script for the first data collection session is provided in Appendix 8.1. The participant read each sentence aloud and then explained it or commented on it aloud, as one might do to oneself (see Example (1)).

Example (1): Excerpt of self-explanation from warm-up

> (1) Uh, basically there are four forms of definite articles in French, uh, three of which are used for singular and *les* which is the plural form. *La ... le*, or *la* is the singular feminine form, *le* is for the singular masculine form and *l'* is for the singular and the next, the ... the, the first letter of the word already starts with a mute *h* or a vowel. (P5, turn 64)

The pretest followed. Students were given a text that they should have been familiar with as it came from the first unit in their textbook (the *Sophie Mercier* text – Part 1). They would have been exposed to

Table 8.2. Study design

Warm-up	*Pretest*	*Self-explanation*	*Break*	*Immediate posttest*	*Interview posttest (one week later)*	*Delayed posttest (one week later)*
Short text with several highlighted determiners	*Sophie Mercier* text with 13 highlighted verbs	Advance organizer introducing concept and providing instructions		Participants explain highlighted items in *Sophie Mercier* text (we 'push' without providing feedback)	Participants talk about their backgrounds and perceptions of the task	Participants define the concept of voice*
Short explanatory text that participants explain	Ask participants to define the concept of voice (we provide some metalinguistic terms)*	Self explanation activity, card by card, using content-free prompts as needed		Participants define concept of voice. We provide some metalinguistic terms*		Participants complete a contextualized cloze test
						Participants do a stimulated recall on the cloze test (push for metalinguistic terms)
50-75 minutes			10 min	15- 30 minutes		20 minutes
Session 1: The first data collection session lasted about 80 minutes						Session 2

*The metalinguistic terms are active/passive/middle/agent/patient.

this text in their French class about seven months prior to our data collection. Each participant read through the text, taking as much time as he/she needed. Thirteen verbs in the text were bolded and the student talked through the text, saying as much as he/she could about the form and meaning of each bolded verb. For example, when we asked P4 to read through the text, her first explanation focused strictly on the form of the verb:

Example (2): Excerpt from pretest

(2) So *je prépare* is uh the *je* form of the verb *préparer*... and conjugated in the present. (P4, turns 80-82)

We then asked each participant to define the concept of voice. We prompted them by providing five key metalinguistic terms: active, passive, middle, agent and patient. The prompts consisted of questions (e.g., Can you define the concept of voice in French? What is your understanding of the concept of voice in French? Can you define the term agent/patient?) and aimed to assess the participants' prior knowledge of these terms.

During the self-explanation stage (column 3), we presented our explanatory text on voice, sentence by sentence, or chunk by chunk (see Appendix 8.2[2]). Here are the instructions, read aloud by the participants:

> The following activity is designed to teach you something about the concept of voice in French. There is research to suggest that explaining grammatical *concepts* rather than focusing on 'rules of thumb' leads to a deeper understanding of the grammar of the second language. This process is more effective when learners get a chance to 'think aloud' about the concept. So the attached sheets present information about the concept of voice in 'chunks,' allowing you time to think about each piece of information and explain it out loud.

There were 36 explanatory cards, including two charts. Wherever we felt the participant needed prompting, we used content-free prompts (Chi *et al.* 2001) (e.g., Can you explain what you are thinking? Could you be a little bit more specific? Could you elaborate on what you have just said?). The prompts were intended to scaffold and elicit as much information as possible. In key places in the explanation, we 'pushed' the participants to apply what they were learning. For example, after verbalizing the idea that, in the passive voice, the patient occupies the subject position and is followed by the auxiliary *être* conjugated in the same tense as the verb of the active sentence, the research assistant asked 'Can you change sentence 1 into the passive voice?' (see footnotes in Appendix 8.2). The participants were given a break after the self-explanation activity. The final stage of session 1 was an immediate posttest where we provided the participants with the pretest text and its bolded verbs and asked again that they explain the forms used to express the active, passive or middle voice. Finally we asked them to try to explain the concept of voice once more and again we prompted them using the key metalinguistic terms of the explanatory text.

The delayed posttest, administered approximately one week later, consisted of part 2 of the *Sophie Mercier* text, published in the participants' textbook. This time however, certain verbs were provided in the infinitive form and students had to fill in 11 blanks, using the appropriate verb form. We then asked the participants to do a stimulated recall and tell us what they were thinking as they filled in each blank. Finally, for the third and last time we asked them to define the concept of voice and provided the five key metalinguistic terms if it seemed necessary to do so.

Materials preparation

In this section we describe in detail three main stages that shaped the instructional unit shown in Appendix 8.2. We explain the criteria of selection of the target grammatical concept, namely the concept of voice in French. We then review the different ways this concept is usually presented in grammars and textbooks, outlining the limitations of some presentations. Finally, this section documents the development of our explanatory text and its validation.

Selecting a grammatical concept: the concept of voice in French

We selected the concept of voice in French for three main reasons. First, it is relatively systematic and can therefore be presented in a coherent instructional unit within one self-explanation session. Second, it represents a system of three interrelated voices (active, passive and middle voice) that serve specific structural and semantic functions. Third, even though the three voices are marked by different surface-level structures (insertion of auxiliary *être* for the passive voice and use of the pronominal clitic for the middle voice), it is the semantic relations between sentence constituents that determine to a large extent the choice of the voice of a given sentence. Moreover, we assumed that intermediate French university students would be familiar with some aspects of the concept of voice. For instance, P5's definition of the concept during the pretest seems to indicate some knowledge about the active and passive voices (Example 3) even though it is incomplete. Our expectation was that the participants would be able to integrate the new explanation we provided to them with their existing knowledge about the grammatical concept of voice. It is to be noted however, that while most participants were able to draw on some previous knowledge about the concept of voice (see Example 3), others were not familiar with the concept or at least with the metalinguistic terms we used for prompting (Example 4, p. 241).

Example (3): P5's understanding of the concept of voice before reading the explanatory text

> (3) Ah, active voice you would have a subject like for example in a sentence like 'I ate your chocolate', I would be the subject and that would be the active voice whereas passive voice you would not have ah-sub-have a however it is, you won't have I for example, like you would say you would use the the object and you would inverse it in such a way that you can make it be the subject like 'the chocolate was eaten by me' and I would become the object. (P5, turn 117)

Reviews of grammars and textbooks

A review of some of the most frequently used grammars and French textbooks (Jarausch and Tufts 2006; Compain, Courchêne, Knoerr and Weinberg 1998; L'Huillier 1999) revealed that the explanation of the concept of voice is often fragmented, incomplete and sometimes misleading. In addition, there is often a preoccupation with the formal manifestations of each voice at the expense of the semantic properties of sentences that determine the choice of voice.

For instance, in *Sur le vif* (Jarausch and Tufts 2006), the textbook used by the participants in their course and *Points de rencontre* (Compain *et al.* 1998), another text that was used previously in this course, pronominal verbs are presented as separate grammatical items. The textbook descriptions focus especially on distinguishing among the reflexive, reciprocal and intrinsic interpretations of pronominals. The few allusions to the use of pronominal verbs to express a passive-like meaning are often vague or misleading. For instance, in explaining the middle voice *Sur le vif* states that 'a reflexive construction is frequently used in French to avoid having a passive construction' (Compain *et al.*

1998: 146). In fact, the construction is not 'reflexive'; it is a pronominal verb with a passive meaning (Connors and Ouellette 1996) used in middle voice sentences. It is to be noted that the middle voice is not mentioned in *Sur le vif.*

We also consulted some reference grammars designed for students and others at a reasonably advanced level of proficiency. *French Grammar and Usage* (Hawkins and Towell 1996: 206) points out that 'pronominal verbs are increasingly used with a meaning equivalent to an English passive.' The authors do not refer to the concept of middle voice. Similarly, *Advanced French grammar* (L'Huillier 1999) explains accurately the difference between the active and passive voices in terms of the agent and patient relationship. However, in the latter grammar text, the middle voice is introduced by means of a rule of thumb that predicts the use of the middle voice when the patient is inanimate, the agentive complement (*par* + agent) is not expressed and the sentence describes a commonplace or expected action (L'Huillier 1999: 243). As Connors and Ouellette (1996) illustrate, in fact, some middle voice sentences indeed have animate patients and do not always express commonplace actions. They give the following example: '*Ces types de personnes se rencontrent dans ce bar*' (p. 215). Connors and Ouellette explain that this sentence can have both a reciprocal (These types of people meet each other in this bar) and a passive (These types of people can be met in this bar) interpretation.

In brief, the understanding one gets from these textbooks and reference grammars is fragmented because: 1) the three voices are often presented separately (as separate linguistic items/categories); 2) voice is defined as a property of the main verb with a special emphasis on the verb-level transformations that take place when one converts sentences from one voice to another; and 3) only the reflexive and intrinsic readings of the pronominals are highlighted, while their passive meaning may be ignored.

The treatment of the grammatical concept of voice seen in grammatical textbooks such as those referred to above corresponds to what Negueruela and Lantolf (2006: 82) call 'incomplete and unsystematic rules of thumb.' Rules of thumb may mix semantic, functional and structural aspects of concepts and present linguistic items independently of their communicative functions. We found a more thorough explanation of the concept of voice in stylistics textbooks (e.g. Ruwet 1972). However, here again the authors used different terminology and did not always agree on the explanation/function of each voice. While Darbelnet (1969) distinguishes between the active, passive and 'pronominal' voices, Ruwet (1972) differentiates between 'constructions' that use the pronominal clitic and refers to pronominal, neutral and middle constructions.

In spite of all these limitations in the existing literature, our review helped establish several basic elements/principles of the concept of voice in French:

1) Voice is a property of the sentence not of the verb. The selection of voice also depends on the speaker/writer's intentionality.

2) The voice of a sentence encodes the relation between patient and agent.

3) The structural changes in passive and middle-voice sentences reflect a change in the emphasis the speaker/writer places on the agent or patient of the sentence.

4) Pronominal verbs have several functions: one of them is to express a passive-like meaning in middle-voice sentences where the agent is not mentioned/is not known.[3]

Validation of the explanatory text

We integrated the four principles listed above into a coherent explanatory text that we presented to the participants in 'chunks' (Appendix 8.2). While they were reading this text, participants also referred to a sheet of 12 examples (Appendix 8.2) of French sentences in the active, passive and middle voice and two didactic diagrams that illustrate the relations between agent and patient in exemplar sentences. The text was revised several times to insure coherence and accessibility. We also sought the feedback of several experts who read and commented on the content, organization and presentation of the text.

A recurrent critique of the text was aimed at the didactic diagrams, which were interpreted in terms of transformational movements characteristic of universal grammar (Chomsky 1965). It is important, however, to note that, following Gal'perin's STI principles, the diagrams are didactic models provided to help the participants internalize the concept of voice; they represent the structural, procedural, functional and content properties (Negueruela and Lantolf 2006) of the target concept. The arrows in the diagrams do not represent 'transformations' and the two exemplar sentences in each diagram are not deep and surface structure models of each other. Rather, the arrows were used as 'mediating tools [of mind]' to help the participants visualize the relations between patient and agent and understand the different roles they play in active/passive/middle voice sentences.

Our colleagues' feedback helped refine our text, identify ambiguous statements and revise some problems with wording. As we started collecting the pilot data, we continued to refine the text in response to questions raised by the participants about the meanings of some terms or the interpretations of sub-concepts. For instance, we added the last section (cards 32 to 36) about the four readings of pronominal verbs (Connors and Ouellette 1996) because we felt that the students found it difficult to integrate the passive-like meaning of pronominal verbs with their existing knowledge about the reflexive meaning. It seemed necessary to make the distinction more explicit and draw the participants' attention to the fact that the use of pronominal verbs to form middle-voice sentences is only *one* of the possible functions of this verb form.

Refining the design

A few revisions to the initial design of the study were necessary to gain a better understanding of the learning process and the role of verbalization in helping the participants internalize the concept of voice in French. Indeed, the original design consisted of a single session divided into three parts: 1) a pretest stage where the participants were asked to identify the form/function of the verbs highlighted in the *Sophie Mercier* text; 2) the verbalization stage where the participants read the explanatory text, including the diagrams, aloud and self-explained each sentence as well as the diagrams; and 3) a posttest that consisted of asking the participants to identify the form/function of the verbs in the *Sophie Mercier* text again.

Based on our observation of the first pilot participants' sessions, we decided to add another measure of comprehension, involving asking our participants to provide a conceptual definition of voice. We also decided to schedule a delayed posttest session with each participant one week after the intervention session to assess the long-term effect of the intervention. The following sections explain the procedures and rationale for these two revisions.

The conceptual definitions

The immediate posttest showed that the participants made some progress. In the pretest they focused on the aspect and tense of the highlighted verbs, but during the posttest their attention shifted more to verbal voice. Table 8.3 presents a few examples of the responses of our first participant (P1) in the pre- and immediate-posttest stages. While P1's pretest answers were focused exclusively on the verb (tense, literal translation), her posttest answers suggest that she was considering the entire sentence and was more aware of the role, position and function of each item in the sentence. It is true that for the form 's'*observe*' she 'guesses' the voice of the sentence thanks to the pronominal clitic. Nonetheless, the evidence of learning is clear.

In order to assess the depth of learning, following Negueruela and Lantolf (2006), we decided to ask the participants to define the concept of voice as part of the pretests and posttests. These conceptual definitions 'play a crucial role in guiding development of performance ability because [they] serve to orient learners to the meaning making possibilities offered by the language' (Valisner, quoted in Negueruela and Lantolf 2006: 84). They 'give access' to the mental representations or mental models (Chi, De Leeuw, Chiu, and LaVancher 1994) that the participants had of the concept of voice before and after the intervention.

The following two quotes present P6's conceptual definitions of the concept of voice. The first definition (Example 4) was collected during the pretest before he read and self-explained the explanatory text; the second quote (Example 5) was collected during the immediate posttest.

Example (4): P6's conceptual definition during the pretest

> (4) Voice um I guess would just be whether you're speaking in the first person so like um I play I run I went to the movies yesterday. Um and otherwise you'd be speaking in the third person

Table 8.3 P1's explanations at pre- and posttest stages

Verb	Pretest	Posttest
Prépare	The verb is used with *je*, it's in present tense, it means she' preparing	This is present tense, active voice, because *je* comes before the verb
Est usée	Present tense, describing	Present tense, passive voice, uses auxiliary *être*, *murs* is the object that the verb is describing
S'observe	To observe oneself, it's a reflexive verb in the present tense	Middle voice because pronominal, agitation goes before the verb, it's agentless

beginning of the session or to their pre-existing knowledge. In an attempt to elicit as much information as possible, the research assistant conducting the session introduced four 'pushing' prompts at strategic points in the explanatory text (see footnotes 1, 2, 3 and 4 in Appendix 8.2). These prompts aimed to encourage the participants to recapitulate their understanding, use their new knowledge or elaborate on what they had just learned. On the rare occasions where the learners responded inaccurately to these prompts, the research assistant provided the necessary scaffolding to help the learner review his/her answer. This procedure is in line with Swain's (e.g., 1995) output hypothesis that stipulates that language learners need to be pushed beyond their current level of expertise. The learner's ability to respond to these pushing prompts is more indicative of development (or lack thereof) than responses to traditional discrete item questions (Aljaafreh and Lantolf 1994).

Instances of learning

The pilot data suggest self-explaining helped the students engage with the conceptual expository text. Not only did we note instances of 'insight'/a-ha moments as the participants 'talked their way through the text,' but we also recorded clear evidence of learning in the posttests. However, we identified other instances where the participant either resisted the procedure and failed to integrate the new information, resorting instead to old rules of thumb (see Example 10, p. 246), or simply failed to understand the explanation.

Example 7 illustrates how P4, by talking her way through the explanation, successfully made a fine distinction between the meanings expressed by two exemplar sentences. It shows that she not only was making predictions as she was reading the text based on her newly acquired knowledge (i.e. her ability to recognize sentence 8 as an active sentence) but she also challenged the explanatory text when her predictions were not borne out. However, by rereading and talking it through she reached a better understanding of the conceptual unit expressed and the illustrating examples.

Example (7): P4 talking her way through a 'confusing' statement

(7) 'Consider examples 8 and 9'. For 8 'On mange le saumon froid'. 9 is 'Le saumon se mange froid'. So 8 would probably mean one eats salmon cold and in 9 the salmon is eaten cold. 'In 8 and 9, English would use the passive: Salmon is eaten or can

where it's you're like a sort of omniscient narrator and you're describing um somebody else so like, um he played, he ran yesterday and it's not from your perspective it's from the people and the action's perspective [...] Um, active vs passive. Um, (2.0) I know, ok passive voice is like it was happening and this this was going on while I was there but then active voice is more like you're you're right in there I am playing and we we played while we were together. (turn 137-144)

It is clear that the participant's understanding of the concept of voice is incorrect. He is apparently familiar with the terms active and passive voice but seems to confuse the concept of voice with another one.[4] Moreover, he said that he did not know anything about middle voice, agent or patient when asked by one of the research assistants. The second quote below shows the development in P6's understanding; it would have been impossible to gauge this development had we relied solely on the participant's immediate posttest responses. P6's second conceptual definition shows a clearly more sophisticated understanding of the uses of the three voices. It is important to note how he presents (and conceptualizes) active, passive and middle voices as interrelated concepts. Also interesting is his ability to self-correct (line 5) which reflects a deep understanding of the difference between patient and object. This second conceptual definition shows P6's mastery of the concept.

Example (5): P6's conceptual definition during the immediate posttest

(5) Ok, so the passive voice, the passive voice um, happens when, you can like I guess you can really only get a passive sentence if you consider the active sentence first. And then, you kind of, if you, if you can realize that the that the um that the subject in the original sentence isn't really so important and you want to place more emphasis on the object? Then you'd move the um sorry the patient? Then you'd move the patient to the front and then that becomes like the new agent or like the new subject and that is what you place more emphasis on. So, if you wanna, like, if you wanna talk about, if you wanna talk about um, the girls who wear the skirt, then you'd use the active voice but if you wanna talk about the skirts themselves and how they're worn, then you'd use the passive voice [...] the middle voice is um still a passive representation of the active of an active phrase, but instead of like and you're still emphasizing the, um, you're still emphasizing the importance of the s- of the object? Um and so again you

just move the object to the front. And then instead of doing like taking *être* as your auxiliary, you just um, you apply like, you turn old verb into a pronominal verb and then the subject, the-sorry the the object of the original sentence has become the original subject or you can or you don't have to, like, based on the context of the phrase. (P6, turns 354 and 360)

Modifying the delayed posttest

We noticed a significant development in the participants' understanding of the concept of voice during the immediate posttest as shown by the above quotes by P6. However, we wanted to know if the intervention had any long-term effects on the participants. In other words, we wanted to assess if self-explaining a concept would result in a longer-term, deep understanding of the target concept. We therefore asked the participants to come back for a delayed posttest one week later.

Here again, we had to refine our design in response to the participants' performance. Initially, we devised a free-production test that consisted of asking the participants to write a short paragraph in French to describe their homes by using sentences in the three voices they learned. The composition was followed by a stimulated-recall session in which we asked the participant to go back to each sentence s/he wrote and explain why s/he chose a particular voice.

The free production task proved to be difficult for the participants because: 1) their lexical repertoire in French is quite limited; and 2) it is difficult to create an obligatory context for the production of a given voice. Indeed, even when we changed the prompt to one that would call for the use of the passive (reporting a robbery), some participants were still able to write sound and acceptable sentences while avoiding using the passive or middle voices, while others, in an attempt to comply with the researcher's instructions, 'created' verb forms that do not exist in French (as in Example 6 below). These forms were particularly problematic because we could not use them to either support or refute our hypothesis. In some instances, both the verbs and the explanation that the participant gave in the stimulated recall were wrong. However, in some cases, the wrong form was used for the right reasons. Poehner (personal communication, November 2006) suggests that this might be due to the fact that learners may have internalized the concept but were unable to use it to regulate their languaging activity. Using these data would have called for a subjective judgment on the part of the researchers.

Example (6): P1's delayed posttest based on first version of the delayed posttest (excerpt)

(6) *Elle se semble nouvelle. [...] La fenetre se face un petit Jardin*[5]

To avoid these problems, we experimented with a guided production task using the second part of the *Sophie Mercier* text as a cloze test. We adapted the text so that sentences in the three voices were included. We then asked the participants to fill in 11 blanks, choosing from among 18 verbs provided in a list below the passage. The list included conjugated verbs and distracters (pronominal verbs that conveyed a reciprocal, reflexive or intrinsic reading). Limited vocabulary was once again a major obstacle as participants failed to understand the meaning of some sentences and seemed to fill in the blanks in a random fashion.

Consequently, we decided to pilot test three delayed posttest alternatives. In the first, participants were given the infinitive form of each missing verb next to the blank, while in the second, blanks were numbered and participants had to choose one of three alternative readings of the sentence (active, passive and middle) in multiple-choice format to fill in the blank. While it might be argued that we 'gave away' part of the answers in these two test types, it is to be recalled that this was the only way to solve the limited vocabulary problem. We modeled the third format on the pretest: we bolded the target features in the second part of the *Sophie Mercier* text and asked the participants to identify and explain the voice of the 11 sentences that contained those features. The stimulated recalls were an additional source of data that we used to gain a better understanding of two participants' performance on these three delayed posttest alternatives. The participants seemed to prefer the first option. We also preferred it because we were uncomfortable with the idea of giving incorrect alternatives in the second test type and the preferred test format, unlike the third option which did not involve production of the target features, allowed for limited 'production' on the part of the learners.

Adding prompts: pushing

The first intervention sessions confirmed one of the most important findings of Chi *et al.* (1994), namely that participants differ in the amount and quality of self-explaining they do. They also differ in the level of involvement they show. While some participants merely paraphrased the expository text, others made more significant inferences and related their newly gained knowledge to what they had learned at the

be eaten.' So it's saying that both 8 and 9 uh could, are used in English as passive, that's from what I understand but it seems like 8 is not a passive sentence. In 8 it says '*On mange*' it says '*In 8 and 9, English would use the passive: Salmon is eaten or can be eaten cold.*' And in 8 '*On mange le saumon froid*' it is an active sentence and I think it's an active sentence which means one eats salmon cold but … okay I see it, it's about the same, roughly the same meaning from English and French. […] uh, salmon because in, when you say one eats salmon cold in English it can also mean salmon is eaten cold. So it it's a general statement. (P4, turn 132)

Example 7, in fact, illustrates how speech is used to explain concepts to oneself. It is in line with Vygotskian theory that asserts the importance of private (Lantolf 2003) and overt (Swain 2000) speech in helping learners internalize target concepts. Talking the explanation through with the self-facilitated learning.

The development in the conceptual definition provided by P6 (Examples 4 and 5) above is evidence of development in the quality of P6's understanding of the concept of voice. It is important to note that this development stems from an internalization of the concept and not a mere memorization of the explanation. In fact, P6's conceptual definition of voice in French at the beginning of the delayed posttest (scheduled one week after the intervention session) confirms this (see Example 8).

Example 8: P6's conceptual definition at the beginning of the delayed posttest

(8) Voice is like, I know it's divided into like active, passive and middle and I guess it's just the way that you're talking about something whether you're emphasizing the importance of the subject or the object. Should I talk about each one? So active voice is like when you're referring, when you're directly talking about the agent, the doer of the object, so he plays guitar that would be active. The passive voice is kind of like when you place more emphasis on the object or the patient and that patient gets moved to the front of the phrase and it becomes the subject so the guitar was played would be a passive voice and then the middle voice is still like a passive representation but instead of using the auxiliary *être* and then the past participle of the verb, you use instead a pronominal verb to describe the middle voice. (P6, turn 8)

Another example comes also from P6 who was also able to provide a thorough and sound explanation for the use of different voices in the second *Sophie Mercier* text when he helped us pilot test the three alternative versions of the delayed posttest ten days after the first session. Example 9 is taken from his response to the third version (accurate forms presented to the participants who had to justify the use of each voice).

Example (9): P6 explains the use of the passive and middle voice in the delayed posttest

> (9) In the sentence *je suis entourée*, it's in the passive voice because E.T. [Extra-terrestres] would serve as the subject in the active voice and *la Tour Eiffel se voit de partout* since there is no, the object does not appear in this middle voice sentence I mean the subject does not appear in this middle voice sentence and the *Tour Eiffel* serves as the object in the active sentence.
> (P6, turn 45)

However, as mentioned above, some students struggled with the concept and failed to reach the same level of understanding as P6 and P4. P5, for instance, was able to distinguish active and passive voice but could not grasp the concept of middle voice (Example 10).

Example 10: Instance of apparent failure to learn (P5: immediate posttest)

> (10) The only way that I even guess that it's middle voice is by looking at reflexive verbs where verbs have a has a will have a direct object pronoun like *se* or *me* or any of those, I would either think it's passive or um it's either passive or middle voice unless I see a subject pronoun which I think is not a good rule to use. (P5, turn 603)

Moreover, while P5 was actively engaged with the explanatory text and successfully self-explained most of the statements he read, he resorted to his rules of thumb when he answered the immediate and delayed posttests (Example 11).

Example 11: P5 resorting to rules of thumb to answer delayed posttest

> (11) The reason I put this as a passive voice is because there is a preposition following the blank. I can't say the wine drinks. [...] and next one, *la Tour Eiffel est vue*. Again there's a there is a preposition *de* following the blank and that's why I need to use the passive voice. (P5, turn 72)

It is not clear, based on the pilot data, what determines the participant's success in engaging in self-explanation and subsequently internalizing the target concept. While most participants said that they are not used to verbalizing their thoughts as they focus on grammar explanations, they all reported that they found the procedure interesting, some even helpful. P4 said 'I guess it's easier to learn something when you actually say it out loud.' Indeed, a few participants said that they would consider verbalizing their thoughts when working at home (e.g., P6). The participants also liked the way the explanatory text 'spelled things out' (P6) for them:

Example 12: P6 talks about his learning in the interview

> (12) Ok, let's see. I learnt that there were four types of pronominal verbs, which I did not know before. I was actually pretty confused by that before. And, yes, I guess I just learnt the difference between the active and the passive voice, like I knew, I kinda knew that some difference existed between two types of phrases but I didn't really know how to give that a name or like point it out so clearly, so, that's what I learnt. (P6, turn 15)

Pedagogical implications

Unlike the Negueruela (2003) study where data were collected over a 16-week period, our study involved only two data collection sessions in two consecutive weeks. On the assumption that it will take some time before curricula are designed so that an entire syllabus is organized around language concepts, it is useful to speculate about what smaller-scale interventions might be implemented to move learners along in their development of grammatical concepts.

Negueruela (2003) suggests that the concept is the appropriate unit of instruction, adding that:

> the complex task of finding good explanations of grammar ... is not enough to promote L2 development. One also needs to materialize these concepts through appropriate didactic models that offer learners a complete orientation to the learning task. (p. 216)

The development of our explanation of the grammatical concept of voice in French was a lengthy, iterative process; the piloting of the material was essential. Our experience suggests that it will take time to develop descriptions of the many concepts that are needed as learners engaged in meaningful activities meet linguistic problems they need to solve.

We have seen the dramatic impact of verbalization in some of the examples reviewed in this chapter. A further example comes from P6 (Interview, turn 22) who explains: 'it's nice to talk about it in English, actually. Like, I think I can understand a lot better if we're starting off in my native tongue. It, it was ok, talking aloud, sure.' These examples suggest that encouraging languaging in the postsecondary second/foreign language classroom is productive and may lead to the internalization of important concepts. Providing students with explanatory texts such as the one we developed for this study and with opportunities to self-explain and explain to peers during class time (or outside of class time, as Negueruela did) may result in enhanced learning. Our pilot participants seemed to value the list of examples they were given along with the explanatory text; 'talking through' such examples in small groups and with the explanatory text and charts close at hand, is a source of learning.

In our study, the research assistant interacting with each participant was asked not to help him or her by providing answers to questions or feedback on the learners' verbalizations (except in the case of prompts). In the classroom, of course, the instructor can circulate and keep track of misperceptions or misunderstandings on the part of the students and provide targeted feedback in the ZPD where indicated.

Acknowledgments

This research was made possible by a grant to Merrill Swain and Sharon Lapkin from the Social Sciences and Humanities Research Council of Canada (#410-04-2099). We are grateful to members of our research team who assisted in developing materials, collecting data and transcribing: Lindsay Brooks, Julie Byrd Clark, Catherine Gaughan, Wataru Suzuki. We wish to thank Birgit Harley, Rena Helms-Park, Jim Lantolf, Jeffrey Steele and Paul Toth for input to the explanation of the grammatical concept of voice in French that we developed for this study and Eduardo Negueruela for consulting with us at an early stage of the project. The editors of this volume also provided valuable feedback.

Notes

1. This research was made possible by a grant to Merrill Swain and Sharon Lapkin from the Social Sciences and Humanities Research Council of Canada

(#410-04-2099). We are grateful to members of our research team who assisted in developing materials, collecting data, and transcribing: Lindsay Brooks, Julie Byrd Clark, Catherine Gaughan, Wataru Suzuki. We wish to thank Birgit Harley, Rena Helms-Park, Jim Lantolf, Jeffrey Steele and Paul Toth for input to the explanation of the grammatical concept of voice in French that we developed for this study, and Eduardo Negueruela for consulting with us at an early stage of the project. The editors of this volume also provided valuable feedback.

2. Appendix 8.2 presents the final version of the explanatory text. In some places, it differs from versions tried out during the pilot test because of confusions we observed among our pilot students, or because of suggestions made by those we consulted.

3. See Toth (2000) for a coherent account of 'anticausative' clitics in Spanish, a language in which *se* is also used to form pronominal verbs with reflexive, passive, intrinsic and middle-voice readings.

4. The larger context suggests that P6 was thinking of direct/indirect speech.

5. Literal translation: It [reflexive form] seems new. [...] The window [reflexive form] faces a small garden. Written in standard French, this example could read: *Elle semble nouvelle* [.] *La fenêtre donne sur un petit jardin.* The participant appears to have overgeneralized the pronominal form of the verb to *sembler*, a verb that does not exist in the pronominal form. In the case of *se face*, the participant has created a verb, perhaps calqued on English 'faces on to'.

References

Aljaafreh, A. and Lantolf, J. P. (1994) Negative feedback as regulation and second language learning in the zone of proximal development. *The Modern Language Journal* 78: 465–83.

Chi, M. T. H. (2000) Self-explaining expository texts: The dual processes of generating inferences and repairing mental models. In R. Glaser (ed.) *Advances in Instructional Psychology* 161–238. Mahwah, NJ: Lawrence Erlbaum.

Chi, M. T. H., De Leeuw, N., Chiu, M. and LaVancher, C. (1994) Eliciting self-explanations improves understanding. *Cognitive Science* 18: 439–77.

Chi, M. T. H., Siler, S. A., Jeong, H., Yamauchi, T. and Hausman, R. G. (2001) Learning from human tutoring. *Cognitive Science* 25: 471–533.

Chomsky, N. (1965) *Aspects of the Theory of Syntax.* Cambridge, MA: MIT Press.

Compain, J., Courchêne, B., Knoerr, H. and Weinberg, A. (1998) *Points de Rencontre.* Scarborough, ON: Prentice Hall.

Connors, K. and Ouellette, B. (1996) Describing the meanings of French pronominal-verbal constructions for students of French translation. *Language Sciences* 18: 213–26.

Darbelnet, J. (1969) *Pensée et Structure.* New York: Scribner's Sons.

Gal'perin, P. Ya. (1966) On the notion of internalization. *A Handbook of Soviet Psychology* 4: 28–33.

Hawkins, R. and Towell, R. (1996) *French Grammar and Usage.* London: Arnold.

Jarausch, H. and Tufts, C. (2006) *Sur le vif. Niveau Intermédiaire* (4th Edn). Southbank, Australia: Thomson Heinle.

Lantolf, J. P. (2003) Intrapersonal communication and internalization in the second language classroom. In A. Kozulin, B.Gindis, V. S. Ageyeu and S. M. Miller (eds) *Vygotsky's Educational Theory in Cultural Context* 349–70. Cambridge: Cambridge University Press.

L'Huillier, M. (1999) *Advanced French Grammar.* Cambridge: Cambridge University Press.

Negueruela, E. (2003) Systemic-theoretical Instruction and L2 Development: A Sociocultural Approach to Teaching-learning and Researching L2 Learning. Unpublished doctoral dissertation, Pennsylvania State University. University Park, PA.

Negueruela, E. and Lantolf, J. P. (2006) Concept-based instruction and the acquisition of L2 Spanish. In R. Salaberry and R. Lafford (eds) *Spanish Second Language Acquisition: From Research to Application* 79–102. Washington, DC: Georgetown University Press.

Odlin, T. (ed.) (1994) *Perspectives on Pedagogical Grammar.* New York: Cambridge University Press.

Ruwet, N. (1972) *Théorie Syntactique et Syntaxe du Français.* Paris: Editions du Seuil.

Swain, M. (1995) Three functions of output in second language learning. In G. Cook and B. Seidlhofer (eds) *Principle and Practice in Applied Linguistics: Studies in Honour of H. G. Widdowson* 125–44. Oxford: Oxford University Press.

Swain, M. (2000) The output hypothesis and beyond: Mediating acquisition through collaborative dialogue. In J. P. Lantolf (ed.) *Sociocultural Theory and Second Language Learning* 97–114 Oxford: Oxford University Press.

Swain, M. (2006) Languaging, agency and collaboration in advanced second language learning. In H. Byrnes (ed.) *Advanced Language Learning: The Contributions of Halliday and Vygotsky* 95–108. London: Continuum.

Swain, M., Lapkin, S., Knouzi, I., Suzuki, W. and Brooks, L. (submitted) Languaging: university students learn the grammatical concept of voice in French. Toronto: OISE/UT Modern Language Centre.

Toth, P. (2000) The interaction of instruction and learner-internal factors in the acquisition of L2 morphosyntax. *Studies in Second Language Acquisition* 22: 169–208.

Valisner, J. (2001) Process structure of semiotic mediation in human development. *Human Development* 44: 84–97.

Vygotsky, L. S. (1978) *Mind in Society: The Development of Higher Mental Processes.* Cambridge, MA: Harvard University Press.

Vygotsky, L.S. (1986) *Thought and Language.* Cambridge, MA: MIT Press.

Appendix 8.1. Script for the first data collection session

1- Sign forms
- Ask participant to read and sign the consent form (2 copies, one for him/her to keep)
- Ask him/her to fill out a form to get information necessary to pay him/her.

2- Introduction
Thanks for agreeing to participate in this pilot study. Today we're going to ask you to do three things. We will start with a practice or warm-up exercise, then we will focus on the main text and we will finish with a short interview.

3- Warm-up
    a- We will now do a practice exercise just to get familiar with the research procedure. In this text, you will see certain grammatical features highlighted in the text. Take a few minutes to read the text, then go back to the highlighted/bolded features and, one by one, please explain out loud what these features mean and why they are used (why they take the form they do).

    b- Now I'm giving you a text that explains articles in French. Please read this text aloud. Stop at the end of each 'card' and say aloud what your understanding of the sentence(s) on the card is.

4- Sophie Mercier text
Ok, thanks. Now we will move to a text describing the experience of a young woman named Sophie Mercier. You have seen this text before, in your FR161 textbook.

Again, you will notice that certain verb forms in the text are highlighted/bolded. Please take some time (as long as you wish) to read through the text. Then go back to the bolded verbs and one by one, please explain out loud what they mean and what grammatical form they take.

5- Define concept of voice
Now, can you please define the concept of voice in French.
(If participant does not understand what we mean by 'concept of voice' or refers to 'sounds,' tone, pronunciation, give him/her the five key terms: active/passive/middle/agent/patient)

6- Explanation cards
Now I'm giving you a text that explains the active, passive and middle voices in French. Please read this text aloud. Stop at the end of each

card and say aloud what your understanding of the sentence(s) in the card is.
[Research assistant 'pushed' to elaborate after card 5, 11, 14 and 24. See APPENDIX 8.2]

10-15 minutes break

7- Sophie Mercier text
Now, I'm going to give you the initial Sophie Mercier passage again. Would you please look especially at the bolded verb forms and describe to me what they mean and what form is being used to express the active, passive or middle voice.

8- Define metalinguistic terms
Can you please define the following terms: *agent, patient, active voice, passive voice, middle voice.*

9- Interview
Finally we'd like to conduct a short interview with you to just ask you some questions about how you found this whole process

Appendix 8.2. Teaching the concept of voice in French

Note: Each 'chunk' is numbered in bold so that the reader will know what appeared on each card. The script for this session was: Now I am giving you a text that explains the active, passive and middle voices in French. Please read this text aloud. Stop at the end of each card and say aloud what your understanding of the sentence(s) on the card is.

> The following activity is designed to teach you something about the concept of voice in French. There is research to suggest that explaining grammatical concepts rather than focusing on 'rules of thumb' leads to a deeper understanding of the grammar of the second language. This process is more effective when learners get a chance to 'think aloud' about the concept. So the attached sheets present information about the concept of voice in 'chunks', allowing you time to think about each piece of information and explain it out loud.

1 Most sentences in French consist of a subject, a verb and an object; these are grammatical categories. **2** The subject and object also have semantic roles (i.e., they contribute to the meaning of the sentence). **3** So in (1) below, *le joueur de baseball* is the grammatical subject of the sentence and its semantic role is that of agent, the 'doer' of the action.

4 The noun *la balle* is the grammatical object; its semantic role is that of patient, the 'undergoer' of the action of throwing.

5 In French, most of the sentences we write or the utterances we speak are in the active voice, like examples (1) and (2).

1. *Le joueur de baseball lance la balle.*
2. *Le chat a mangé toutes les souris.*[1]

6 In the case of sentences like (1) and (2), there is an agent (the 'doer' of the action) that serves as the grammatical subject, a verb and a 'patient' that is the grammatical object. **7** The initial noun or noun phrase is the subject; the main verb follows; and the patient (the 'undergoer' of the action) is the grammatical object.

8 Using the passive voice enables us to put the emphasis on the patient, in order to focus on it, as illustrated in diagram A:

9 Another way of explaining sentences like (3) is that the passive allows the direct object, i.e., the patient (toutes les souris), to occupy the subject position; the subject (le chat) appears optionally in the agent phrase (par + agent). **10** That is, in (3) the phrase par le chat could have been omitted. **11** In other words, the passive voice does not require the

Diagram A (see sentence 2 above):

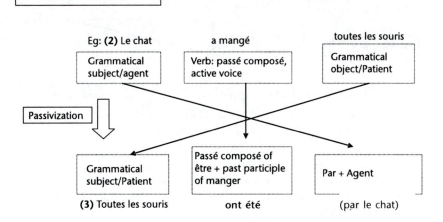

1 The first prompt is inserted here:

* *Can you tell me about sentence (2) in terms of semantic roles?*

If participant does not understand the question, or gives a brief (or wrong) answer, prompt further.

* *Can you tell me about sentence (2) in terms of object, subject, agent, patient?*

agent to be mentioned: in (4) we assume that members of parliament voted in a particular law; but the agent is not specified.[2]

12 In (5), the person who stole the bicycle is unknown and therefore not specified.

4.   *La loi a été votée.*

5.   *Sa bicyclette a été volée (on ne sait pas par qui).*

13 We obtain the passive by moving the object (patient) to the subject position and inserting the auxiliary être. **14** The auxiliary takes the tense of the main verb of the active sentence, followed by the past participle of that verb.[3]

15 Another way of expressing a passive-like meaning without using the type of structure illustrated in diagram A is through what is known as the middle voice. **16** Even though the agent is not expressed, we understand that an agent is the doer of the action. **17** In the middle voice, we do not insert the auxiliary être, but the meaning is passive-like. **18** Sentence 6 below is in the active voice; sentence 7 has a passive meaning, expressed in the middle voice, using a pronominal verb.

6.   *Les filles portent des jupes courtes (cette année).*

7.   *Les jupes se portent courtes cette année.*

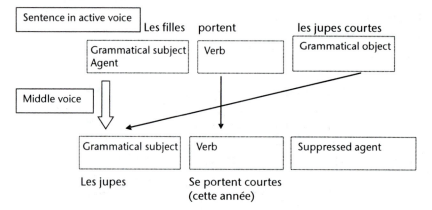

2 The second prompt occurs at this point:
* *Can you tell me about sentence (5) in terms of semantic roles ?*
If participant does not understand the question, or gives a brief (or wrong) answer, prompt further.
* *Can you tell me about sentence (5) in terms of object, subject, agent, patient ?*
3 The third prompt is inserted here:
* *Can you change sentence (1) into the passive voice?*
If participant does not understand the question, or gives a brief (or wrong) answer, prompt further.
* *You can refer back to diagram A (p. 253) if you want ?*

19 In middle-voice sentence (7), the pronominal verb *se porter* would be translated into English as 'are worn': Skirts are worn short this year. **20** Again, the agent is not expressed. **21** Rather, the grammatical object (the patient) *'les jupes'* is highlighted or emphasized and becomes the subject. **22** This is illustrated in Diagram B.

23 Consider examples (8) and (9).

8. *On mange le saumon froid.*
9. *Le saumon se mange froid.*

24 Sentence (8) is in the active voice; sentence (9) is in the middle voice, which gives the sentence a passive-like meaning.[4]

25 For (9), English uses the passive: Salmon is eaten cold. **26** Some grammars refer to this as the agent-less passive. **27** French prefers the middle voice in sentences like (9).

28 Sentence (10) may be seen as a passive counterpart of active voice sentences (11) and (12). **29** In the case of passive AND middle voice sentences, it is important to remember that they allow us to place emphasis on the element of the sentence that we want to highlight by putting it in the subject position.

10. *Les tomates se sont bien vendues cette année.* [Tomatoes sold well this year.]
11. *La vente de tomates a été bonne cette année.*
12. *On a bien vendu les tomates cette année.*

30 It is important to note that not all pronominal verbs in French are used in middle voice sentences. **31** There are four main types of pronominal verbs. **32** One is the type we have been discussing, those used to form sentences in the middle voice. **33** Here are the three others:

34 (a) reflexive pronominal verbs such as *s'habiller* ('to dress oneself' or 'to get dressed'), *se laver, se peigner*. Example: *Je me lave les mains.*

35 (b) reciprocal pronominal verbs such as *se rencontrer* ('to meet each other' or simply 'to meet'), *se parler*. Example: *Nous nous parlons chaque soir.*

36 (c) inherently or intrinsically pronominal verbs that never appear without the pronoun *se*, for example *s'évanouir, se souvenir*. Example: *Il se souvient fréquemment de son premier voyage à Paris.*

---

4 The fourth prompt occurs here:
*Please explain sentence (9)
If participant does not understand the question, or gives a brief (or wrong) answer, prompt further.
* Is there an agent, patient in sentence (9)? What is it?

9 Mediation as objectification in the development of professional academic discourse: a corpus-informed curricular innovation

Steven L. Thorne, Jonathon Reinhardt and Paula Golombek

Introduction

Gaining the ability to appropriately and successfully communicate in professional work contexts presents challenges for native/expert speakers as well as for second language (L2) learners at all levels. Nuances characterizing professional discourse contexts and competencies have been detailed in a number of settings, including specific activity types such as genetic counseling (Sarangi 2000), physicians' opening questions as they affect patients' presentations of medical problems (Heritage and Robinson 2006) and attempts to create collaboratively forged care solutions between physicians, medical administrators and patients (Engeström, Engeström, and Kerosuo 2003). Broader analyses of discourse have addressed professional talk in institutional workplaces (e.g., Drew and Heritage, 1992), language use across work, family and social situations (e.g., Cameron 2000) and intercultural pragmatics research describing interactions between native and non-native speakers of English in counseling, advising and writing center contexts (Bardovi-Harlig and Hartford 1990, 1993, 2005; Thonus 1999; He 1993; Williams 2005)

Drawing from descriptive, developmental and praxiological traditions, this chapter addresses language use in the arena of higher education. Specifically, we present a corpus-informed assessment of professional academic discourse practices that forms the foundation for a Vygotsky-inspired curricular innovation to an International Teaching Assistants' (ITA) English language preparation course at a major research university. While there is a significant body of corpus-informed assessments of written learner English (Granger 2002; Flowerdew 2002), much less researched are the interactional and pragmalinguistic demands associated with American spoken academic discourse genres. It is no wonder that ITAs, as well as native/expert[1] speakers new to university level teaching, experience difficulty negotiating the many spoken genres that comprise instructional activity. A non-comprehensive list of expected discourse competencies common to ITA duties include lecturing, leading discussion and/or lab sections, advising, holding office hours consultations and providing tutorials and exam preparation sessions. In addition, ITAs face a complex of fluid and overlapping social and professional roles including those of instructor, disciplinarian, tutor, advisor, fellow student, confidante, researcher, adjudicator and acting as the mediator between the lead professor and/or department and the course section students he or she is responsible for.

Based on learner corpus analysis (see Granger 1998, 2002) of ITA language use, we have identified several high frequency features of professional academic discourse that are problematic for many ITAs. In response, we have developed pedagogical resources that highlight genre awareness and that include conceptual-theoretical materializations of language use associated with teaching and interpersonal interaction with students. We have based the content of these materializations on data from a corpus of expert and native speaker academic language use and have structured them according to Vygotskian pedagogical principles (e.g., Arievitch and Stetsenko 2000; Negueruela 2003; Lantolf and Thorne 2006; Vygotsky 1997), specifically the use of explicit and conceptually framed objectifications of the units of language that expert speakers utilize to achieve particular social actions in high frequency academic contexts. In this sense, the project is structured as a mediated corpus-informed approach to advanced ESL pedagogy, but one that qualitatively differs from earlier inductive methods of data-driven learning (see Johns 1991; Seidlhofer 2002; Chambers 2005). Our method, described at length below, attempts to dialectically unite development and instruction by focusing on high-level conceptual aspects of grammar while concomitantly fostering conditions for communicative practice. For each of these interrelated enterprises, we rely upon corpus data that represent actual language use in the precise academic contexts that comprise the focal themes of the ITA training course.

Description of the political origins of the 'ITA problem' and *ITAcorp* project

Since 1990, over 20 US state legislatures, responding to student and parent complaints, have mandated that post-secondary institutions develop policy to certify oral English language proficiency of ITAs. The so-called 'ITA problem,' despite widespread implementation of systematic language proficiency assessments and language courses, persists in public debate (see North Dakota bill HB1364 from 2005) and in research on speaker intelligibility and ITA effectiveness. Complaints concerning ITAs have been characterized as linguistic, cultural and pedagogical (Jacobs and Friedman 1988). The common undergraduate refrain is that ITAs speak 'not a lick of English' (Fitch and Morgan 2003). Undergraduates evaluate ITAs as distant, due to their inability to exploit American English tonal structure for referential and pragmatic functions (Pickering 2001) and have also highlighted extralinguistic factors such as delivery and non-verbals (Orth 1982) and teaching styles (Bailey 1984) as limitations to ITA effectiveness.

The institutional solution to the purported 'ITA problem' has included university preparation courses and the production of a variety of pedagogical texts. A cursory review of textbooks used in ITA preparation classrooms demonstrates a focus on cultural awareness and teaching skills (Byrd, Constantinides and Pennington 1989; Pica, Barnes and Finger 1990; Smith, Meyers and Burkhalter 1992). These texts in particular somewhat reductively emphasize pronunciation segmentals and suprasegmentals as the primary focus in developing ITA communication abilities. Furthermore, they present a prescriptivist version of grammar and vocabulary that generally does not draw from or adequately represent actual language use (e.g., corpus approaches to spoken language, see McCarthy 1998). It is our belief that the characterization of ITAs as a 'problem' and the orientation of attendant pedagogical materials are themselves problematic on a number of levels. For example, in a world of growing diaspora populations and wide dispersion of world Englishes (e.g., Canagarajah, 2007a, 2007b), the reaction of North American students, parents and legislatures can, in many instances, be typified as xenophobic. However, it is also the case that ITAs play a vital role in university education, with 50 percent of graduate students in engineering being foreign born and 41 percent in math and the physical sciences (Finder 2005). Additionally, ITAs' professional development and future job prospects will hinge, in part, on their capacity to fully participate in spoken genres of communication comprising everyday teaching activity. Thus there is a compelling need to develop innovative pedagogical approaches specifically designed to enhance discourse awareness and to expand communicative repertoires that would enable ITAs, as well as expert speakers of English who are inexperienced teachers, to satisfactorily and satisfyingly perform complex professional roles and functions within higher education.

Our current project, *ITAcorp*, responds to this need by coupling contrastive corpus analysis research – ITA language use contrasted with a genre-comparable benchmark corpus of spoken academic English – with pedagogical innovation in the domain of academic discourse competence. We should like to make clear at the outset that we are aware of past problems associated with contrastive and comparative approaches to language pedagogy and to challenges to the construct of the 'native speaker' as the most appropriate and useful benchmark for second and foreign language learners (e.g., Kramsch 1997; Rampton 1990; Train 2003). Our project is critically framed in that the contrastive analyses are not meant to suggest deficiency on the part of ITAs nor valorization of 'expert' language use – rather within a framework of grammar as choice (e.g., Larsen-Freeman 2003) and language use as a form of social action (Heritage 1984; Thorne and Lantolf 2007; Wittgenstein 1958), we emphasize critical language awareness and the making visible of linguistic resources that may augment ITAs' professional communication repertoires.

Description of the ITA preparation course and language corpora informing the project

The *ITAcorp* project,[2] initiated in the Fall of 2005, involves the building of a corpus of advanced ESL use in role-play situations[3] designed to mirror university instructional contexts. The corpus is comprised of the language production of advanced ESL learners in ITA language and skills development classes as they engage in a number of classroom and computer-mediated activities that include office hour role plays, brief lecture/concept presentations and discussion leading role plays. The course (our intervention focuses on only one course within the series) emphasizes oral skills development, especially in the genres of advising and lecturing, for international graduate students who either advanced from an earlier ITA preparation course or received a score between 230 and 250 on our university's international student proficiency test, which, following legislative mandate, all non-American graduate students at our university must pass in order to become teaching assistants. To meet course goals and prepare participants for the post-evaluation exam, the course activities include a face-to-face office hours role play and two lecturette presentations in front of the class, all three of which are recorded onto mini DVD-R disks for purposes of transcription.[4] Currently, the corpus includes nearly 300,000 tokens produced by approximately 115 ITA preparation course participants.

The Michigan Corpus of Academic Spoken English (MICASE) (Simpson, Briggs, Ovens and Swales 2002) was utilized as baseline data for comparison with the learner data.[5] MICASE is comprised of the transcriptions of 152 academic speech events from a variety of types,[6] e.g. advising, colloquia, discussion sections, lectures, office hours and tutorials. Speech events of a particular type, for example the focus of our initial efforts reported here – office hours interactions – can be analyzed as a discrete subcorpus, allowing us to contrastively study ITA and expert speaker language use in functionally similar contexts. The speech events represent a balance of university academic disciplines and total approximately 1,695,540 tokens produced by 1,571 individuals. According to the MICASE website (2006), corpus development began in 1997 and was completed in 2002. The purpose of the MICASE corpus is fourfold: 1) to fill a gap in available corpus resources, since no spoken academic corpus has existed previously; 2) to develop descriptions of language features that may diverge from current explanations of grammar and vocabulary, since those explanations may have been based on intuition and written language; 3) to analyze development of academic speech patterns over time; and 4) to allow for the development of more appropriate, corpus-informed ESL and EAP materials than are currently available. Participants include 160 faculty, 257 graduate students and 782 undergraduates and each is identified with the metadata categories of rank (senior faculty, graduate student, undergraduate student, etc.), age-group, gender and native-speaker status (native, near-native and non-native). MICASE can be accessed through its web interface, which allows searching for words or phrases and co-text with any combination of metadata parameters.

MICASE was chosen for the current project because of the overall genre compatibility and the similarity between its subcorpora and those being developed in *ITAcorp*. These subcorpora serve as the baseline data for the comparative analyses, as well as the source of the transcripts of actual language use that are part of the pedagogical materials forming the intervention.

Our corpus-informed intervention, which was motivated in part by the work of Reinhardt (2007), focuses on the grammatical constructions associated with the use of directive modality by expert speakers represented in MICASE. Using contrastive corpus analysis (described in detail below), ITAcorp and MICASE together provide resources for the design, implementation and evaluation of a corpus-informed curriculum of advanced ESL grammar within the context of an ITA professional development course.

Theoretical frameworks

A number of research, pedagogical and developmental theories have informed our work. These are introduced below and then briefly revisited in juxtaposition to the discussion of the pedagogical materializations.

Vygotskian developmental theory and Gal'perin's pedagogical approach

In many of his writings, Vygotsky showed commitment to what in his professional lifetime (primarily the 1920s and early 1930s) was the nascent mass intervention of public education, an enterprise he hoped would provide a cognitively and socially progressive function in society (see Prawat, 2000). Key elements of formal education include mediating tools such as literacy and numeracy and more concretely, texts, notation systems for math, music and design and a wide array of schematizations such as diagrams, figures, tables, annotated renderings and the like. Due in part to his truncated professional life (he died at the age of 38), Vygotsky was limited in his opportunity to experiment with pedagogical innovation. However, pedagogical extensions of his work have been elaborated by others within the cultural-historical tradition, one of the more prominent of whom was Piotr Gal'perin. Arievitch and Haenen (2005: 155) describe Gal'perin as focusing on three areas in his work: 1) the relationship of teaching and learning to development; 2) the use of concept-based materializations to foster efficient and specific lines of cognitive development; and 3) the overall importance of cultural tools and participation in culturally organized practices in development. Learning in well-structured educational contexts involves engagement with concepts, content and processes that are in advance of participants' current abilities yet within their zone of proximal development. Note that Gal'perin, like Vygotsky, does not equate learning with development. Rather, learning precedes and shapes what can be described as the staging ground for development.

At the heart of cultural-historical approaches to development is the notion that higher order mental functions are creatively transformed and internalized forms of initially inter-mental and socially enacted collective systems of activity. Called the 'genetic law of cultural development' (Vygotsky 1978: 57), the principle idea, as stated by Vygotsky, is that 'social relations or relations among people genetically underlie all higher functions and their relationships' (Vygotsky 1981: 163). In this sense, internalization describes the developmental process whereby humans gain the capacity to perform complex cognitive and physical-motor functions with progressively decreasing reliance on overt social assistance, or mediation. In modern societies, specially engineered institutions have emerged to organize, facilitate and also to normalize the progressive mastery of content knowledge and problem solving, the primary example of which is compulsory education.

Within Gal'perin's approach, pedagogical materials are conceived of as cognitive-cultural tools and great emphasis is placed on their quality and the responsibility of educators to procedurally implement them in specific fashion. Arievitch and Stetsenko (2000: 71) note that many developmental researchers, both within and outside of the cultural-historical school, have emphasized 'the forms and specifics of shared activity but not ... how what is taught ... affects development.' This is precisely the issue that Gal'perin addressed in his pedagogical research. In particular, Gal'perin emphasized the importance of orienting students to the rationality and systemic structuring of complex domains of knowledge and/or action, what has been translated as providing the 'orienting basis' (similar to planning or anticipatory preparation for action) which necessarily precedes guided exploration and practice (Arievitch and Stetsenko 2000: 86). Gal'perin's model of human action proposes that without a proper orienting basis, learners are not able to plan their participation in pedagogical activities and thus their contributions to such activities as well as resultant development are not optimized and occur instead on a hit-or-miss basis. Examples of the consequences of this would include the partial or simply inaccurate understandings of the conceptual structure of domains of human practice (see, for example, Negueruela's (2003) analysis of incomplete conceptual understanding of verbal aspect among learners of L2 Spanish).

In our efforts to combine corpus data, contrastive corpus analyses and principles of language awareness (discussion of each below) with sociocultural theory, we draw upon select elements of Gal'perin's model of systemic-theoretical instruction[7] to produce a three-stage process. Synoptically described, these are:

> Phase 1: Orienting Basis – Building upon an overview of genre theory and language as discourse, specific lexical-grammatical realizations are presented within functional contexts of use.

> Phase 2: Use of high-level conceptual materializations – Awareness that discrete choices in language use correlate to differing social actions (directness, politeness, enhancing or restricting student agency).

> Phase 3: Individual and group verbalization activities to foster internalization of an expanded repertoire of linguistic resources associated with academic professional discourse in classroom contexts.

To describe these in more detail, phase one begins at the start of the ITA preparation course when we introduce the students to the framework of genre theory. As Hanks describes them, 'genres can be defined as the historically specific conventions and ideals according to which authors compose discourse and audiences receive it' (Hanks 1999: 135). As our project is corpus-informed, we emphasize the most commonly used lexico-grammatical formulations that are associated with specific communicative purposes within instructional discourse.[8] In regard to interaction with undergraduate students, we use the notion of genre to heighten awareness of instructional language use in the areas of style and register. We also emphasize that classroom discourse practices can be immensely diverse, but equally, that language use in formal educational contexts is often predictable, recurrent and systematic. In other words, for ITAs, the message of hope is that professional academic discourse associated with teaching situations is learnable. This phase builds from Gal'perin's emphasis on orienting students through a systematic and conceptual treatment of the subject to be studied (Haenen 2000).

The second phase is based on materializing the higher-level conceptual frameworks of genre and emphasizing the importance of the fact that discrete choices in language use correlate with constructing differing levels of directness, politeness and opportunities for agency on the part of students being addressed. Gal'perin proposed that interaction with external, object-related materializations provide an efficient method for promoting internalization within educational contexts. As described by Arievitch and van der Veer (1995: 124), Gal'perin's non-dualistic view of the formation of the 'internal plane of action', or internalization, implies 'the transformation of certain forms of human external activity (with certain possibilities for the individual) into other forms (with other possibilities) [that] reflect a new level of flexibility in performing certain actions.' For our project, the materializations take the form of interrelated sets of flow charts inspired by a Gal'perin-based research and pedagogical project on the teaching of aspect in a Spanish foreign language course by Negueruela (2003) using a procedure he called 'Schema for Complete Orienting Basis of Action,' or SCOBA. The materializations we describe in this chapter focus on directive language use in the context of holding office hours.

The third and final Gal'perin-informed implementation phase, still to be fully realized in our project, includes a series of individual as well as small group verbalization activities meant to assist in the internalization of the linguistic choices schematically represented in the materializations. It is important to note that in his work, Gal'perin stressed only the private speech function of verbalization as it related to internalization. We are interested in exploring the potential of both private speech through individual rehearsal as well as social speech through small group discussions of the materializations. For the latter, the rationale is that discussion with others may provoke opportunities for metacognitive problem solving and language awareness that align with what Swain and colleagues have described as 'collaborative dialogue' (e.g., Swain 2000; Swain and Lapkin 2001; Swain, Brooks and Tocalli-Beller 2002). In addition to the reported benefits of peer assistance within the ZPD (Donato 1994; see Lantolf and Thorne 2006, for discussion), collaborative dialog sparked by the materializations may, to paraphrase Swain, create conditions whereby the students' performance will outstrip their competence (2000: 113). This scenario is a concrete example of the interactive process of learning (through 'collaborative dialogue') leading development, with development defined as progressive internalization of linguistic repertoires that over time enhance self-regulation in the area of purposeful choices of directive language use.

In the sections to follow, we detail additional components of our pedagogical framework that synergistically unite Vygotskian developmental theory with principles of language awareness and contrastive corpus analysis.

Language as discourse and language awareness

Carter (1998: 52) explains that language awareness is about 'understanding of tendencies, variable rules and choices according to context
and interpersonal relations.' Language awareness has its roots in the
UK in the 1970s as part of a movement to introduce knowledge about
language across the curriculum in response to a fall in literacy rates.
Concurrent with this movement, in the US the Chomsky-inspired mentalist models (1965) and Krashen's Monitor Model (1982) were growing
in popularity, both of which downplayed the role of higher cognitive
functions in acquisition. This, along with misinterpretations within communicative language teaching principles that grammar did not need to
be taught explicitly, may account for why language awareness did not
establish itself among US L2 researchers and educators.

Crucial to discourse awareness is an understanding of spoken genres,
which have core yet negotiated structures and are highly contingent on
participant goals and relationships (McCarthy 1998: 47). A view of language as discourse 'focuses, where appropriate, on complete spoken
and written texts and on the social and cultural contexts in which such
language operates' (McCarthy and Carter 1994: 1). Translated into a
pedagogical approach, this involves raising learner awareness of grammatical and lexical choices available to realize different meanings at
textual, interpersonal and ideological levels. Within this composite
systemic-theoretical instruction and language awareness framework,
learners are provided with conceptual schemata and attendant exege-
sis, extended excerpts of actual language use and are guided in their
exploration of the relationships between features of spoken discourse,
the social contexts in which they function (genre) and the social realities specific language choices will tend to instantiate. McCarthy and
Carter (1994) offer several principles that aim to develop awareness of
language-as-discourse. These include the contrastive principle, which
focuses on differences within comparable text types and/or language
used to achieve particular social actions; the continuum principle, involving exposure to a variety of texts in the same genre but produced
by different authors; and the inferencing principle which teaches strategies for cultural and literary understanding, or interpretative skills.

Because of their focus on consciousness-raising and making explicit
knowledge about interactive language use, language awareness principles are highly congruent to our use of corpus- and Gal'perin-informed
materials development. Also crucial to remaking the ITA course curriculum is to acknowledge and explicitly differentiate spoken academic

communication from its written counterpart at the level of concrete grammatical realizations (McCarthy 1998). This has been particularly important in the pragmatically sensitive areas of deontics and directives, the focal point of our efforts reported here.

Research on contrastive learner corpus analysis and pedagogical mediation

A pioneer in corpus-driven language pedagogy, Johns (1991; 1994) describes a pedagogical application of concordance analysis he termed 'data-driven learning' (DDL), where the language learner is 'essentially a research worker whose learning needs to be driven by access to linguistic data' (1994: 2). In a DDL approach, learners examine concordances of data from expert speakers to discover language facts and rules inductively, developing metalinguistic awareness based on evidence from authentic language use (Johns 1994: 3). As we discuss later, our approach differs from DDL in that we are using corpora as the empirical foundation for the materializations, but our focus is to highlight concepts structuring grammatical choice in relation to semantic and pragmatic function. In this sense, we present a theoretically mediated corpus informed approach that does not preclude learner exploration of corpus data, but that foregrounds the importance of conceptual understanding of the kind argued by Vygotsky and Gal'perin.

More recent corpus-informed pedagogy has had learners compare corpus data from expert speakers with that from learners, including their own production (what Seidlhofer (2002) terms 'learner-driven data'). Learner corpus analysis has been applied in combination with a variety of theoretical frameworks, including genre theory (Upton and Connor 2001), cognitive linguistics (Waara 2004), Relevance Theory (Hasselgren 2002), developmental sequence theory (Housen 2002), systemic-functional appraisal theory (Flowerdew 2003) and sociocultural theory (Belz 2004). Meunier (2002) notes the benefits of exposing learners to both expert and learner corpora and corpora-based materials, including the opportunity to notice the differences between their own and expert production and to negotiate and interact with other students, teachers and experts during the learning process. Recent corpus-based studies have demonstrated how learners were able to develop awareness of the pragmatic consequences of their own usage (Belz and Vyatkina 2005) and to experience 'technology-enhanced rhetorical consciousness raising' (Lee and Swales 2006: 72). For research involving linguistic description and lexicography, large corpora are preferred. However, Flowerdew (2005: 329) argues that small corpora are useful for pedagogic purposes, explaining that 'the more the corpus draws on features from the students' own socio-cultural environment, the easier it should be for the teacher to act as a kind of mediating specialist informant of the raw corpus data, thereby authenticating the data for classroom use to fit the students' reality' (see also Thorne and Reinhardt, in press). Emphasizing this point, Braun (2005) has argued, and we agree, that substantial 'pedagogic mediation' is required for teachers and learners to overcome the potential shortcomings of corpora.

As briefly described above, the project addresses the criticism that DDL and concordance-based materials decontextualize language use (Widdowson 2003) by building upon what McCarthy (1998) describes as a 'corpus-informed' approach that emphasizes the careful pedagogical framing of corpus-rendered language data into purposeful and contextualized illustrations of actual communicative activity. The incorporation of Vygotskian principles, specifically the use of explicit and conceptually framed objectifications of the units of language that expert speakers utilize to achieve particular social actions, reconciles corpus-informed pedagogy with the goal of enhancing discourse awareness. Our development of conceptual materializations also addresses Gal'perin's emphasis on efficiency and establishing a systemic 'orienting basis' as necessary elements for generating qualitative shifts to new forms of cognitive, and in this case, communicative functioning (Arievitch and Stetsenko 2000). In this sense, the current project develops a mediated corpus-informed approach to advanced ESL pedagogy that is more theoretically and developmentally informed than both straight corpus-driven materials development and the pedagogical use of corpus as a mere data source facilitating inductive learning.

Processes of intervention: contrastive corpus analysis of directive language use

Before we could know precisely how to begin reforming the ITA training course curriculum and materials, we needed to know how ITA language use differed from expert/native language use in comparable professional activity settings. Fundamental to learner corpus analysis is the comparison of learner data to expert or other learner data, using techniques such as Granger's (1998, 2002) contrastive interlanguage analysis, which combines elements of contrastive and error analysis. In this approach, corpus techniques mostly involving frequency analyses are applied to two corpora sharing a genre and speech event context and the results are compared for relative over- and under-use by the two groups. Our ITA course innovations are built upon such contrastive analyses comparing ITA language use and expert MICASE corpora. The contrastive corpus analyses that inform the focal intervention reported in this chapter are specifically based on aggregative and individual use of directives in office hours contexts, an example of which is excerpted below (drawn from Reinhardt 2007).

In Table 9.1, the Learner Office Hours (LOH, from *ITAcorp*) and Expert Office Hours (EOH, from MICASE) corpora are contrasted with one another in the area of modal and periphrastic modal (or p-modal) constructions. The table empirically demonstrates that learners and experts are using directive language in strikingly different ways. Of particular interest to us are the upper-most and lower-most rows of the table. The upper rows indicate that the LOH corpus shows higher frequencies of two strongly deontic constructions: 1) 'you had better'; and 2) 'you should.' The lower three rows show that the EOH corpus includes high frequencies of three different constructions: 1) 'you could'; 2) 'I would'; and 3) 'you want to.' A number of such contrastive analyses were used to ascertain areas of lexical and construction divergence between the two corpora and to generate the lexico-grammatical and conceptual content of the materializations.

Table 9.1. Learner and expert use of directives during office hours

Modal or p-modal construction	Learner office hours		Expert office hours		log-l LOHvEOH*
	Total	Freq/10K	Total	Freq/10K	
You can (undiff.)	536	52.137	340	27.126	+91.67*
You had better	29	2.918	0	0.000	+46.24*
You should	103	10.019	46	3.670	+35.13*
I want you to	9	0.875	6	0.479	+1.35
You don't need to	17	1.654	16	1.276	+0.14
You have to	55	5.350	87	6.941	−2.32
You need to	41	3.988	76	6.063	−4.84*
You could	9	0.875	59	4.707	−31.87*
I would	1	0.095	38	3.032	−45.52*
You want to (wanna)	12	1.167	173	13.802	−137.51*

Directives defined

Directives can be generally described as speech situations 'where we try to get others to do things' (Searle 1983). Reinhardt (2007) operationalizes such language as 'directive constructions,' which he defines as 'a social-functional device comprised of one or more discrete, lexico-grammatical units which index directive illocutionary force.' In a recent monograph, Biber (2006) describes 'university' language from a largely textual metafunction perspective while our project, in complementary contrast, focuses on directives from the vantage point of the interpersonal metafunction (Halliday and Matthiesen, 2004). Hence while directive constructions may correspond to formulaic sequences (e.g., Schmitt 2004) and lexical bundles (e.g., Biber, Conrad and Cortez 2004), we emphasize the social-functional role of directive constructions rather than their frequency or distribution alone.

As expressed in the choice of directive vocabulary, pronouns and adjuncts (or 'small words') that act as mitigators and intensifiers, Reinhardt found that learners generally made less use of directive constructions illustrating independence strategies (or negative politeness, the understanding that you are imposing on your interlocutor) and involvement strategies (positive politeness, emphasizing reciprocity and a friendly relationship (Brown and Levinson 1987; Scollon and Scollon 1995: 46)) strategies than did experts in comparable office hours situations. Learners preferred constructions that directly appealed to the listener's dependence, e.g. 'you should' and 'you had better' over forms that may indirectly appeal to the listener's involvement, e.g. 'you want to,' 'I would' and 'let's.' Learners made greater use than experts of directive vocabulary constructions that restrict listener choice such as 'students are required' and 'I suggest,' while making less use of directives like 'you could' that index choice and mitigators that appeal to negative politeness. As part of the language awareness intervention, select findings from the ITA and MICASE contrastive corpus analyses were presented to participants in the ITA training course (see Tables 9.1 and 9.4).

Examples of mediated corpus-informed materials development

In this section, we describe the pedagogical materials we have developed illustrating elements of directive language use in the context of office hours consultations. Due to space limitations, we present selective examples that represent the balance of systemic-theoretical materializations, functional explanations of directive constructions with examples, corpus analyses of usage frequencies and activities that draw attention to directive constructions within extended excerpts of expert language use from MICASE.

Table 9.2. MICASE excerpt: anthropology office hours

T: um, okay that's good, okay here you go ... okay this is a very awkward sentence. <LAUGH>

S: yeah it is <SS LAUGH>

T: right. okay, i um ... okay i want you to ... well maybe i should see how you, do this okay. um ... it seems to me like in this paragraph there are lots of totally different things going on. um, and in general you should do this throughout the paper too. you need to go through and ask yourself what the point of each paragraph is, right? um and make sure it has a point, and make sure it says what its point is, okay? um, cuz here we've got, okay. the first sentence which is to me a really important point that you should talk more about, right?

1. Who are the participants? What do you think their relationship is?
2. Where do you think the session could be taking place?
3. What is the teacher (T) trying to get the student (S) to do?
4. What language does the T use to accomplish this?

The materials below are used in the latter half of the semester. Leading up to this point, the ITA participants will have engaged in discussion and activities addressing the concept of genre, been introduced to public and undergraduate perspectives on ITAs through newspaper articles and activities utilizing ratemyprofessor.com and practiced monologic presentation skills (e.g., lectures and explanations) and dialogic situations such as question and answer sessions. The intervention on directive language use specifically addresses office-hours scenarios and begins with an excerpt of an office-hours encounter in an Anthropology course drawn from MICASE (see Table 9.2, above). The purpose of the opening exercise is to expose ITAs to spoken data from an actual office-hours interaction. The excerpt exhibits the messy nature of spoken interaction and focuses on directives used by the teacher (T). Basic questions are then posed that are meant to heighten the learners' awareness of directive language within a context that is relevant to their past experience as students and future careers as teaching assistants and faculty/instructors.

At this point in a true data-driven approach, the learners would be encouraged to analyze the data (although most likely more data samples than this, including concordances) and to hypothesize the function and collocational patterns of the target elements. In contrast, our corpus-informed concept-based instruction approach provides explicit descriptions of directive language use to aid conceptual understanding. The first explanation is titled 'What is a directive?' in which the following bullet points are presented:

- A directive is a phrase or a group of words that we use to tell or suggest to others what we want them to do.

- Directives can be statements and indirect requests.

- The addressee of the directive is usually the listener ('you').

- In educational environments, teachers and advisors usually give directives to students.

Learners are then instructed to identify directives in the first excerpt (Table 9.2) and to reflect on their purpose in office hours contexts. To make visible available linguistic resources, a paradigm of forms is presented according to three primary elements of directive language use: 1) pronoun/subject choice, which is presented in terms of appealing to or restricting a listener's sense of involvement; 2) main directive element, emphasizing choice of grammatical form; and 3) modifier choice, explained as either appealing toward or restricting a listener's sense of agency and independence.

(1) Pronoun /subject
   - neutral
     - **You** should go to the library.
     - I recommend you go to the library.
   - appeal to listener's sense of involvement
     - **We** should go to the library.
     - I would go to the library.
   - restrict listener's sense of involvement
     - **We** recommend you go to the library.
     - **It** is recommended that you go to the library.

(2) The main element, containing the main action
   - simple imperative
     - **Go** to the library.
   - modal or semi-modal
     - You **should go** to the library.
     - You **need to go** to the library.
   - directive vocabulary
     - I **recommend** you **go** to the library.
   - hypothetical situation
     - I **would go** to the library.

(3) Modifier
- appeal to listener's sense of independence (hedge)
  - **I think** you should **maybe** go to the library.
- restrict listener's sense of independence (intensifier)
  - **Wow**, you **definitely** need to go to the library.

This is followed by a discussion of politeness to introduce the learn-ers to the aforementioned concepts of involvement (i.e. rapport, or posi-tive politeness) and independence (i.e. respect, or negative politeness) and to encourage them to draw from their own experience to help rec-ognize both the universality of the concepts and the different ways that they are enacted and linguistically expressed cross-linguistically.

The remaining materials present several activities for each of the three areas, pronoun/subject, main element and modifier. For each, a linear outline of questions focusing on the role of speaker choice is presented first. This is followed by conceptual materialization flow charts to aid conceptual understanding, guide subsequent performance and ultimately lead to the internalization of the conceptual choices instantiated in spe-cific directive constructions (see also Neguereula 2003). Each of the choices in the chart is then explicitly described with exemplar uses and questions are posed focused on building actionable understanding of the information in the chart, descriptions and examples. An application activity using an excerpt from MICASE follows, with instructions to identify the context and directives, while paying attention to the target elements of directive constructions (pronoun/subject, main element and modifier). Because of space limitations, we present representative materials for pronoun choice and the concept of building listener in-volvement and then include only the materialization flow charts from the main element and modifier materials. In the complete intervention, the organization and structure of the activities for main directive ele-ment and modifiers mirror the pronoun materials presented below.

Pronoun/subject choice materials

The section begins with a list of questions that focuses the learner on the notion of speaker choice, implying that choice of pronoun/subject is dependent on a variety of factors. Moreover, we emphasize that this choice can dynamically shift in response to changes in speaker intent along the clines of involvement and dependence-independence and in conjunction with use of the other directive construction elements.

Pronoun/Subject Choice:

One way of building solidarity with your listener, or giving them a sense of involvement, is to make strategic use of pronouns that you use in directives. The choice of a pronoun (or subject):

- happens in conjunction with choice of main element and modifier
- may change during conversation depending on the reaction of the listener
- depends on speaker choices:
  - Do you want to appeal to listener involvement?
  - Do you want to include yourself in the directive?
  - Do you want to allow the listener to identify with you?
  - Do you want to restrict listener involvement?
  - Do you want to exclude yourself from the directive?

The materialization flow chart (Figure 9.1) is then presented, which graphically represents the implications of pronoun choice. In the materialization, diamonds represent choices, while rectangles represent outcomes. The purpose of the materialization is to act as a conceptual heuristic that will ultimately assist with the internalization of pronoun use within directive constructions in the context of real time communication. As a heuristic, the materialization is not meant to represent 'right' and 'wrong,' but rather to act as a conceptual tool with the potential to

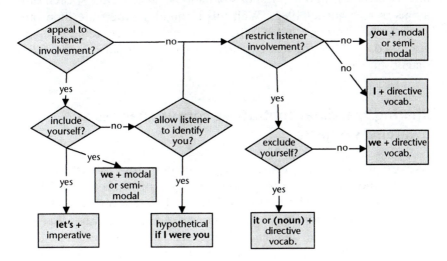

Figure 9.1. Materialization 1 – dynamic system of pronoun choice in directives.

raise awareness of the possible effects of pronoun choice and to imbue learners with sense of agency.

Each of the choices in the materialization is then explicitly described with cases of actual use. For example, the description of the 'yes' branch from the first, upper-left 'appeal toward listener involvement' is as follows:

Appealing to listener involvement:
'Let's' and 'inclusive we' can appeal toward listener involvement if the speaker is part of the directive

a. let's + imperative
Let's see what you have here.

b. we + modal/semi-modal
So **we** need to multiply this quantity by this fraction.

c. Allowing listener to identify with speaker:

a. hypothetical 'if I were you'-like statement
can appeal toward listener involvement by putting the speaker in the listener's place
I would first check with the registrar.

Moving between materializations and examples of usage, between conceptual understanding and real-time application is a critically important method we are employing to heighten awareness of available linguistic choices and implications of their use in academic speech situations (see Vygotsky 1987). With this in mind, learners are then presented with another MICASE office hours excerpt (see Table 9.3) and are asked to utilize the text explanations and conceptual schematic as diagnostic aids.

Sharing real data: contrastive corpus analyses as awareness objects

As part of our move toward transparent pedagogy, we share with students the same contrastive corpus analyses that have informed the design of the materializations. We have had significant support from participating ITAs for the use of contrastive corpus analyses that numerically illustrate the differences between ITA language use (based on our growing ITA corpus) and the expert/native usage represented in MICASE. Learner enthusiasm for exposure to actual corpus analyses

Table 9.3. MICASE excerpt: statistics office hours

T: mkay negative-two-point-five-seven, is good? [S1: how do yo-] mhm, negative-two-point-five-seven, is your test statistic. you wanna still find the P-values
you normally would, and then, point-O-five is a good rule of thumb to use in
general. what I would do though is check the answer with both one five and ten
percent all three, because then you might say well if i make the decision that it's
the same for all three of those then i pretty much know what my decision should
be, okay? if your P-value turns out to be so small that you'd reject for all those
levels then go ahead and say so. if it's in between, for some alphas you'd reject
for some you wouldn't, then say you know for alpha point-O-five we would
reject H-naught however, if alpha were one percent we would not quite reject
H-naught, and then you're recording your results you're telling me you know
how to do a test if alpha were given, [S7: mhm.] in an exam we generally will
give you the specified alpha cuz in any clinical study or anything there is a
determined alpha that is set ahead of time.

1. What is the teacher (T) trying to get the student (S) to do?
2. Identify the directives. What different pronoun choices does the teacher
   make? What are the effects of these choices?

may be because many of them were graduate students in quantitative
and data-oriented fields like math, science and engineering. Table 9.4
illustrates an example of one of the contrastive corpus analyses we
used in the course. Note that frequency counts from ITA corpus and
MICASE are contrasted in both raw numbers and relativized to show
frequency of occurrence per 10,000 words.

Table 9.4. Pronoun use in the ITA corpus versus MICASE corpus

Directive construction word/phrase	ITA corpus	Rate per 10K	MICASE	Rate per 10K	Ratio of over/ underuse
I suggest OR my suggestion	30	3.35	5	0.28	12.0314
You should	94	10.50	83	4.63	2.2710
let's	41	4.58	118	6.58	0.6967
we	146	16.31	881	49.1	0.3308
I would	0	0.00	64	3.57	–
Total words	89,489		179,446		

*Discuss the observations below. Can you offer any explanation of the
data? What other observations can you make of the data?*

1. The ESL 118 students used 'I + directive vocab' in the case of
   'suggest' seven times more frequently than the experts in MICASE.

2.   The MICASE expert speakers (including non-native speakers) used 'I would' much more frequently than the ESL 118 students.
3.   Your observation:

As explained above, the mediated corpus-informed materials for the main directive element and modifier choice in the directive constructions office hours unit mirror these activities in structure and organization and were designed to help raise awareness of the role of choice in language use as it relates to different meanings, interlocutor relationships, degree of social distance and potentials for social-pragmatic effects. Below, we present a materialization outlining main directive elements. The design goal of the materialization is to create a high-level conceptual map that illustrates the linguistic choices available and possible outcomes and interpretations of each lexico-grammatical realization.

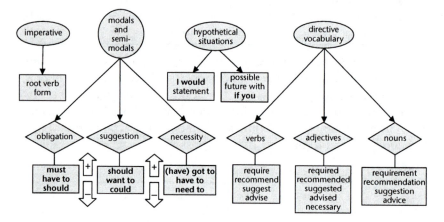

Figure 9.2. Flow chart – schematic of main directive elements.

Preliminary Assessment

In a pilot study that formed the starting point for the current revision of the ITA preparation course curriculum, an alpha-version of the corpus-informed concept-based instructional materials was presented (see Reinhardt, 2007). Two experimental sections ($N = 20$ students), taught by different instructors, were presented with the directives office hours alpha-materials and an additional section ($N = 13$), taught by one of the experimental section instructors, used the conventional materials. In the experimental sections, students were exposed to MICASE transcripts of office hours consultations and were asked to identify directive constructions, discuss how instructors made suggestions and identify patterns in the discourse. The experimental sections were then presented with a graphical representation of elements comprising directives (alpha-versions of the pronoun choice, main directive element and modifier materializations described above) and were engaged in a discussion about how specific directive constructions convey differences in source of authority (e.g., speaker/ITA, lead professor, department/ institution), vary in intensity and constitute different sorts of social actions. Students were also presented with concordances of high-frequency directive constructions drawn from MICASE. To take one example, the learners were presented with a contrastive corpus analysis showing the high frequency of expert speaker (MICASE) use of the directive construction: you [+ hedge] want to / wanna [+ hedge], MICASE examples of which are:

- You just wanna get a ...
- You may wanna think about ...
- You might wanna sort of ...
- You wanna just ...

None of the ITA participants in any of the sections had used this construction in the earlier semester office hours role-plays. However, in the final high-stakes office hours role-play exit exam that followed the course, ten of the ITAs in the experimental sections and none in the control group, used the 'you [+ hedge] want to / wanna [+ hedge]' construction in varied and accurate ways, examples of which are represented in Table 9.5.

Additionally, in comparison to the control group, the experimental groups made substantially greater use of other constructions presented

Table 9.5. Examples of ITA directives post-intervention

you	also	wanna	say,	what,
you	also	want to	i	mean
you	just	wanna	get	a
you	just	wanna	draw	out
you	just	wanna	think	about
you	may	wanna	think	about
you	maybe	wanna	highlight,	why
you	might	wanna	summarize	here
you	do	wanna	make,	but
you	might	wanna	think	about

from MICASE, such as 'you could' and 'you have to,' and produced fewer MICASE low frequency constructions such as 'I suggest,' 'I recommend' and 'you can.'

Within the limited scope of the data presented here, the directives used in late-semester role play activities represent visible shifts in experimental section ITA language use that are traceable to the mediated corpus-informed materials. It is an encouraging indication that a concerted focus on developing awareness of high frequency constructions across various materials, including actual spoken language extracts from MICASE, explicit linguistic and pragmatic descriptions of constructions, conceptual flow chart materializations mapping functionally specific linguistic choices and contrastive corpus analyses presenting evidence of differences between ITA and expert-MICASE language use, holds promise as an instructional framework. A primary hypothesis is that propagating high frequency and high utility constructions across divergent representational media helps to make linguistic resources more salient (or noticeable in the sense of Schmitt 1993) and ultimately, more readily internalizable. This sequence is not unique to Vygotksian pedagogical and developmental theory and aligns with other research on language awareness and frequency effects in second language acquisition, for example that of N. Ellis. When challenged about his argument for frequency effects in implicit adult second language acquisition (see Gass and Mackey 2002), Ellis noted that frequency not withstanding, explicit instruction may play an important role in second language development. As Ellis (2002: 297) pithily states, 'what you seize is what you get.' Drawing from cultural-historical developmental theory, our emphasis has been to provide explicit conceptual knowledge representations in tandem with contextualized examples of use, opportunities for private rehearsal and public performance, to the end of aiding internalization of a larger repertoire of professional academic discourse. In turn, greater linguistic resources should assist ITAs in their movement toward self-regulation in the many speech situations expected in academic professional life.

Future developments

As a next step we will develop learning modules for our ITA training course classroom teachers that will include orientations for how the ITAs should and could use the materializations, for example silently verbalizing the materializations to oneself, having students talk through the materializations independently and in groups (e.g., Swain 2000), using the materializations as heuristics to help analyze the linguistic choices made by expert/native speakers in the MICASE examples and utilizing the materializations to examine collected examples of professional academic discourse that arise in the ITAs' own experiences.

We will create sets of materials that include high-level conceptual materializations of grammatical and lexical choices in the areas of lecturing, classroom management and interactive classroom discussion and question-and-answer sessions. In each case, the conceptual materializations will be informed by attested language use and accompanied by transcripts of actual instructional discourse (drawn from MICASE and ITA corpus data). The materializations will assist with the internalization of new repertoires of purpose-specific, pragmatically attuned and consciously chosen language use within professional academic teaching situations. In our estimation, the combination of conceptual flow chart materializations and selected examples of actual usage will reinforce the movement from the level of conscious reflective action to procedural knowledge and eventually to automatized performance (following Leontiev 1981; see also DeKeyser 2007). In design and application, the *ITAcorp* project attempts to combine the strengths of Vygotskian developmental theory with the attributes of a mediated corpus-based approach and genre and situationally sensitive perspectives provided by discourse- and usage-based approaches to grammar.

Notes

1. Following the debates within the applied linguistics literature regarding the difficulty of operationalizing the definition of 'native speaker', hereafter we will use 'expert speaker' to describe the professional discourse of experienced university instructors.
2. The ITAcorp project has received generous research assistant and technology support from the Center for Language Acquisition at Penn State University.
3. Although we term these 'role plays,' they are more accurately 'teaching tasks' as they are identical to the peer teaching tasks that may be found in many teacher preparation courses.
4. The ITAcorp project received Penn State IRB approval as part of project #21429.
5. The database is free and publicly accessible on the WWW. The developers were informed of the current project and will be provided with a copy of the current project upon completion.
6. These could be considered 'genres' or 'registers.'

7. Gal'perin has been criticized for the rigidity of his framework (see for example van der Veer 2000) and indeed, some aspects have seemed too constraining for our purposes. Thus, while we wish to acknowledge our debt to Gal'perin, our materializations, in-development implementation plan and hybrid pedagogical model (including as it does language awareness and corpus-informed principles) are inspired by, but do not fully conform to, the strictures of his formalized method.
8. Genre suggests that language use is realized by means of a systematic relationship between cultural context, situational context and linguistic features (known collectively within the Hallidayan framework as the text-context model, e.g., Halliday 1978).

References

Arievitch, I. and Haenen, J. (2005) Connecting sociocultural theory and education practice: Galperin's approach. *Educational Researcher* 40: 155–65.

Arievitch, I. and Stetsenko, A. (2000) The quality of cultural tools and cognitive development: Gal'perin's perspective and its implications. *Human Development* 43: 69–92.

Arievitch, I. and van der Veer, R. (1995) Furthering the internalization debate: Gal'perin's contribution. *Human Development* 38: 113–26.

Bailey, K. M. (1984) The 'foreign TA problem.' In K. M. Bailey, F. Pialorsi and J. Zukowski-Faust (eds) *Foreign Teaching Assistants in US Universities* 3–15. Washington, DC: National Association for Foreign Student Affairs.

Bardovi-Harlig, K. and Hartford, B. (1990) Congruence in native and nonnative conversations: status balance in the academic advising session. *Language Learning* 40: 467–500.

Bardovi-Harlig, K. and Hartford, B. (1993) Learning the rules of academic talk: a longitudinal study of pragmatic change. *Studies in Second Language Acquisition* 15: 279–304.

Bardovi-Harlig, K. and Hartford, B. S. (2005) Institutional discourse and interlanguage pragmatics. In K. Bardovi-Harlig and B. S. Hartford (eds) *Interlanguage Pragmatics: Exploring Institutional Talk* 7–36. Mahwah, NJ: Erlbaum.

Belz, J. (2002) The myth of the deficient communicator. *Language Teaching Research* 6: 59–82.

Belz, J. A. and Vyatkina, N. (2005) Learner corpus research and the development of L2 pragmatic competence in networked intercultural language study: the case of German modal particles. *Canadian Modern Language Review/Revue canadienne des langues vivantes* 62: 17–48.

Biber, D. (2006) *University Language: A Corpus-based Study of Spoken and Written Registers*. Philadelphia, PA: John Benjamins.

Biber, D., Conrad, S. and Cortes, V. (2004) If you look at...: lexical bundles in university teaching and textbooks. *Applied Linguistics* 25: 371–405.

Braun, S. (2005) From pedagogically relevant corpora to authentic language learning contents. *ReCALL* 17: 47–64.

Brown, P. and Levinson, S. (1987) *Politeness: Some Universals in Language Usage.* Cambridge: Cambridge University Press.

Byrd, P., Constantinides, J. C. and Pennington, M. (1989) *The Foreign Teaching Assistant's Manual.* New York: Collier Macmillan.

Cameron, D. (2000) *Good to Talk?: Living and Working in a Communication Culture.* London: Sage Publications.

Canagarajah, S. (2007a) The ecology of global English. *International Multilingual Research Journal* 1: 89–100.

Canagarajah, S. (2007b) Lingua franca English, multilingual communities, and language acquisition. *Modern Language Journal* 91: 921–937.

Carter, R. (1998) Orders of reality: CANCODE, communication and culture. *ELT Journal* 52: 43–56.

Chambers, A. (2005) Integrating corpus consultation in language studies. *Language Learning and Technology* 9: 111–25.

Chomsky, N. (1965) *Cartesian Linguistics.* New York: Harper and Row.

DeKeyser, R. (2007) Skill acquisition theory. In B. VanPatten and J. Williams (eds), *Theories in Second Language Acquisition* 97–114. Mahwah, NJ: Lawrence Erlbaum.

Donato, R. (1994) Collective scaffolding in second language learning. In J. Lantolf and G. Appel (eds) *Vygotskian Approaches to Second Language Acquisition* 33–56. Norwood, NJ: Ablex Publishing.

Drew, P. and Heritage, J. (1992) *Talk at Work.* New York: Cambridge University Press.

Ellis, N. (2002) Reflections on frequency effects in language processing. *Studies in Second Language Acquisition* 24: 297–339.

Engeström, Y., Engeström, R. and Kerosuo, H. (2003) The discursive construction of collaborative care. *Applied Linguistics* 24: 286–315.

Finder, A. (2005, June 24) Unclear on American campus: What the foreign teacher said. *The New York Times,* p. A1.

Fitch, F. and Morgan, S. E. (2003) 'Not a lick of English': Constructing the ITA identity through student narratives. *Communication Education* 52: 297–310.

Flowerdew, L. (2002) Corpus-based analyses in EAP. In J. Flowerdew (ed.) *Academic Discourse* 95–114. Harlow, UK: Longman.

Flowerdew, L. (2003) A combined corpus and systemic-functional analysis of the problem-solution pattern in a student and professional corpus of technical writing. *TESOL Quarterly* 37: 489–511.

Flowerdew, L. (2005) An integration of corpus-based and genre-based approaches to text analysis in EAP/ESP: countering criticisms against corpus-based methodologies. *English for Specific Purposes* 24: 321–32.

Gal'perin, P. I. (1992) The problem of activity in Soviet psychology. *Journal of Russian and East European Psychology* 30/4: 37–59.

Gass, S. and Mackey, A. (2002) Frequency effects and second language acquisition. *Studies in Second Language Acquisition* 24: 249–60.

Granger, S. (1998) The computer learner corpus: a versatile new source of data for SLA research. In S. Granger (ed.) *Learner English on Computer* 3–18. New York: Longman.

Granger, S. (2002) A bird's-eye view of learner corpus research. In S. Granger, J. Hung and S. Petch-Tyson (eds) *Computer Learner Corpora, Second Language Acquisition and Foreign Language Teaching* 2–33. Amsterdam: John Benjamins.

Haenen, J. (2000) Gal'perin and instruction in the ZPD. *Human Development* 43: 93–8.

Halliday, M. A. K. (1978) *Language as Social Semiotic: The Social Interpretation of Language and Meaning.* London: Arnold.

Halliday, M. A. K., and Matthiesen, C. (2004) *An Introduction to Functional Grammar.* London: Arnold.

Hanks, W. (1999) *Intertexts, Writings on Language, Utterance and Context.* Denver, CO: Rowman and Littlefield.

Hasselgren, A. (2002) Learner corpora and language testing: smallwords as markers of learner fluency. In S. Granger, J. Hung and S. Petch-Tyson (eds) *Computer Learner Corpora, Second Language Acquisition and Foreign Language Teaching* 143–74. Amsterdam: John Benjamins.

He, A. (1993) Exploring modality in institutional interactions: cases from academic counselling encounters. *Text* 13: 503–28.

Heritage, J. (1984) *Garfinkel and Ethnomethodology.* Cambridge: Polity Press.

Heritage, J. and Robinson, J. (2006) The structure of patients' presenting concerns: physicians' opening questions. *Health Communication* 19: 89–102.

Housen, A. (2002) A corpus-based study of the L2-acquisition of the English verb system. In S. Granger, J. Hung and S. Petch-Tyson (eds) *Computer Learner Corpora, Second Language Acquisition and Foreign Language Teaching* 77–116. Amsterdam: John Benjamins.

Jacobs, L. C. and Friedman, C. B. (1988) Student achievement under foreign teaching associates compared with native teaching associates. *Journal of Higher Education* 59: 521–63.

Johns, T. (1991) Should you be persuaded – two examples of data-driven learning materials. *English Language Research Journal* 4: 1–16.

Johns, T. (1994) From printout to handout: grammar and vocabulary teaching in the context of data-driven learning. In T. Odlin (ed.) *Perspectives on Pedagogical Grammar* 193–212. New York: Cambridge University Press.

Kramsch, C. (1997) The privilege of the nonnative speaker. *PMLA* 112: 359–69.

Krashen, S. (1982) *Principles and Practice in Second Language Acquisition.* New York: Prentice Hall.

Lantolf, J. P. and Thorne, S. L. (2006) *Sociocultural Theory and the Genesis of Second Language Development.* Oxford: Oxford University Press.

Larsen-Freeman, D. (2003) *Teaching Language: From Grammar to Grammaring.* Boston, MA: Thomson/Heinle.

Lee, D. and Swales, J. (2006) A corpus-based EAP course for NNS doctoral students: Moving from available specialized corpora to self-compiled corpora. *English for Specific Purposes* 25: 56–75.

Legislative Assembly of North Dakota. (2005) *House Bill 1364*. Enrollment. Retrieved March 15, 2006, from http://www/state.nd.us/lr/asse,b;u/59-2005/bill-text/FBGB0300.pdf.

Leontiev, A. N. (1981) The problem of activity in Soviet psychology. In J. V. Wertsch (ed.) *The Concept of Activity in Soviet Psychology* 37–71. Armonk, NY: Sharpe.

McCarthy, M. (1998) *Spoken Language and Applied Linguistics*. Cambridge: Cambridge University Press.

McCarthy, M. and Carter, R. (1994) *Language as Discourse: Perspectives for Language Teaching*. London: Longman.

Meunier, F. (2002). The pedagogical value of native and learner corpora in EFL grammar teaching. In S. Granger, J. Hung and S. Petch-Tyson (eds) *Computer Learner Corpora, Second Language Acquisition and Foreign Language Teaching* 119–42. Amsterdam: John Benjamins.

Negueruela, E. (2003) A Sociocultural Approach to the Teaching and Learning of Second Languages: Systemic-theoretical Instruction and L2 Development. Unpublished doctroal dissertation. The Pennsylvania State University, University Park, PA.

Orth, J. L. (1982) University Undergraduate Evaluational Reactions to the Speech of Foreign Teaching Assistants. Unpublished doctoral dissertation, University of Texas – Austin. Dissertation Abstracts International, 43, 3897A.

Pica, T., Barnes, G. A. and Finger, A. G. (1990) *Teaching Matters: Skills and Strategies for International Teaching Assistants*. Rowley, MA: Newbury House.

Pickering, L. (2001) The role of tone choice in improving ITA communication in the classroom. *TESOL Quarterly* 35: 233–55.

Prawat, R. (2000) Dewey meets the 'Mozart of psychology' in Moscow: the untold story. *American Education Research Journal* 37: 663–96.

Rampton, B. (1990) Displacing the 'native speaker': expertise, affiliation and inheritance. *ELT Journal* 44: 338–43.

Reinhardt, J. (2007) Directives Usage by ITAs: An Applied Learner Corpus Analysis. Unpublished doctoral dissertation. The Pennsylvania State University, University Park, PA.

Sarangi, S. (2000) Activity types, discourse types and interactional hybridity: the case of genetic counseling. In S. Sarangi and M. Coulthard (eds) *Discourse and Social Life* 1–27. New York: Longman.

Schmitt, N. (ed.) (2004) *Formulaic Sequences*. Amsterdam: John Benjamins.

Scollon, R. and Scollon, S.W. (1995) *Intercultural Communication*. Blackwell: Malden, MA.

Searle, J. (1983) *Intentionality: An Essay in the Philosophy of Mind*. Cambridge: Cambridge University Press.

Seidlhofer, B. (2002) Pedagogy and local learner corpora: working with learning-driven data. S. Granger, J. Hung and S. Petch-Tyson (eds) *Computer Learner Corpora, Second Language Acquisition and Foreign Language Teaching* 213–33. Amsterdam: John Benjamins.

Simpson, R. C., Briggs, S. L., Ovens, J. and Swales, J. M. (2002) *The Michigan Corpus of Academic Spoken English*. Ann Arbor, MI: The Regents of the University of Michigan.

Smith, J., Meyers, C. M. and Burkhalter, A. J. (1992) *Communicate: Strategies for International Teaching Assistants*. Englewood Cliffs, NJ: Regents/Prentice Hall.

Swain, M. (2000) The output hypothesis and beyond: mediating acquisition through collaborative dialogue. In J. P. Lantolf (ed.) *Sociocultural Theory and Second Language Learning* 97–114. Oxford: Oxford University Press.

Swain, M. and Lapkin, S. (2001) Focus on form through collaborative dialogue: exploring task effects. In M. Bygate, P. Skehan and M. Swain (eds) *Researching Pedagogic Tasks: Second Language Learning, Teaching and Assessment* 99–118. London: Pearson International.

Swain, M., Brooks, L. and Tocalli-Beller, A. (2002) Peer-peer dialogue as a means of second language learning. *Annual Review of Applied Linguistics* 22: 171–85.

Thonus, T. (1999) How to communicate politely and be a tutor, too: NS-NNS interaction and writing center practice. *Text* 19: 253–79.

Thorne, S. L. and Lantolf, J. P. (2007) A linguistics of communicative activity. In S. Makoni and A. Pennycook (eds) *Disinventing and Reconstituting Languages* 170–96. Clevedon: Multilingual Matters.

Thorne, S. L. & Reinhardt, J. (in press) "Bridging activities," new media literacies and advanced foreign language proficiency. *The CALICO Journal* 25 (3).

Train, R. (2003) The (non)native standard language in foreign language education: A critical perspective. In C. Blyth (ed.) *The Sociolinguistics of Foreign Language Classrooms: Contributions of the Native, the Near-native and the Non-native Speaker* 3–9. Boston, MA: Thomson Heinle.

Upton, T. and Connor, U. (2001) Using computerized corpus analysis to investigate the textlinguistic discourse moves of a genre. *English for Specific Purposes* 20: 313–29.

van der Veer, R. (2000) Some reflections concerning Gal'perin's theory. *Human Development* 43: 99–102.

Vygotsky, L. S. (1978) Mind in Society. The Development of Higher Psychological Processes. Cambridge, MA: Harvard University Press.

Vygotsky, L. S. (1981) The genesis of higher mental functions. In J. V. Wertsch (ed.) The Concept of Activity in Soviet Psychology 144–88. Armonk, NY: M.E. Sharpe.

Vygotsky, L. S. (1987) *The Collected Works of L. S. Vygotsky (Vol. 1): Problems of General Psychology. Including the Volume Thinking and Speech*. New York: Plenum.

Vygotsky, L. S. (1997) *The Collected Works of L. S. Vygotsky (Vol. 4): The History of the Development of Higher Mental Functions*. New York: Plenum.

Waara, R. (2004) Construal, convention and constructions in L2 speech. In M. Achard and S. Niemeier (eds) *Cognitive Linguistics, Second Language Acquisition and Foreign Language Teaching* 51–75. Berlin: Walter De Gruyter.

Widdowson, H. (2003) *Defining Issues in English Language Teaching*. Oxford, UK: Oxford University Press.

Williams, J. (2005) Writing center interaction: institutional discourse and the role of peer tutors. In B. Hartford (ed.) *Interlanguage Pragmatics* 37–65. Mahwah, NJ, Lawrence Erlbaum.

Wittgenstein, L. (1958) *Philosophical Investigations*. New York: Blackwell.

10 A concept-based approach to teaching writing through genre analysis

Marilia M. Ferreira and James P. Lantolf

Introduction

The previous chapters in this subsection focus on concept-based instruction as conceived by Piotr Gal'perin. In this chapter we discuss a study carried out within a concept-based framework developed by Vladimir Davydov, a contemporary of Gal'perin and also an important interpreter of Vygotsky's educational theory. As we think will become clear throughout the chapter, in comparison to Gal'perin's approach, Davydov's theory is less rigid to the extent that it does not adhere to a fixed set of sequentially arranged procedures designed to promote internalization of a particular concept. Nevertheless, as with Gal'perin's model, Davydov underscores the importance of theoretical thinking as the starting point of educationally grounded development. For Davydov, the key to effective education is to help learners connect theoretical knowledge to specific concrete goal directed activity guided by this knowledge. Davydov's (1999) general approach is often characterized as 'movement from the abstract to the concrete' (see editors' introductory discussion of dialectics). For convenience, we use the abbreviation MAC pedagogy. According to MAC, learners are presented with systematic conceptual knowledge in a particular domain (e.g., physics, chemistry, mathematics, language, etc.) and are then encouraged, with guidance, to proceduralize this knowledge in concrete circumstances that are relevant to their own interests. In the case at hand, the particular concept under study was the general concept of communication, as realized in the notion of genre and the practical activity was the production of texts typical of specific genres, the details of which are fleshed out later in the chapter.

As a way of proceeding, we begin by outlining the principles of MAC pedagogy and briefly review some of the studies carried out within this framework. We then report on the implementation of a MAC-based approach to L2 writing instruction organized around the Systemic-Functional model of genre, as developed in the writings of James Martin and his colleagues.

MAC pedagogy

Following Vygotsky, Davydov proposed theoretical knowledge as a tool for thinking and for carrying out systemic practical activity. The goal of MAC education is to take account of the functionality of theoretical concepts as symbolic tools for carrying out concrete practical activity in the various disciplines comprising the educational curriculum. Davydov (1988b) thus recommends that instruction should make clear to students the importance of the central concepts within a discipline and should help learners bring these to bear in practical activity. In MAC, as in Gal'perin's approach, conceptual knowledge is not offered to students solely in verbal form, but it must be materialized in an easily accessible, integrated and concise format. Davydov referred to this format as a *germ-cell model* – the visual representation of theoretical knowledge aimed at helping students develop theoretical thinking. We will illustrate the germ-cell model when we discuss the study itself.

Beginning in the 1950's Davydov and his colleagues studied the effect of MAC pedagogy on student development using Vygotsky's research methodology known as the *genetic* or *formative experiment* in which the history of mental abilities is traced as learners appropriate theoretical concepts to mediate their thinking in specific disciplinary domains (see Vygotsky 1978; Davydov 1988; Lantolf and Thorne 2006). Davydov's initial investigation revealed that children enrolled in Russian elementary schools had more cognitive potential than was being realized through current pedagogies. In the 1960's experimental syllabi in math and language were introduced into some of the schools and eventually a series of experimental schools that employed MAC pedagogy was established. Throughout the 1970's Davydov and colleagues conducted a number of studies of how MAC pedagogy impacted the full personality of children, including not only cognitive, but also moral and emotional development.

For Davydov educational activity is not about making students become scientists and walking them through a rediscovery of the findings of previous generations. Rather, it is a 'quasi-investigation in which pupils reproduce real investigatory and search acts in only a compressed form' (Davydov and Markova 1984: 67). This quasi-investigation is the way of providing students with the genesis of the knowledge being taught and to make them active learners. The components of educational activity are learning actions materialized through tasks whose aim is to move learners from the abstract to the concrete (Davydov and Markova 1983: 61) and include the following: 1) problem situation; 2) modeling; 3) modifying the model; 4) applying the model to solve tasks; 5) monitoring the actions; and 6) evaluating the actions.

An extensive example of MAC instruction applied to the development of mathematical knowledge is documented in Davydov (1988b). In order to teach the concept of numbers to first graders, the theoretical concept of quantity was first introduced by means of comparisons (equal to, greater than, less than) of quantities. Then ways to represent these comparisons were taught: $c + a = b$, $a = b - c$ (Davydov 1988b: 34). Next, by putting the students into a situation in which these representations of quantity could not be used efficiently as a way of representing relationships among quantities, the teacher led the students to perceive the need for the concept of number. For example, how is it possible to express the equality or inequality of segments? The students were then able to understand that the concept of number functions as a form of mediation for comparing different measures of substances or items. Along with numbers, the concept of multiplicity was introduced as the students verified how many times a certain quantity fits in what is being measured ($A/c = 4$, $B/c = 5$, then $4 < 5$) (Davydov 1988b: 36). This is followed by a modification of the multiplicity concept: a change in c with the same quantity in A alters the number.

As we can see from this example the teacher provides the students with tasks that lead them to the need for a concept – number – to mediate the relationships among quantities. In this case, the abstract theoretical concept that is the focus of instruction is quantity, followed by the concrete concept of number, which then leads students to the concrete concept of multiplicity. In this way students come to understand that number is a tool to facilitate measurements and comparison of measurements. This approach proved to be much more effective than beginning with the notion of using numbers to count individual items, such as apples or oranges where the reason why numbers as useful tools is not immediately apparent.

Another groundbreaking study based on Davydov's approach is Markova's (1979) implementation of a MAC curriculum for teaching

Russian as L1 in the schools of Moscow. In her book, she extensively describes the curriculum, which followed MAC principles. The study focused on the theoretical concept of utterance, defined as an 'expository statement' (Markova 1979: 66) that can be expressed in a group of words, a sentence, or a whole text, along with its constitutive relations: form – function and form – meaning. Several concrete examples of language use were utilized to reveal how these elements relate to one another and constitute the utterance. The concept was also investigated as a tool for communication. The study was carried out over a ten-year period (from 1962 to 1972) in grades 4 through 8 with over 3,000 children participating. One of the most interesting results was that children developed the ability to use their language in exceptionally creative ways to express complex and often quite figurative meanings, much in the way novelists and poets do. They came to realize that language was a tool for mediating their thinking and that the grammatical and even lexical norms did not have to be rigidly followed but could be pushed and even ruptured in systematic and quite effective ways.

Aidarova (1982) employed Davydov's approach to teach Russian morphology and spelling to seven-year-old children. The basic relation taught was form – meaning at the word level and linked to the broader activity of communication (Aidarova 1982: 106). Using tests designed to detect children's level of theoretical thinking and orientation, she reported significant improvement in their performance in subsequent grade levels. The author also extensively explored the impact of models on the development of theoretical thinking (see Serran-Lopez and Poehner, Chapter 11, this volume).

Lompscher (1984) also conducted a 30-hour study with fourth graders to teach the natural sciences. The abstract concept of energy was introduced to students as the basis of all natural processes and was described as follows:

> there are permanent changes in nature; these processes are
> evoked by certain conditions and in their turn, they evoke certain
> effects in the sense of interaction, not only simple causal relations;
> a necessary condition for all processes of nature is the existence of
> energy; there are different forms of energy, which are based on
> different carriers and can be transferred and changed. (Lompscher
> 1984: 337–8)

As a continuation of this course, the fifth graders in the subject of biology were taught the basic relations below:

the permanent contact and exchange (of matter, energy and information) between living beings and the environment is the necessary condition for the building up and upholding of the body and for procreation; the presupposition of this exchange is the adaptation of living beings to their environment; modifications of the environment have, in the course of very long timespaces, effected the adaptation to modified circumstances and thus the development of living beings. (Lompscher 1984: 345)

Lompscher (1984, 1999a) and Giest and Lompscher (2003) report significant improvements in the classes participating in their experimental project compared with control groups in terms of performance in tasks (planning, describing and observing the outcome of an experiment), development of theoretical thinking and motivation.

Hedegaard's research (Hedegaard 1987, 1989, 1990, 1999, 2002; Hedegaard, Chaiklin and Pedraza 2001; Hedegaard and Sigersted 1992) represents the most accessible and comprehensive work on MAC to date. In one particularly ambitious project, Hedegaard's team implemented a three-year course of study extending from third through fifth grade in Danish schools where biology, history and geography were integrated into a single curriculum. The focus of the course was on the evolution of the species, the origin of humans and historical changes in society. The project dealt with a wide range of topics, including goal formation, motive formation, development of theoretical thinking, use of models to solve tasks, methodological aspects of data collection, along with personality development and cultural identity. Rather than using an experimental design, Hedegaard conducted analyses of case studies of individual students paying particular attention to various aspects of their personality development (e.g., motivation, theoretical thinking, emotion, etc.).

The present study: MAC in an ESL writing course

The study was carried out for a 16 week period in a university ESL writing course. A total of 14 students participated in the course. Their first language backgrounds were as follows: one Korean, two Vietnamese, four Spanish (from Central America), six Chinese (Mandarin), one Somali. Except for the Korean L1 speaker, all of the students had come to the US as members of immigrant families. They all began to study English in their early- to mid-teen years, which, with the exception of the Korean speaker, had taken place in the US setting.

The course comprised three units organized according to three genres: unit 1 – invitation by means of a public announcement; unit 2 – cover letters; unit 3 – argumentative texts. These genres represented the concrete manifestation of the *abstract communicative principle* (ACP), in the present case the interrelationship between language and culture (LANGUAGE ↔ CONTEXT) as explained below. As the course sought to develop writing ability through theoretical thinking about genre, the seven learning actions developed by Davydov and Markova (as listed in the previous section) were implemented in the class. We will discuss how each of these was concretely realized and responded to by the students. Before we do this, however, we will present a brief description of the course syllabus in order to give the reader an idea of the general framework in which the actions were carried out.

In the study two important components of development were examined: the extent to which students showed signs of a shift away from empirical, context-bound thinking and toward more general theoretical thinking and the extent to which their actual writing performance improved over the course of the semester. To anticipate the findings of the study, we note that while the majority of students had a difficult time shifting from empirical to theoretical thinking, at least some of the participants did manifest clear evidence of the emergence of the developmental change in orientation, which in turn appeared to impact positively on their writing ability.[2]

The course syllabus

The content of the syllabus was organized around the concept of genre as it is understood in Systemtic Functional Linguistics (henceforth, SFL). The concept was taught by relating it to the more general activity of communication. We will explain this important point later in the chapter. Three genres were selected as the major focus of instruction; these were announcements, job application cover letters and argumentation/expository texts. These were selected because it was believed that they represent genres university students are likely to need to produce at some time during their studies. Announcements, for instance are an important means through which various activities on a North American university campus are made public, including academic club events (e.g., math club, science, history club, etc.), visiting speakers, career related activities, social clubs and the like. It was also believed that announcements would allow the instructor to more easily introduce students for the first time to the concepts of field, tenor, mode and generic moves. Field refers to the content or the social action involved in the text; tenor is the relationship between the language users; and mode refers to how language is employed in a particular text (e.g., cohesion and thematic progression) (Martin 1993). The cover letter was introduced because it is linked to the students' vocational activity. Also, it has a medium level of complexity that would allow the instructor to expand upon the concept of mode via cohesion and thematic progression. The argumentative/expository genre was chosen because it is one of the major text types students are expected to master in tertiary education. As it has a more complex schematic structure than the others, it was introduced as the final genre. The course also exposed the students to several other genres, including invitation letters, obituaries, wedding invitations, letters to the editor and research abstracts. The students were not asked to analyze these genres and their schematic structure extensively, nevertheless they had the opportunity to at least try to understand how the general concept of genre could be concretized in an array of texts beyond those that were the primary focus of the course.

Several types of exercises were incorporated into the syllabus. These were designed to: 1) develop theoretical thinking; 2) improve writing; 3) analyze language; and 4) promote reading. The first type consisted of problem situations to be solved by employing the germ-cell models the students created (discussed below in learning activities). These problems related to linguistic phenomena. Three were given in the course: 1) an activity in which students were asked to compare the genre of wedding invitation in their own country with that of the United States; 2) an activity adopted from Bhatia (1993), which asked students to first compare job application cover letters from South Asia with those of North America and then to do the same between their home country and North America. In this case they were asked to make explicit note of differences in field, tenor and mode; and 3) an obituary task whereby the students had to read two obituaries taken from a local newspaper and explain the differences in information content (one was much longer than the other) and its impact on the reader.

The course offered the learners several opportunities to practice their writing in three types of tasks: short answers to questions, long writing assignments (one page or more), including the major assignment of each unit and the writing report and transformed practice (Kern 2000). Transformed practice relates to tasks that require students to rewrite a text following new parameters. These parameters can be to write to a different audience or to the same audience but with a different intent in mind. The students also engaged in a review exercise given during the 11th week of class where they had to correct their classmates' letters for sentence structure and excessive use of the first-person pronoun.

The first major assignment consisted of writing two announcements of an event. In each case the event remained the same but the targeted audience shifted. One audience was real and one was imagined. In the first assignment the students had to find a real event announced on campus and write an alternative announcement for the audience targeted by the sponsors of the event. For the second assignment, they had to write an announcement for an event they created, which was aimed at an audience of their choosing. For the second writing assignment the students had to write a cover letter for a job they would like to apply for. This was to be based on a real advertisement, which they took from the local newspaper. For the third major writing activity, the students had to write a three-page text where they supported a thesis statement regarding the influence of culture on genres. Through this third assignment, students were led to review the entire course and to verbalize in writing their understanding of what was taught.

The linguistic analysis exercises were aimed at helping students develop an understanding of the concepts of field, tenor and mode, which form the basis of genre in the SFL framework. To realize this goal, the information provided in Table 10.1 was presented to the students. At first the instructor and the students worked together to complete the Language portion of the chart where it was necessary to provide concrete examples of language. Students were then required to fill in the missing language component of in the table. Eventually, students were given primary responsibility for completing the chart when new texts were introduced.

To assist students in carrying out the writing activities, conferences with the teacher took place throughout the semester. These encounters mainly focused on discussing and repairing the students textual problems, but they also included discussions of the students' models of the three genres taught and the students' doubts about these models and the conceptual focus of the course (i.e., field, tenor and mode).

The reading opportunities consisted mainly of students reading samples of the genre under study as well as texts that explained the properties of these genres (cover letter as discussed in Besson (1996) and the construction of argumentative/expository texts as presented by Hacker (2003)). The course employed the readings to promote discussions in the classroom, to teach the generic moves of a given genre and

Table 10.1. Linguistic analysis chart (version 1)

Context	Questions	Language
Field (content)	1) What is the content of …? 2) What is its goal? 3) What are the parts of…? (generic moves). In other words, divide the text into parts and indicate what is happening in each part.	
Tenor (reader/ writer relationship)	1) Who is the writer? 2) Who is the text addressed to? 3) How does the writer approach the audience?	
Mode	Mode – written text to be read – … (letter or announcement) How is the text constructed? Are there fully developed sentences with subject + verb + complement, use of connectors (because, although, but, and) or are key words more often employed? Why (not)?	

to carry out linguistic analysis of a particular text; that is, to analyze the field, the tenor and the mode of the text.

We now turn to a discussion of the specific learning actions the students were asked to carry out over the duration of the course. As already mentioned, we will present some data samples to illustrate how each of the actions was carried out.

Learning actions

In this section, we present representative data that relate to the various learning actions introduced during the course. Clearly, we are unable to present all of the data here; however, we consider evidence that indicates how the students carried out the activities and the impact these had on their understanding of genre and how this knowledge could help them improve their concrete writing ability. We focus on six of the 14 students who participated in the course because these six showed evidence of development of their theoretical thinking as related to the general concept of communication and genre.

Learning action 1: the problem situation

MAC education begins with the principle that students should be placed in a situation in which they perceive the need for the content to be taught in the discipline under focus (Aidarova 1982; Markova 1979; Lompscher 1999a, b). They should accordingly be exposed to problems that they cannot solve without first receiving instruction in the relevant content. They should also be presented with a general question or questions that relate to the particular theoretical concept that informs the entire course of study as well as a series of unit-specific questions that connect the general question to concrete topics. These questions were either responded to jointly by the instructor and the students in class or by the students alone as a homework assignment.

Since the course was based on the concept of genre as elaborated in systemic-functional linguistics, the problem situation questions related to this particular theory of genre and therefore focused on the basic LANGUAGE $\leftrightarrow$ CONTEXT relationship and how understanding this can help students use language effectively. It was clear that the students knew that language is used differently according to context; for example, that one speaks with a boss differently than with a friend. However, because of their low level of writing ability in English they did not know precisely how to realize such variation when producing written texts in their L2.

The general problem situation question for the course was as follows: We use language in a variety of situations and to achieve a wide range of goals. How do we use language to achieve these goals and how does the social situation affect our use of language? For each of the instructional units covered in the course, which corresponded to the three genres mentioned above, the problem situation question was: What is the context in which the genre is used and how are language and context related in this genre?

Learning action 2: modeling

Davydov argues for the importance of visually depicting the abstract concept under study in any educational activity (Davydov 1988c). This is because visual depictions are material and as such have more permanence than verbal representations of the concept. Moreover, if done properly they are more concise and coherent than written linguistic representations and therefore more easily used by students to guide their activity and are more readily internalized. The abstract depictions of concepts are called germ-cell models. In addition to depicting the abstract concept in material form, the germ-cell model must also reflect conflicts or tensions present in the concept (Hedegaard 1987).

The germ-cell model developed for the writing course was inspired by research in SFL (e.g., Martin 1993; Eggins 1994). Since this linguistic theory focuses on how language and context influence each another (Eggins 1994), students were given a model depicting the *abstract communicative principle* (ACP) which reflects the fundamental relationship LANGUAGE ↔ CONTEXT. Context, according to SFL, is expanded to take account of the subconcepts of *field, tenor* and *mode*. Following Eggins (1994) an additional concept was incorporated into the model – culture – since culture influences how language and context interrelate. The full germ-cell model is present in Figure 10.1.

The model attempts to capture the tension inherent in concrete language use between creativity on the part of the users and the constraints imposed by context, which demand specific forms of speech, or in the present case, writing. The tension is reflected in the symbol ↔ linking LANGUAGE and CONTEXT. This was further explored with regard to specific genres, such as cover letter for job applications where there exists a tension between the applicant's desire to promote oneself as unique and different from other applicants while at the same time complying with the norms of the genre. In this case, instruction sought

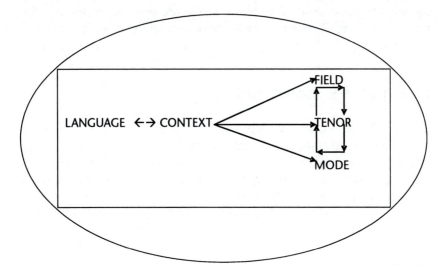

Figure 10.1. Germ-cell model depicting theoretical concept of communication.

to help the students comprehend the conflict (creativity ↔ norms, individual use ↔ social use) which constitutes language use and which is part of the ACP.

The course relied extensively on the use of models to help students understand and concretize the relevant concepts relating to genre. The initial germ-cell model of genre was given to students early in the course. This was accompanied by an in-depth discussion of the concept. As the course developed, students were asked to draw their own models of the abstract concept of genre as well as models to show their understanding of each of the specific genres studied. Figures 10.2 and 10.3 illustrate students' depiction of argumentative and cover-letter genres respectively. Examples of their general models will be presented when we consider the next learning action. The majority of student models tended to indicate procedures for how to produce the relevant text rather than the concept itself. This is indicated by the absence or backgrounding of the basic categories of field, tenor and mode. We interpret this to mean that the students had not developed a high level of theoretical thinking about genre and were instead functioning on an empirical level. We will have more to say about this important matter shortly.

The model in Figure 10.2 relates to argumentative texts and is completely procedural given that it fails to include any of the categories of the ACP. In contrast, Figure 10.3, which depicts the cover letter genre, does include the basic elements of the ACP and links these to the foregrounded schematic structure of the genre. Yet, even in this case, the student appears to conceive of the genre specific model as a formula for writing cover letters rather than conceiving of such letters as a concrete manifestation of a specific combination of field, tenor and mode.

Learning action 3: modifying models

The modification of the students' models of genre took place at three different points throughout the course: at the beginning (week 3 of the course), in the middle (week 11) and near the end of the semester (week 13). Modeling of the three types of genre occurred in two phases: a hypothesized model in which the students modeled their understanding of the genre before reading examples of the genre and a substantive model formulated after they read the examples. The students were also given tasks designed to promote theoretical thinking in order to compel them to revise their models in ways that would link them to the concept of genre while at the same time taking account of ACP.

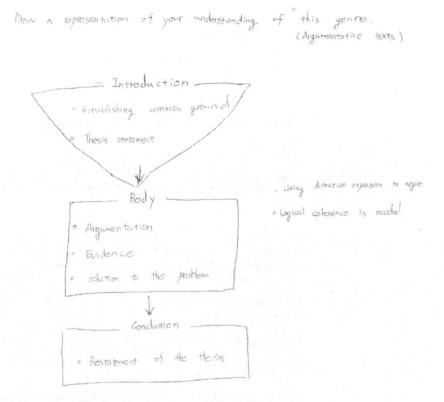

Figure 10.2. Student model of argumentative text.

During instruction and in one-on-one conferences with the instructor, the students were encouraged to construct germ-cell models. Following Davydov's (1988c) notion of 'formative experiment,' the intent was to stimulate the students to develop models that depicted abstract relations rather than to focus on procedures for producing a text within a particular genre. This is important because understanding genre at the abstract theoretical level allows one to be more flexible in manipulating the genre as needed under different circumstances, as often happens when tailoring a cover letter to highlight different aspects of one's qualifications for a position. Following a fixed set of procedures for producing texts in a given genre, on the other hand, is likely to stifle the flexibility needed to cope with changes in concrete circumstances. Despite the instructor's best efforts, with some exceptions (see below)

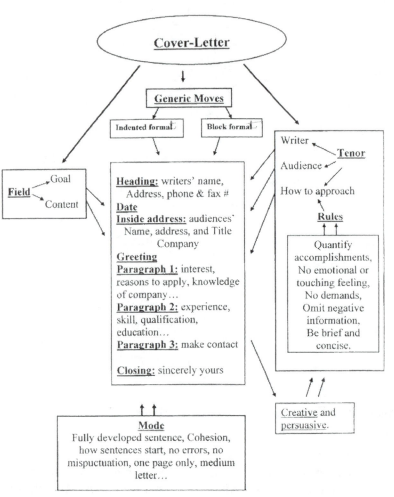

Figure 10.3. Student model of cover letter.

the students tended to produce 'how to' rather than theoretical models of the genres. This happened even when the instructor made direct comparisons between her theoretical model and the student's models and tried to lead them into modifying their models accordingly.

In his first attempt at depicting the abstract concept of genre, the student we will refer to as Chg modeled the abstract concept of genre in an empirical rather than theoretical fashion (see Figure 10.4). That is, his model segmented genre into different classifications – written and oral, formal and informal – and included examples of different genres (e.g., newspaper ads, recipes, news stories). In his second attempt, produced in the 11th week of the course (see Figure 10.5), the same student continued to classify genres as formal and informal; however, the model does attempt to integrate the theoretical categories of field, tenor and mode. Nevertheless, things are rather disjointed as the student appears to confuse mode with tenor as indicated by his inclusion of 'friendly' and 'no emotion' in the domain of mode. Furthermore, the model does not incorporate any understanding of the interaction that occurs among field, tenor and mode in any genre. We consider the model in Figure 10.5 as a transition model, since in week 13, Chg incorporates the interrelatedness of field, tenor and mode in the theoretical concept of genre (see Figure 10.6).

Comparison of the three models shows how Chg's theoretical thinking developed throughout the course. He began with a very empirical understanding which explained through example rather than definition, much in the way that children respond when asked to explain what an 'uncle' is. They usually provide an example of real uncles (e.g., my uncle Fred) rather than with a statement that captures the notion of uncle as 'male sibling of either of my parents.' Chg then realized that field, tenor and mode are essential features of genre, as he included these in his second model, but, as we mentioned, these features were neither well understood nor were they interrelated. In his final model, Chg exhibited a much more sophisticated, if still incomplete, comprehension of the concept as he depicted the interrelated nature of the features and indicated recognition that audience is important in determining tenor.

Learning action 4: applying the models

One of the tasks students were given was to use the germ-cell model given in Figure 10.1 first to explain the similarities and differences between cover letters in the United States and in South Asia and then to describe how this genre is used in his or her home culture.

The exercise follows:

Use the germ-cell model in its four versions to answer the following:

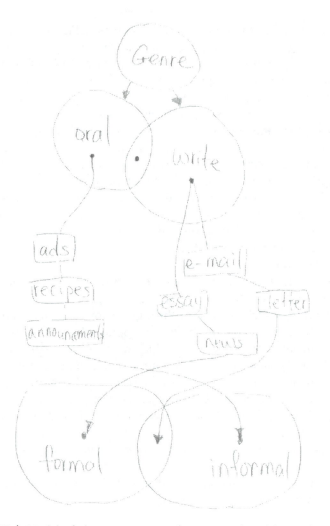

Figure 10.4. Model of abstract concept of genre produced by student Chg at beginning of course.

(a) How do you explain the differences between cover letters in America and in South Asia?

(b) How do you explain the presence of the moves adversary-glorification and self-degradation in South Asian cover letters?

(c) How are field, tenor and mode interrelated in the genre cover letter? Answer this question by comparing South Asian and American cover letters.

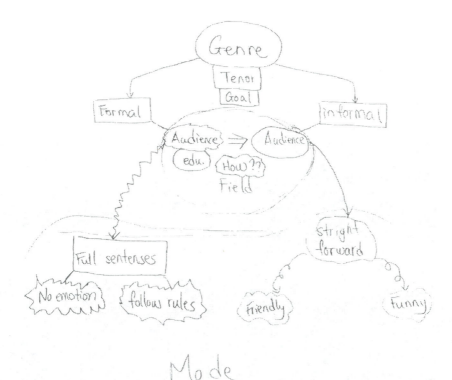

Figure 10.5. Model of abstract concept of genre produced by student Chg in the eleventh week of the course.

(d) Do people in your country write job application letters when they apply for a job? .... yes ....no. Why?

(e) (To be done individually) What are cover letters like in your country? Write at least one double-spaced page.

Two students from China , Ch1 and X, produced the following response to question (b):

> In our opinion, the presence of the moves adversary-glorification and self-degradation in South Asian cover letters is due to the tradition or culture of South Asians. The employers are more likely kind-hearted people who have lots of sympathy and willingness to help others. For this reason, once they read about the plight and difficulties of the applicants, they automatically want to try to help them solve the problem.

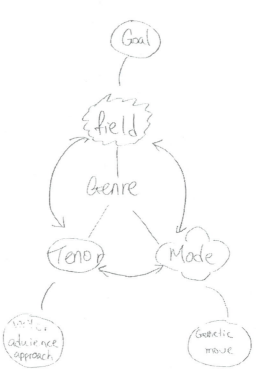

Figure 10.6. Model of abstract concept of genre produced by student Chg in the thirteenth week of the course.

The students at least incorporate an element of the germ-cell model – culture – to explain the difference of the genre cover letter in the two different cultures. Then they explain how culture affects the tenor in this cover letter: employees in South Asia are compassionate and for this reason they accept the moves adversary-glorification and self-degradation in the letter. However, these students did not attempt to explain why culture might compel an employer to be kind-hearted, sympathetic and willing to help.

Another example is from the student referred to as Ma, from Central America, who when responding to question (d), wrote:

> The tenor that they use in these letters is similar to Americans'.
> The tenor has to be persuasive enough so that the recruiter gives you at least an interview and eventually get a job in the company that you want to work in. The word choice (mode) that they use is also very similar to American's way. They try not to use too basic vocabulary and also they try to diversify the way they start their sentences.[1]

Ma's explanation does incorporate the notions of tenor and mode, which we take as an indication of his improved understanding of the theoretical concept.

Learning actions 5 and 6: monitoring and evaluation

The important action of monitoring and evaluating one's own ability as well as what transpired in the course occurred in a variety of ways at several points throughout in the course: 1) the scientific work board (Aidarova 1982); 2) writing reports; 3) review sessions; 4) closing sessions; 5) answers to the problem situation questions; and 6) the final course evaluation, which was written in the students' log. The review and closing sessions occurred at the beginning and at the end of each unit. The students' logs consisted of diaries where they reflected on their learning process. The reports consisted of an evaluation of the writing process that the students engaged in for each of the three major writing assignments.

As a reminder, the general question that framed the course and which was aimed at verifying the students' understanding of ACP was the following: We use language in a variety of situations and to achieve a wide range of goals. How do we use language to achieve these goals? How does the social situation affect our use of language? Student responses to the general question were provided at the conclusion of the course. Below we consider some of these responses.

> H: We use language in many ways to achieve our goals, like for example through News, Ads, Letters, Argumentative texts, Recipes, Essays, etc, which are different kinds of genres. The social situation affects the use of language so much. It is what determines what kind of language we have to use formal, informal, friendly, persuasive, etc. and it is pretty obvious because we would not talk to a president the same way we talk to our friends.

H showed signs of theoretical thinking by revealing his understanding of the basic relation ('The social situation affects the use of language so much') and by providing some examples ('formal, informal, friendly, persuasive'). Another interesting aspect of H's answer is his reference to specific genres in the first sentence. We believe this indicates that even though evidence of theoretical thinking was beginning to emerge, it coexisted with the empirical orientation to learning that was prevalent among all students from the outset of the course. H's use of 'obvious' in his statement is interesting because while it may reflect his general attitude toward the ACP, he does not comment on the inter-relationship between language and context in real writing situations.

The students' logs consist of another source of evaluation data. They maintained logs throughout the entire semester in which they were to comment on or given their impressions of any aspect of the course they considered noteworthy, including both positive and negative aspects. They were also expected to write about what they had learned during a particular week. The following are examples of students' reactions to the three genres taught in the course.

> **J:** I believed what I would learn from the class is what I already know, because the 'announcement' consists of quite simple content. However, it was my misunderstanding. There were many new parts that I didn't know such as the announce, construction, content and the use of language. I knew the difference that came from using different type of language. I mean the full sentence and short sentence. Although I'm learning from class, I wonder how it can be good at my writing skill.

J's remarks indicate a tension between learning and the course content which has helped him to learn. He recognizes he is learning from the unit on announcements but is not able to relate it to any improvement in his writing. Even though J discovered aspects of the announcement genre that he did not know before taking the course, he continues to worry about whether or not he will be able to instantiate this knowledge in concrete writing activities. Again, we construe this as an orientation toward empirical rather than theoretical learning. This same tension is also reflected in N's comments:

> **N:** I told them [parents] that English class in college is so easy but the thing is I'm not learning how to write, but learning how to apply or how do a job application letter.

It is interesting to note that for N writing is not learning different genres; he does not perceive that by learning how to write a cover letter he is also learning how to write and to use language effectively. It is quite plausible that N has a general conception of writing as a unitary process that does not distinguish text types. Related to this is the distinct possibility that in his history as a student of writing he may have considered writing to be the ability to produce a series of grammatically correct sentences rather than a coherent and cohesive text that varies according to the specifications of a particular genre. This in turn may prevent him from perceiving the connection, established by the

of 24 texts. Each rater was asked to read and rate 16 pieces of writing over a two-week period following the conclusion of the course. As it turned out, one rater had to score three additional texts due to discrepancies (see Appendix 10.1 for level descriptors used to rate student writing). The inter-rater reliability coefficients were as follows: for the cover letters, pre-test (0.91); for the argumentative/expository texts, pre-test (0.91); cover letters, post-test (0.83) and argumentative texts, post-test (0.89). Only the correlation for cover letter, post-test was not significant at $p = 0.05$. All correlations were calculated through Spearman Rank Order (Rho). The raters were compensated for their service.

As can be seen from Table 10.2, some of the students showed improvement in the ratings they received from the first to the second set of writing activities. However, as we discussed above, all six of the students showed development in their theoretical thinking. X and Cho showed noticeable improvement in both genres from the pre- to the end-of-course writing activity, while K and H exhibited very little improvement in either genre. M received a higher rating for the cover letter in the second writing activity but did not manifest much improvement in ability to produce argumentative/expository texts. Chl's performance improved quite a bit for job cover letters but did not change with respect to the argumentative/expository genre. On the other hand, Chl seemed to already have considerable ability in this genre at the outset of the course.

From the perspective of MAC pedagogy, it is not all that surprising that there does not appear to be a direct connection between development of theoretical thinking and improvement in writing performance. This is because, as Davydov and Vygotsky before him, argue, the impact of education on development is not causal in the sense of

Table 10.2. Final scores for the pre-tests and post-tests

Students	Pre-course activity		End-of-course activity	
	CL	*A/ET*	*CL*	*A/ET*
K	1	1	1.5	1.5
Cho	1.5	1.5	2.5	2.5
M	1	1	2.5	1.5
H	1.5	2	2	2
Chl	1.5	3	3	3
X	1.5	1.5	3.5	3

CL = Job application cover letter
A/ET = Argumentative/Expository text

procedure A causing performance B. This does not mean, however, that there is no relationship between A and B. For Vygotsky (see Negueruela, Chapter 7, this volume) development is a revolutionary and not an evolutionary process that cannot be predicted and progresses in fits and starts. What we would anticipate therefore is that over time and with consistent experience with theoretical concepts, the students' capacity to engage in effective writing activity would indeed continue to improve (see Karpov (2005) for further discussion of theoretical thinking in educational contexts).

Conclusion

The syllabus designed for the ESL freshman composition course utilized two theoretical frameworks: systemic functional linguistics (SFL), to describe the object of study and 'the movement from the abstract to the concrete' (MAC), to provide the pedagogical procedure for promoting the learning process. The first pedagogical goal of the course was to promote the development of theoretical thinking through MAC procedures, whereby the basic abstract relationship (the ACP) that defines the function of language (LANGUAGE $\leftrightarrow$ CONTEXT) was realized at the concrete level through the specific genres of announcements, cover letters and argumentative texts. These genres constitute the concrete manifestation of the theoretical concept of genre, based on the SFL view of genre and as a manifestation of the ACP.

The second and related, pedagogical goal consisted of improving students' writing in specific textual genres. The course pushed students to develop a conceptual understanding of the communicative function of language, which, when coupled with concrete instantiations of genres and implemented through principles of MAC pedagogy, aimed to improve students' writing proficiency.

The Australian school of genre analysis, with Martin at its core, focuses solely on language learning; it is concerned with language acquisition, in general and with language proficiency, in particular. There is no explicit pedagogical action that consciously targets the learner's psychological development. In general, genre-based pedagogies consider development to be a by-product of instruction. The utilization of the MAC pedagogy (a concept based approach) attempts to directly address the matter of cognitive development during genre-based writing instruction. To this end it supplements the Australian genre-based pedagogy with the pedagogical ideas developed by Davydov and his colleagues – an approach that focuses on theoretical thinking based on conceptual instruction.

The concept-based approach to writing aims fundamentally to teach genre as a theoretical concept. This perspective adopts Vygotsky's notion of concept as a tool to solve a problem (Vygotsky 1987: 164). By application, genre is a tool to achieve more effective communication. It cannot be seen as just one more empirical category in foreign language education like functions and notions from the communicative approach to language teaching or grammatical structures. Instead, genre is a manifestation of the communicative principle we call ACP (abstract communicative principle), which is the basic relationship (abstract) of language functioning.

From the data considered in this chapter, it can be seen that students provided some indications that they were beginning to think theoretically about writing and how this relates to the abstract communicative principle. They often managed to recognize the power of the ACP to explain certain linguistic phenomena and to understand genre but they were sometimes unable to apprehend how it was realized in specific genres and how it could assist writing in these specific genres. In other words, theoretical thinking developed at the level of the conceptualization of genre but not at the level of a tool to write. Overall, the students improved their writing in the genres taught; however, they did not utilize theoretical thinking as a type of knowledge to assist themselves in this activity. Teaching writing in this approach means going beyond linguistic/genre analysis of samples of the genre under focus (the empirical aspect) and joint or individual (re)construction of texts, following empirical principles detected in the analysis. It is also extremely relevant to lead students to perceive that genre is a manifestation of the ACP and of its intrinsic dialectical relationship between rules and creativity and that this principle can explain an array of other linguistic phenomena.

The potential for student learning of the theoretical, concept-based, approach we considered in the chapter is supported by a number of studies in other educational domains surveyed by Karpov (2005). Karpov stresses that the true advantage to theoretical learning is not attested merely in students' ability to master a specific body of knowledge, but is its impact on the cognitive development of students such that when they approach new tasks and problems they follow a theoretical and systematic orientation (Karpov 2005: 189). For instance, in a study that compared the performance of second- and fourth-graders from a traditional school with those from an experimental school organized around the principles of concept-based instruction, it was reported that the latter group of students not only out-performed their traditional counterparts on specific problem sets but the experimental students oriented themselves to new problems in a far more systematic and theoretical way. In the study, students had to solve a series of problems whereby they had to rearrange a sequence of numbered chips into a new sequence using a maximum of eight moves. Not only did the experimental students do better than their traditional colleagues in solving each concrete problem but, according to Karpov (2005: 191), 75 percent of them at both grade levels immediately realized that 'the optimal solution of all the problems involved the same sequence of moves,' while only 20 percent of the second-graders and 30 percent of the fourth graders receiving traditional instruction discovered and used the general principle to solve the problems.

Ideally, something analogous should have occurred in the writing course under consideration here. That is, as a result of theoretical instruction the students were expected to be able to improve their writing for the genres actually studied while at the same time develop an understanding of the concepts of genre and communication that would enable them to approach the production of texts in new genres in a systematic and coherent way. Unfortunately, it was not possible to assess whether or not the students had achieved this ability, although based on their performance on the genres studied in the course, we suspect this would not have occurred. The reason it was not feasible to investigate this important matter was because the students had problems coping with the new approach, as we have mentioned earlier in the chapter. Far more time than anticipated at the outset of the course had to be spent on helping the students understand the theoretical concepts at issue. This is because most of the students resisted the new pedagogical approach to writing instruction. Unlike the students in the study mentioned by Karpov, the students in the present study had a long history of traditional, empirically-based schooling where learning to write meant following models for how to produce specific kinds of texts rather than approaching the writing process in a systematic and theoretical way. Consequently, a great deal of time was required to help the students appreciate the potential of the new approach and to convince them that it would, in the long run, result in improved writing. This was no easy task as many of the students resisted the approach as not relevant to their interests and needs, which was to learn how to write. Thus, while theoretical instruction has indeed proven to be a powerful way of learning in the case of children whose first exposure to schooling is through such an approach, it remains to be seen if it can have similar impact on adult learning. Our belief is that it can but it will take more time for this to happen, if the adults in question have been through years of empirical- rather than theoretically-based learning.

Notes

1. All student texts are not edited and are reproduced as written.
2. One of the problems Ferreira encountered as instruction and researcher emanated from the university's Institutional Review Board. When the project was approved, the IRB did not allow Ferreira as course instructor to have access to the students' logs in which they wrote about their attitudes toward the new methodology they encountered during the course. This was a procedure used to safeguard the students since the Board did not feel it was appropriate for the instructor to know which students had agreed to participate in the research portion of the project. Those students who had agreed were then expected to keep a log expressing their thoughts on the way the course was being conducted. Because Ferreira did not have access to the logs until after the course was completed and grades assigned, she was unable to interact with those students who expressed either a negative orientation or lack of understanding of what was transpiring in the course. This is an unfortunate but understandable consequence of the researcher-as-teacher design of the study. Future research will need to find a way of dealing with the matter without of course compromising the rights of the students.

References

Aidarova, L. (1982) *Child Development and Education.* Moscow: Progress Publishers.

Bakhurst, D. (1991) *Consciousness and Revolution in Soviet Philosophy.* Cambridge: Cambridge University Press.

Besson, T. (1996) *Cover Letters.* New York: John Wiley and Sons, Inc.

Bhatia, V. K. (1993) *Analyzing Genre: Language in Professional Settings.* London: Longman.

Davydov, V. V. (1984) Substantial generalization and the dialectical-materialistic theory of thinking. In M. Hedegaard, P. Hakkarainen and Y. Engström (eds), *Learning and Teaching on a Scientific Basis* 11–32. Aarhus, Denmark: Aarhus University Press.

Davydov, V. V. (1988a) The concept of theoretical generalization and problems of educational psychology. *Studies in Soviet Thought* 36: 169–202.

Davydov, V. V. (1988b) Problems of developmental teaching: the experience of theoretical and experimental psychology research. *Soviet Education* 30: (1) 6–97.

Davydov, V. V. (1988c) Problems of developmental teaching: the experience of theoretical and experimental psychological research. *Soviet Education* 30: (2) 3–83.

Davydov, V. V. (1988d) Problems of developmental teaching: the experience of theoretical and experimental psychological research. *Soviet Education* 30: (3) 3–77.

Davydov, V. V. (1999a) The content and unsolved problems of activity theory. In Y. Engström (ed.) *Perspectives on Activity Theory* 39–52. Cambridge: Cambridge University Press.

Davydov, V. V. (1999b) What is real learning activity? In M. Hedegaard and J. Lompscher (eds) *Learning Activity and Development* 123–38. Aarhus: Aarhus University Press.

Davydov, V. V. and Markova, A. K. (1983) A concept of educational activity for school children. *Soviet Psychology* 21: 50–76.

Eggins, S. (1994) *An Introduction to Systemic Functional Linguistics.* London: Pinter Publishers.

Engeström, Y., Hakkarainen, P. and Hedegaard, M. (1984) On the methodological basis of research in teaching and learning. In M. Hedegaard, P. Hakkarainen and Y. Engström (eds) *Learning and Teaching on a Scientific Basis* 119–89. Aarhus: Aarhus University Press.

Ferreira, M. M. (2005) A Concept-based Approach to Writing Instruction: From the Abstract Concept to the Concrete Performance. Unpublished doctoral dissertation. The Pennsylvania State University. University Park, PA.

Gal'perin, P. Y. (1992) Stage-by-stage formation as a method of psychological investigation. *Journal of Russian and Eastern European Psychology,* 30: 60–80.

Giest, H. and Lompscher, J. (2003) Formation of learning activity and theoretical thinking in science teaching. In A. Kozulim, B. Gindis, V. S. Ageyev and S. M. Miller (eds) *Vygotsky's Educational Theory in Cultural Context* 267–88. Cambridge: Cambridge University Press.

Hacker, D. (1999) *A Writer's Reference* (4th ed.). Boston: Bedford/St. Martin's.

Hacker, D. (2003) *A Writer's Reference* (5th ed.). New York: Bedford/St Martins.

Hall, R. (1967) Dialectic. In P. Edwards (ed.) *The Encyclopedia of Philosophy (Vol. 2)* 385–9. New York: Macmillan and the Free Press.

Hedegaard, M. (1987) Methodology in evaluative research on teaching and learning. In F. J. van Zuuren, F. F. Wertz and B. Mook (eds) *Advances in Qualitative Psychology* 53–8. Berwyn, PA: Swetz & Zeitlinger.

Hedegaard, M. (1990) The zone of proximal development as basis for instruction. In L. C. Moll and J. B. Greenberg (eds), *Vygotsky and Education* 349–71. Cambridge: Cambridge University Press.

Hedegaard, M. (1995) The qualitative analyses of the development of a child's theoretical knowledge and thinking. In L. Martin, K. Nelson and E. Tobach (eds) *Sociocultural Psychology. Theory and Practice of Doing and Knowing.* New York: Cambridge University Press.

Hedegaard, M. (1999) Activity theory and history teaching. In Y. Engström, R. Miettinen and R. L. Punamaki (eds) *Perspectives on Activity Theory* 282–97. Cambridge: Cambridge University Press.

Hedegaard, M. (2002) *Learning and Child Development: A Cultural-historical Study.* Aarhus: Aarhus University Press.

Hedegaard, M. and Sigersted, G. (1992) Experimental classroom teaching in history and anthropological geography. *Activity Theory* 11: 13–23.

Hedegaard, M., Chaiklin, S. and Pedraza, P. (2001) Culturally sensitive teaching within a Vygotskian perspective. In M. Hedegaard (ed.) *Learning in Classrooms: A Cultural Historical Approach* 121–43. Aarhus: Aarhus University Press.

Ilyenkov, E. V. (1982) *The Dialectics of the Abstract and the Concrete in Marx's Capital.* Moscow: Progress.

Karpov, Y. V. (2003) Vygotsky's doctrine of scientific concepts: its role for contemporary education. In A. Kozulim, B. Gindis, V. S. Ageyev and S. M. Miller (eds) *Vygotsky's Educational Theory in Cultural Context* 65–82. Cambridge: Cambridge University Press.

Karpov, Y. V. (2005) *The neo-Vygotskian Approach to Child Development.* Cambridge: Cambridge University Press.

Kern, R. (2000) *Literacy and Language Teaching.* Oxford: Oxford University Press.

Kozulin, A. (1986) The concept of activity in Soviet psychology: Vygotsky, his disciples and critics. *American Psychologist,* 41: 264–74.

Kozulin, A. (1995) The learning process: Vygotsky's theory in the mirror of its interpretations. *School Psychology International* 16: 117–29.

Kussman, T. (1976) The Soviet concept of development and the problem of activity. In K. F. Riegel and J. S. Meacham (eds), *The Developing Individual in a Changing World* 122-30. Chicago, IL: Mouton.

Lantolf, J. P. and S. L. Thorne (2006) *Sociocultural Theory and the Genesis of Second Language Development.* Oxford: Oxford University Press.

Leontiev, A. N. (1981) *Problems of the Development of the Mind.* Moscow: Progress.

Lompscher, J. (1984). Problems and results of experimental research on the formation of theoretical thinking through instruction. In M. Hedegaard, P. Hakkarainen and Y. Engström (eds) *Learning and Teaching on a Scientific Basis* 293–357. Aarhus: Aarhus University Press.

Lompscher, J. (1999a) Learning activity and its formation. In M. Hedegaard and J. Lompscher (eds) *Learning Activity and Development* 139–66. Aarhus: Aarhus University Press.

Lompscher, J. (1999b) Activity formation as an alternative strategy of instruction. In Y. Engström, R. Miettinen and R. L. Punamaki (eds) *Perspectives on Activity Theory* 264–81. Cambridge: Cambridge University Press.

Macken, M. and Slade, D. (1993) Assessment: a foundation for effective learning in the school context. In B. Cope and M. Kalantzis (eds) *The Powers of Literacy: A Genre Approach to Teaching Writing* 203-230. Pittsburgh, PA: University of Pittsburgh Press.

Markova, A. K. (1979) *The Teaching and Mastery of Language*. White Plains, NY: M. E. Sharpe Inc.

Martin, J. (1993) Genre and literacy: modeling context in educational linguistics. *Annual Review of Applied Linguistics* 13: 141–72.

Newman, F. and Holzman, L. (1993) *Lev Vygotsky: Revolutionary Scientist*. London: Routledge.

Schneuwly, B. (2004) *Gêneros e tipos de discurso: considerações psicológicas e ontogenéticas* [Genre and types of discourse: psychological and ontogenetic considerations]. In Schneuwly, B. and Dolz, J. (eds) *Gêneros orais e escritos na escola* 21–39. São Paulo: Mercado de Letras.

Tedick, D. J. (1990) ESL writing assessment: subject-matter knowledge and its impact on performance. *English for Specific Purposes* 9: 123–43.

Vygotsky, L. S. (1978) *Mind in Society. The Development of Higher Psychological Processes*. Cambridge, MA: Harvard University Press.

Vygotsky, L. S. (1987) *The Collected Works of L. S. Vygotsky: Vol 1. Problems in General Psychology. Including the Volume Thinking and Speech*. New York: Plenum.

Vygotsky, L. S. (1997) *Educational Psychology*. Boca Raton, FL: St Lucie Press.

Wells, G. (1993) Commentary: the complementary contributions of Halliday and Vygotsky to a 'language-based theory of learning.' *Linguistics and Education* 6: 41–90.

Wells, G. (1995) Language and the Inquiry-oriented curriculum. *Curriculum Inquiry,* 25(3), 233–69.

Wells, G. (1999) *Dialogic Inquiry: Toward a Sociocultural Practice and Theory of Education*. Cambridge: Cambridge University Press.

Wertsch, J. V. (1981) Editor's introduction. In J. V. Wertsch (ed.) *The Concept of Activity in Soviet Psychology* 37–40. Armonk, NY: Sharpe.

Appendix 10.1. Level descriptors for scoring writing performance

A. Holistic scoring 4-point scale for cover letters:

4 (very good) A cover letter in this category has the following:

- The cover letter is a very good sample of the genre. It contains all the following moves: (minor) – Heading, Inside address, Greeting, Closing – and (major) – Explanation of why one is contacting the employer, Summary of one's experience, accomplishments and qualifications, Initiative to make contact with the employer. The letter can have mistakes in the minor moves but not in the major ones.

- The message required by each generic move is fully conveyed. The sequence of information is very appropriate to the genre. Information is appropriately extended, enhanced or further elaborated.

- The writer efficiently tailors the letter to the employer's needs. The linguistic forms (lexical items, verbs, adjectives, adverbs) used are very appropriate to the audience, i.e., they provide a formal and polite tone to the letter. The letter is concise, non-demanding, emotionally neutral and refers to the quality of the company.

- The clauses are fully integrated within the sentence. There is use of different types of sentences (simple, complex, compound). Sentences do not always start with I. The text is cohesive. No linguistic errors (word choice, grammar, punctuation, spelling, etc.) are found in the text.

3 (good) A cover letter in this category has the following:

- The cover letter is a good sample of the genre. It contains more than half of the seven moves. Two of the major moves (Explanation of why one is contacting the employer, Summary of one's experience, accomplishments and qualifications, Initiative to make contact with the employer) have a quality ranging from high to medium.

- The message required by one major move is not fully conveyed. The sequence of information is somewhat appropriate to the genre. Information is somewhat extended, enhanced and further elaborated.

- The writer somewhat tailors the letter to the employer's needs. The linguistic forms (lexical items, verbs, adjectives, adverbs) used are almost totally appropriate to the audience, i.e., they provide an almost formal and polite tone to the letter. The letter is not one of the following: concise, non-demanding, emotionally neutral and refers to the quality of the company.

- The clauses are almost fully integrated within the sentence. Sentences do not always start with I. The text is almost totally cohesive. Some linguistic errors (word choice, grammar, punctuation, spelling, etc.) are found in the text, but they do not interfere with its comprehensibility.

2 (reasonable) A cover letter in this category has the following:

- The cover letter is partially satisfactory. It contains half of the seven moves. The letter has one to two of the major moves (Explanation of why you're contacting the employer, Summary of your experience, accomplishments and qualifications, Initiative to make contact with the employer) present but its quality will be from medium to low.

- The message required by two of the three major generic moves are not fully conveyed. The sequence of information is somewhat appropriate to the genre. There is some use of language which extends, enhances or elaborates on the information.

- The writer partially tailors the letter to the employer's needs. The linguistic forms (lexical items, verbs, adjectives, adverbs) used are somewhat appropriate to the audience, i.e., the letter is somewhat informal, but the tone is still polite. The letter is not two of the following: concise, non-demanding, emotionally neutral and refers to the quality of the company.

- The clauses are somewhat integrated within the sentence. The text is somewhat cohesive. The layout of the text partially resembles a formal letter. The letter tends to be I centered. A considerable number of linguistic errors (word choice, grammar, punctuation, spelling, etc.) are found in the text which may or may not interfere with comprehensibility.

1 (poor) A cover letter in this category has the following:

- The cover letter is poor. It contains less than half of the seven moves. In addition, none of the major moves (Explanation of why one is contacting the employer, Summary of one's experience, accomplishments and qualifications, Initiative to make contact with the employer) will be present or all the major moves are realized with poor quality.

- The message required by each major generic move is conveyed in a restricted way. The sequence of information is inappropriate to the genre. Information is inefficiently extended, enhanced or elaborated.

- The writer tailors the letter to the employer's needs in a limited way. The linguistic forms (lexical items, verbs, adjectives, adverbs) used are inappropriate to the audience, i.e., the letter is very informal, but the tone is still polite. The letter is not three or more of the following: concise, non-demanding, emotionally neutral and refers to the quality of the company.

- The clauses are integrated within the sentence in a limited way. The text is barely cohesive. The lay out resembles a formal letter in a limited way. The letter is I centered. A lot of linguistic errors (word choice, grammar, punctuation, spelling, etc.) are found in the text and which interfere with comprehensibility.

B. Holistic scoring 4-point scale for argumentative texts:

4 (very good) An argumentative text in this category contains the following:

- The text is a very good sample of the genre. It contains all of the major generic moves (setting the context for the thesis statement (i.e., introduction); thesis statement; argumentation supporting the thesis statement and conclusion) and at least two of the four minor moves (opponent's view, rebuttal to the opponent's view, establishing common ground, restatement of the thesis). All or almost all of them are developed well.

- The message required by each generic move is fully conveyed. The sequence of information is very appropriate to the genre. Information is appropriately extended, enhanced or further elaborated. The introduction sets the context for the thesis. The thesis has almost all the following features (contains 'generalization demanding proof of further development,' (Hacker 1999) is narrowed enough to be fully developed in the number of pages allotted, is sharply focused, reveals the writer's stance about the issue). The argumentation fully supports the thesis with plenty of evidence (statistics, testimonies, examples, invented examples, personal experiences, stories). The conclusion provides a strong sense of closure to the text.

- The text efficiently entices the audience. The linguistic forms (nouns, verbs, adjectives, adverbs) used are very appropriate to the audience and to the writer's goal. The opponent's views are represented in a strategic way. If rebutted by the writer, the rebuttal should be polite and convincing.

- The clauses are almost fully integrated within the sentence. There is a wide variety of sentences (simple, complex, compound). Sentences start with a variety of different words. The text is considerably cohesive. Almost no linguistic errors (word choice, grammar, punctuation, spelling, etc.) are found in the text.

3 (good) An argumentative text in this category contains the following:

- The text is a good sample of the genre. It contains either: a) a thesis + argumentation + either an introduction or conclusion + one minor move, or b) it contains the four major moves without the minor ones.

- The message required by three to four of the major moves is fully conveyed. The sequence of information is appropriate to the purpose of the genre. Information is somewhat extended, enhanced and further elaborated. The introduction somewhat sets the context for the thesis. The thesis has three of the following features ('contains generalization demanding proof of further development,' (Hacker 1999) is narrowed enough to be fully developed in the number of pages allotted, is sharply focused, reveals the writer's stance about the issue). The argumentation almost fully supports the thesis with plenty of evidence (statistics, testimonies, examples, invented examples, personal experiences, stories). The conclusion provides a good sense of closure to the text.

- The text almost efficiently entices the audience. The linguistic forms (nouns, verbs, adjectives, adverbs) used are somewhat appropriate to the audience and to the goal of the writer. If the opponent's views are represented they are represented in a strategic way.

- The clauses are almost fully integrated within the sentences. There is variety of sentences (simple, complex, compound). Sentences start in somewhat different ways. The text is considerably cohesive. Almost no linguistic errors (word choice, grammar, punctuation, spelling, etc.) are found in the text.

2 (reasonable) An argumentative text in this category contains the following:

- The text is partially satisfactory. It contains three of the major moves or it contains either a thesis without support or argumentation without a clearly stated thesis but with an introduction and a conclusion.

- The message required by two of the generic moves is partially conveyed. The sequence of information is somewhat appropriate to the genre. Information is partially extended, enhanced or elaborated. If there is thesis it has two of the following features (contains 'generalization demanding proof of further development,' (Hacker 1999) is narrowed enough to be fully developed in the number of pages allotted, is sharply focused, reveals the writer's stance about the issue). The argumentation partially supports the thesis with some evidence (statistics, testimonies, examples, invented examples, personal experiences, stories). The conclusion provides some sense of closure to the text.

- The text barely entices the audience. Most of the linguistic forms (nouns, verbs, adjectives, adverbs) used are inappropriate to the audience and to the goal of the writer. If the opponent's views are represented they are not represented in a strategic way.

- The clauses are not always integrated within the sentence. There is little variety of sentences (simple, complex, compound). There is some variation in how sentences start. The text is somewhat cohesive. A considerable number of linguistic errors (word choice, grammar, punctuation, spelling, etc.) are found in the text.

1 (poor) An argumentative text in this category contains the following:

- The text is poor. It contains two of the major moves.

- The message required by all the major generic moves is conveyed in a restricted way. The sequence of information is inappropriate to the genre. Information is inefficiently extended, enhanced or elaborated. There is no thesis and if there is one it has one or none of the following features (contains 'generalization demanding proof of further development,' (Hacker 1999) is narrowed enough to be fully developed in the number of pages allotted, is sharply focused, reveals the writer's stance about the issue). The argumentation supports the thesis in a very limited way or not at all. There is little evidence. The conclusion barely provides a sense of closure to the text or does not close the text at all.

- The text does not entice the audience. The linguistic forms (nouns, verbs, adjectives, adverbs) used are very inappropriate to the audience and to the writer's goal. The opponent's views are not represented.

- Most of the clauses are not integrated within the sentence. There is no variety of sentences (simple, complex, compound). There is limited variation in the way sentences start. The text is barely cohesive. A lot of linguistic errors (word choice, grammar, punctuation, spelling, etc.) are found in the text and they interfere with comprehensibility.

11 Materializing linguistic concepts through 3-D clay modeling: a tool-and-result approach to mediating L2 Spanish development

Maria Serrano-Lopez and Matthew E. Poehner

Introduction

Prepositions are among the most difficult grammatical features for L2 learners to master, in part because the relations among individuals, objects and activities represented by prepositions are conceptualized in myriad ways across languages (Lightbown 1987: 185). As a case in point, consider the spatial relations represented by the Spanish locatives *en, sobre, de* and *a.* Grammar books have traditionally translated these expressions for English-speaking learners as *in* and *on,* although as Gonzalez-Pueyo (1995: 86) explains, there is strong semantic overlapping between these prepositions as well as syntactic incompatibilities between Spanish and English. For example, L2 learners of Spanish wishing to situate some event or action 'at night' are challenged by semantic polysemy and synonymy as they must select one of several alternatives: *de noche, por la noche, durante la noche* and *en la noche.* As a result of such complexities, various pedagogical 'rules' have been devised that describe instances when one preposition should be used over another (e.g., *en la noche* refers to set up time while *durante la noche* is reserved for unestablished time). Nevertheless, Spanish locative constructions continue to pose problems for English-speaking learners even at advanced levels of study, when they have presumably had hours of explicit instruction and practice. Is it that even more 'seat time' is necessary before learners are able to control these features? Or could better results be obtained if a different pedagogical approach were followed?

In the present chapter, we argue in favor of the latter option. Specifically, we suggest that the difficulty experienced by English-speaking learners of L2 Spanish prepositions stems from a lack of conceptual congruence between locatives in each language. That is, the spatial relations represented by Spanish prepositions differ conceptually from English spatial relations and so cannot be resolved by grammatical rules of thumb. Instead, a new orienting basis is required that makes clear to learners the underlying conceptualizations realized through *en, sobre, de* and *a*. This chapter describes the implementation of a pedagogical innovation for teaching prepositions based on the pioneering work of Davis (1997) with dyslexic individuals in which learning activities are mediated through the creation of 3-D clay models to represent difficult concepts. Although the *Davis Method* does not explicitly refer to Vygotskian theory, it resonates well with the systemic theoretical approach to instruction developed by Vygotsky's colleague, Piotr Gal'perin (1967, 1989, 1992). In systemic-theoretical instruction, or *concept-based instruction* (CBI) as it has come to be known, learners pass through a series of stages as they internalize theoretical knowledge. Recently, CBI has begun to attract the attention of L2 researchers (e.g., Negueruela 2003; Lantolf and Thorne 2006; Negueruela and Lantolf 2006). Our discussion focuses on one stage of Gal'perin's internalization model, *materialization*, which entails the presentation of abstract knowledge to learners in a concrete form. Whereas Gal'perin emphasized the use of charts and diagrams prepared by a teacher or other expert, we contend that learner-created artifacts can function as powerful mediators of learning as well. In our view, learner-generated 3-D clay models are an important extension of Gal'perin's approach. We present examples of 3-D clay models developed by L2 learners to represent the Spanish locatives and discuss how they mediated the learners' understanding of the spatial relations represented by the prepositions.

Gal'perin's stage-by-stage model of internalization

Although the relevance of teaching and learning for cognitive development was a subject of keen interest for Vygotsky and was central to many of his well-known proposals, including the Zone of Proximal Development, his untimely death meant that he was not able to fully elucidate the specifics of this relationship. Kozulin (1998, 2003) submits that the implications of Vygotsky's work for education stem directly from his core principle that human mental abilities are always mediated. He explains that just as individuals make use of physical tools when engaging in labor activities, they rely on symbolic tools during school activities, in which they encounter abstract knowledge, usually organized according to specific domains such as history, mathematics and language. In school, the cultural artifacts that enable individuals to interact with the abstract in a mediated, rather than direct, manner include signs, numeric systems, writing systems, graphs, charts and tables (Kozulin 2003: 18). According to Kozulin (1998), through extensive and intensive use of these symbolic tools, learners develop *internalized* versions of them, which he refers to as psychological tools (Kozulin 1998: 89). Psychological tools afford learners greater awareness and control of cognitive processes, which from a Vygotskian perspective *is* development (ibid.). The significance of psychological tools is that they enable learners to engage more fully and more expertly in activities that require hypothetical reasoning, problem solving, experimentation and related abilities (Kozulin 1998: 84–5).

Moreover, 'because sociocultural theory emphasizes the historical character of human cognition, the conceptual structure of disciplinary knowledge appears here as a veritable form of human thinking' (Kozulin 2003: 33). In other words, the conceptual study of history teaches one to think like an historian and the conceptual study of math teaches one to think like a mathematician. Domains of knowledge, then, each have their own underlying logic, their own unique concepts that serve as 'symbolic devices' for representing their object of study, for highlighting essential characteristics of that object and for organizing relationships among the various categories and principles that form the domain. In fact, van der Veer (2000: 99) attributes the poor academic performance of many learners to pedagogical approaches that fail to provide a proper orienting basis to the subject matter. He argues that instruction that privileges memorization over conceptual understanding of content results in learners' inability to apply their knowledge to topics and problems that differ only slightly from those they have previously encountered.

Gal'perin's CBI is a highly systematic approach to promoting the internalization of conceptual knowledge. Based on Gal'perin's analysis of human mental action CBI emphasizes the importance of the quality of concepts presented to learners and prescribes stages through which learners must pass to fully internalize theoretical knowledge (see Talyzina 1981). Briefly, CBI contrasts with many traditional pedagogies by advocating that learners be introduced to the essential characteristics of their subject matter at the outset of study rather than focusing on narrower sub-topics that might appear easy to learn (Arievitch and Stetsenko 2000: 77).

In the case of mathematics instruction, for instance, one begins with notions of quantification and measurement. Students initially are asked to describe concrete objects and are introduced to the concept of measuring objects' dimensions. At first, they may take measurements using bits of string and report their results in terms of string-units (e.g., the length of the table is eight bits of string). This lays the groundwork for both thinking about quantities more abstractly (i.e., where eight is a symbol that need not refer to any actual units) and for performing basic operations such as addition and subtraction. Crucially, this orienting basis helps learners to more fully and accurately grasp the meaning of numbers and operations and this will affect how they approach mathematics even at advanced levels of study. In more traditional approaches to mathematics instruction learners are often left with only a partial understanding of the relations among quantities, addition, multiplication, fractions, square roots, etc. Only by learning the guiding principles at the outset of study can learners formulate the necessary 'concrete orientation basis to solve any specific problem in a given subject domain' (Arievitch and Stetsenko 2000: 77). In this way, learners develop a theoretical rather than an empirical understanding of the relevant domain. That is, their understanding is conceptual (i.e., a general understanding of the essence of the object of study) rather than based upon a series of isolated empirical experiences.

According to Gal'perin, full internalization of conceptual knowledge is preceded by two stages: materialization and verbalization. During the first, concepts are presented to learners in a concrete form, which may be either material or materialized (Talyzina 1981). The former refers to representations of conceptual knowledge that learners can physically manipulate, as in the case of models, while the latter includes graphs, tables, charts and other symbolic tools as described above. An interesting example of the mediating potential of a material artifact is found in the work of Kabanova (1985), who used colored plates arranged in various configurations to help L1 Russian children learn the concept of word and syntactic ordering. The importance of rendering the abstract in a material or materialized form is that it helps learners to identify essential characteristics of concepts. As they work through tasks and problems, learners rely on these external forms of mediation to help them understand the operations necessary for carrying out and evaluating their performance. As they become more proficient, the material or materialized artifact is internalized and their dependence on its fully external form is replaced by self-mediating private speech. That is, mediation is still required but this is achieved by 'talking themselves through' problems. In some instances, learners find written language, which is more material than spoken language, to be a helpful intermediary step as they move toward greater autonomy. Eventually, private speech disappears and the process is carried out internally, on what Vygotsky described as the intramental plane of inner speech – the plane where meaning predominates over form (Vygotsky 1978). Of course, we may also re-access earlier stages of our development under conditions of intense cognitive activity (see Frawley and Lantolf 1985). This can be observed, for example, when advanced language learners resort to talking through problems in their L1, as might happen when calculating currency exchange rates or using a map to find one's way.

To illustrate the value of Gal'perin's framework for helping us to understand development and design appropriate pedagogical interventions, consider the following study reported by Karpov and Gindis (2000). Their research seeks to identify learners' current stage of internalization in order to determine the form of mediational support needed to move them to the next stage. Karpov and Gindis used their procedure to support the development of analogical reasoning abilities of school-aged children with learning disabilities. Given the learners' special needs, the researchers quickly found that material, rather than materialized, support proved especially useful because it enabled the children to physically manipulate objects that represented elements in the analogies. The authors developed a three-level hierarchy of mediational support which they termed visual-motor, visual-imagery and symbolic. At the visual-motor level, the children required physical objects that they could manipulate while solving the analogies. Learners at the visual-imagery level still required the presence of physical objects but no longer needed to physically move them. At the final stage, physical objects were irrelevant as learners were able to complete the tasks by self-mediating (either using private speech or completely internally). Learners were first assessed to determine their current level of analogical reasoning, defined according to the level of mediation required to complete the analogies and subsequent intervention was aimed at helping them move beyond that stage. According to Karpov and Gindis, this method produced impressive results. One particularly compelling case involved a seven year-old girl who had been identified with attention-deficit-hyperactivity-disorder (ADHD) and was described by her teachers as having marked limitations in her cognitive and linguistic abilities. Initially, the child was unable to solve the analogies even at the visual-motor level, but through an intervention in which she received dialogic support from a mediator she was eventually able to progress to the symbolic stage of thinking (Karpov and Gindis 2000: 151).

Tool-and-result methodology

Despite these and other successes reported by proponents of Gal'perin-inspired pedagogies (see Kabanova 1985; Karpova 1977; Markóva 1979; Talyzina 1981), they have not escaped criticism. Van der Veer (2000: 101), for example, worries about the plausibility of identifying key organizing principles and concepts within a domain, noting that this is a culturally-embedded process, with different cultures likely generating their own organizational schemas. This is no doubt a legitimate concern and fits well with Vygotsky's understanding of genetic domains. Even in well-established disciplines that would appear to have clear organizing principles and concepts, as with the natural sciences, new discoveries and theoretical perspectives sometimes require a re-thinking of the basic paradigm (e.g., the impact of Einstein's work on centuries worth of thinking in physics). The point is that the concepts introduced to students should not be reified as immutable representations of reality but should constitute a theoretically-informed, research-grounded, best (though contingent) understanding of the object of study available.

A critique more relevant to the present study concerns the highly structured nature of CBI. Does this leave adequate room for adaptability on the part of both teachers and learners? Other approaches to promoting learner development, such as Reuven Feuerstein's Instrumental Enrichment program, follow highly flexible procedures, arguing that adaptation is a defining feature of life in late Modern, rapidly changing, technological societies (Feuerstein, Rand and Rynders 1988: 62). The notion of a systematic but emergent approach rather than a highly structured one articulates well with the interpretation of Vygotsky's writings proposed by Newman and Holzman (1993), psychologists and educators who have formulated principles for implementing Vygotsky's ideas on development through education in a variety of contexts.

Newman and Holzman (1993: 38–9) distinguish between what they refer to as *tool-for-result* and *tool-and-result* methodologies. They illustrate the difference between these by pointing out that some physical tools, such as hammers, are pre-designed to carry out specific kinds of actions (e.g., hammering nails into boards to build a wall) and are readily available in hardware stores, while other tools are manufactured in the process of carrying out a given activity, such as happens when tool-and-die makers build unique tools to the specifications of a particular task. According to Newman and Holzman, tools in this latter category 'are inseparable from results in that their essential character (their defining feature) is the activity of their development rather than their function ... They are defined in and by the process of their production' (ibid.). This type of *tool-and-result* does not have a purpose or identity (or name even) that is generalized beyond the activity for which it was created. The tool both emerges from and serves as an affordance that enables the tool-and-dye maker's activity.

Returning to our discussion of education, a core tenet of Vygotskian theory is that individuals use tools to transform their environment and, in the process, are themselves transformed. Indeed, as we explained above, Vygotsky-based instructional programs are predicated on the notion that activity mediated by symbolic tools gives rise to new cognitive functions as these tools are assigned psychological status. Following Newman and Holzman, only a tool-and-result approach to mediation fully realizes human development as a transformative, revolutionary activity. From this perspective, engaging learners in the creation of their own symbolic tools opens the door to developmental trajectories that cannot be predicted a priori or mapped onto a pre-determined course syllabus.

In the remainder of this chapter we report the results of a pedagogical innovation that we believe is congruent with Newman and Holzman's notion of tool-and-result methodology. Specifically, the Davis Method of 3-D clay modeling (Davis 1997) was used to materialize the spatial relations represented by the Spanish locatives *en, sobre, de* and *a*. Importantly, the models were generated by L2 learners themselves, who also explained how the models instantiated the use of these prepositions. In the following section, we detail the specifics of this program and its implementation with learners of L2 Spanish. We then provide examples of the clay models that were produced by the learners and we present evidence of learners' subsequent enhanced control over the relevant locatives, as indicated by their performance on pre- and post-tests and in comparison with a control group.

3-D clay modeling instruction

Davis (1997: 21) explains that when dyslexic individuals learn to read in their L1, they often experience confusion identifying what he terms *trigger words*, which include function words such as prepositions. In Davis' view, these trigger words are problematic because dyslexic individuals are unable to link them to an accurate concept or mental picture (ibid.). To help learners overcome this problem, Davis proposes a visual-kinesthetic method that employs three dimensional (3-D) clay figures and models to link the concept represented by the preposition to a physical reality, a 'picture' of the concept that the individual did not have before (see Phoenix 2006 for additional discussion).

Davis argues that the problem dyslexics experience learning to read trigger words actually stems from a poorly developed conceptual understanding of the relations they represent (Davis 1997: 21). He maintains that this confusion exacerbates the dyslexia, leading to *perceptual instability* and contends that 3-D models function to reduce the confusion by helping learners to create new mental pictures of the words' underlying concept. Following Davis, we submit that while 'perceptions' among dyslexics learning to read their L1 are unstable, for adult L2 learners they are often impoverished. Indeed, as Gal'perin noted, many learners needlessly fail because instructional methods do not provide a proper orienting basis to the object of study (van der Veer 2000: 99).

Although Davis developed the 3-D modeling method independent of Gal'perin's model of internalization, we believe it is not only commensurable with CBI but that it also extends it in important ways. Davis's method offers an even more concrete instantiation of the concept to be learned than do charts and diagrams because it not only stimulates learners' visual but also their tactile and auditory (through verbalization) senses and directly engages their creativity. In fact, Davis comments that his clay modeling method emerged from his clinical experience using simple visual images with dyslexics, an approach that was not effective at all (Davis, personal communication). He further notes that earlier interventions in which learners drew representations of concepts (see Ferreira and Lantolf, Chapter 10, this volume) were also not quite as successful as clay modelling (ibid.).

3-D clay modeling may provide an additional benefit beyond the additional (haptic) channel. Unlike pre-manufactured manipulatives, students are required to make their own models using the clay (i.e., tool-and-result). This process of external, physical model creation may serve as a focus, inspiration and reinforcement for the process of internal modeling that is necessary for learning the explicit knowledge of the preposition. Clay work helps create a 'bridge' between the consciously accessible (e.g. dictionary definition) and preverbal (e.g. kinesthetic) understanding. The combination of verbal, visual and kinesthetic creation and learning in a single learning session allows a deep, multi-level understanding of the concept.

The process of guided 3-D clay modeling appears to allow the explicit conceptual system to be used to build a physical model. The model generally is built of open-class concepts (i.e., nouns) but can express non-verbal spatial information. It is concrete but expresses abstractions, thus it has a dialectical quality. The abstractions or spatial elements expressed in the model are readily accessible, having been made explicit, tangible and enduring. This model and the kinesthetic and cognitive memories of its creation can thus be accessed by the closed-class system. In addition, having been engaged in building the model, the student may be able to learn from memory of the process or its result at a later time.

3-D clay modeling of L2 Spanish locatives

Context

The data described in this study are part of a larger study conducted by Serrano-Lopez (2003) that investigated the effects of 3-D clay modeling as an intervention in the teaching of Spanish locatives to L2 learners. In this section we present data of L2 learners' developing understanding of uses of Spanish prepositions in cases where they cannot rely on their L1 to generate appropriate uses.

Participants in the study included 241 advanced university learners of L2 Spanish enrolled in 12 sections of a fourth-semester Spanish language course, the highest level required needed to fulfill the requirement at the university where the data were collected. The sections of this course were divided into three groups, two experimental and one that served as a control. Both experimental groups were introduced to the locative concepts through a formal lecture and given written practice exercises. One of the groups, which we refer to as the CBI group, also engaged in 3-D clay modeling of the concepts. Students in the control group received no classroom instruction or assignments related to the relevant prepositions during the study. In fact, the course from which participants were recruited was oriented toward reading and culture and grammar was neither studied explicitly nor discussed in the course textbook. Of course, students in this group had studied grammar, including use of prepositions, in other courses and may have consulted reference books outside of class. The control group functioned to evaluate the effectiveness of both experimental groups.

For students in the two experimental groups, presentation of the concepts was conducted in English. Students were given a sheet that explained the underlying spatial concepts represented by the prepositions (Appendix 11.1). For example, they were instructed that the Spanish preposition *a* can be used to specify a relation that requires movement from an object's original location to some other point and that this can be rendered in English as *in, through* and *into*. This relation was then illustrated with the Spanish sentence *El paracaidista se lanzó a el vacio* and its English equivalent, *The skydiver jumped into the air*. Additional explanations and examples are provided in Appendix 11.1.

Students were encouraged to ask questions and to consider how use of Spanish prepositions differed from English. They were then referred to the handouts (Appendix 11.1) that summarized the information presented during the lecture and offered contrastive examples. The learners next worked independently through written exercises that required them to use the Spanish locatives. The CBI group also participated in an extra session designed to familiarize them with Davis' clay modeling method. These learners were given a worksheet (Appendix 11.2) that explained the rationale behind the approach and offered hints about how to create their models. An additional handout (Appendix 11.3) provided guidelines to help learners verbalize the definition and signification of their models once they were completed (this phase was referred to as 'Talk to your clay').

During the clay modeling session, the students created their models to correspond to self-generated sentences illustrating use of Spanish locatives. They presented their sentence and model to the instructor to ensure that they had appropriately understood the concept. This was followed by the 'Talk to your clay' exercise. They were also encouraged to make a mental picture of their model. Due to scheduling limitations, there was no time for the final planned stage that required learners to invent and share additional sentences illustrating the concepts.

All participants were administered the Spatial Prepositions Usage Test, a non-standardized assessment designed by the researcher to evaluate learners' ability to correctly use spatial prepositions in English and Spanish. Each of the 11 items on the test presents a picture accompanied by a descriptive sentence that learners must complete by providing the appropriate preposition. The English and Spanish versions of the test were trialed using native speakers of each language in order to identify problematic items. Figure 11.1 is a typical item from the test.

The same questions were used in both languages (translations), although they were arranged in a different order. The test was administered in both languages (first in English, then in Spanish) prior to instruction, immediately following instruction and again two weeks after instruction. An analysis of covariance (ANCOVA) was performed to control pre-existing differences among the groups, if any. The ANCOCA of the pre- and follow-up tests allowed adjustments for the pretest measurement when it covaried with the outcome measurement. Unless specified otherwise, the ANCOVA analyses were performed at a level of significance of 0.05 (α = 0.05) to decide whether to reject the null hypothesis. Post hoc Bonferroni tests were performed whenever ANCOVA found significant results.

Examples of 3-D clay models of Spanish locatives

Before turning to an analysis of the results we will present examples of 3-D clay models so that the reader may better appreciate how models

I presume the judoka _____top will be the champion (Answer: on)
Presumo que el judoka _____arriba será el vencedor (Answer: de)

Figure 11.1. Sample item from spatial prepositions usage test.

can be used to represent spatial relations. It is worth noting that although the relationship between a given clay model and Spanish locative is not always apparent, it nevertheless expresses a meaning for the learner-sculptor, who was able to explain the signification to the researcher and others in the class.

The model in Figure 11.2 represents the action of diving into a swimming pool. The diver disappearing into the water shows the active nature of the preposition. The model emphasizes the concept of entering a volume, region, or substance. Thus, although *a* is usually translated as 'to' this model reminds its creator that people jump 'into' water or air.

Figure 11.3 represents the use of the Spanish preposition *sobre* to express a spatial relation that is difficult for English-speaking learners. In this model, a person leans on a table while reading. The preposition *sobre* describes the position of the reader 'over the book.' In this case, one can refer to the book as either *en* or *sobre* the table, but the reader's higher, dominating position over the book can only be expressed using *sobre*.

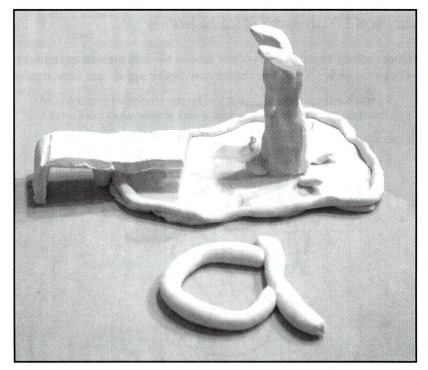

Figure 11.2. Example of model representing preposition *a*.

Figure 11.3. Example of model representing preposition *sobre*.

Turning to the clay models in Figures 11.4 and 11.5, we see representations of the preposition *de* to portray a spatial relation of attachment
that is difficult for English-speaking learners to conceptualize. The
English structure 'the flowers in the corner,' for example, is problematic
for learners of L2 Spanish, who often attempt to translate 'in' using *en*
when the correct preposition is in fact *de*. The model in Figure 11.4
shows little plants connected to the corner itself to signify that these
plants are attached to, or belong to, the corner. In this way, the model
helps the learner remember this concept and to associate it with
the preposition *de*. Similarly, Figure 11.5 invokes a strong sense of
permanence-in-place, as the tree is clearly rooted to the ground and
therefore occupying a fixed position in the garden. While a movable
object would be *en el jardín* it would be incorrect to use this structure
for the tree in the garden because it does not convey the tree's spatial
relationship to the garden; it is unlikely that someone would move the
tree because of its attached position. In Figure 11.6 we see a simple,
straightforward, model to reinforce the notion that although Spanish *en*
is usually translated as *in*, the phrase 'on TV' is correctly rendered as
'en la TV.'
    Once the students finished their models they took turns sharing them
with their classmates. When asked to explain the 'story' behind the
model, some students initially had difficulties communicating the meaning of their creation even though it was evident that the models had a
clear signification for them. In one particularly revealing instance, a
learner remarked: 'It may not mean much to you but it is very clear to
me, [i.e., it had a private, intramental, function] and this is the exact
representation of the concept I am learning.' Eventually, all the learners

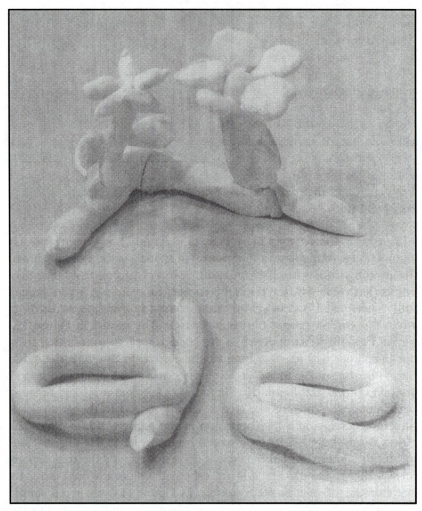

Figure 11.4. Example of model representing preposition *de*.

were able to share the meaning of their creation and this in itself was an enjoyable activity.

Results

Analyses of the three groups' performances on the pre- and post-tests revealed the following: 1) the CBI intervention had a significant immediate and delayed general effect over both instruction alone and no

Figure 11.5. Example of model representing preposition *de*.

instruction for the mixed spatial concepts; 2) CBI can both help resolve confusion regarding overlapping spatial concepts between the L1 and L2 and create new mental representations that do not exist in the L1; and 3) instruction without the clay modeling component had no significant immediate or delayed effect over no instruction.

More specifically, an ANCOVA analysis of the relevant questions (those involving prepositions expected to cause confusion) on the post-test

Figure 11.6. Example of model representing preposition *en*.

and the follow-up test using the pre-test as the covariate showed for a majority of those questions a significant relationship between the covariate and the dependent variable (Post-test F (1,182) = 17.94; $p < 0.001$ and follow-up test F (1,189) = 23.69; $p < 0.001$). This indicates that previous knowledge of Spanish prepositions accounted for a significant portion of the variance of the immediate and delayed measures of Spanish prepositional knowledge. Performing an ANCOVA test of the effects of instruction method (post-test F (2,182) = 11.23; $p < 0.001$ and follow-up test F (2,189) = 9.71; $p < 0.001$) revealed a significant difference in the dependent variable after the impact of previous knowledge was controlled for by the covariate. In other words, when previous knowledge was accounted for, there remained a significant effect of different instructional methods.

A Bonferroni post-hoc test was then performed on post-test and follow-up test scores for all three groups (see Table 11.1). The results showed that there was no significant difference between the No Instruction group and the Instruction only group ($p = 0.041$) or between the Instruction only and the CBI group ($p = 0.086$). However, a significant difference was found between the No Instruction group and the CBI group ($p < 0.001$). Moreover, a Bonferroni post-hoc test of the scores on the follow-up test showed a significant difference between the No

Table 11.1. Bonferroni post-hoc analysis of posttest and follow-up test scores

	No instruction group vs instruction only group	Instruction only group vs CBI group	No instruction group vs CBI group
Posttest	No (p = 0.041)	No (p = 0.086)	Yes (p < 0.001)
Follow-up test	No (p = 0.434)	Yes (p < 0.016)	Yes (p < 0.001)

Instruction group and the CBI group (p < 0.001) but not between the No Instruction group and the Instruction only group (p = 0.434). A significant difference on the follow-up test was also found between Instruction only and CBI groups (p < 0.016).

For the delayed effect, as indicated by follow-up test scores, the CBI group performed significantly better than the Instruction only group. The effects of instruction without clay modeling faded after only two weeks, as indicated by the significant p value for the No Instruction versus Instruction only groups on the follow-up test as compared to the post-test. The addition of the clay modeling stage resulted in a longer lasting effect on learners' performance. We conclude from this that although instruction in general had a positive effect on learners' acquisition of Spanish locatives, CBI, with its 3-D clay modeling intervention, led to qualitatively deeper learning of the concepts. Clay modeling enabled learners to more fully internalize the meaning of the locatives and internalization of course entails incorporating knowledge into long term memory. The potential of clay modeling to support learners' creation of new mental representations that do not exist in the L1 and to help resolve confusion of concepts overlapping between languages is an exciting contribution to L2 teaching and learning. We remind the reader that the learners in the present study were given very little time to acquaint themselves with 3-D clay modeling. Furthermore, given the significant time pressure under which the method was delivered, we find these results all the more encouraging.

Discussion and conclusion

The present study offers compelling evidence of the Davis (1997) Method's potential to enhance learners' development of conceptual knowledge. The gains made by the students who engaged in clay modeling of Spanish locatives relative to the group that received only instruction confirm Gal'perin's (1967) argument that the presentation of conceptual knowledge alone does not lead to full internalization but that this process is significantly enhanced by external mediation that progressively moves toward less material forms of support as learners develop internal symbolic representations. In the present study, learners initially relied on 3-D clay models they had created and later on verbalized explanations of the meanings behind their models; finally, during the posttests, they completed the tasks on the intramental plane. Of course, it is possible that some learners verbalized spontaneously during the posttests although this was not observed by the researchers. Learners' use of private speech during a clay modeling intervention is an interesting matter that might be explored in future research.

We acknowledge that the study described here had limitations with regard to time and resources. While one-on-one instruction is usually preferred in the Davis Method so that teachers may interact with and optimally support learners' modeling, this was not possible given the limited class time allotted to clay modeling in the Spanish L2 courses. In our view, the fact that clay modeling was found to positively impact student learning despite there being no one-on-one intervention is a strong indicator of the approach's instructional potential. Similarly, because the Spanish instructors were required to follow the same syllabus and maintain the same schedule as the other sections, learners did not have time to gain familiarity with clay modeling. If this method were integrated as a regular part of language instruction, learners might become more adept at understanding the production of clay models not as an activity unto itself but as a component of the larger activity of developing new understandings of the L2. A final point worth noting is that the Davis Method typically deals with one concept at a time, while four spatial concepts were targeted in this study. Using a new method to simultaneously learn four new concepts may have been overwhelming for some students. In light of these limitations, we believe the results obtained using this method are all the more impressive.

The Davis Method, as it was implemented with learners of L2 Spanish, departs from Gal'perin's original inception of CBI in important ways. Specifically, we have argued that engaging learners in the creation of their own mediating tools breaks with Gal'perin's relatively rigid approach to internalization but aligns well with Newman and Holzman's (1993) tool-and-result methodology. In some respects, Gal'perin and Newman and Holzman represent divergent interpretations of Vygotsky's writings on the development of higher mental functions. In Gal'perin's view, presenting learners with carefully constructed cultural artifacts that must be used in a prescribed manner is the most efficient approach to ensuring internalization of academic concepts. For Gal'perin, the content to be internalized is pre-specified and thus development has clear stages and endpoints (i.e., when the concept has been fully internalized). Indeed, Gal'perin's preference for highly specified, lock-step procedures is motivated by a concern that in a less rigid approach not all learners will fully develop the concepts in question. A tool-and-result methodology, in contrast, underscores the transformative potential of supporting individuals' engagement in the activity of creating their own mediating artifacts. That is, the very act of creating artifacts helps learners to mediate their development of conceptual knowledge. Because the process is inherently creative its precise outcomes cannot be predicted a priori and the process itself is ongoing, without fixed endpoints. The result can perhaps be best understood with reference to Vygotsky's (1986) distinction between *meaning* (socially shared understandings) and *sense* (understandings specific to the individual) and the resultant tension between them. This perspective recognizes external forces (in this case, the classroom teacher who engaged dialogically with students) that help to bring learners' understandings in line with the larger community but also allows for learners' individual, emergent understandings.

An important question that emerges from this discussion concerns the practical consequences for learners of using ready-made or student-generated artifacts. In their analysis, Newman and Holzman (1993: 38) cast serious doubt as to whether mediating tools that are 'complete (fully manufactured) and usable for a particular purpose' lead to the same kinds of 'cognitive equipment' as tools whose development is a part of the activity they mediate. In the present study, learners were not left to 'discover' the concepts inductively on their own but were instead provided with conceptual explanations and examples. Learner creativity came into play as they produced their own representations of the concepts through clay modeling. Although this study did not include a group of learners who received pre-fabricated or ready-made artifacts, we are inclined to agree with Newman and Holzman that such instruments will not have the same mediating potential as artifacts developed by the learners themselves. Recall that the learners' models in this study often did not make sense to other students or to the instructor; their mediating potential was a function of the personal meanings imbued by their creators. An interesting topic for future research is how the mediating potential of clay artifacts might be affected by asking learners to consciously try to make their models comprehensible to others. In other words, is it better for the models to be as individualized as possible or to conform to some shared symbolism? It may be the case that the manner in which conceptual knowledge is presented to learners and the approach followed to internalization – including the use and creation of cultural artifacts – will need to vary according to learners' needs. Of course, these matters will only be illuminated through future empirical investigations.

References

Arievitch, I. M. and Stetsenko, A. (2000) The quality of cultural tools and cognitive development: Gal'perin's perspective and its implications. *Human Development* 43: 69–92.

Davis, R. (1997) *The Gift of Dyslexia* (revised edition). New York: Perigee.

Feuerstein, R., Rand, Y. and Rynders, J. E. (1988) *Don't Accept Me as I Am. Helping Retarded Performers Excel*. New York: Plenum.

Frawley, W. and Lantolf, J. P. (1985) Second language discourse: A Vygotskian perspective. *Applied Linguistics* 6: 19–44.

Gal'perin, P. Ya. (1967) On the notion of internalization. *Soviet Psychology* 5: 28–33.

Gal'perin, P. Ya. (1989) Study of the intellectual development of the child. *Soviet Psychology* 27: 26–44.

Gal'perin, P. Ya. (1992) Linguistic consciousness and some questions of the relationships between language and thought. *Journal of Russian and East European Psychology* 30: 28–49.

Gonzalez-Pueyo, M. I. (1995) Translation of in, on, at and over into Spanish in a technical context. *Meta* 40: 81–90.

Kabanova, O. Ya. (1985) The teaching of foreign languages. *Instructional Science* 14: 1–47.

Karpov, Y. V. and Gindis, B. (2000). Dynamic Assessment of the level of internalization of elementary school children's problem-solving activity. In C. S. Lidz and J. G. Elliott (eds) *Dynamic Assessment: Prevailing Models and Applications* 133–54. Amsterdam: Elsevier.

Karpova, S. N. (1977) *The Realization of Language in Children*. Paris: Mouton.

Kozulin, A. (1998) *Psychological Tools: A Sociocultural Approach to Education*. Cambridge, MA: Harvard University Press.

Kozulin, A. (2003) Psychological tools and mediated learning. In A. Kozulin, B. Gindis, V. S. Ageyev and S. M. Miller (eds) *Vygotsky's Educational Theory in Cultural Context* 15–38. Cambridge: Cambridge University Press.

Lantolf, J. and Thorne, S. L. (2006) *Sociocultural Theory and the Genesis of Second Language Development*. Oxford: Oxford University Press.

Lightbown, P. (1987) Classroom language as input to SLA. In C. W. Pfaff (ed.) *First and Second Language Acquisition Processes* 169–87. Cambridge: Newbury House.

Marková, A. K. (1979) *The Teaching and Mastery of Language*. B. B. Szekely (ed.). White Plains, NY: M. E. Sharpe, Inc.

Negueruela, E. (2003) A Sociocultural Approach to Teaching and Researching Second Language: Systemic-theoretical Instruction and Second Language Development. Unpublished doctoral dissertation. The Pennsylvania State University.

Negueruela, E. and Lantolf, J. P. (2006) A concept-based approach to teaching Spanish grammar. In R Salaberry and R. Lafford (eds) *Spanish Second Language Acquisition: State of the Art* 79–102. Washington, DC: Georgetown University Press.

Newman, F. and Holzman, L. (1993). *Lev Vygotsky. Revolutionary Scientist.* London: Routledge.

Phoenix, C. (2006) A multi-level synthesis of dyslexia. Proceedings of the Fourth International Conference On Complex Systems. Retrieved May, 2006 from http://necsi.org/events/iccs/2002/proceedings.html

Serrano-Lopez, M. (2003) 3-D Clay Modeling Instruction: A Pathway to Spatial Concept Formation in Second Language Learners. Unpublished doctoral dissertation. The University of Arizona.

Talyzina, N. (1981) *The Psychology of Learning. Theories of Learning and Programmed Instruction.* Moscow: Progress Publishers.

van der Veer, R. (2000) Some reflections concerning Gal'perin's theory. *Human Development* 43: 99–102.

Vygotsky, L. S. (1978) *Mind in Society: The Development of Higher Psychological Processes.* Cambridge, MA: Harvard University Press.

Vygotsky, L. S. (1986) *Thought and Language. Newly revised and edited by A. Kozulin.* Cambridge, MA: MIT Press.

Appendix 1. Explanation of underlying spatial concepts

3-D Clay Intervention Handout

Create models that describe the following concepts. The sentences are given just as examples, use your own imagination to create your own models. You do not have to create models for the 'usage' part, just read it. Give yourself seven minutes for each model. BE CREATIVE BUT QUICK. HAVE FUN :-)

1) IN/ON————————> DE

Situation 1 (Choosing involved)

CONCEPT A: When a specific object is in a specific place and there is no question of the speaker moving the object we use DE
Ex. Me gusta la planta de la esquina. I like the plant in the comer.
(You go into a room and you see an object that is already in the comer and you just point out to the fact that you like the one that IS SITTING IN THAT PARTICULAR PLACE)
CONCEPT B: When a specific object is in a specific place and there is the possibility of placement from the part of the speaker we use EN
Ex. Me gusta la planta en la esquina. I like the plant in the comer.
(You go into a room and you see an object that is already in the comer but you do not like it there and you point out to ANOTHER PLACE where the object should be placed)

Situation 2 (Parts of the whole)

CONCEPT C: When we are talking about the parts of a whole we use DE. The parts are not conceptualized as being inside of the whole, but as BELONGING to it.

Ex. Las paginas del libro. (de el libro) (The pages on the book.)

2) IN/THROUGH/INTO————————>A

CONCEPT D: When the place where the object is requires movement to get there we use A. EX. El paracaidista se lanzó al vacio (The skydiver jumped into the air.)

3) IN/ON———————>EN <u>Only</u>

CONCEPT E: When the object is contained within the place we use only EN Ex. El libro está en la caja. The book is in the box.

4) IN/ON/ON TOP OF/OVER ————————> EN/SOBRE

CONCEPT F: If the surface is flat and there is a separation between the object and the place where the object is we use EN/ SOBRE Ex. El libro está sobre/en la cama. The book is on the bed.

Usage

1. <u>**EN**</u> is used when we refer to **means of transportation**.
Monto en bicicleta todos los dias. I ride on a bicycle every day.
2. <u>A</u> is used when we talk about **games or musical instruments**.
Me gusta bailar al son del tambor. I like to dance **to** the beats of the drums.
3. We **<u>do not use anv preposition</u>** when we talk about <u>dates.</u>
Voy a clase los lunes. I go to class **on** Mondays

Appendix 2. Hints about how to create clay models

3-D CLAY MODELING: LEARNING WITH CLAY

Traditional language instruction is almost completely verbal: you hear definitions made out of words. Unfortunately, not all words can be easily defined in terms of a different language – or even the same language (try describing the difference between 'above' and 'over') And even when you can hear and learn a definition, it's quite difficult to think through the defining phrase(s) every time you want to use a word.

When you learned English, no one told you the definition of 'the' or 'in,' or even 'run' or 'sing'. You learned by example. You saw how the word was supposed to be used-and for many words, you learned visually/spatially, while interacting with your environment.

In class, we can't recreate the years of experience it takes to learn a language naturally. But we can, to some extent, recreate the process of learning by example rather than by definition. With the clay learning technique (adapted from Davis Symbol Mastery), you will create your own examples. The process will give you a deeper, more accurate, more usable and more permanent understanding of the words than you could get simply by memorizing their definitions.

1. **Understand the word.** Read the definition; discuss the word with classmates; make up example sentences using the word. Be careful! Some words have many definitions and you need to learn only one at a time.

2. **Create your example.** Build a clay model that shows the meaning of the word.

3. **Build the word.** Make the word out of clay.

4. **Learn the word.** Say to the model, 'You are meaning (definition in English).' Say to the word, 'You say _.' Then say to the model, 'Tu eres y significas (definition in Spanish).' Say to the word, 'Tu dices'

5. **Lock it in.** Make a mental picture of the model and word you've created and say the word and definition to yourself. Make sure you can remember the model (and definition) well enough to 'look' at your memory and know how the word is used.

Helpful Hints:

- Make sure that the model is related to the word and shows what it means and how it is used. If the word is 'cat' and you come up with a sentence like 'The cat is up a tree,' don't just make a model of the tree!

- Notice the wording in step 4. This is important. The model *is* the word/concept you're trying to learn. The letters are simply a set of symbols that *say* the word. Why go through all these steps? When you learn a word naturally, you have many chances to hear it and you can gradually create your own definition. In class, you feed yourself all the pieces at once.

- If you have trouble thinking of a picture, make up more example sentences and look for the common theme. Is the word expressing action? Relative location? Description?

- Remember to stick to *one* definition at a time. If the word is 'throw' and the definition is 'propel through the air,' 'Throw out the trash' is *not* a good sentence.

- It works best if you think up your own picture, rather than using someone else's.

Appendix 11.3. Talking to your clay

1 - Situation 1

'You are <u>**DE**</u> meaning <u>**BELONGING TO**</u>'
'You say <u>**DE**</u>'

'Tu eres <u>**DE**</u> y significas <u>**PERTENECES A**</u>'
'Tu dices <u>**DE**</u>'

1 - Situation 2

'You are <u>**EN**</u> meaning <u>**CHOOSING THE PLACEMENT OF**</u>'
'You say <u>**EN**</u>'

'Tu eres <u>**EN**</u> y significas <u>**ESCOGER EL LUGAR**</u>'
'Tu dices <u>**EN**</u>'

2

'You are <u>**A**</u> meaning <u>**MOTION TO A DESTINATION**</u>'
'You say <u>**A**</u>'

'Tu eres <u>**A**</u> y significas <u>**MOVIMIENTO A UN LUGAR**</u>'
'Tu dices <u>**A**</u>'

3

'You are <u>**SOBRE**</u> meaning <u>**SITTING ON TOP OF**</u>'
'You say <u>**SOBRE**</u>'

'Tu eres <u>**SOBRE**</u> y significas <u>**EN UNA SUPERFICIE PLANA**</u>'
'Tu dices <u>**SOBRE**</u>'

Part III
The classroom-world nexus

12 The unfulfilled promise of teaching for communicative competence: insights from sociocultural theory

Sally Sieloff Magnan

Introduction

What does *communicative competence* mean in terms of language teaching today? Has its promise to revolutionize foreign language learning been fulfilled through Communicative Language Teaching (CLT)? Can we fulfill our goals for foreign language education today through this instructional frame? In this chapter, I challenge the fit between the notion of communicative competence and the nature of CLT that has become associated with it over the past 30 years. Questioning the lack of a social and cultural framework in our teaching practices, I examine the limiting nature of classroom interaction inherent in CLT and suggest how socially based notions of second language acquisition, particularly sociocultural theory (SCT), might lead us to a broader, more culturally dependent notion of what and how our students need to learn. Expanded goals for language learning would include developing a greater intellectual and analytical intercultural competence in the sense of Kramsch's (1993) *third space* and of Cook's (1992, 2003) *multicompetence,* both of which are seen as important to identity formation. I conclude with considerations for reorienting foreign language education in terms of communities of practice, which may bring us closer to a desired outcome in line with the thinking of Vygotsky: meaning making as an 'organic and dialectical unity forged between communities and individuals' (Lantolf 2006: 103). Inherent in these suggestions are implications for research to discover to what degree language and cultural systems are learnable and thereby, on what level the promise of language teaching for intercultural and multicompetence may be an obtainable goal.

What is our expressed goal for foreign language education?

As a nation, we have reconsidered many times our methodologies and goals for foreign language teaching as we moved from grammar-translation to audiolingual methods, through curricula influenced by the ACTFL *Guidelines* for proficiency assessment and to the content goals found in the *National Standards for Foreign Language Learning* (ACTFL 1996). In the United States, we have made this journey under the auspices of one consistent force: the foreign language requirement, which has been extended downward from university to high school to many middle and elementary school levels. The rationale underlying language requirements is typically that students need to be able to converse and read in a multilingual world and to appreciate and respect cultural difference. The first part of the rationale, relating to language skill, is clearly reflected in the 'be able to do' part of the National Standards. The second part relates to the 'should know' part of the Standards and implies that students develop an analytical stance to that knowledge, evoking the notion of a third space (Kramsch 1993) where learners have a reflective critical awareness of and engagement with communities that extend beyond their own. The language requirement thus suggests that students learn another language and culture in addition to their native one(s) and also achieve an intellectual, international identity to complement their national one.

Are models of communicative competence pertinent to our educational goals?

This ambitious, dual outcome of foreign language programs would appear to accord well with the far-reaching, sociolinguistic concept of communicative competence. This notion is generally first attributed to Dell Hymes (1971, 1972, 1974), who departed from the Chomskian focus on the ideal speaker-listener which underlines *linguistic competence* to focus more broadly on sociolinguistic competence or on how meaning is made in social interactions within speech communities. Hymes (1974: 75) defined *communicative competence* as the ability 'to participate in [the child's] society as not only a speaking, but also a communicating member.' Membership in the community in which the interaction occurs and on which meaning is dependent is critical to this theory 'within which socio-cultural factors have an explicit and constitutive role' (Hymes 1972: 271). Given an educational objective of having students interact with members of other cultures, the notion of interaction in social communities is highly pertinent to our instructional mission.

Drawing on the work of Hymes, Canale and Swain (1980) proposed a four-part framework for communicative competence: grammatical competence, sociolinguistic competence, discourse competence and strategic competence. By teasing out four individual competences, their work gave separate focal lenses for different instructional objectives and, through the subsequent work of Bachman (1990), stimulated related orientations for assessment. It reaffirmed the interest in context, reminding teachers that meaning is bound to a particular discourse in a particular community. The focus on discourse encouraged syllabuses written, often after the European model, around linguistic notions and functions rather than around grammar points (Munby 1978; Wilkins 1976; Yalden 1983; see also Lightbown 2000 for a summary). It also helped focus attention on the individual learner and strategies that he or she uses to communicate and learn.

Bachman's (1990) model of communicative language ability included a tri-partite expansion of language competence, strategic competence and psychophysiological mechanisms. Particularly in the first area, he expanded the notion of language competence to include organizational competence (grammatical and textual competence) and pragmatic competence (illocutionary and sociolinguistic competence). This expanded framework emphasized how the interdependent competences each relied, individually and jointly, on an individual's understanding and ability to interact with and manipulate culturally-based notions.

Littlemore and Low (2006: 268) drew heavily on Bachman's model to argue that metaphorical competence is an important part of communicative language ability and that 'metaphor is therefore highly relevant to second language learning, teaching and testing, from the earliest to the most advanced stages of learning.' As Littlemore and Low explain, ability to understand and use metaphors 'represents an important way in which learners can develop a "voice" in the second language' (p. 290). Considering that conceptual metaphors come from cultural models of how society is organized and the world-view it holds, they go beyond linguistic or other behavioral patterns (Lantolf 2006). When learners acquire conceptual metaphors as well as linguistic metaphors stemming from them, their voices echo the cultures from which their foreign words come and their communicative ability should allow more culturally based interactions with native speakers.

Moving steadily toward a pedagogical model, Celce-Murcia, Zoltan and Thurrell (1995) arranged communicative competence in five interrelated areas of knowledge. Discourse competence moved to the core of the model, where it shapes and is shaped by sociocultural competence, linguistic competence and actional competence. Their conception recalled Hymes' vision by focusing on how sociocultural competence interacts with discourse competence: how utterances and texts are products of societies that create them and also act upon those societies through the messages they produce. Celce-Murcia *et al.*'s (1995) fifth domain, strategic competence, includes skills for negotiating and resolving communicative problems (Hall 1999).

Taken together, we find in these portrayals of communicative competence a reliance on the social before the linguistic – whether portrayed through speech, documents, or other language products – because language is bound by the society that creates it. We also find an iterative system: competencies reflect what language users do in society and they also create what is done, a creation that becomes the basis of future reflections. It is easy to see then that the notion of communicative competence is well suited to situating instructional goals in different sociocultural worlds and to having learners' reflect on communal identities. It is also important to see that this notion of communicative competence lies in the interactive framing of thought that occurs at the intersection of cultures, as members of one society interact with members of another, creating a new discourse about new content and new meaning which they construct together through their interactions.

We might conceive this new, analytical ability in terms of Kramsch's (1993) third space of understanding, where learners can mediate between cultural norms and expectations with sensitivity and insight. With a cultural third space we might associate Cook's concept of multicompetence, a sort of linguistic third space in which users of two languages possess not only knowledge and ability in each language, but also an added knowledge that comes from knowing two language systems. Much as Kramsch's third space exists beyond the borders of monocultural knowledge, Cook's multicompetence is a 'language supersystem' (Cook 2003: 2) that exceeds the linguistic knowledge system of monolinguals. Hall, Cheng and Carlson (2006) reconceived Cook's concept of multicompetence to ground it firmly in social activity within communities of practice. Reliance on social situation is compatible with Kramsch's notion of third space, which suggests that learners move between social spaces while maintaining an analytical distance among them. Our educational goal might then include bringing students to both a state of third space and of multicompetence, an ambitious outcome in the limited time available for foreign language learning in the US context.

How has research guided notions of communicative competence into teaching?

Once we accept that theories of communicative competence hold promise for our educational mission, we might look to SLA research to see what pedagogical questions have been asked of these theories. According to Lightbown (2000), the discipline of SLA has grown in the past 15 years to a point where it exerts an influence on textbooks, teacher training programs and curriculum design. Block (2003) explains that the primary line of research over this period has been the Input-Interaction-Output (IIO) model, championed by Gass, Long and others (for an overview, see Mackey and Gass 2006). This model has responded, Block believes, to two of Hymes's main orientations: considering the *social as well as the linguistic* and developing *socially realistic linguistics*. Some IIO researchers have approached the first orientation in their observations about the context of language use and classroom learning, but they have not, he charges, adequately focused on the problems that are socially dependent. The concern of IIO researchers with data from language communities focusing on language variation in societal context involves the second orientation, but it too has fallen short in IIO research because when the data is applied to teaching, the classroom has not itself been recognized as a community. The most serious lacunae in IIO research, according to Block, relates to Hymes's third orientation, *socially constituted linguistics*, which expresses 'the view that social function gives form to the ways in which linguistic features are encountered in actual life' (Hymes 1974: 196). Because it is concerned with social as well as referential meaning, recognition of *socially constituted linguistics* would mean that language is not separated from social action. It reverses the IIO approach to research and the standard view of teaching in which linguistic questions are primary and the social comes into play only secondarily, if at all. Mackey (2006: 375) noted that, although most interaction research has focused 'primarily on cognition and learning as opposed to language use,' literature is beginning to reflect a move toward taking up 'the design challenges involved in incorporating the insights and questions of those who focus on social context' (p. 375). She noted, in particular, studies focusing on language-related episodes or talk about language, on the relationship between interactional processes and classroom discourse contexts and on the impact of learner factors on opportunities for learning. In her view, this trend is a positive one toward incorporating 'some understanding of social factors ... into designs that examine learning' (ibid.).

This movement of IIO research toward recognition of the social dimension does not yet go far enough to respond to Block's concern. To follow the tenet of *socially constituted linguistics,* we need to recognize that language develops from a social foundation in which the individual resides. In teaching we would need to start with the dynamics of the learning community, which entails not only learners, but teachers and learners involved in the activity of teaching-learning. As Block (2003: 64) explained, 'interactional and interpersonal communication [would be] at the service of the social construction of self-identity, group membership, solidarity, support, trust and so on.'

CLT has moved language pedagogy from a teacher to a learner focus in terms of having students work regularly in pair and group interactions, allowing students to suggest vocabulary pertinent to their lives and building lessons around internet sites identified by learners. But how much of the lesson's focus is really on those activities and what kind of activity is involved?

From a sociocultural perspective, the instructional focus should not be on either the teacher or the learner. It should be on the activity of teaching-learning itself, that is, on the *instructional conversation* (van Lier 1996: 164–6). Deriving the concept of the instructional conversation from Vygotsky's *zone of proximal development* (1978), van Lier regards teaching as primarily assisted performance in task completion which provides mediated development in language learning. In the classroom, conversation springs necessarily from the student-participants and the school context in which they interact. It must take into account the students' family backgrounds and social connections, the institutional forces of school and society and sociocultural influences of the historical time in which the conversation occurs. Wertsch, Tulviste and Hagstrom (1993) suggested that the change from teacher- to student-centered instruction results in a new social language for learners because the relationship between the students and their classroom interlocutors is fundamentally changed. Agency and expertise should be no longer attributed to an isolated individual (the teacher) but must be socially distributed across learners. Teaching and learning become more reciprocal; negotiations in the learners' zone of proximal development involve more players, making theoretically for a richer learning environment.

But despite this lauded shift in classroom dynamics, have we escaped the paradox between learning through classroom interactions and routines and the authentic instructional conversations that CLT aims to create? In our classrooms, we can strive for symmetry among conversational participants including peers and the teacher, but we have not been able to achieve genuine conversational interactions because the classroom is traditionally not set up to foster them. If the authenticity of an interaction depends on the personal characteristics of the learners and on how they engage in the learning situation, the classroom can be authentic only within the identities of the learners and the socially situated school setting. Pedagogical social interaction remains locally constructed (van Lier 1996).

The unmet challenge for teaching, then, is that our individual students are members of cultures other than the target ones and their community is that of the foreign classroom. Classroom interactions are thus grounded in the students' sociocultural backgrounds and contexts, as Sullivan (2000) demonstrated. In US classrooms, we might expect to find students from a variety of cultural backgrounds, most of which are not associated with the target language being studied. Van Lier (1996) pointed out that if the gap is too great between what is done inside the classroom (such as the study of the foreign language) and what occurs outside of it (such as students living in the United States and perhaps from remotely different cultural backgrounds), 'the possibilities of learning anything at all are very seriously impaired' (p. 43). The gap includes the learners' values, aspirations and personal histories as compared to those assumed by the social structure of the classroom. Might we question the degree to which American and other perspectives impose themselves on those of the target language? Following the Vygotskian notion that mediated activity prepares development (understood as the ability to regulate oneself in order to create intended meanings in goal-directed activity), we might question how much of what is learned is truly foreign and how much remains American. The reality of the foreign language learning experience is that instruction does not provide learners an entrance into communities of practice in the target language society. This reality contrasts sharply with the explicit goals of language education: helping learners become sensitive, understanding interactants in other languages and societies.

To illustrate further, consider the role of *tasks* in both CLT and in IIO research. In CLT, teachers use tasks to create an environment in which students exchange and negotiate meaning (Bygate, Skehan and Swain 2001), making them the pedagogical starting point for learning. During the task teachers or peers negotiate the conversation to help learners create their personal meanings. The task-based lesson tends to be uni-directional: help the learner get his or her meaning across, not make meaning together as would be typical of a natural social interaction. In IIO research, tasks are the site in which negotiation of meaning and change in the interlanguage system occur (Bygate *et al.* 2001). Both these conceptions assume implicitly a preferred manner in which a task is carried out toward an anticipated outcome. But Coughlan and Duff (1994) demonstrated how learners define tasks differently – from each other and often from the intentions of the teacher – and how the same learner can interpret and execute a task differently on different occa-sions. As Lantolf and Thorne (2006) subsequently argued, this individually variable interpretation suggests that instructional tasks are centered on the collaborative activity of learners and teacher.

If activity forms the foundation and the center of learning, it is par-ticularly worrisome for cultural growth to have all learners doing an activity anchored in the same language and culture (e.g., all American learners in an American classroom learning Russian). This anchoring in the native or classroom culture would make it likely that the foreign words and expressions used in instructional activity reflect the mono-culture of the students, rather than the foreign cultures they are suppos-edly learning. Similarly, Block explained that the IIO line of research reinforced the tendency toward monoculturalism, by looking only at language disassociated from social perspectives. He claimed that 'SLA researchers fell short of taking on Hymes's social view of language, the socially realistic study of language and a socially constituted applied linguistics … The result has been a relatively partial view of language and this partial view has become foundational to the IIO model where two concepts, "task" and "negotiation for meaning," are fundamental' (Block 2003: 5). We are led to conclude then that Hymes's notion of communicative competence and that of others who have followed him, is realized only partially in the IIO line of research and teaching drawn from it. The critical component of social factors has not been consid-ered central enough to the process, or, at least, has not been scruti-nized as intensely as linguistic factors have been.

Why is CLT failing?

According to Savignon (1983), whose doctoral thesis (1971) is an early adaptation of Hymes's notion to language pedagogy, teaching for communicative competence must: 1) focus on meaning in addition to form (cf. Paulston 1974); and 2) ensure spontaneity of expression (cf. Rivers 1972). On this premise CLT was built around three main themes: 1) CLT is 'a post-method approach ... in which the principles underlying the use of different classroom procedures were of paramount importance, rather than a package of teaching materials'; 2) the most fundamental element was 'its explicit emphasis on the role of authentic communication within classroom contexts'; and 3) the measure of effectiveness was 'the ability to use language accurately and appropriately in communicative contexts' (Bygate *et al.* 2001: 2). Teachers followed these themes to transform their form-focused exercises into meaning-rich activities, such as personalized questions, role-plays in which students simulate routines of everyday life in the target culture and interactive conversational activities in which students and classmates exchange information about their own lives. Through these activities, CLT attempts to emulate a target-culture environment and 'to create in the classroom the conditions which exist in "natural" language learning' (Hughes 1983: 1). It nonetheless remains an open question how much CLT adheres to these three themes in the sense of intercultural, multicompetence as Hymes might have imagined it.

As a post-methods approach focusing on procedures rather than materials, CLT has struggled. Readings and other authentic documents were first decentered in favor of conversation and then returned to the classroom as a means of introducing cultural authenticity. But the tasks applied to them often did not change: personal reaction, from the monocultural perspective of the students, continued to dominate over reflection, creating what I have criticized elsewhere (Magnan 2006) as ego-centric expression consistent with the American focus on individual rights and needs. This emphasis on oral, transactional language anchored in an American perspective perpetuates the archetypal US norms of rugged individualism and personal stake. Indeed, the association of CLT with Western values of choice, independence, freedom and equality has led scholars to question its fit with some non-Western cultures (see Sullivan 2000). Furthermore, in these tasks, instructional outcome still relates to accuracy, albeit accuracy of language use in situation, rather than merely accuracy of linguistic form. Such a focus articulates well with the skills development rationale of the foreign language requirement but lacks a means of realizing the analytical, reflective stance associated with critical thinking from an intercultural perspective.

Although CLT founded itself on the concept of *authenticity*, through its use of documents for cultural authenticity and through its real-life, personalized interactions among classmates for communicative authenticity, a simple problem remained. The world of the classroom had its own unique discourse and its own interactional norms, an authenticity grounded in the worldview of students who were, for the most part, if not exclusively, monolingual and monocultural individuals. Recalling van Lier's (1996) conception of authenticity grounded in the history of the conversational participants and their sociocultural situation, we realize that instructed conversations in US classrooms and the meanings they generate likely remain essentially American although the words are foreign.

It is ironic that, as it upheld Hymes's basic tenets that communicative competence is directed by and responds to social constraints, CLT undermined itself. Because the communicative situation of the classroom was defined by its community of learners, it became, as one might have predicted, a place in which the social constraints, discourse patterns and strategies of interaction remained true to the nature of the learner participants. The linguistics changed, but the meanings did not: students used foreign words and structures to talk about their own cultural concepts. Liddicoat and Crozet (2001) offer a striking example in their study of how French and Australians consider the question 'How was your weekend?' For the French, this conversational routine is an opportunity to get to know someone and make personal connections, whereas for Australians it serves primarily to open an interaction for another purpose, or to make polite, but small talk. For the French, the subsequent conversation is expected to have some substance; for Australians it is expected to be short, with interlocutors remaining distant. Through a classroom experiment, Liddicoat and Crozet showed that specific instruction in interactional norms was needed for Australian students to respond to this question through French rather than their own cultural norms. Without this specific instructional intervention, the Australian students used French words to express Australian pragmatic routines representing underlying Australian expectations for modes of human interaction. As this example shows, it is possible for learners to have sufficient control of language as a tool to engage in a communicative action and yet not have the necessary understanding of the cultural concepts tying communities together to enable them to perform activities with true communicative competence. In sociocultural terms, such learners are yet unable to bring together activities, artifacts and concepts into an integrated organic system (Lantolf 2006; Lantolf and Thorne 2006).

Another example comes from immersion classrooms. Tarone and Swain (1995) found that the students in school immersion settings who did not have out-of-school exposure to French failed to learn the informal register appropriate for use with adolescent francophone peers. Yet, Lyster (1994) found that the students' immersion community provided insufficient opportunities for them to learn the formal registers needed for interacting with adults. As Lightbown (2000) pointed out, language learning is enormously complex. Even immersion does not seem to fulfill the need for an appropriate community in which to learn the full range of target-culture interactional norms. What these examples have in common is a classroom community composed primarily of language learners. The unmet challenge for CLT is to defy the apparently rigid monocultural boundaries that define interaction and thinking in classroom communities and inadvertently reinforce students' own perspectives and values.

Wenger (1998) offered insight into this phenomenon in his explanation of how communities of practice can create and maintain stereotypes. We might consider a classroom of learners to be a community of practice, which Wenger described as social groups that exist everywhere in society and shape identity through the ways they exercise power over members to conform with or change expected social patterns of interaction. He explained that communities of practice entail three modes of belonging: engagement (actual involvement in mutual negotiation), imagination (creating images and connections by extrapolating from personal experience) and alignment (coordinating energies and activities to fit in a broader enterprise). A typical community of students will engage each other within their own monocultural bounds of understanding and expectations. Imagination in this restricted community then proceeds from monocultural engagement. As Wenger explains, when imagination projects experience beyond the sounding board of mutual engagement, or in the case of classroom communities where the engagement is limited to a monocultural view, overgeneralizations or stereotypes can be formed, especially about images upon which engagement cannot act because it is not within the cultural spheres of the community of practice.

Whereas Hymes's notion envisioned authentic cultural communities in which different, individual members would communicate about the diverse interests that linked them as a society, the communicative foreign language classroom offers a practice ground primarily for students to talk about themselves from their own perspectives. Because the typical community of practice in foreign language education does not include members of target communities who engage with the learners, CLT has not fulfilled its promise to bring learners to communicative competence, defined in social terms. Kramsch (2006) recognized the failure of CLT in her claim that 'foreign language education, under the pressure to show evidence of efficiency and accountability, has … diverged from the original pursuit of social justice through communicative competence, as envisaged by Hymes, Breen and Candlin and others in the 1970s and is being put to the service of instrumental goals' (p. 250).

In US education, the greatest challenge for CLT to date can be found in the *National Standards for Foreign Language Learning*. Phillips (1999: 3) advised that the *Standards* provide a 'major shift' in language learning because they require 'teachers to focus more on what students are learning than on what they are teaching – making output what counts rather than input.' We can take this statement two ways: 1) to reinforce CLT's primary focus on students' personal expression of ideas, which leads us back to the conclusion that input from the target culture is a stimulus for students' own language use; or 2) that output and input are inseparable as community members determine them both and thereby shape together the construction of meaning and through it language learning. Both interpretations move the profession from a Krashenesque model of input first and foremost. But the first interpretation maintains the status quo on personalization in CLT and, I suggest, will yield no better educational results than we presently enjoy. The second interpretation, in contrast, has the potential for revolutionizing foreign language education by anchoring it in a constellation of target communities which become the site and the very makings of learning.

Indeed, the *Standards* pave the way for moving in the second direction through their focus on Communities and Connections, both against the backdrop of Culture and in their three communicative modes (interpersonal, interpretive and presentational). From the point of view of socially based theories of language learning, the interpersonal and interpretive modes are especially interconnected: it is through interpersonal interaction that meaning is both made and interpreted. In her explanation of how the *Standards* can work for teaching, Hall (1999) drove the point home by explaining that the type of discourse interaction students have in classrooms (e.g., teacher initiative; student response; teacher evaluation or theme-based, instructed conversations engaging teachers and students together) shapes both what they learn and the process of learning itself. For foreign language education to advance toward truly meeting the identity-charged goals of foreign language requirements, we need to understand much more about how communities of practice function in language learning. As Schulz (2006: 254) contended, communicative competence as it is practiced today 'is neither a realistic nor a sufficient goal for the general education FL requirement.'

What can sociocultural theories offer to teaching?

To re-examine the role of community in instructed language learning, it would seem appropriate to look toward socially based approaches to how languages are used and learned. Compatible with the view expressed by Firth and Wagner (1997) that use and learning are inseparable because they are part of the same dialectically organized activity, SCT recognizes the community as the entity enabling and creating the language mediation that is fundamental to both language acquisition and use. An examination of a few basic tenets of SCT leads us to more troubling insights about CLT as it is currently practiced. First, consciousness emerges from practice. As Lantolf and Thorne (2006: 213) explained, this tenet means that 'the thought structures of individual and communities are tied to the social and material conditions of their everyday practice.' For instructional situations, it would suggest that the language interaction in our classrooms is founded in the students' already established individual identities and culturally sedimented meanings and is mediated by the peers with whom they interact. The fact that interaction takes place in a code other than English does not mean that the transmission of meaning would be inherently different from what it would have been in English. In other words, foreign words and new, foreign consciousness are not necessarily linked; foreign words, used by L1 speakers in an L1 community, continue to make meaning anchored in the L1 social culture in which they are artificially imbedded. Lantolf and Thorne (2006) suggested that part of the reason the foreign words do not convey foreign thinking is that inner speech remains in the L1. Ushakova (1994: 154) put it figuratively: 'second language is looking into the windows cut out by the first language.' We could speculate that this window or frame of reference would be magnified in proportion to the lack of individuals from the target culture and the lack of an authentic cultural situation in the interaction.

Activity Theory, a primary component of SCT, offers an explanation of why learning an L2 can be restricted by L1 concepts and cultural values associated with them (see Lantolf and Thorne 2006, for a review of Activity Theory applied to language learning). Lantolf and Thorne contend that, according to Activity Theory: 'It is through activity that new forms of reality are created, including the transformation of self' (2003: 215). *Activity* is the contextualizing framework for interaction and is motivated by a biological or social need or desire. *Actions* or, in pedagogical terms, communicative goals and *operations* or again in pedagogical terms, communicative tasks, flow from *activity* because activity forms the center of learning. To apply the principle to instruction, we might consider a typical classroom task as a pedagogical attempt to evoke the activity framework. We could then put that task into a contextual frame that simulates the physical setting, the purpose of the exchange, the roles of the participants and the socially acceptable norms of interaction, as recommended by Omaggio Hadley (2001), Shrum and Glisan (1994) and other CLT pedagogues. We might assume that the learners would work through the task, accomplishing it successfully, with help from the teacher and peers.

However, recalling that learners' execution of tasks is not homogeneous or predictable and is always dynamic, we might question what type of learning (or more appropriately development) these tasks will promote. Perhaps the authenticized frame that CLT teachers create for classroom tasks is insufficient for teaching authentic interactions. Referring to work by Wertsch (1985), Lantolf and Thorne (2006: 215) explained that 'the context is not a setting within which activity takes place, rather it is activity that produces the very arena of human conduct.' Meaning is created by how students work through the instructional tasks, how they set their goals and what they do to accomplish them. Hence individual learners can interpret and perform the same task very differently (Coughlan and Duff 1994); in other words, learners 'involved in the same task are necessarily involved in different activity because they bring their unique histories, goals and capacities' to the task (Roebuck 2000: 79; see also Roebuck 1998). These learners would also then develop differentially from doing what instructors might consider the same task. It is unlikely, therefore, that an artificially imposed contextual frame that aims to situate activity in a foreign community would affect, to any great degree, how learners sitting in an American classroom think and work through that activity and thereby greatly influence identity growth formation achieved by doing that activity. Furthermore, if we accept, as does Activity Theory, that all learners construct activities through the lens of their individual identities mediated by the communities in which the activity takes place, then we must conclude that each activity will potentially be different for each student and will be highly dependent on the instructional environment in which it occurs (on the relationship between identity and instructional environment, see Lantolf and Genung 2002). In fact, we should have reached this conclusion long before now. As Bygate *et al.* (2001) summarized in their review of the literature on tasks, scholarly thinking in the 1990s concluded that tasks are done by learners in different ways and, in fact, the mark of a good task, is one that lends itself to interpretation by the groups of learners doing it. SCT takes us one step further to argue that different interpretations lead to different learning. According to Lantolf and Thorne (2006), in SCT social activity is psychological activity because the source of mind resides in social activity and in interaction with social artifacts.

In fact, individualization in how activity is realized formed part of Hymes's conception of *communicative competence,* although he explained it in different terms. He pointed out in 1972 that a 'normal member of a community' has knowledge of many aspects of communicative systems and 'will interpret or assess the conduct of others and himself in ways that reflect [that] knowledge.' Because individuals and their relationships in communities are not identical, it cannot be assumed, Hymes (1972: 282) further explained, 'that the knowledge acquired by different individuals is identical, despite identity of manifestation and apparent system.' To return to rhetoric associated with Activity Theory, the ways an individual interprets and actualizes activity exists within a constellation of his or her consciousness, which is founded in his or her community. For English-dominant students in the US classroom, it is normal then to interpret and convey meaning in accordance with US- and English-based norms and expectations. It would be doubtful that changing the code used to express that meaning would essentially change the communicative nature of the interaction through which meaning is co-constructed. Attaining a goal of communicative competence, in the original sociolinguistic and sociohistorical sense put forth by Hymes, may not be possible within the boundaries of instructional situations such as the typical US classroom because the ethnography of the symbolic forms that interrelate with speech in the communicative life of the society of the classroom remain too limited.

Framework for re-conceiving foreign language education

What can we do? With new scholars in SLA being trained in socially based approaches, we may be nearing a time when we can re-conceive foreign language education around social influences as well as for social objectives. Breen (2001: 180, cited in Block 2003: 126) offered a useful profile of learner contributions to language learning through a communicative perspective. It consists of four embedded layers:

1. Learner attributes, conceptualizations and affects that the individual learner brings to language learning, including innate attributes such as intelligence and socially dependent attributes such as beliefs and attitudes.

2. Learner action in context, which relates with how the learner engages with the language in the learning context, including his or her autonomy, strategies, self-regulation and participation.

3. Classroom context, representing the learning community in which the learner participates.

4. The wider community identity and participation, which forms a continuum of states of transition from the state to which the learner previously belonged through the current state to the state to which he or she seeks to belong.

Current CLT pedagogy accesses these levels from layer 1, the most micro level focusing on the individual learner, to layer 4, the macro level focusing on the sociocultural context. The focus is on the learner, to whom all learning is directed and around whom the teaching is focused. Classroom practice activates level 2 and takes place in level 3. The hope of CLT is that these levels are anchored in level 4, but as previously discussed, we must question whether this assumption is realistic in the US educational structure. If we apply a SCT perspective from SLA research to teaching, we would need to reverse the application of Breen's four layers: first and foremost, we would need to situate learning in wider communities so that learners can shape their evolving identities through a co-constructive relationship with others in social groups beyond their own.

In that a SCT perspective would not necessarily downplay the role of the teacher as CLT or Breen do, the teacher could be an active part of that community, both as a member of the language class and as someone with expert knowledge of the target culture. Within the wider community, we would need to create a learning environment in which the classroom is less rigidly defined so that students can reach into the target communities and contribute actively to meaningful exchanges there. Once this multi-faceted environment for learning is established, it is natural to reconceive learning activities in terms of real world inter-actions where co-construction of meaning and identity occurs. The in-dividual learner, then, the last layer, becomes the evolving outcome on which the forces of the other layers act, rather than the pre-established entity from which all else comes. When we look at the learner, we need to focus on socially mediated attributes, including biological traits and social factors and consider how learner histories influence the activities in which they become involved. This outlook, in teaching as well as in research, brings us back to the all encompassing layer of the wider community, which makes learning a fluid and dynamic process of inter-acting individuals in diverse social groups, rather than a hierarchical development starting from the individual and reaching toward the target society.

Such reconceptualization of foreign language education would include the full range of educational choices inherent in a curriculum. We need to look beyond classrooms, teachers and individual learners to create a learning environment and structure that promotes a new way of learning and knowing, evoking linguistic and cultural growth in the expansive sense of both Kramsch's third space and Cook's multicompetence. An initial step in creating a new learning community is to abandon the notions of monolingualism and monoculturalism as a starting point for instruction. Studies of heritage learners (see Byrnes 2005) and discussion following the Firth and Wagner debate (1997; cf. Block 2003), enhanced by Cook's (1992, 2003) work on multicompetence, has seriously challenged this norm. Even linguistically sheltered stu-dents from my Midwestern institution have some background in a language other than English when they come to foreign language courses. For example, Magnan, Frantzen and Worth (2004) surveyed first-semester learners of French, Spanish and Italian to find that 55 percent, 49 percent and 41 percent respectively had already studied another language previously in college; and this percentage would be even higher if we had considered high school foreign language study that is mandated for university entrance. It is no longer accurate to say that the United States is a monolingual or monocultural nation, if those terms mean no sustained exposure to languages other than English or cultural homogeneity whether or not it is language bound. Furthermore, the notions of American monolingualism and monoculturalism fail to recognize the great variety of American Englishes and American cultures routinely navigated by our students.

If we were to soften our insistence in CLT on target language only in the classroom, we could allow learners to benefit from their multicompetences as they add another language and confront yet another culture. From a SCT perspective it seems reasonable to allow space for the LI. Lee (2006) demonstrated the mixing of L1 and L2 in private speech although it is not clear in the data whether the meanings that emerge in the participants' L2 private speech are L2 or L1. Ushakova (1994) showed how learners use L1 in their inner speech, suggesting that the L1 is needed to mediate the learning of the new language, a point made by Vygotsky (1962). If we opened the classroom door to code-switching, a natural linguistic occurrence in multilingual environments, learners would become resources for learning as they bring different competencies to the co-construction of knowledge through interaction. In addition, abandoning the monolingual and monocultural norms would open the way for critical comparison among languages and cultures and, by extension, for developing multiple identities. As Kramsch (2003: 120) said, 'The notion of "linguistic identity," that takes into account the historical, social and cultural meanings of various languages for individual language users, suggests that current approaches [to teaching] might unnecessarily deprive language study of important personal and emotional dimensions.'

What is unclear is how code-switching might affect the underlying meanings of interactions. Can speakers switch codes without switching underlying meanings, that is, can the formal properties of language be different but not the semantic, pragmatic and metaphorical properties? In what ways will code-switching contribute to meaning making in language classes, to the community created in them and to how learner activity unfolds? Answers to these questions will come only when curricular reform is underway, creating an environment in which code-switching will spontaneously occur.

Following are seven curricular avenues that we might wish to pursue to situate language learning in multiple, authentic communities of practice where learners can both develop their language abilities and explore their intercultural identities.

1) *Make authentic cultural documents, in their historical and social contexts, the impetus for learning.* CLT has long insisted on the use of authentic documents (e.g., Omaggio Hadley 2001). In the

language of the National Standards these documents fulfill part of the cultural triangle: they are the cultural *products* that teachers use to present societal *practices* to students in order for them to gain new *perspectives* on the worlds of the language they are learning (Phillips 1999). In this scenario, the authentic document originates outside of teaching, an artifact that the instructor brings into the classroom community for students to interpret and analyze. SCT brings a sharp contrast to this line of thinking: the authentic document is a cultural tool that provides the impetus, the site and the source for learning; learning cannot exist apart from culture because learning and communication occur only through interaction, which is always culturally dependent. Thus, culture cannot be 'brought more fully' into a curriculum; the curriculum flows from and through the culture by way of the social communities that make learning possible. We need to preserve the authentic document in its historical, cultural home. Learners need to identify its value for specific purposes of the learning community, privileging their agency and defining their activity. Ideally, that learning community would be integrated into a community of practice including native or high-level target language speakers, which would have its own goals beyond those of language learning. In this activity system, learners and other community members would use the authentic document as a tool to mediate the goal-directed activity of their group. It would be evident that language learning must relate to development of higher mental processes.

2) *Promote virtual communities.* In the 1980s and 1990s we put our faith in Computer Assisted Language Learning (CALL), hoping that it would take grammar out of the classroom and allow more teaching time to be devoted to comprehensible input. Both of these technological initiatives, for their successes and failures, involved *linguistic competence,* even though CALL thrived in hope of providing time to develop communicative competence in language classes. We need to harness technology toward a socially based communicative competence, more in line with Hymes's original notion of a *socially constituted linguistics,* to move the profession from communicative competence to intercultural competence (Thorne 2006; Train 2006). We now have the technological ability to create virtual communities through telecollaborations using asynchronous bulletin board postings with video, images,

text, wikis and through synchronous chat (see Belz and Thorne 2006 for a review). In these virtual communities of practice learners can, with group members, mediate their identity and social activity, which will also foster linguistic development, as Dussias (2006), von Hoene (1995) and Kinginger and Belz (2005) demonstrated in their studies of students engaged in border-crossings through telecollaborations. In creating virtual communities, we should reach out to disciplines beyond language education, involving our learners in communities of practice in many fields, for, as Wertsch *et al.* (1993) explained, mediated agency cannot be grounded in the perspective of any single academic discipline. Given the nature of non-teacher directed virtual interaction, telecollaboration would also be likely involve code-switching and the use of a variety of culturally dependent tools, demanding that learners mediate their interaction toward both self- and other-directed goals. The teaching profession would need to confront the impact on language development of multilingual language use, learner agency and activity that transforms higher mental processes (Belz and Thorne 2006; Train 2006).

3) *Maximize service learning.* Situating interaction in diverse communities of practice would give a priority to service learning, in which students go where target languages are spoken (see also Grabois, Chapter 13, this volume). We need to understand that interactions in service learning situations provide opportunities for co-construction of language and identity; they should no longer be conceived just as places where students practice their language skills. Students need to become members of these communities; in Wenger's (1998) terms, they need to invest their engagement, imagination and, when social relations allow it, their alignment with the broader enterprises of the communities. Pairing students with service partners to discuss ways of living or knowing or including them in the communities' efforts to alter existing patterns of behavior would provide students with opportunities to negotiate meaning mutually with community members, see cultural connections and confront identity issues. Critical pedagogy (cf. Norton and Toohey 2004) with its goal of social change could come to play here, as learning is mediated by issues of power and when action is intended to change social systems.

4) *Re-orient study abroad toward new community building.* Common belief is that study abroad fosters students' engagement in target-culture communities of practice, especially if students live within the social network of a family. Wilkinson (1998), Hoffman-Hicks (1999) and Segalowitz and Freed (2004), however, questioned whether family stays necessarily lead to language gain, noting that lack of linguistic gain is often associated with the student's lack of opportunity or ability to integrate socially into the family. Magnan and Back (2007) showed that time spent with other Americans correlated negatively with French-language gains during study abroad in France, suggesting that the site of language acquisition might be less the surrounding culture than the immediate social community in which the learner interacts. Such findings call into question orientation sessions where Americans studying abroad meet each other and subsequently share group trips and sheltered classes, all of which transplant abroad the American community with its Americanized activity systems. Could it be that this restricted community reduces the potential for language development in the zone of proximal development because American classmates, even though they speak French, do not offer the range of mediation that can occur with native speakers? Such thinking suggests that the study abroad experience be re-focused toward community building with members of the target culture and toward a concomitant distance from other Americans.

   Study abroad is advocated for personal growth as well as linguistic development. Keeping in mind that activity is founded in social histories, study abroad is a prime site for challenging ideologies and for transforming activity into learning associated with higher mental processes. For example, Kinginger (2005) described how American learners in France reacted initially from an American perspective when they encountered gender-related differences because they failed to understand that the conflict related to local interactional norms and how broader and historically-situated ideologies of gender are instantiated in the United States and France. Eventual interaction with French communities influenced their development of constructs of gendered identity and their motives for learning French.

5) *Enhance reflection on identity building.* Language study has long been purported to enhance individual openness toward other

cultures, personal growth and self-understanding. Penuel and Wertsch (1995: 84) suggested how SCT's understanding of human mental functioning informs identity formation, which is 'viewed as shaped by and shaping forms of action, involving a complex interplay among cultural tools employed in the action, the sociocultural and institutional context of the action and the purposes embedded in the action.' They recommended integrating the dynamic poles of individual functioning and sociocultural processes into a mediated-action approach to identity formation, building on life stories present in a society as artifact, images and myths. Returning to Kramsch's (1993) metaphor of a third space where learners mediate between language and cultures, we might introduce learners to language-learning life stories of others who occupy such spaces. With a goal toward helping students become 'cross-cultural and cross-linguistic ethnographers in the contemplative process of applied difference' (von Hoene 1999: 28), von Hoene suggests adding to the curriculum texts that look at border crossings and identity shifts, such as Alice Kaplan's *French Lessons*, Eva Hoffman's *Lost in Translation*, or Josef Breuer's case study of Anna O, for first-year courses and texts that present a more analytical stance, such as Edward Said's *Orientalism* or Mary Louise Pratt's *Imperial Eyes*, for second-year courses. Once we open the classroom doors to interdisciplinarity, to use of the L1 and to learning goals beyond linguistic skill, we could use such readings, personal reflections and broad academic experiences to help students gain the critical distance often associated with multilingualism and multiculturalism. In line with SCT, we could ask students 'to focus on specific questions about the mediational means or cultural tools that people employ to construct their identities in the course of different activities and how they are put to use in particular actions' (Penuel and Wertsch 1995: 91). In looking at others and their activity systems, students are encouraged to self-reflection. Introspection about culturally dependent activity provides a new interpretation to the personalized focus of CLT, more in line with the notions of transformations of agency of individuals and groups (Wertsch *et al.* 1993) and of activity leading to greater understanding.

6) *Develop interdisciplinary constellations of courses.* The previous suggestions would make obsolete the notion of one

language class bounded by four classroom walls with one teacher and one textbook. Given that many practices of current CLT succeed in helping students develop basic linguistic skills, we likely do not want to abandon language courses, but we need to seek ways of enhancing students' cultural knowledge and critically reflective stances. We need also to relate these goals and thereby relate language learning directly to the development of higher-level mental processes. Despite serious efforts to integrate culture into a skills-based language curriculum, our language courses typically offer disjointed, pedestrian views of culture with stereotypic edges. Moreover, our profession has suffered from a bifurcation of foreign language programs into language courses and content courses, as well as from a separation of language courses lodged in the humanities from culturally related courses in other disciplines (von Hoene 1999; Scullion 2005).

To change this paradigm, we might partner language courses with other courses aimed at providing students with more knowledge about target cultures and giving them more time to use their L1s to interpret and discuss cultural comparisons. Efforts in language across the curriculum (LAC) have provided the most promising combinations of language and content skill development to date. Where LAC is not possible, or in addition to it, we might create constellations of interdisciplinary courses. One model would be the first-year interest groups (FIGs) initiated a few years ago at my institution. The FIG is a set of three courses that about 20 first-year students take together. The courses are linked thematically, each having its own class meetings, readings and assignments. For example, *Latin American Culture, History and Society*, which includes a third-year Spanish class (Introduction to Hispanic Cultures), a history course (Modern Latin America: From Independence to the Present) and an anthropology course (Cultural Anthropology and Human Diversity) or *Language, Culture and Experience: Perspectives from Asia*, which includes an anthropology course (Language, Culture and the Social Imagination), a first-semester Indonesian language course and a religious studies course (Religion in History and Culture: The East). Within the larger classes, the FIG students benefit from their own learning community, in which they co-construct knowledge and internalize meaning to shape their developing intercultural identities.

7) *Monitor learning*. Taking inspiration from the European language portfolio associated with the Common European Framework of Reference, we might monitor learning in a more individual manner than current testing provides. As the European language portfolio seeks to foster learner autonomy for life-long learning, our portfolios could be created by the learner and for the learner, as much or more than for a potential employer (see example of Linguafolio projects, Cummins 2007). Much like the published biographies of language learners, student portfolios could serve as texts for analytical examination and reflections on identity development. They could also help students, teachers and researchers understand the relationship between acquiring linguistic skill and developing higher-mental processes associated with cultural reflection.

Conclusions and future directions

Hymes (1972: 287) suggested that we might construct a 'short' and a 'long' range view of competency, 'the short range view being interested primarily in … the first years of life and the long range view in understanding the continuing socialization and change of competence through life.' Might we not think of our foreign language teaching also in terms of short-range and long-range objectives? If we take the short range as the earliest experience of a language student and, by necessity, place that life in the US classroom, we will acknowledge students' successful learning of linguistic tools (e.g., vocabulary, grammar, basic pragmatic routines) through CLT methods and we might allow ourselves to accept that the promise of attaining communicative competence cannot be fulfilled in our current instructional settings. Then, for the long range, we could turn to developing a competence that is responsive to foreign communities because it is developed through them. It is this long-range goal that will move us beyond our current national drive for enhanced language-skill ability toward a policy of language education leading to intercultural competence.

For developing that long-range view, SCT encourages us to ask questions that have not yet entered into our mainline pedagogical discussions. As our courses take an interdisciplinary turn, we will be asking our students to mediate their learning toward different types of learning outcome, those of multicompetence and intercultural competence. These competences are more in line with Hymes's original concept of communicative competence than are the more linguistically oriented and functionally oriented goals of CLT as it is generally practiced today. SCT would ask: Can instructors accept and even foster, the individual variation that is inherent in instructional tasks? How can they embed these tasks in a social environment – that is, in an activity system – where the division of labor between the L2 and L1 users responds simultaneously to the likely different objectives of each group for their conversational interactions? Can instructed situations be reconstrued so that natural social forces of a community of practice mediate the dynamic process of language acquisition? Conceiving instruction in this way would broaden what students learn to include culturally bound notions of social models and conceptual metaphors (Lantolf 2006)?

Lantolf (2006) wondered if all SCT concepts can be fruitfully applied to L2 instruction. Specifically, he asked whether 'appropriate pedagogical interventions can be designed to promote the development of conceptual and associated linguistic knowledge to enable learners to use the L2 as a mediational artifact' (Lantolf 2006: 103). Before we can answer this question, we need to consider how notions from SCT reframe three key components of CLT in the past two decades: teaching language in context with a focus on meaning, teaching language through interpersonal exchanges and putting the learner at the center of instruction. It is these components, I argue, which have undermined CLT's attempt to lead learners to communicative competence, in the sense of Hymes and his followers.

CLT has often operationalized the notion of authentic context for language learning as using documents designed for target-culture audiences. SCT suggests that cultural artifacts are socially bound. If CLT releases them from their social constraints by introducing them into the classroom, often to serve linguistic purposes, is the contextual frame they promise lost? CLT typically asks students to imagine real-world interactions and transform them into tasks for in-class role plays. Activity theory suggests that tasks too are culturally bound, that individuals respond to situational demands in performing them and that how tasks are mediated relates directly to the histories and agencies of individuals involved in them. It would appear that tasks carried out by students in a US classroom can be authentic only to that situation, which, because it is a learner community and not a target-language one, can lead only to linguistic skill development and not acquisition of more culturally bound notions associated with communication, such as conceptual metaphors (cf. Lantolf 2006). At present, these limitations of our CLT classrooms have not allowed us to answer the most critical questions: Is an L2 conceptual system learnable? What meanings are learned? What would we take as evidence that learning has occurred?

Through its extensive reliance on pair and small group work, CLT has put spontaneous, interpersonal expression at the center of teaching. Given that Vygotsky argued that speaking completed the thinking process, we might question whether our students are led to think like Americans with foreign words rather than to develop intercultural competence. Using SCT as a research frame, we might investigate if and how, the L2 is used to make meaning. Does private speech in the L2 lead to inner speech in the L2, that is, does it show developing analytical perspectives, comparative perspectives and an ability to internalize information in new ways that are sensitive to two languages and their cultures? As Lantolf (2006) asked, can instruction promote this internalization process? If it can, how can we identify and develop this emerging state of meaning-making from the inadequate state of L2 acquisition where it is necessary to resort to the L1 in order to process thought? At what point of learning, can understanding, comparison and analysis be dually mediated by artifacts and tools of more than one language and culture?

Related to extensive student-to-student talk in the classroom is the CLT tenet of putting the learner at the center of instruction. As shown in Breen's (2001) four-layer schema, learner histories have strong influences on individual learning, a notion that accords well with thinking in SCT. But the self-regulation of learning in CLT is more limited than SCT would allow. Agency in CLT is most often considered in terms of learners' individual goals and momentary emotions and desires. The object of the work of the classroom activity system typically remains with course materials, the teachers and the tests; when an individual student envisions a different outcome, it is often seen as resistance (Worth 2006). Evolution of the work of the activity system according to changing agencies of the learner members is discouraged. As Lantolf (2006) suggests, studies of private speech might yield insights into the dynamic, individual nature of agency and the tension with which it exists in the community of classrooms and in noninstructed learning situations. In understanding this organic dialectic better, we should gain insight into why students in our classrooms are not achieving the multifaceted communicative competence that Hymes described.

In summation, the lack of a community outside the borders of the classroom, with only its students and teacher, defies acquisition of communicative competence in Hymes's sense. SCT would suggest that an authentic community of practice in which all members – language learners and native speakers – share a stake, negotiate meaning together and work toward common, dynamic goals is missing in our pedagogies and in our classrooms. The borders of our classrooms and the dynamic processes occurring in them need to be re-examined in order for us to redirect foreign language learning toward the promise of communicative competence.

References

ACTFL (1999) *ACTFL Proficiency Guidelines* (revised). Alexandria, VA: ACTFL.

ACTFL (1996) *National Standards for Foreign Language Learning: Preparing for the 21st Century.* Alexandria, VA: ACTFL.

Bachman, L. (1990) *Fundamental Considerations in Language Testing.* Oxford: Oxford University Press.

Belz, J. and Thorne, S. (eds) (2006) *Internet-Mediated Intercultural Foreign Language Education.* Boston, MA: Heinle.

Block, D. (2003) *The Social Turn in Second Language Acquisition.* Washington, DC: Georgetown University Press.

Breen, M. (2001) Postscript: new directions for research on learner contributions. In M. Breen (ed.) *Learner Contribution to Language Learning* 172–82. London: Longman.

Breen, M. and Candlin, C. (1980) The essentials of a communicative curriculum in language teaching. *Applied Linguistics* 1: 89–112.

Breuer, J. and Freud, S. (1966) *Studies on Hysteria.* New York: Avon. (Reprint of volume 2 of the Standard edition of the Complete Psychological Works of Sigmund Freud). New York: Hogarth Press 1955.

Bygate, M., Skehan, P. and Swain, M. (2001) Introduction. In M. Bygate, P. Skehan and M. Swain (eds) *Researching Pedagogic Tasks: Second Language Learning, Teaching and Testing* 1–20. New York: Longman.

Byrnes, H. (2005) Perspectives. *The Modern Language Journal* 89: 582–616.

Canale, M. and Swain, M. (1980) Theoretical bases of communicative approaches to second language teaching and testing. *Applied Linguistics* 1: 1–47.

Celce-Murcia, M., Zoltan, D. and Thurrel, S. (1995) Communicative competence: a pedagogically motivated model with content specifications. *Issues in Applied Linguistics* 6: 5–35.

Cook, V. (1992) Evidence for multi-competence. *Language Learning* 42: 557–91.

Cook, V. (2003) The changing L1 in the L2 users mind. In V. Cook (ed.) *Effects of the Second Language on the First* 1–18. Clevedon: Multilingual Matters.

Coughlan, P. and Duff, P. (1994) Same task, different activities: analysis of SLA task from an Activity Theory perspective. In J. Lantolf and G. Appel (eds) *Vygotskian Approaches to Second Language Research* 173–193. Norwood, NJ: Ablex.

Cummins, P. (2007) LinguaFolio: American model for the European language portfolio. *The Modern Language Journal* 91: 117–21.

Dussias, P. (2006) Morphological development in Spanish-American telecollaboration. In J. Belz and S. Thorne (eds) *Internet-Mediated Intercultural Foreign Language Education* 121–46. Boston, MA: Heinle.

Firth, A. and Wagner, J. (1997) On discourse, communication and (some) fundamental concepts in SLA research. *The Modern Language Journal* 81: 285–300.

Hall, J. K. (1999) The communication standards. In. J. Phillips and R. Terry (eds) *Foreign Language Standards: Linking Research, Theories and Practices* 15–56. Lincolnwood, IL: National Textbook.

Hall, J. K., Cheng, A. and Carlson, M. (2006) Reconceptualizing multicompetence as a theory of language knowledge. *Applied Linguistics* 27: 220–40.

Hoffman, E. (1990) *Lost in Translation: A Life in a New Language*. New York: Penguin Books.

Hoffman-Hicks, S. (1999) The Longitudinal Development of French Foreign Language Pragmatic Competence: Evidence from Study Abroad Participants. Unpublished doctoral dissertation, Indiana University. Bloomington, IN.

Hughes, A. (1983) Second language learning and communicative language teaching. In K. Johnson and D. Porter (eds) *Perspectives in Communicative Language Teaching* 1–22 London: Academic Press.

Hymes, D. (1971) *On Communicative Competence*. Philadelphia, PA: University of Pennsylvania Press.

Hymes, D. (1972) On communicative competence. In J. Pride and J. Holmes (eds) *Sociolinguistics: Selected Readings* 269–93. Harmondsworth: Penguin.

Hymes, D. (1974) *Foundations in Sociolinguistics: An Ethnographic Approach*. Philadelphia, PA: University of Pennsylvania Press.

Kaplan, A. (1994) *French Lessons*. Chicago, IL: University of Chicago Press.

Kinginger, C. (2005) 'Language development and negotiation of gendered identities in study abroad.' Presented at the International Congress of Applied Linguistics, July 2005. Madison, WI.

Kinginger, C. and Belz, J. (2005) Socio-cultural perspectives on pragmatic development in foreign language learning: Microgenetic case studies from telecollaboration and residence abroad. *Intercultural Pragmatics* 2–4: 369–421.

Kramsch, C. (1993) *Context and Culture in Language Teaching*. Oxford: Oxford University Press.

Kramsch, C. (2003) The multilingual subject. In I. de Florio-Hansen and A. Hu (eds) *Plurilingualitaet und Identitaet* 107–24. Tuebingen: Stauffenburg Verlag.

Kramsch, C. (2006) From communicative competence to symbolic competence. *The Modern Language Journal* 90: 249–52.

Lantolf, J. P. (2006) Sociocultural Theory and L2: State of the Art. *Studies in Second Language Acquisition* 28: 67–109.

Lantolf, J. and Genung, P. (2002) 'I'd rather switch than fight': An activity-theoretic study of power, success and failure in a foreign language classroom.

In C. Kramsch (ed.) *Language Acquisition and Language Socialization* 175–96. New York: Continuum.

Lantolf, J. P. and Thorne, S. L. (2006) *Sociocultural Theory and the Genesis of Second Language Development*. Oxford: Oxford University Press.

Lee, J. (2006) Talking to the Self: A Study of the Private Speech of Adult Bilinguals. Unpublished doctoral dissertation. University of Wisconsin-Madison.

Liddicoat, A. and Crozet, C. (2001) Acquiring French interactional norms through instruction. In K. Rose and G. Kasper (eds) *Pragmatics in Language Teaching* 125–44. New York: Cambridge University Press.

Lightbown, P. (2000) Classroom SLA research and second language teaching. *Applied Linguistics* 21: 431–62.

Littlemore, J. and Low, G. (2006) Metaphoric competence and communicative language ability. *Applied Linguistics* 27: 268–94.

Lyster, R. (1994) *La négotiation de la forme stratégie analytique en classe d'immersion*. *Canadian Modern Language Review* 50: 446–65.

Mackey, A. (2006) Epilogue. From introspections, brain scans and memory tests to the role of social context: Advancing research on interaction and learning. *Studies in Second Language Acquisition* 28: 369–79.

Mackey, A. and Gass, S. (2006) Introduction. Interaction research: extending the methodological boundaries. *Studies in Second Language Acquisition* 28: 169–78.

Magnan, S. (2006) *Enjeux et défis de l'enseignement du français langue étrangère en France et aux Etats-Unis*. *French Review* 80: 332–52.

Magnan, S. and Back, M. (2007) Social interaction and linguistic gain during study abroad. *Foreign Language Annals* 40(1): 43–61.

Magnan, S., Frantzen, D. and Worth, R. (2004) Factoring in previous study of other foreign languages when designing introductory courses. In C. Barrett and K. Paesani (eds) *Language Program Articulation: Developing a Theoretical Foundation* 149–71. Boston, MA: Heinle.

Munby, J. (1978) *Communicative Syllabus Design*. New York: Cambridge University Press.

Norton, B. and Toohey, K. (2004) *Critical Pedagogies and Language Learning*. Cambridge: Cambridge University Press.

Omaggio Hadley, A. (2001) *Teaching Language in Context*, 3rd edition. Boston, MA: Heinle/Thomson Learning.

Paulston, C. (1974) Linguistic and communicative competence. *TESOL Quarterly* 8: 347–62.

Penuel, W. and Wertsch, J. (1995) Vygotsky and identity formation: A sociocultural approach. *Educational Psychologist* 30: 83–92.

Phillips, J. (1999) Introduction: standards for world language – on a firm foundation. In J. Phillips and R. Terry (eds) *Foreign Language Standards: Linking Research, Theories and Practices* 1–14. Lincolnwood, IL: National Textbook.

Pratt, M. (1992) *Imperial Eyes: Travel Writing and Transculturation*. New York: Routledge.

Rivers, W. (1972) *Speaking in Many Tongues*. Rowley, MA: Newbury House.

Roebuck, R. (1998) *Reading and Recall in L1 and L2: A Sociocultural Approach.* Stamford, CT: Ablex.

Roebuck, R. (2000) Subjects speak out: how learners position themselves in psycholinguistic task. In J. Lantolf (ed.) *Sociocultural Theory and Second Language Learning* 79–96. Oxford: University Press.

Saïd, E. (1978) *Orientalism.* New York: Vintage Books.

Savignon, S. J. (1971) A Study of the Effect of Training in Communicative Skills as Part of a Beginning College French Course on Student Attitude and Achievement in Linguistic and Communicative Competence. Unpublished Doctoral Dissertation. University of Illinois, Champaign, Urbana. Expanded and published as *Communicative Competence: an Experiment in Foreign Language Teaching*, Philadelphia, PA: Center for Curriculum Development, 1972.

Savignon, S. J. (1983) *Communicative Competence: Theory and Classroom Practice.* Reading, MA: Addison-Wesley.

Schulz, R. (2006) Reevaluating communicative competence as a major goal in postsecondary language requirement courses. *The Modern Language Journal* 90: 252–5.

Scullion, R. (2005) Reaching out: interdisciplinarity, foreign language departments and the liberal arts curriculum. *ADFL Bulletin* 36: 5–9.

Segalowitz, N. and Freed, B. (2004) Context, contact and cognition in oral fluency acquisition: learning Spanish in at home and study abroad contexts. *Studies in Second Language Acquisition* 26: 173–99.

Shrum, J. and Glisan, E. (1994) *Teacher's Handbook: Contextualized Language Instruction.* Boston, MA: Heinle/Thomson Learning.

Sullivan, P. (2000) Playfulness as mediation in communicative language teaching in a Vietnamese classroom. In J. Lantolf (ed.) *Sociocultural Theory and Second Language Learning* 114–31. Oxford: Oxford University Press.

Tarone, E. and Swain, M. (1995) A sociolinguistic perspective on second language use in immersion classrooms. *The Modern Language Journal* 79: 166–78.

Thorne, S. (2006) Pedagogical and praxiological lessons from internet-mediated intercultural foreign language education research. In J. Belz and S. Thorne (eds) *Internet-Mediated Intercultural Foreign Language Education* 2–30. Boston, MA: Heinle.

Train, R. (2006) Epilogue: a critical look at technologies and ideologies in internet-mediated intercultural foreign language education. In J. Belz and S. Thorne (eds) *Internet-Mediated Intercultural Foreign Language Education* 247–84. Boston, MA: Heinle.

Ushakova, T. (1994) Inner speech and second language acquisition: an experimental-theoretical approach. In J. Lantolf and G. Appel (eds) *Vygotskian Approaches to Second Language Research* 135–56. Norwood, NJ: Ablex.

van Lier, L. (1996) *Interaction in the Language Curriculum: Awareness, Autonomy and Authenticity.* New York: Longman.

von Hoene, L. (1995) Redefining the boundaries of foreign language literacy. In C. Kramsch (ed.) *Redefining the Boundaries of Language Study* 39–57. Boston, MA: Heinle.

von Hoene, L. (1999) Imagining otherwise: rethinking departments of foreign languages and literatures as departments of cross-cultural difference. *ADFL Bulletin* 30: 26–9.

Vygotsky, L. S. (1962) *Thought and Language.* Edited and translated by Eugenia Hanfmann and Gertrude Vakar. Cambridge, MA: MIT Press.

Vygotsky, L. (1978) *Mind in Society. The Development of Higher Psychological Processes.* Cambridge, MA: Harvard University Press.

Wenger, E. (1998) *Communities of Practice: Learning, Meaning and Identity.* Cambridge: Cambridge University Press.

Wertsch, J. (1985) *Vygotsky and the Social Formation of Mind.* Cambridge, MA: Harvard University Press.

Wertsch, J., Tulviste, P. and Hagstrom, F. (1993) A sociocultural approach to agency. In E. Forman, N. Minick, and C. A. Stone (eds) *Contexts for Learning: Sociocultural Dynamics in Children's Development* 336–56. Oxford: Oxford University Press.

Wilkins, D. (1976) *Notional Syllabuses.* London: Oxford University Press.

Wilkinson, S. (1998) Study abroad from the participants' perspective: a challenge to common beliefs. *Foreign Language Annals* 31: 23–39.

Worth, R. (2006) Resistance in the Foreign Language Classroom. Unpublished doctoral dissertation. University of Wisconsin–Madison.

Yalden, J. (1983) *The Communicative Syllabus: Evolution, Design and Implementation.* New York: Pergamon Press.

13 Contribution and language learning: service-learning from a sociocultural perspective

Howard Grabois

Introduction

In recent years service-learning (SL) as a pedagogical tool has received ever increasing attention by educational institutions at all levels. SL has been employed successfully in courses ranging from engineering to veterinary medicine to landscape architecture, to mention just some examples in relation to very diverse community contexts. It is hardly surprising that many institutions earnestly promote SL, as it is not only a powerful pedagogical tool, but also helps to enhance relationships between universities and the communities that surround them.

SL has also been integrated into language instruction, particularly L2 Spanish. Given the social and demographic developments related to Spanish in the United States, it is not surprising that SL is perceived as a potentially satisfying and enriching experience for students while simultaneously allowing them to help address real needs of people who are struggling to become integrated into educational, social and economic institutions. This is reflected in the large number of service learning opportunities offered in Spanish courses throughout the country and the attention that Spanish service-learning has received in recent years in scholarly publications (Hellebrandt and Varona 1999; Plann 2002; Weldon and Trautmann 2003; Hellebrandt, Arries and Varona 2004; Kaplan and Gamboa 2004; Grabois 2007).

Given the success and increasing popularity of SL for language instruction, developing a greater understanding of the cognitive processes that allow it to enhance student learning can help us to better understand language learning as well. This will entail discussion of not only second language theory, but also of the metaphors that inform them.

Metaphors for learning

In a review article that discusses the multiplicity of orientations toward language instruction in the twentieth century, Mitchell and Vidal (2002) note that 'one of the things that the 20th century has brought to consciousness with regard to language and language teaching is the idea of metaphor and how metaphors shape our thinking, including our psychological and emotional responses.' Lantolf (2006) highlights the profound importance of metaphor in relation to the learning of language and culture, suggesting that 'the acquisition of culture is also about the appropriation of cultural models ... above all, conceptual metaphors.' But if we are to take seriously metaphor as a significant aspect of cognition, we must consider not only issues relating directly to language and language learning, but also those related to questions of epistemology and theory construction. Sfard (1998: 4) describes metaphors for learning as 'the most primitive, most elusive and yet amazingly informative objects of analysis. Their special power stems from the fact that they often cross the borders between the spontaneous and the scientific, between the intuitive and the formal.' Lantolf (1996) describes how virtually all scholarly pursuits, even within the natural sciences, are framed to a large extent by metaphorical constructs. This is particularly true of L2 research and pedagogy as evidenced by the diversity of theoretical orientations the field currently enjoys and the sensitivity toward language issues of its practitioners.[1]

Metaphor and mapping

Research on metaphor as a cognitive tool (Lakoff and Johnson 1980; Lakoff 1987) highlights how metaphor can be used to construct cognitive relationships between distinct domains, allowing us to gain a better understanding of one domain in terms of the other. This is done by way of mapping between the two domains, such that relevant similarities between the domains are highlighted. Common metaphors of this sort include ARGUMENT IS WAR, allowing us to understand argument in terms of physical confrontation and the possibility of victory, or UP IS GOOD, portraying values of well being in relation to embodied spatial relationships. However, metaphorical mapping not only highlights similarities between domains, but may also obscure differences. For example, in a web log that discusses the Bush administration's use of the term 'war on terrorism' (http://www.huffingtonpost.com/george-lakoff)

Lakoff points out that the use of the war metaphor serves a variety of political purposes, including allowing the President to assume certain powers that are appropriate only in a time of war. But the use of this metaphor also obscures important differences between the war on terror and actual war, such as the fact that terror is an emotional state and not an army, not something you can defeat militarily or sign a peace treaty with, as you can with opposing forces in a non-metaphorical war.

Just as language and metaphors matter in political forums, they also matter in relation to how we construct our understanding of learning. A variety of metaphors have been discussed in this context, including THE MIND IS A COMPUTER (Searle 1992) and THE MIND IS A CONTAINER (Lakoff and Johnson 1980). Most directly relevant to the current discussion are metaphors of *acquisition* and *participation* in relation to learning (Sfard 1998). Like all metaphors, these may not only serve to elucidate how we understand learning and construct learning environments; they may also fail to recognize significant aspects of the learning process. This is particularly important since learning, like all cognition, is situated (Wertsch 1991, 1995, 1998). Different situations and contexts may require different constructs and means of analysis: learning does not lend itself to a universal one-size-fits-all metaphor and conceptualizing it this way may obfuscate significant aspects of specific learning environments.

Acquisition and participation

The acquisition metaphor, as described by Sfard (1998) is a historically long-standing and entrenched way of conceptualizing learning that sees the mind as a container to be filled with knowledge and concepts. This includes the notions that 'learning means acquisition and accumulation of goods' and implies 'gaining ownership over some kind of self-sustained entity' (Sfard 1998: 4). Within this metaphor she further postulates that knowledge is understood as akin to a commodity, having the same functional attributes as material possessions.

The participation metaphor represents a significant shift from its predecessor, as it emphasizes activities rather than states and doing rather than having. Echoing apprenticeship theory (Lave and Wenger 1991; Rogoff 1990), Sfard (1998: 6) describes the participation metaphor as moving towards membership in a community. She states that it 'shifts the focus to the evolving bond between the individual and others' and 'makes salient the dialectic nature of the learning interaction.' There is a foundational shift in emphasis from possession to becoming and from the decontextualized learner to the learner as part of a larger group that engages in shared activities. Sfard concludes that, while the participation metaphor may offer certain advantages over the acquisition metaphor, both are necessary and need not be mutually exclusive.

Contribution is learning

While the acquisition and participation metaphors articulated by Sfard elucidate and inform our understanding of different aspects of learning, they are by no means the only possible metaphorical means of constructing an epistemology of learning. Sfard (1998: 5) explicitly recognizes the pitfalls of remaining within accepted metaphors as they may keep 'human experience within the confines of former experience and conceptions,' and cautions that 'old foundational assumptions and deeply rooted beliefs, being tacit rather than explicit, prove particularly inert.' In fact, while established metaphors and their associated theories may be used to inform pedagogical practices, they may not be sufficient to fully describe the cognitive processes of powerful pedagogies which arise without connection to traditional metaphors. Service-learning appears to be one such case. As we shall see below, student responses to the SL experience indicate an enhancement of commitment, personal development and understanding of subject matter in the deepest and broadest senses. While the learning that takes place in this context could be partially elucidated by the participation metaphor – and to a lesser extent the acquisition metaphor – the metaphor of *contribution* may provide even greater insights.

A schematic conceptualization of these metaphors reveals that the contribution and acquisition metaphors are symmetrically opposite. While the acquisition metaphor emphasizes first person singular possession, the contribution metaphor highlights the enrichment of second person interlocutors as much as that of first person contributors. While the acquisition metaphor is predicated on the individual accumulation of knowledge, the contribution metaphor is predicated on the sharing of socially distributed knowledge. Although one might assume that the contribution metaphor has more in common with the participation metaphor, this is misleading. The participation metaphor conceptualizes learning as doing rather than having; the contribution metaphor in many ways encompasses both, including not only activity, but also the accumulation of cultural capital (Bourdieu 1991). The participation metaphor as commonly constructed within educational contexts typically implies a group of people collaborating to achieve common goals, or moving toward a common center in relation to a community of practice. In language classes this may mean constructing a dialog, making sense out of a text, or in the broadest sense, learning a language. In contrast, the contribution metaphor prioritizes the goals and interests of others as much as or more than those of the first person individual, although indeed these goals may turn out to be complimentary. Furthermore, the contribution metaphor may be of particular interest for language learning if we consider the centrality of agency in relation to discourse and the social construction of meaning. Language use as contribution to meaning is wholly consistent with notions such as dialogism and interpersonal mediation (Lantolf and Thorne 2006) that are central to SCT. This is very different from participation through turn-taking that other metaphors may allow. Finally, the contribution metaphor differs fundamentally from the participation metaphor (as informed by apprenticeship theory) by emphasizing engagement in emergent communities of practice rather than movement toward the center of established ones.

In their discussion of apprenticeship as a model for learning, Lave and Wenger (1991) develop the idea of legitimate peripheral participation. This is the ability of the novice to be a recognized and accepted participant in relation to the community they would like to join and where a particular expertise resides. Examples of apprenticeship that Lave and Wenger present include West African tailors, supermarket butchers, Navy midshipmen and Alcoholics Anonymous.

Lave and Wenger are not unique in promoting the notion that learning and cognition take place in relation to communities of practice as this is highlighted in a variety of ways within the Vygotskian tradition. Cole and Engeström (1993) for example, place community of practice at the base of their activity diagram. In his discussion of the embeddedness of actions within activity, Leontiev (1978) clearly places culturally constructed values and practices at the center of Activity Theory. Where apprenticeship theory is unique however, is in schematizing knowledge as residing exclusively within one group. While it provides a powerful representation of movement toward the center of a community of practice, it is also a representation that conceptualizes learning in terms of a one way street, with unidirectional movement only.

In service-learning however, learning is a two way street with mutual movement between complementary communities. Instead of expertise being uniquely situated within the center of one group, it is distributed differentially among diverse groups, thereby radically chang-ing conceptions of knowledge and power. Learners are no longer out-siders striving toward a center where they seek to become enfranchised, but rather are contributors to emergent communities of practice where their voices, life experiences and knowledge form an essential part of the learning dynamic. The notion of emergent communities may be par-ticularly useful for an understanding of the cognitive processes related to SL and highlights a crucial distinction between the participation and contribution metaphors of learning.

Sociocultural theory and contribution

Sociocultural theory (henceforth, SCT), with its emphasis on cognition as institutionally, historically and culturally situated (Wertsch 1985, 1998), as well as distributed (Cole and Engeström 1993; Cole 1996; Salomon 1993), is in many ways better equipped to provide a coherent analysis of the cognitive process involved in SL than mentalist approaches that emphasize self-contained aspects of cognition and highlight universal rather than situated properties of learning. Many mainstream theoreti-cal approaches are largely predicated on Krashen's (1981, 1982) assump-tions that language acquisition is primarily an unconscious process where most if not all significant development takes place through the operation of a genetically endowed language acquisition device and while affective factors may influence cognitive mechanisms (allowing input to become intake, for example) they remain essentially separate from them. In this way affective factors are seen as intervening vari-ables in relation to cognitive processes and not an integral part of cognition itself. This separation of affect from cognition is consistent with and perhaps influenced by, Chomskian assumptions concerning the modularity of cognitive processes (Chomsky 1980). From a SCT per-spective, however, the interaction of cultures in SL situates the central aspects of the learning process directly in relation to affective concerns such as motivation, personal intersubjective relationships and partici-pants' intentions. Furthermore, the centrality of notions such as the zone of proximal development (Vygotsky 1978, 1986; Kinginger 2002) or the use of language as an internalized psychological tool (Newman and Holzman 1993) clearly posit mental activity as socially constructed and culturally mediated, such that values, beliefs and affect must be seen as central to cognition and not merely a peripheral influence.

The goals of SCT historically have been generated in relation to questions of how to make a difference in the world and how to positively influence people's lives, at times on a scale that overwhelms the more narrowly focused interests of mainstream research on second language acquisition. Stetskenko and Arievitch (2004) remind us that the theoretical developments elaborated by Vygotsky and his collaborators took place in the historical context of addressing issues of extensive illiteracy in many of the newly formed Soviet Socialist Republics, particularly in Asia. Their theories were elaborated very much in relation to questions of educational policy that had the potential to affect large segments of the population. It is no coincidence that one of the landmark studies within Vygotsky's circle was Luria's (1976) research on the influence of educational literacy on cognition in Uzbekistan.

More contemporary research in the Vygotskian tradition also emphasizes making a difference in the world and in people's lives. Engeström (2000, 2003), for example, has conducted extensive research (with many of the same attributes as community based action research) on how to enhance health care delivery in Finland and on issues regarding the organization of activity in the workplace. Wertsch (1998) has investigated the significance of narrative schema for teaching history to children and on comparing mother/child and teacher/child dyads in rural Brazil and how interaction within these dyads differentially influences children's development (Wertsch, Minick, and Arns 1984). The Fifth Dimension program organized by Cole (http://www.whittierfifthdimension.org/theoretical.html) is directly concerned with enhancing educational outcomes for marginalized populations. Within the context of second language studies, the emphasis of researchers in the sociocultural tradition on agency and the individual's learning in context rather than on the learner as object in the abstract (Roebuck 2000), research in dynamic assessment (Lantolf and Poehner 2004) and studies on the sociopolitical context of learning in immersion programs (Swain and Lapkin 2005) are examples of SCT research that fall firmly within this tradition.

Overview of the program

The service-learning program discussed in this chapter is articulated in relation to a Spanish language program at Purdue University. Unlike many SL programs, which are designed for particular classes or course sections, this program accepts students from a variety of courses and

sections, thus allowing for a relatively large cohort of student participants. Fifth and sixth semester language students are encouraged, but
not required, to take part in the program known as *Ayuda y Aprende*
(Help and Learn.) In addition, more advanced and even some third and
fourth semester students have also participated in the program. Well
over 100 students regularly enroll each semester. Students who choose
to take part in the program are expected to spend two hours per week
with a community partner, attend a series of discussion sessions designed specifically for the program, respond to a series of on-line guided
reflections and write a composition on a topic related to SL. Involvement in the program is reflected in course grades in a variety of ways:
as part of periodically submitted language learning portfolios and in
place of other types of content-based learning that are part of the course
structure. Partnerships vary somewhat from semester to semester, but
have recently included: an after-school program for Hispanic elementary school children, in-class and study-hall assistance for Hispanic high
school students, ESL assistance for Hispanic students at a middle school,
tutoring at The Lafayette Adult Resource Academy (LARA) a local not-
for-profit institution that provides ESL instruction for adults, helping
the Hispanic clientele at a not-for-profit neighborhood housing association that provides assistance to low-income residents and the Girl Scouts
of America, where students fulfilled leadership roles for primarily
Hispanic troops. Students who participate are encouraged to use the SL
experience not only to improve their Spanish, but also to gain a heightened awareness of local and national issues having to do with Hispanic
communities. Many of the students also develop strong affective ties to
the people that they work with, an important aspect of the reflexive
nature of learning through contribution and the simultaneous benefit
to both first person contributors and their interlocutors.

Student reflections on service-learning

One activity that is generally considered to be central to SL (Foos and
Hatcher 1999; Zlotkowski 1998) and language learning in general
(Richards and Lockhardt 1996) is reflection. For SL this includes
reflection on the SL experience itself, how it relates to the learning of
course content and how it relates to issues of civic responsibility or
awareness. Drawing upon written student responses to on-line reflection questions, a variety of themes stand out and help to better
elucidate the centrality of contribution to learning from the students'

own perspective.[2] All of the protocols in the sections that follow are from different students who have engaged in SL with a variety of community partners, such that recurring themes are the expression of a variety of student voices.

Included among the themes that stand out in student reflection are the degree to which the SL experience enhances language learning, the development of greater confidence and ease of expression, enhanced cultural understanding, the importance of contributing to the well-being of others, academic and personal growth, the development of empathetic interpersonal relations and heightened civic awareness. In the following sections, I will consider in more detail the contribution metaphor and its implications for SL in a second language.

Learning

One issue that must be taken into consideration *a priori* is whether the service-learning experience is in fact useful for language learning. It is important to consider not only the development of language skills and proficiency, but also comparisons of SL to classroom learning, as well as the interaction between affect and learning in SL.

Language skills, goals and confidence

Student self-reports consistently show that SL is one of the most important language learning experiences they have had. Improvement in vocabulary, grammar, fluency and confidence are frequently reported:

1) When I'm helping at LARA I'm constantly using my Spanish to explain concepts or vocabulary to people that don't understand English very well. Of course that may not at first seem like learning; however, the more I'm able to talk there the more I will be able to be comfortable in situations later if I need to speak in Spanish. Also, while I'm there, I learn a lot of new vocabulary and using that vocabulary. For example we've done exercises about shopping in a mall. So fashion was something I hadn't studied for a long time in Spanish. While I was there I learned quite a few new words and had to use them when talking.

2) Being a part of the service-learning program had a huge influence on my learning of Spanish. Before participating with *Ayuda y Aprende*, I was not the most confident in my Spanish speaking

capabilities. Although we did not talk in Spanish the entire time I was helping the little girl I was assigned to, this experience gave me the most real life communication with another person of Hispanic race [*sic*] and it made me have to practice my speaking with her. Now, I feel that I am a little more confident, the most I have ever been, with my speaking capabilities and I have this service-learning experience and the little girl I worked with to thank for that. The gain in confidence will be of great help because now I want to practice speaking to others and I can only get better with the practice.

The positive influence on language learning also has an influence on students' learning goals. The following student's comments suggest that the learner has moved beyond the institutionally mediated goal of fulfilling course requirements and is personally involved in both service and learning, having established higher level goals relating to improving language skills and engaging with the local culture.

3) Service-learning has greatly influenced my learning of Spanish. For the first time in my life, I have had a chance to use my Spanish to benefit others. Participating in Service-learning has not only greatly increased my understanding of the Spanish language, but it has also increased my reading, writing and speaking abilities as well. I was forced into a situation where I had to speak Spanish or the adults I was working with would not understand me. So as I helped them learn English they helped me speak better Spanish! I plan on continuing to volunteer at LARA even though I will not be receiving any points or anything like that next semester. Service-learning increased my abilities in Spanish and simultaneously increased my love for the Hispanic culture as a whole.

For SL students language learning and learning about cultures and the life experiences of people from other backgrounds are not simply independent parts of a cumulative acquisition of knowledge, but rather are intimately related:

4) *Ayuda y Aprende* has been one of the most amazing experiences I received this year at Purdue. I learned a lot not only about Spanish and the Hispanic culture, but I learned a lot about community service and volunteerism as well. *Ayuda y Aprende* combines a new level of foreign language learning with valuable life experiences. Community service and volunteering are things

that everyone should contribute to. Giving back to the community is part of becoming a well rounded adult. Volunteering teaches people compassion and respect for others. *Ayuda y Aprende* is a fabulous program. It combines this community service and volunteering setting with a cultural learning experience as well. Through *Ayuda y Aprende* I have learned to value community service and I have realized the importance of volunteering. Helping others teaches you to understand and respect people from all walks of life. Working at LARA I have gained experience with people from different cultural backgrounds, different financial situations and a variety of different educational backgrounds. The more I work in this setting, the more I respect each of the students.

Service-learning and classroom learning

Students frequently compare the language learning that takes place during their SL experience with other language learning experiences. They typically draw these comparisons in order to highlight the greater usefulness of SL as compared to more conventional language learning experiences:

5) I think that this past semester in service-learning has had a huge influence on my Spanish learning. Working with the high school girls proved to be a challenge because they talked a lot and I had to really pay attention to stay with their conversation. This challenge caused me to work much harder at learning new words and picking up on phrases. It has also helped reduce the amount of literal translation I do when I speak Spanish. I have learned more conversational Spanish through talking to the girls than I ever have in class. Just talking to them helps me to really pick up on the language and has made me nearly fluent.

As part of the comparison between service-learning and classroom learning, students also highlight the development of greater learner autonomy as a result of engagement with the Hispanic community. Learning is no longer something that is merely assigned, but becomes an activity for which the student takes personal responsibility. Furthermore, as described in the following reflection, the learning that takes place in SL can also have a positive influence on classroom learning.

6) Service-learning has influenced my learning of the Spanish language dramatically. I feel like I never have a better grasp of the

language than I do when I am at LARA. When I am there, I notice that I talk more fluidly in Spanish, I am quicker to process ideas and I make less [*sic*] grammatical mistakes compared to situations in the classroom. I cannot say enough about how valuable it is to simply be immersed in the language for two hours per week. When I am at LARA, there is no teacher standing in the same room to help me if I do not understand something or cannot articulate something. The practice of being able to think one's way through the language barrier and express thoughts is a truly valuable part of any language. Also, I find myself comprehending classroom dialogue and grammatical concepts better since I have been attending LARA. The language just seems to have a more natural feel to it now.

Affect and learning

Beyond improvement in their language skills and speaking ability, students frequently discuss how the SL experience influences their affective relationship to language learning itself. Common themes have to do with their motivation and attitudes:

> 7) Since I have participated in Service Learning, I have become more serious about learning Spanish. It's one thing for me to know that there are a lot of Spanish speakers in our country, but it's entirely different to immerse myself in the Hispanic community of Lafayette, IN. It became even more apparent to me how many Hispanics we really do have in our country and [how] much of a need there is for Spanish speakers. Service Learning was also great for me too because I got to see the language being used in every day situations with children. Moreover, it was rather humbling to see children half my age speaking with one another in Spanish and then holding a conversation with me perfectly fine in English. It has really made me want to really learn the language.

In the following reflection we can also observe that success generates motivation as much as motivation is a requisite for success and the importance of affect as a positive and central aspect of learning (Leontiev 1981). This is in direct contrast to the affective filter posited by Krashen (1981, 1982) that limits input into independent cognitive processes. Furthermore, while Krashen explicitly accepts the acquisition metaphor, prioritizing it as an unconscious process that is distinct from learning, we can see the importance of conscious intentions as central to a process of doing.

8) Service-learning has been a positive influence on my own learning of Spanish. I feel as though, even though I'm supposed to be helping the students learn English, that they've done a better job of teaching me Spanish than I have done teaching them. I feel a lot more confident speaking now, because I am able to communicate in the language. Also, knowing that I am able to help those people who speak Spanish natively, I am now very motivated to learn more Spanish so I am able to help more and more people, especially in the future when I work in a hospital.

Contribution

If we are to take seriously the metaphor that *contribution is learning* it is important to understand student perceptions of their role in SL in relation to the communities that they work with. This includes not only the value that they place on contributing to the well being of others, but also their understanding of the dynamic that is formed amongst all participants during the SL experience.

Contributing to well being of others

A recurring theme in student reflections is the importance of contributing to the well being of others. While this may represent an expression of students' values, their comments demonstrate that something more profound than what ordinarily takes place in a language class is occurring during the SL experience. Making a contribution has an influence not only on the members of the Hispanic community students work with, but also on the students themselves.

9) I feel like I am really making a difference in these kid's lives. I know that most of their parents know little or no English and that makes it difficult for them to receive much help at home. I have such an amazing time with the kids. They make me smile everyday and I really do enjoy spending time with them and it really helps knowing that while I am learning so much from them, they are learning from me. I feel like a big sister to these girls and I am hoping to continue with this next year.

10) Service-learning has influenced my learning in many ways. The most important way has been that I have been able to judge my level and fluency of Spanish as compared with native speakers. When you are in a classroom setting it is hard to judge how well you actually know the language because for everyone in the room English is his first language. I think that doing the service-learning program has instilled a new purpose for learning Spanish. Seeing the impact of not being able to communicate in daily life put things in perspective. Communication is something that many of us take for granted. I think that my learning after service-learning is more for the prospect of helping people than just for my benefit.

Legitimate central contribution

Service-learning brings together members of diverse linguistic and cultural communities who, despite the fact that they often inhabit the same geographical spaces, may have minimal opportunity to interact in significant and meaningful ways with members of other groups. Unlike the examples provided by Lave and Wenger (1991) however, SL students and community members not only have the opportunity to access the expertise of linguistic, cultural and even educational communities to which they would not normally have access, but also do so within a context which values the knowledge and expertise that they have upon entering the process.

One student described the situation in far simpler and perhaps more eloquent terms:

11) The most important thing that I have learned through Service Learning is how segregated we all are here. It just seems crazy that people can live here for 10 or 20 years and be able to almost completely avoid the majority of the population. Likewise it's sad that English speakers really don't have any interaction with the Hispanic population. I guess I just never realized this before and it has been cool to see a different side of things and meet a really different group of people that I wouldn't have come in contact with had I not gone to LARA.

While not all students are so explicit in their recognition of how SL provides mutual entry into communities of practice, there is often recognition that the SL experience provides unique opportunities to tap into expertise that students do not typically have access to:

12) I have always found that the true proof of knowing something is to be able to teach it to someone else and have them understand what I am saying. I believe this is a big part of what this program is. By trying to explain things to another person, we find out what we still need to learn. Because these people are 'experts' in what we are trying to learn, they can explain to us what we need to know. Also, by doing a project like this, we discover non-academic things about ourselves too. I know I have learned patience and flexibility. Without participating, you can not learn some of these things.

While many students recognize the access to linguistic and cultural expertise that they gain through SL, other narratives show a much broader scope in relation to their learning experiences. The quotations below show how having access to life experiences and narratives very different from their own can influence students' personal development:

13) There is one special child that stands out in my mind after this semester in service-learning. His name is Daniel. The reason he stands out so much in my mind is because one day while I was helping him with his homework he told me that he doesn't like to speak Spanish because the kids down the block from his house make fun of him. He also told me that he was ashamed to be Hispanic. This made me sick at my stomach. I know in my heart that the only reason the kids that tease him do so is because they have heard someone else (most likely one of their parents or other relatives) do the same and think it's an OK thing to do. I told Daniel that he should be proud of his background. I told him he was blessed to come from such a history (he is Mexican) and that he should be proud to be able to speak 2 languages (English and Spanish) fluently. I hope I contributed to his life by helping him believe in himself. He contributed to my life by making me a little more proud of my background. Hearing him say those heartbreaking words made me realize how proud I am to be who I am. I only hope I helped him be proud of who he is.

14) One girl who stood out to me is Flor. Flor, also from Mexico, is very involved in immigration rights and informs the other Hispanic girls in the class about different acts and laws that are trying to be passed. Flor is also the most outspoken girl in the group. For example, in class the other week, the teacher asked for volunteers to read out loud and specifically asked the

Hispanic girls in the class. A boy in the class made the comment, 'They can't read, they can't even speak English.' After that comment, none of the Hispanic girls wanted to read, but Flor said, 'Yes I can,' and read to the class. She shows a strength that is amazing to witness. I don't know how much of an impact I have on her life, but she has definitely impacted mine.

Empathy

If we are to understand contribution as a conceptual metaphor: LEARNING IS MAKING A CONTRIBUTION, perhaps the crucial cognitive mechanisms that come into play are not simply those traditionally associated with second language acquisition, but also have to do with issues concerning the nature of the personal relationships that students develop. While the above quotations often discuss broader affective and social issues such as being a role model, a striking number of students highlight the empathetic nature of the relationships they develop with members of the Hispanic community as a significant aspect of their learning:

15) I guess that contributing to the community is a good way to look at what we are doing through the program, but I like to think of it on a more personal level. I work at the high school with the same girl every week and I have learned about her and her family and have become, I would hope, a friend. My helping her may in turn benefit the community, but as long as I help her I will feel accomplished.

16) I think that one of the most beneficial learning experiences in service-learning comes from the contributions you give to the community. This program provides students with an opportunity to give something back. I learn life lessons at LARA. I am learning respect and empathy for a cultural group that I may have never interacted with without *Ayuda y Aprende*. Contributing to the community by tutoring at LARA provides me with many valuable life lessons. I have felt the genuine satisfaction that only comes from helping someone in need and truly caring about their success. *Ayuda y Aprende* has convinced me to continue volunteering and helping in my community throughout my life. Giving back to the community in this way provides more than just help in learning Spanish, it has taught me the importance and great personal satisfaction that comes from volunteer work.

Attaining the perspective of others

One of the aspects of the developing personal relationships that students experience and see as important to their own learning, as mentioned in reflections above, is empathy for others. Often this is cast in terms of attaining an appreciation for others' perspectives and life experiences.

> 17) The most important thing that I have learned during my experiences in *Ayuda y Aprende* is empathy. Because of *Ayuda y Aprende*, I more fully understand the hardships the Hispanic people go through to try and stay here, learn English and try to adapt and get used to a completely different culture. I am also more sympathetic of what they are going through after hearing countless stories of hardship and perseverance. Also, because of my experiences in *Ayuda y Aprende*, I have decided to pursue a career in Spanish so that I can continue to help Hispanic migrants adapt to their new surroundings.

> 18) I often put myself in their shoes. I imagine how I would feel if I moved to Mexico, knowing absolutely no Spanish. I would feel very scared and shy. Having someone sit with me and help me learn Spanish and also talking with me in English would mean the world to me. I feel it is the same in their shoes. I like to talk with them about their jobs and their families and help them in those situations if at all possible.

Empathy and learning

The sense of empathy that students develop, while significant in its own right, is also presented as an important aspect of student learning in ways that often go far beyond the development of language skills. The empathy that many students develop in relation to the Hispanics they work with in SL is consistent with what Kramsch (1993) describes as teaching along the cultural fault line. This is centered on the ability to not only see another culture with recognition of one's own perspective, but also to see one's own culture from a different perspective. The SL experience promotes this for members of both communities – university students and Hispanics – to overcome cultural divides in a way that may not be possible under other circumstances:

> 19) The most important thing I have learned through Service-learning is how hard it is for people to adjust to a culture where they do not know the language. In the classes where there are a

lot of Spanish speaking people, they all hang out with each other. I think it is because they feel most comfortable with those they can relate to, like with the language, but at the same time it separated the class to the extent that at the end of the year they do not even know each other's names. I never realized how strong a language barrier actually is, both verbally and physically.

20) I think that the most important thing that I learned while participating in *Ayuda y Aprende* is how the kids feel about being Hispanic and how they are so embarrassed to speak it. I think that is the most important thing because I didn't realize that kids like them felt that way, when I think of it I think it is amazing that they can speak two languages fluently especially since I want to be able to speak Spanish so bad and they were just basically born with it. I never really noticed that they sort of had a stigma that came along with being the way they are and I never realized that people in school would make fun of them and would make them feel ashamed to speak Spanish. It was the most important thing for me to learn because I had never realized that aspect of their lives before.

Emergent communities

As discussed above, one of the fundamental differences between the participation and contribution metaphors is that while the former highlights movement toward the center of an existing community of practice, the latter highlights interaction within emergent communities. The notion of emergent communities allows us to understand distributed cognition (Cole and Engeström 1993; Cole 1996) not only in terms of collaboration in working toward common goals, but also in terms of collaboratively working toward complimentary goals, with consciousness of their inter-related nature.

The two way street

Because students perceive a relationship between the contribution they are making and their own learning, they often cast their thoughts in relation to what might be called a 'two way street': they discuss a learning process that goes in both directions. While several of the above reflections allude to this, many students explicitly comment on the fact that all participants have expertise that they contribute to the process.

Crucially, differential contributions by individuals are able to accomplish far more together than they can independently. In this way all parties can experience significant personal development, although perhaps in different ways.

21) In this case with *Ayuda y Aprende*, while I am making a contribution, I at the same time am learning. The best part of *Ayuda y Aprende* is that you do not even realize that you are learning while you are making the contribution. The contribution that you are making is providing someone with the knowledge of how to speak English – you think to yourself that THEY are the ones who are learning. But in reality, you are learning, too. You are using your Spanish with native Spanish speakers and through the process are improving it by adding vocabulary and learning different grammatical patterns. It's great!

22) I feel that we are not only helping out the community, but we are also increasing our knowledge at the same time. In essence, this is a win-win situation. Overall, I feel that the time spent at the service learning destination helps out my learning and understanding of the Spanish language, as well helping out the community in which we live. I believe that providing service to the community is something which everybody should try to do and this is an excellent way for me to do that as well as improve upon my learning of the Spanish language.

Interpersonal relationships

As the two-way street metaphor suggests, students see their own learning in broader terms than improving language skills or gathering knowledge about culture. They understand that their contribution is not limited to the immediate content of instruction, but also includes affective aspects of the relationships they develop with the people they work with. Several reflections show that these relationships are not simply contributing factors to learning, but rather are central to it.

23) My participation in *Ayuda y Aprende* allows me to have a very unique experience with the Spanish culture and language. My student is Mexican and I have, therefore, learned much about the immigrant Mexican family and home environment. The experience is quite unique, however, in that I am not simply benefiting from it. My student is also receiving the benefits of having a role

model and someone to help her with her studies and learning of the English language.

24) The kids do help us too. They tell me about what is going on in their lives and this makes me feel as if I have actually gotten to know them. They let me know what is traditional for their culture and based on these aspects, I can better relate to not only why they act the way they do, but also their life goals. I learn about the individual children as well as the Hispanic culture as a whole. The local Hispanic community needs to be represented not only in the school setting but also in many other places such as at social school functions and school sports. It is an eye-opening experience to learn about how these children feel in their environment. I feel as though I am helping them in some aspects while they are helping me in others.

Personal development

Student reflections often suggest that the notion of learning is not limited to more traditional language course content during the SL experience, but also extends to personal development. This includes issues related to values, language and identity and experiences that are so powerful as to be transformative.

Values and civic responsibility

Within service-learning we can see the elaboration of an evolving set of values and an understanding of civic responsibility:

25) I think that when you give a contribution, such as participating in service-learning, you end up learning a lesson. A lesson, whether it is about life or about yourself, is always learned when you give up your time to help someone else. I feel like I have learned so much just by participating in service-learning. I feel like I have learned my strengths and weaknesses in concern to speaking Spanish. Also, I have learned so much about the actual language. The adults that I work with at LARA are constantly teaching me new sayings and correcting my pronunciation. I have learned so much about the Spanish language and about their culture. I think that it is so much easier to understand Spanish speakers now because I have trained myself to listen to them. I

feel like when you give your time to help others, no matter what you will benefit from it as well.

26) Yes! I definitely believe that there is a direct correlation between helping someone and being able to learn something in return. Both benefit someone in some way. Contributing to the community also helps you to realize the importance of lending a helping hand to others in need. Through this experience one also learns a lot about themselves. They realize many different aspects of life are not as easy as one expects them to be. Also when you contribute to your community you learn a sense of tolerance and acceptance of others because you learn how they are very similar to you and you have an explanation for why things are the way they appear and ignorance becomes out of the question. Through contributing everyone can learn and impact their lives in ways they thought were impossible before!

Learning and identity

Issues surrounding language and identity have been discussed in a variety of ways (Pavlenko and Lantolf 2000; Kramsch 2000) and are generally focused on the relationship between the language one speaks and its relation to the construction of self. This process is often discussed in relation to inner speech. While one would not expect the interactions that students have during their SL experience to lead them to restructure their identity in relation to a different language, it does have an influence on how students construct their identities as language learners and students, as well as the role they see for themselves within society:

27) The most important thing I have learned during my participation in *Ayuda y Aprende* is the courage to be myself, to live up to my potential and to remember how lucky I am to be afforded these wonderful opportunities. I see how these students struggle just to pass their classes let alone excel in them … participating has caused me to reflect on my own life and I see how lucky I am. I learn more and more each day to never take anything for granted.

28) The person I worked with this semester in *Ayuda y Aprende* has contributed to my learning and to my life in many ways. The person I worked with most of the time was Juan. Working with him has enriched my life and he has become a friend. He has taught me a lot about the Spanish language, culture and life in

general. Conversation with him has made me reevaluate some of my values. So many things that I take for granted as a citizen of the United States are some of the main reasons for his migration here. He has shared not only his knowledge of Spanish, but also life stories and friendship.

Transformative experiences

Educational experiences that so profoundly influence students so as to be transformative must be considered among those that are most significant. The transformative aspect of the learning experience may in some cases be apparent, as in cases where students are motivated to change career or educational goals. One example of this sort can be seen in a pre-med student who decided that she would specialize in pediatric medicine after a SL experience with young children. Another student decided to change majors from industrial design to elementary education after a similar experience. Yet another student decided to pursue a career in TESOL after her experience working with adult learners of English.

While not all transformative experiences can be measured in such dramatic ways as the above cases, they can be equally profound as they restructure student attitudes toward learning in general, language learning in particular, enhanced understanding of personal goals, or increased awareness of social issues related to other cultures:

29) The most important thing that I have learned during my participation in *Ayuda y Aprende* is learning to be motivated. It took me awhile to learn that the people that I tutor are highly motivated to learn and I should be this motivated in college. I no longer despise studying and doing homework, but instead I enjoy getting better grades through studying harder and doing homework better. Along with motivation, I have learned that it is also important to better myself whenever possible instead of wasting time. I am learning how to draw and I work instead of watching television or playing videogames.

30) The people that I tutor at LARA all have jobs that do not produce a very comfortable standard of living. One is a gas station attendant, another works in a factory, others do similar things. I am in college to get an education in order to get a better job that will produce a more comfortable standard of living and tutoring these people gives me motivation to get grades that will allow me to

continue my education and, in the end, live a better life later on. This motivation will not die after I stop tutoring, so I have been changed for the rest of my life, or at least educational career.

At times the experience of having a transformative experience is related to a realization of the differences that exist between themselves and those they work with, not only in terms of language and more superficial aspects of culture, but also in terms of profound differences that exist in terms of life experience, goals and expectations; in effect a realization of profoundly different world views:

31) I have learned many important things that I can apply to various aspects of my life. However, the most important thing I have learned is to have compassion for others. If you have true compassion for others, then you will be open-minded and patient. These are qualities one must have to be successful in life. With these characteristics, one can effectively communicate and relate well to others. Service-learning has helped me to gain more compassion for others. This program presents you with people who speak a different language than you, who look different than you and who come from different places than you. You learn to be open-minded and patient. You realize how difficult it is to learn a foreign language and adapt to a different lifestyle and culture. You also learn how important you can be in someone's life just by volunteering your time.

Summary and conclusion

US Supreme Court Justice Potter Stewart, in dealing with a difficult first amendment case, is well known for saying he would not attempt to define obscenity 'but I know it when I see it.' While this may seem to abandon the jurist's role of providing clear definitions within the legal system, it does highlight the fact that, despite the difficulty of defining certain aspects of human experience, these can be recognized by a person of reasonable values within a particular historical and cultural context.[3]

The same holds true for second language learning, which for over a half century has been the object of intense theorizing and attempts at definition within the contexts of those theories (Byrnes 2000). There are language learning environments, however, that provide powerful testament to the fact that learning is indeed taking place, despite not emerging from second language theory. In these cases you can't help knowing it when you see it and service-learning is one such 'it.'

This is not to say that theory is of no use in cases such as these. Indeed, extraordinary learning environments challenge us as a profession to find the theories and metaphors that will help us to understand the phenomenon, beginning inductively from the context rather than deductively from theory. A Vygotskian perspective provides us with a principled way of understanding the success of SL, given its tradition of regarding cognition holistically and its emphasis on the subjectively interpersonal and distributed nature of learning and development. On a more practical level, theoretically principled analysis of exceptionally successful learning experiences may help us to better understand and enhance the learning experience in other contexts as well. Contribution as a metaphor for learning can provide us with one such perspective.

Since the heyday of the audiolingual method a great deal of emphasis has been placed on the importance of meaningful activity as a basis for language learning. Examples of this range from content based learning (Brinton, Snow and Wesche 2004) to task based learning (Willis 1996; Ellis 2003) and from interactionist approaches (Doughty and Varela 1998) to SCT (van Lier 1996). I can think of no activity that provides students with a more meaningful context for learning than contributing to the well being of others. In the process students become contributing members of emergent communities where learning is based on symmetrically distributed expertise, they develop awareness of and empathy for cultures and life experiences that are different from their own and they attain enhanced motivation as language learners, students and citizens. Service-learning may be the most powerful language pedagogy available to students enrolled in foreign language courses. Understanding its success can help us to better understand language learning as well.

Notes

1. Not all in the L2 field agree that theoretical diversity is beneficial, perhaps an indication of the degree to which some metaphors have become entrenched.
2. Student reflections have been edited for spelling and minor grammar corrections. In some cases sections of reflections are presented. There has been no editing of content.

3. Stewart's comment in many ways reflects similar insights to those found in prototype theory (Rosch 1977; Lakoff 1987), with the idea that concepts are often formed not on the basis of necessary and sufficient conditions, but rather on the basis of family resemblance, or similarity to real or idealized central members.

References

Bourdieu, P. (1991) *Language and Symbolic Power*. Cambridge, MA: Harvard University Press.

Brinton, D., Snow, M. and Wesche, M. (2004) *Content-Based Second Language Instruction*. Anne Arbor, MI: University of Anne Arbor Press.

Byrnes, H. (2000) Shaping the discourse of practice: the role of linguistics and psychology in language teaching and learning. *The Modern Language Journal* 84: 472–94.

Chomsky, N. (1980) *Rules and Representations*. New York: Columbia University Press.

Cole, M. (1996) *Cultural Psychology: A Once and Future Discipline*. Cambridge, MA: Harvard University Press.

Cole, M. and Engeström, Y. (1993) A cultural-historical approach to distributed cognition. In G. Salomon (ed.) *Distributed Cognitions: Psychological and Educational Considerations* 1–43. Cambridge, UK and New York: Cambridge University Press.

Doughty, C and Varela, E. (1998) Communicative focus on form. In C. Doughty and J. Williams (eds) *Focus on Form in Classroom Second Language Acquisition* 114–38. Cambridge: Cambridge University Press.

Ellis, R. (2003) *Task-based Language Learning and Teaching*. Oxford: Oxford University Press.

Engeström, Y. (2000) From individual action to collective activity and back: Developmental work research as an interventionist methodology. In P. Luff, J. Hindmarsh and C. Heath (eds) *Workplace Studies: Recovering Work Practice and Informing System Design* 150–66. Cambridge: Cambridge University Press.

Engeström, Y. (2003) The discursive construction of collaborative care. *Applied Linguistics* 24: 286–315.

Foos, C. and Hatcher, J. (1999) *Service-Learning Workshop Curriculum Guide*. Indianapolis, IN: Universities as Citizens.

Grabois, H. (2007) Service-learning throughout the Spanish curriculum: an inclusive and expansive theory driven model. *Service-Learning in Applied Linguistics* 164–89. Boston, MA: Anker Publishing.

Hellebrandt, J. and Varona, L. (eds) (1999) *Construyendo Puentes (Building bridges): Concepts and Models for Service-Learning in Spanish*. Herndon, VA: Stylus Publishing.

Hellebrandt, J., Arries, J. and Varona, L. (eds) (2004) *Juntos: Community Partnerships in Spanish and Portuguese*. Exton, PA: American Association of Teachers of Spanish and Portuguese.

Kaplan, B. and Perez Gamboa, T. (2004) *Más allá del salón de clase: Una experiencia de integración de aprendizaje de español y servicio comunitario en UGA. Hispania*, 87: 137–8.

Kinginger, C. (2002) Defining the zone of proximal development in US foreign language education. *Applied Linguistics* 23: 240–61

Kramsch, C. (1993) *Context and Culture in Language Learning*. Oxford: Oxford University Press.

Kramsch, C. (2000) Social discursive constructions of self in L2 learning. In J. P. Lantolf (ed.) *Sociocultural Theory and Second Language Learning* 133–53. Oxford: Oxford University Press.

Krashen, S. (1981) *Second Language Acquisition and Second Language Learning*. New York: Pergamon Press.

Krashen, S. (1982) *Principles and Practice in Second Language Acquisition*. New York: Pergamon Press.

Lakoff, G. (1987) *Women, Fire and Dangerous Things: What Categories Reveal about the Mind*. Chicago, IL: University of Chicago Press.

Lakoff, G. and Johnson, M. (1980) *Metaphors We Live By*. Chicago, IL: University of Chicago Press.

Lantolf, J. (1996) SLA theory building: 'Letting all the flowers bloom!' *Language Learning* 46: 713–49.

Lantolf, J. (2006) Re(de)fining language proficiency in light of the concept of languaculture. In H. Byrnes (ed.) *Advanced Language Learning: The Contribution of Halliday and Vygotsky* 72–94. London: Continuum Press.

Lantolf, J. and Poehner, M. (2004) Dynamic assessment of L2 development: bringing the past into the future. *Journal of Applied Linguistics* 1: 49–72.

Lantolf, J. and Thorne, S. (2006) *Sociocultural Theory and the Genesis of Second Language Development*. Oxford: Oxford University Press.

Lave, J. and Wenger, E. (1991) *Situated Learning. Legitimate Peripheral Participation*. Cambridge: Cambridge University Press.

Leontiev, A. A. (1981) *Psychology and the Language Learning Process*. Oxford: Pergamon.

Leontiev, A. N. (1978) *Activity, Consciousness and Personality*. Englewood Cliffs, NJ: Prentice-Hall.

Luria, A. R. (1976) *Cognitive Development: Its Cultural and Social Foundations*. Cambridge, MA: Harvard University Press.

Mitchell, C. and Vidal, K. (2001) Weighing the ways of the flow: twentieth century language instruction. *The Modern Language Journal* 85: 26–38.

Newman, F. and Holzman, L. (1993) *Lev Vygotsky: Revolutionary Scientist*. London and New York: Routledge.

Pavlenko, A. and Lantolf, J. P. (2000) Second language learning as participation and the (re)construction of selves. In J. P. Lantolf (ed.) *Sociocultural Theory and Second Language Learning* 155–77. Oxford: Oxford University Press.

Plann, S. (2002) Latinos and literacy: An upper-division Spanish course with service learning. *Hispania,* 85: 330–8.

Richards, J. and Lockhardt, C. (1996) *Reflective Teaching in Second Language Classrooms.* Cambridge, UK and New York: Cambridge University Press.

Roebuck, R. (2000) Subjects speak out: how learners position themselves in a psycholinguistic task. In J. P. Lantolf (ed.) *Sociocultural Theory and Second Language Learning* 179–96. Oxford: Oxford University Press.

Rogoff, B (1990) *Apprenticeship in Thinking: Cognitive Development in Social Context.* New York: Oxford University Press.

Rosch, E. (1977) Human categorization. In N. Warren (ed.) *Advances in Cross Cultural Psychology, Vol. 1* 1–72. New York: Academic Press.

Salomon, G. (ed.) (1993) *Distributed Cognitions: Psychological and Educational Considerations.* Cambridge: Cambridge University Press.

Searle, J. (1992) *The Rediscovery of the Mind.* Cambridge, MA: MIT Press.

Sfard, A. (1998) On two metaphors for learning and the dangers of choosing just one. *Educational Researcher* 27: 4–13.

Stetsenko, A. and Arievitch, I. (2004) Vygotskian collaborative project of social transformation: history, politics and practice in knowledge construction. *Journal of Critical Psychology* 12: 58–60.

Swain, M. and Lapkin, S. (2005) The evolving sociopolitical context of immersion education in Canada: some implications for program development. *International Journal of Applied Linguistics* 15: 169–86.

van Lier, L. (1996) *Interaction in the Language Curriculum: Awareness, Autonomy and Authenticity.* London: Longman.

Vygotsky, L. (1978) *Mind in Society. The Development of Higher Psychological Processes.* (M. Cole and V. John-Stiener, S. Scribner, and E. Souberman, eds). Cambridge, MA: Harvard University Press.

Vygotsky, L. (1986) *Thought and Language.* (Alex Kozulin, ed.). Cambridge, MA: MIT Press.

Weldon, A. and Trautmann, G. (2003) Spanish and service-learning: pedagogy and praxis. *Hispania,* 86: 574–85.

Wertsch, J. (1985) *Vygotsky and the Social Formation of Mind.* Cambridge, MA: Harvard University Press.

Wertsch, J. (1991) *Voices of the Mind. A Sociocultural Approach to Mediated Action.* Cambridge, MA: Harvard University Press.

Wertsch, J. (1998) *Mind as Action.* Oxford: Oxford University Press.

Wertsch, J., Minick N. and Arns, F. (1984) The creation of context in joint problem-solving. In B. Rogoff and J. Lave (eds) *Everyday Cognition: Development in Social Context* 151–71. Cambridge, MA: Harvard University Press.

Willis, J. (1996) *A Framework for Task-Based Learning.* Essex: Longman.

Zlotkowski, E. (1998) *Successful Service-Learning Programs: New Models of Excellence in Higher Education.* Boston, MA: Anker Publishing.

Index

References to notes are entered as follows; 55n. References to tables or figures are entered in italics, e.g. *55*.

Lightning Source UK Ltd.
Milton Keynes UK
UKOW05f2226180115

244683UK00001B/42/P